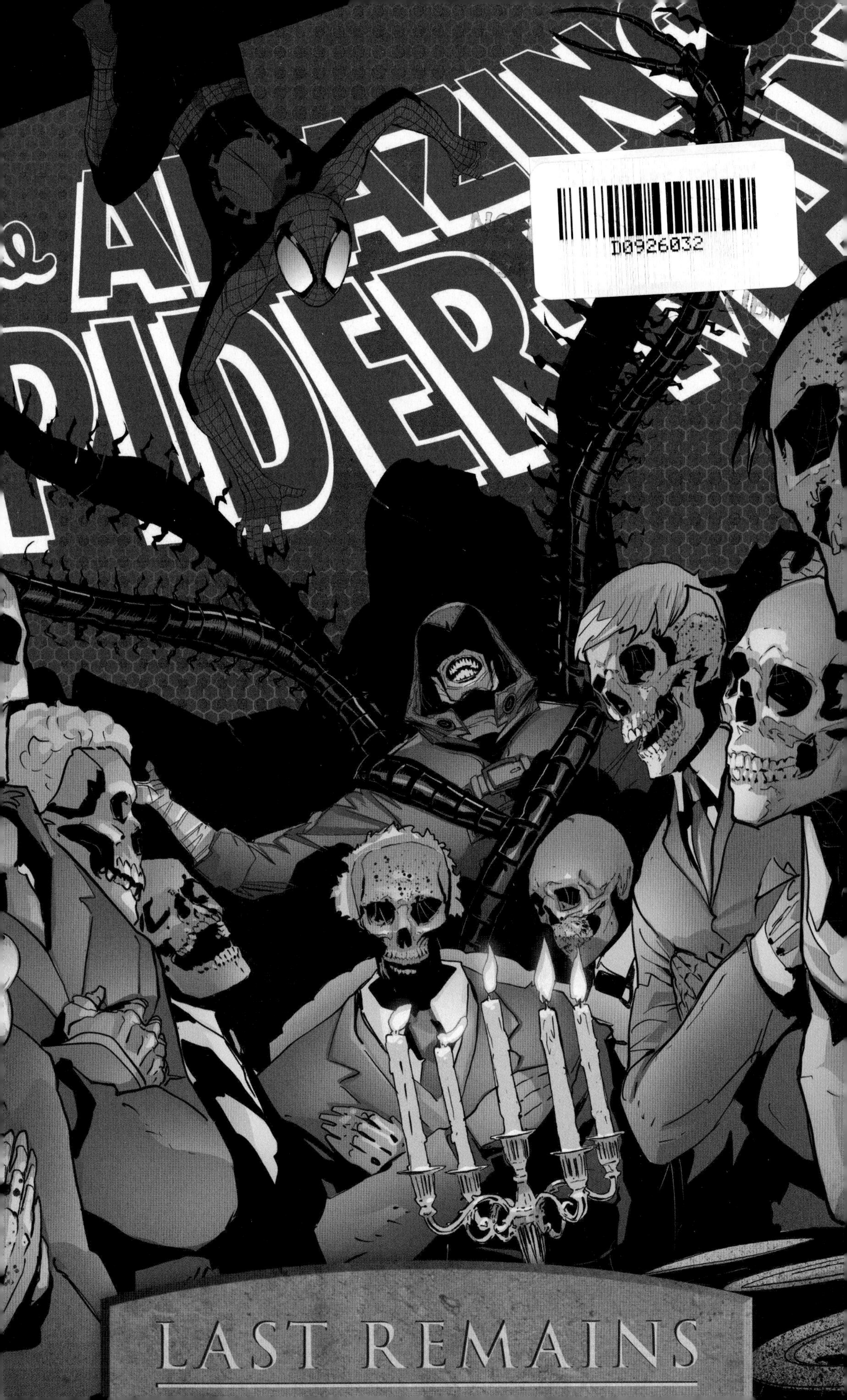
LAST REMAINS

Thanks to the mysterious villain Kindred, Sin-Eater rose from the dead more dangerous than ever. He's "cleansing" criminals of their sins AND their powers, leaving them reformed, but Spider-Man doesn't trust the cop killer. So when Sin-Eater set his sights on Norman Osborn, current director of Ravencroft Institute for the Criminally Insane, Spider-Man swung to the rescue of his archnemesis. Norman donned the Green Goblin suit once again, and he and Spidey teamed up against the souped-up Sin-Eater.

But once Sin-Eater had been stalled, Norman showed his true colors by trying to kill Spider-Man! Fortunately, Peter's Spider-Friends, calling themselves "the Order of the Web," showed up in time to rescue him. In a fit of rage, Spider-Man left Norman behind in the ruins of Ravencroft Institute while he and the Order escaped!

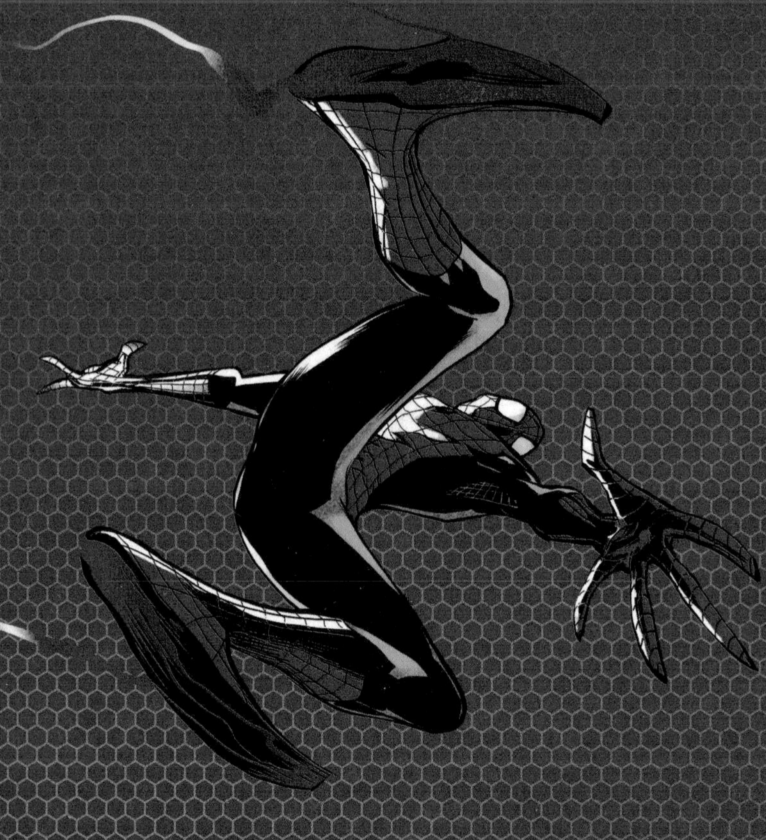

SPIDER-MAN CREATED BY STAN LEE & STEVE DITKO

COLLECTION EDITOR JENNIFER GRÜNWALD
ASSISTANT EDITOR DANIEL KIRCHHOFFER ✱ ASSISTANT MANAGING EDITOR MAIA LOY
ASSISTANT MANAGING EDITOR LISA MONTALBANO ✱ VP PRODUCTION & SPECIAL PROJECTS JEFF YOUNGQUIST
BOOK DESIGNERS ADAM DEL RE WITH JAY BOWEN
SVP PRINT, SALES & MARKETING DAVID GABRIEL ✱ EDITOR IN CHIEF C.B. CEBULSKI

AMAZING SPIDER-MAN BY NICK SPENCER VOL. 11: LAST REMAINS. Contains material originally published in magazine form as AMAZING SPIDER-MAN (2018) #50-55. First printing 2021. ISBN 978-1-302-92587-1. Published by MARVEL WORLDWIDE, INC., a subsidiary of MARVEL ENTERTAINMENT, LLC. OFFICE OF PUBLICATION: 1290 Avenue of the Americas, New York, NY 10104. © 2021 MARVEL No similarity between any of the names, characters, persons, and/or institutions in this magazine with those of any living or dead person or institution is intended, and any such similarity which may exist is purely coincidental. **Printed in the U.S.A.** KEVIN FEIGE, Chief Creative Officer; DAN BUCKLEY, President, Marvel Entertainment; JOE QUESADA, EVP & Creative Director; DAVID BOGART, Associate Publisher & SVP of Talent Affairs; TOM BREVOORT, VP, Executive Editor; NICK LOWE, Executive Editor, VP of Content, Digital Publishing; DAVID GABRIEL, VP of Print & Digital Publishing; JEFF YOUNGQUIST, VP of Production & Special Projects; ALEX MORALES, Director of Publishing Operations; DAN EDINGTON, Managing Editor; RICKEY PURDIN, Director of Talent Relations; JENNIFER GRÜNWALD, Senior Editor, Special Projects; SUSAN CRESPI, Production Manager; STAN LEE, Chairman Emeritus. For information regarding advertising in Marvel Comics or on Marvel.com, please contact Vit DeBellis, Custom Solutions & Integrated Advertising Manager, at vdebellis@marvel.com. For Marvel subscription inquiries, please call 888-511-5480. **Manufactured between 1/8/2021 and 2/9/2021 by FRY COMMUNICATIONS, MECHANICSBURG, PA, USA.**

10 9 8 7 6 5 4 3 2 1

the AMAZING SPIDER-MAN

LAST REMAINS

WRITER **NICK SPENCER**

AMAZING SPIDER-MAN #50-52 & #55

ARTIST **PATRICK GLEASON**

COLOR ARTIST **EDGAR DELGADO**

AMAZING SPIDER-MAN #53-54

PENCILER **MARK BAGLEY**

INKERS **JOHN DELL** WITH **ANDREW HENNESSY** (#54)

COLOR ARTIST **EDGAR DELGADO**

LETTERER **VC's JOE CARAMAGNA**

COVER ART **PATRICK GLEASON** WITH **MORRY HOLLOWELL** (#50) & **EDGAR DELGADO** (#51-54)

ASSISTANT EDITORS **TOM GRONEMAN** & **LINDSEY COHICK**

EDITOR **NICK LOWE**

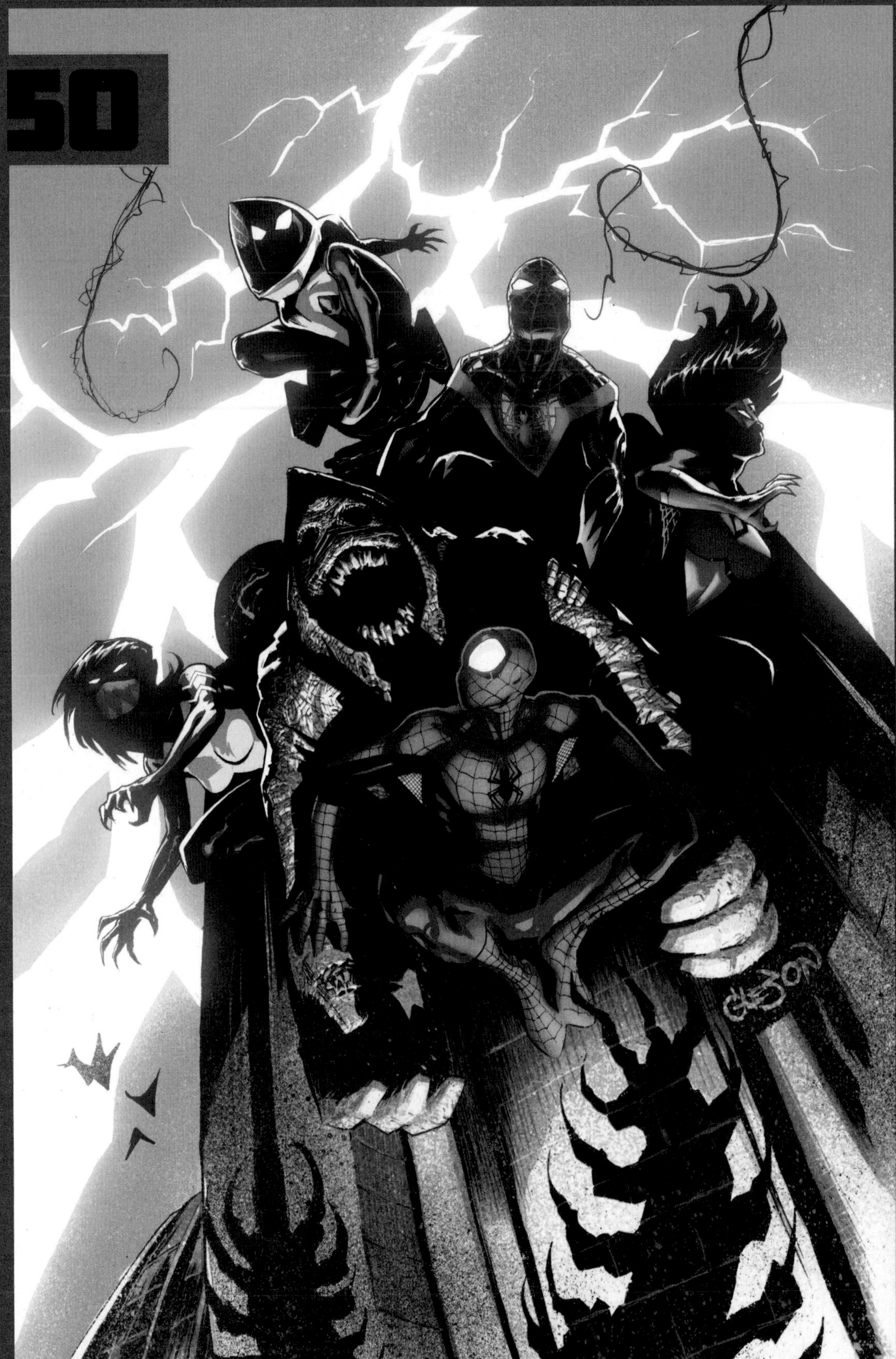
50

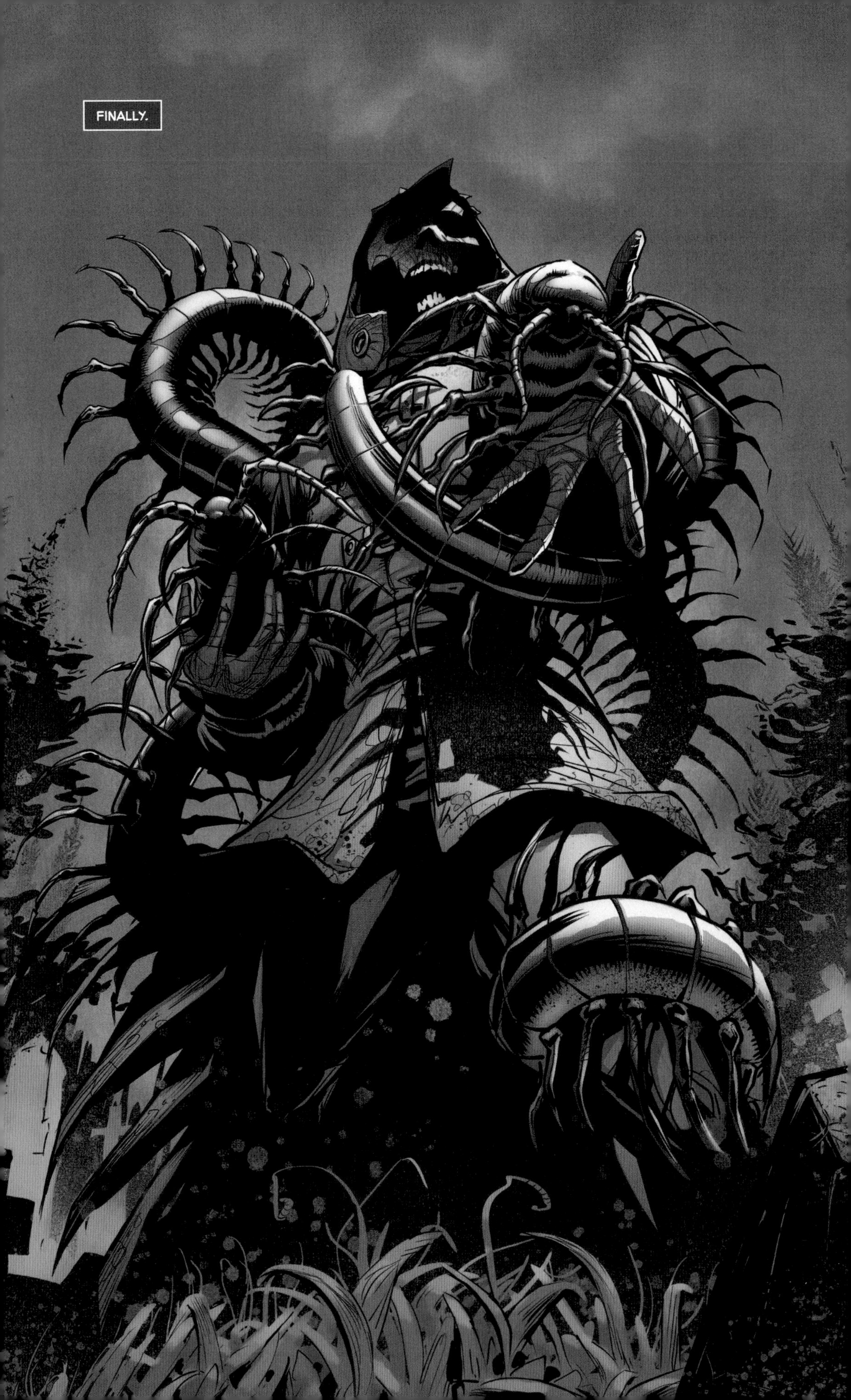
FINALLY.

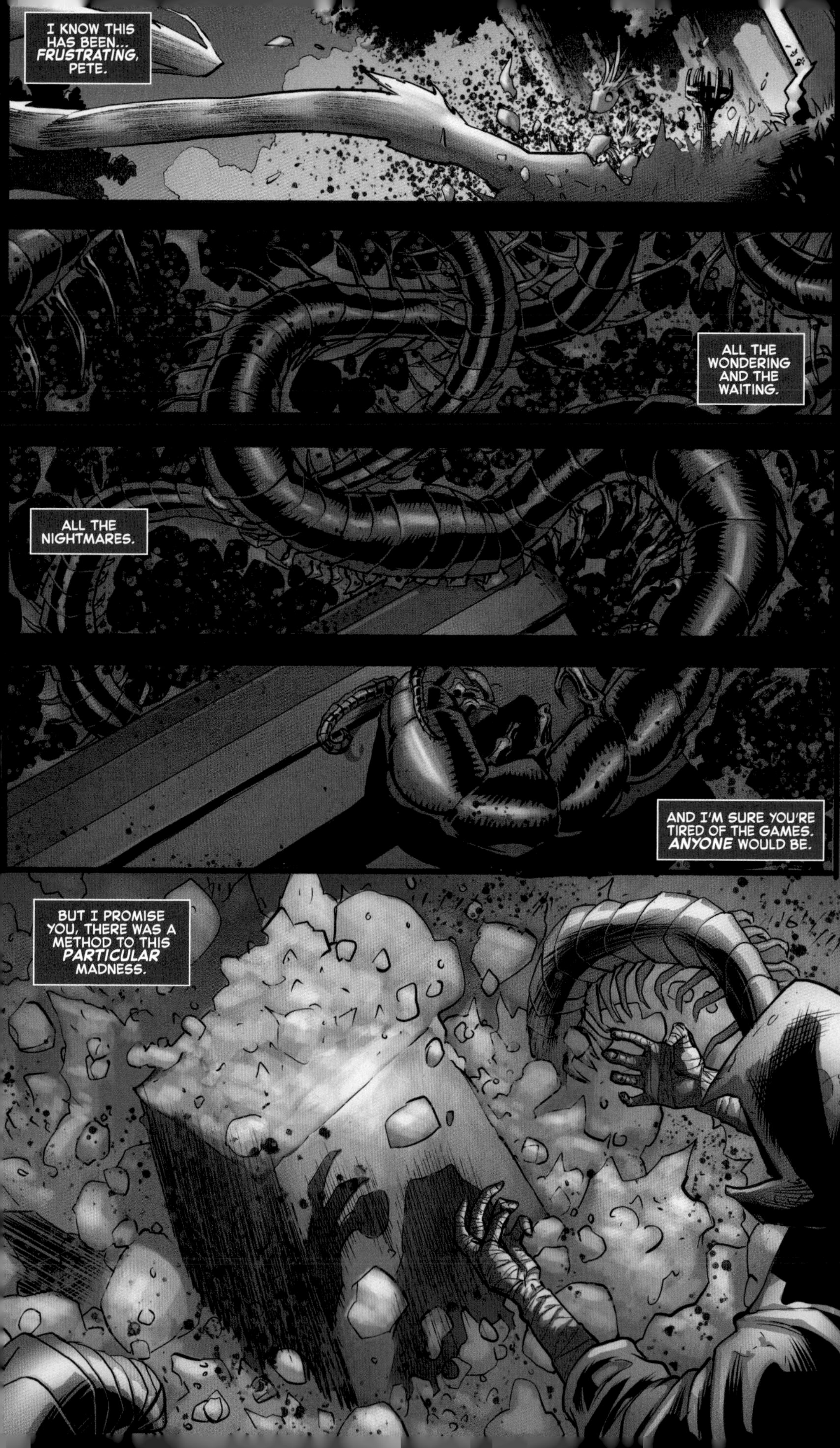
I KNOW THIS HAS BEEN... FRUSTRATING, PETE.
ALL THE WONDERING AND THE WAITING.
ALL THE NIGHTMARES.
AND I'M SURE YOU'RE TIRED OF THE GAMES. ANYONE WOULD BE.
BUT I PROMISE YOU, THERE WAS A METHOD TO THIS PARTICULAR MADNESS.

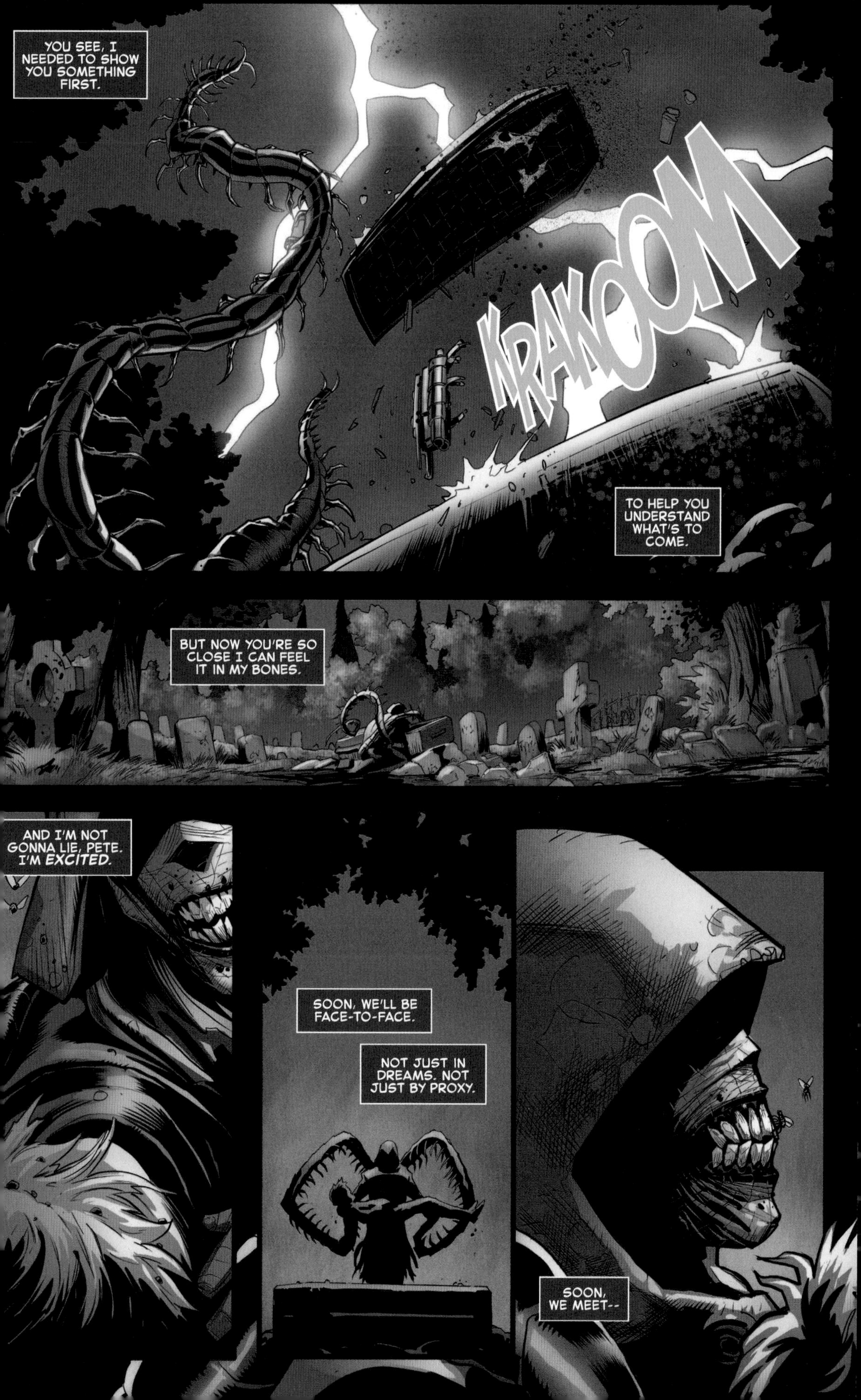
YOU SEE, I NEEDED TO SHOW YOU SOMETHING FIRST.
KRAKOOM
TO HELP YOU UNDERSTAND WHAT'S TO COME.
BUT NOW YOU'RE SO CLOSE I CAN FEEL IT IN MY BONES.
AND I'M NOT GONNA LIE, PETE. I'M EXCITED.
SOON, WE'LL BE FACE-TO-FACE.
NOT JUST IN DREAMS. NOT JUST BY PROXY.
SOON, WE MEET--

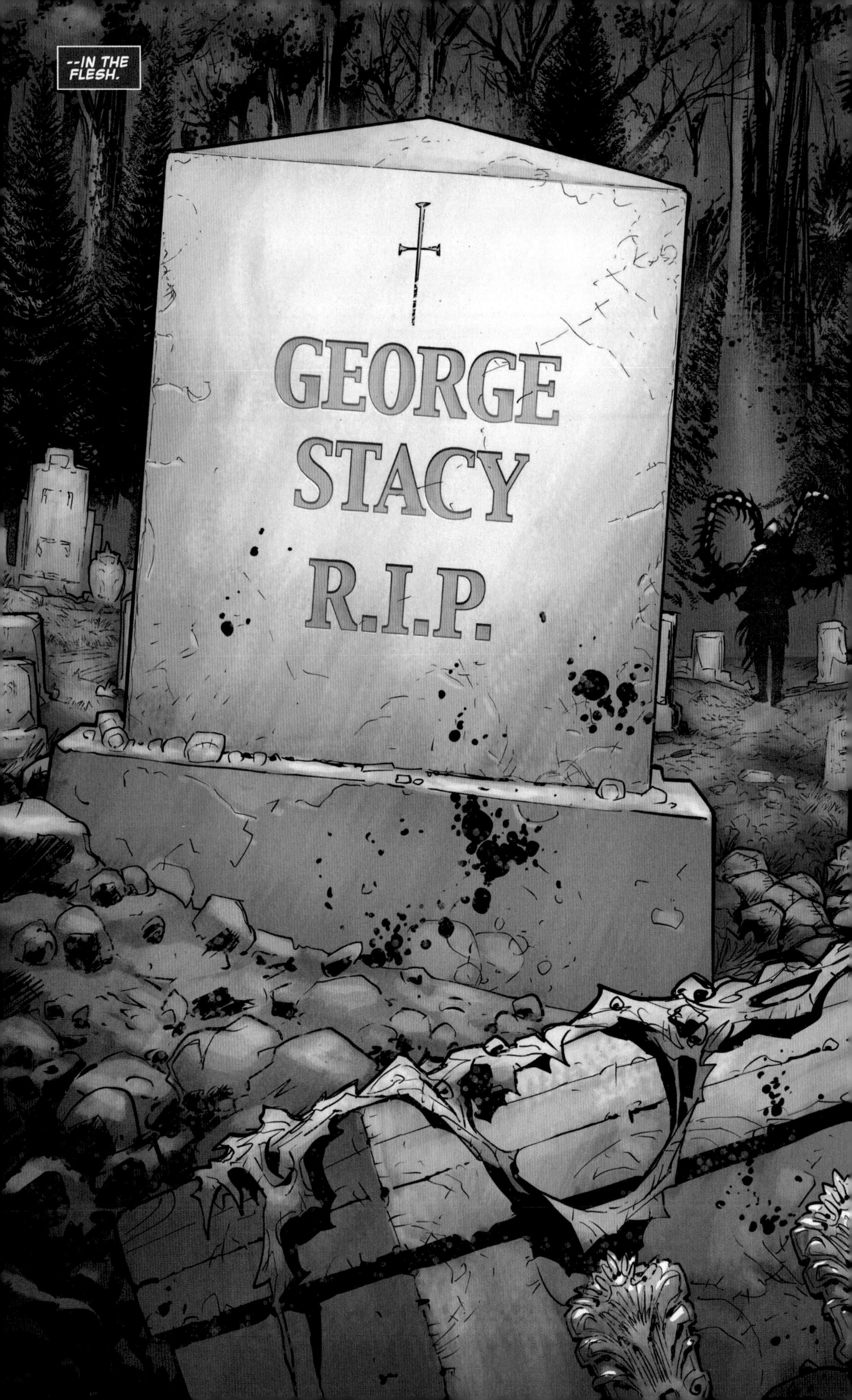
--IN THE FLESH.
GEORGE STACY R.I.P.

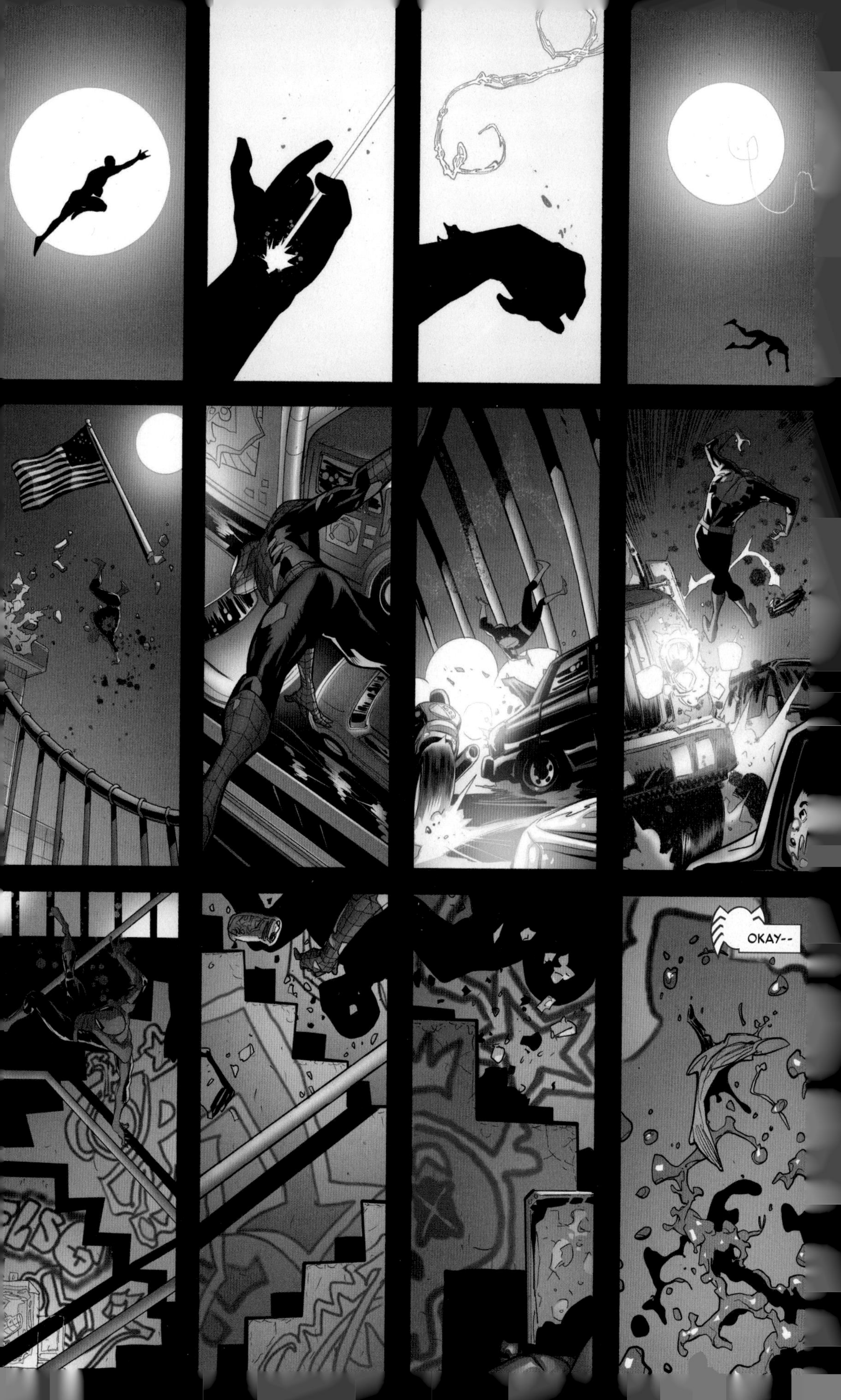
OKAY--

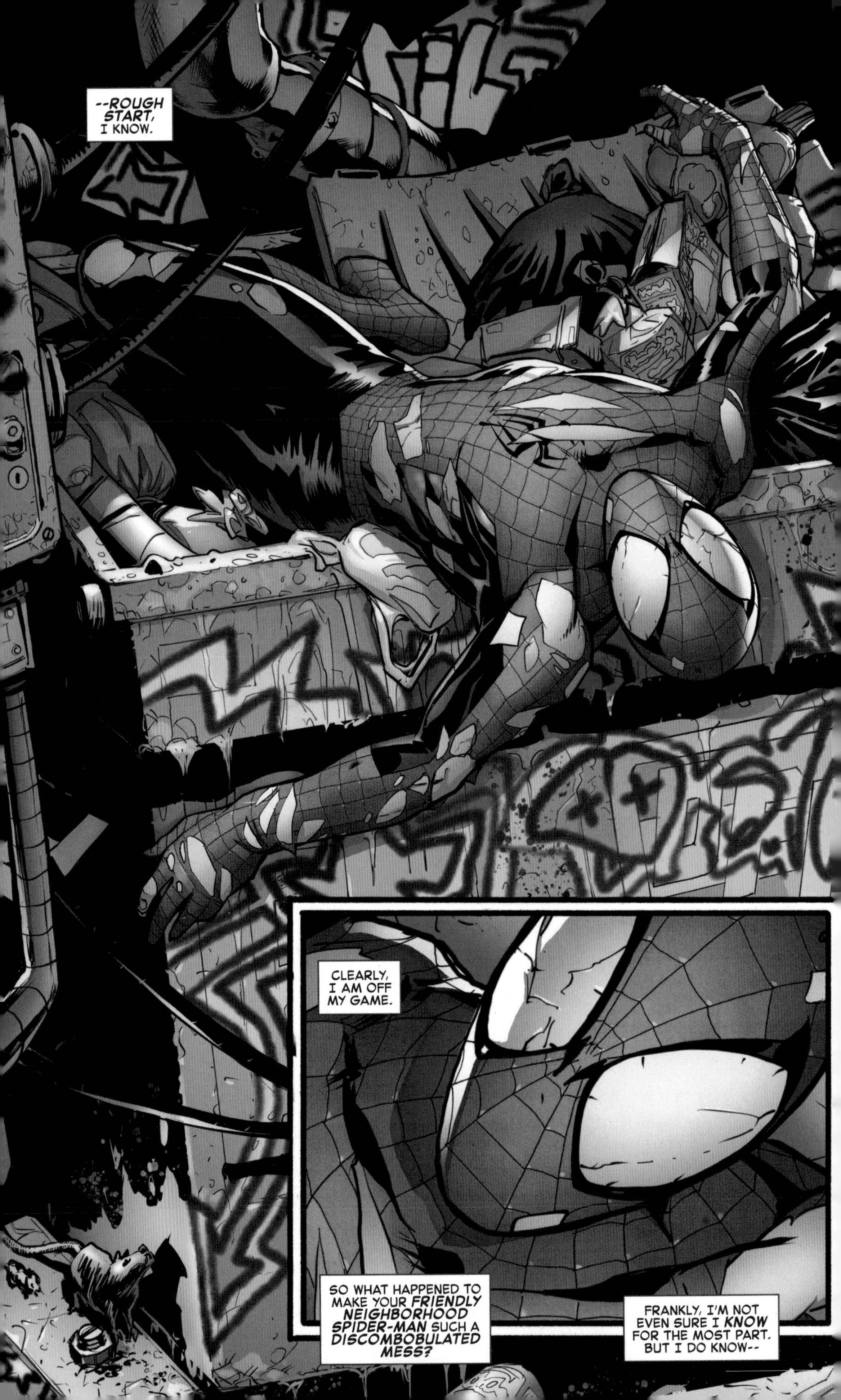
--ROUGH START, I KNOW.
CLEARLY, I AM OFF MY GAME.
SO WHAT HAPPENED TO MAKE YOUR FRIENDLY NEIGHBORHOOD SPIDER-MAN SUCH A DISCOMBOBULATED MESS?
FRANKLY, I'M NOT EVEN SURE I KNOW FOR THE MOST PART. BUT I DO KNOW--

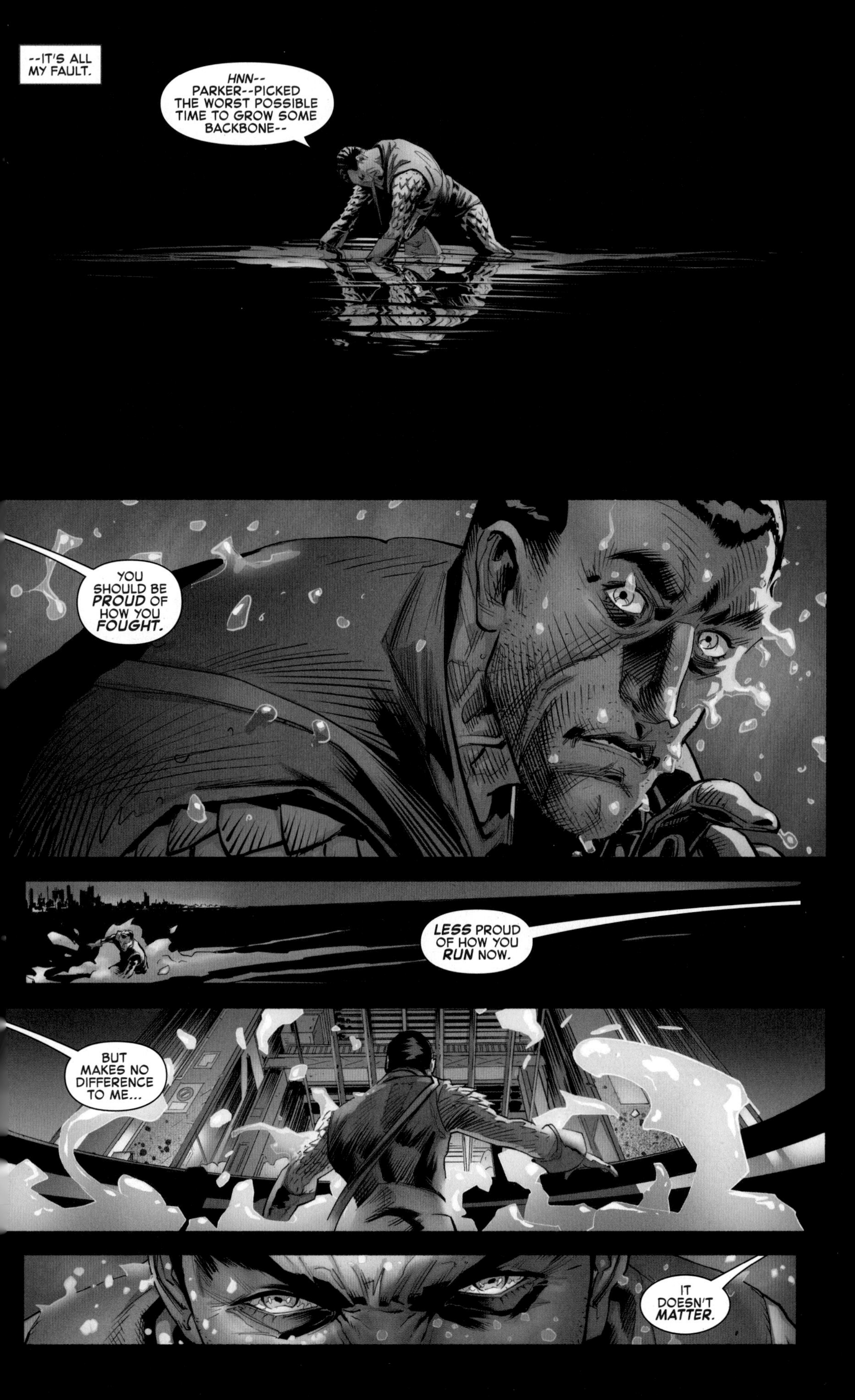
--IT'S ALL MY FAULT.
HNN-- PARKER--PICKED THE WORST POSSIBLE TIME TO GROW SOME BACKBONE--
YOU SHOULD BE PROUD OF HOW YOU FOUGHT.
LESS PROUD OF HOW YOU RUN NOW.
BUT MAKES NO DIFFERENCE TO ME...
IT DOESN'T MATTER.

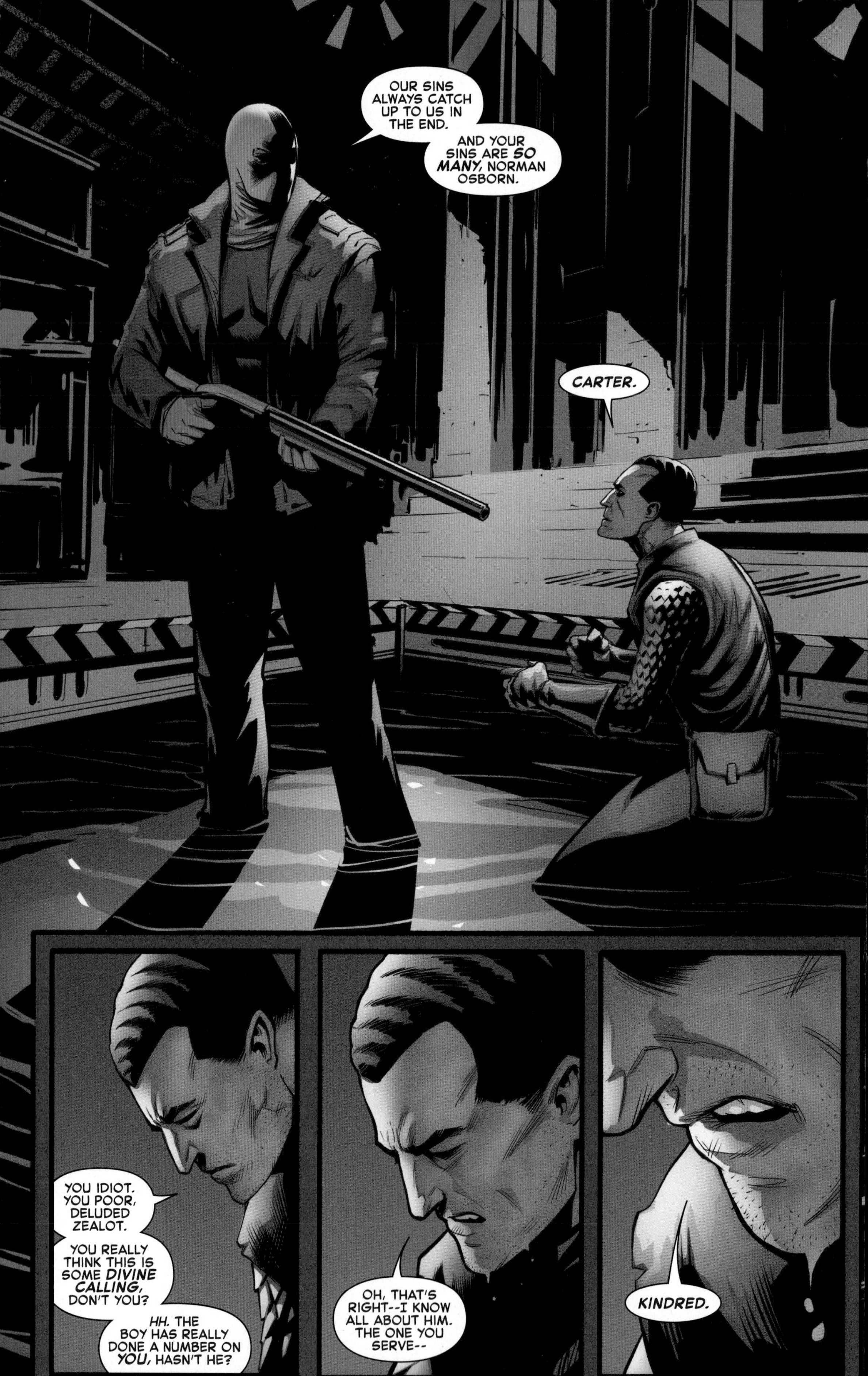
OUR SINS ALWAYS CATCH UP TO US IN THE END.
AND YOUR SINS ARE SO MANY, NORMAN OSBORN.
CARTER.
YOU IDIOT. YOU POOR, DELUDED ZEALOT.
YOU REALLY THINK THIS IS SOME DIVINE CALLING, DON'T YOU?
HH. THE BOY HAS REALLY DONE A NUMBER ON YOU, HASN'T HE?
OH, THAT'S RIGHT--I KNOW ALL ABOUT HIM. THE ONE YOU SERVE--
KINDRED.

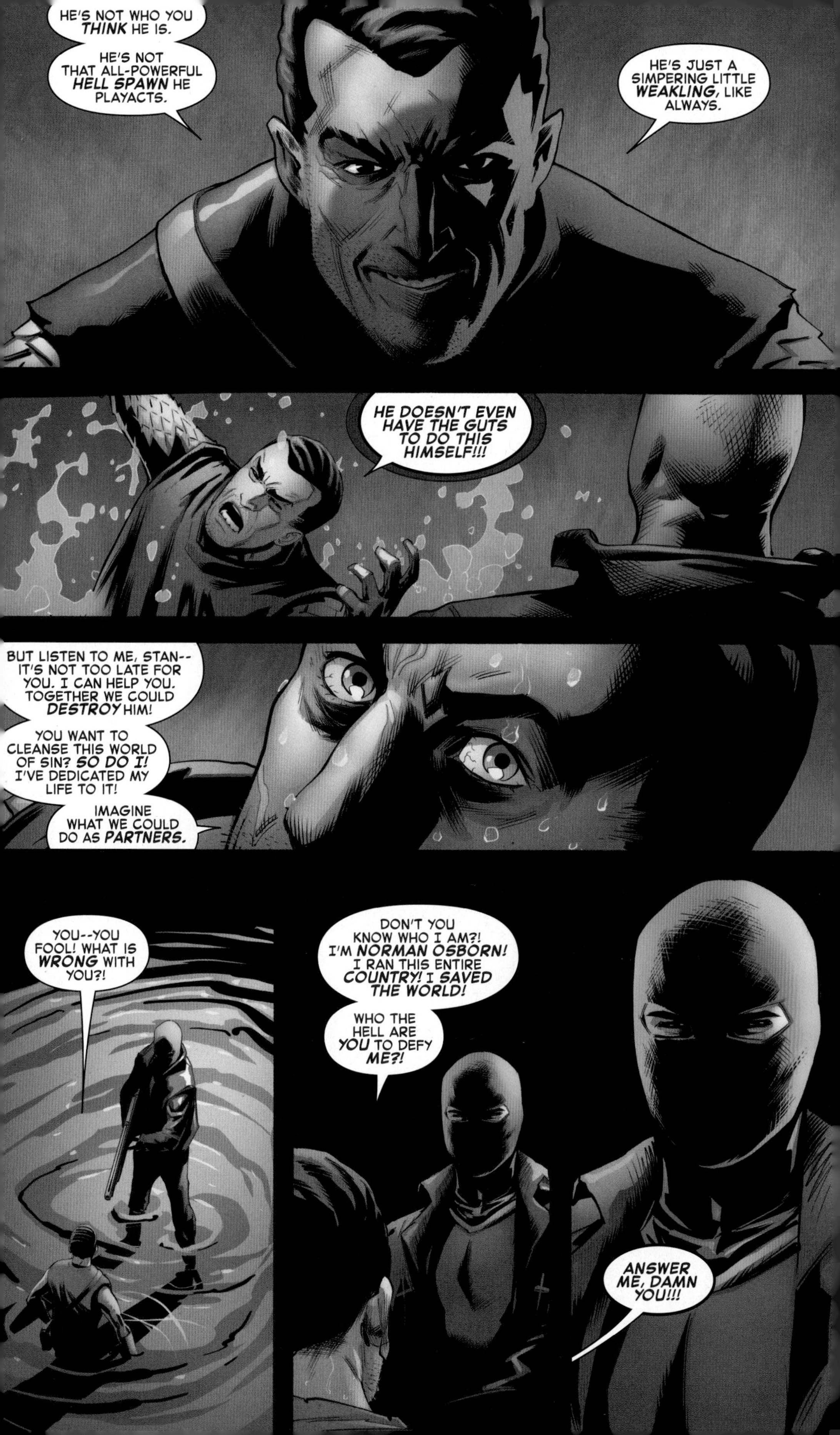
HE'S NOT WHO YOU THINK HE IS.
HE'S NOT THAT ALL-POWERFUL HELL SPAWN HE PLAYACTS.
HE'S JUST A SIMPERING LITTLE WEAKLING, LIKE ALWAYS.
HE DOESN'T EVEN HAVE THE GUTS TO DO THIS HIMSELF!!!
BUT LISTEN TO ME, STAN--IT'S NOT TOO LATE FOR YOU. I CAN HELP YOU. TOGETHER WE COULD DESTROY HIM!
YOU WANT TO CLEANSE THIS WORLD OF SIN? SO DO I! I'VE DEDICATED MY LIFE TO IT!
IMAGINE WHAT WE COULD DO AS PARTNERS.
YOU--YOU FOOL! WHAT IS WRONG WITH YOU?!
DON'T YOU KNOW WHO I AM?! I'M NORMAN OSBORN! I RAN THIS ENTIRE COUNTRY! I SAVED THE WORLD!
WHO THE HELL ARE YOU TO DEFY ME?!
ANSWER ME, DAMN YOU!!!

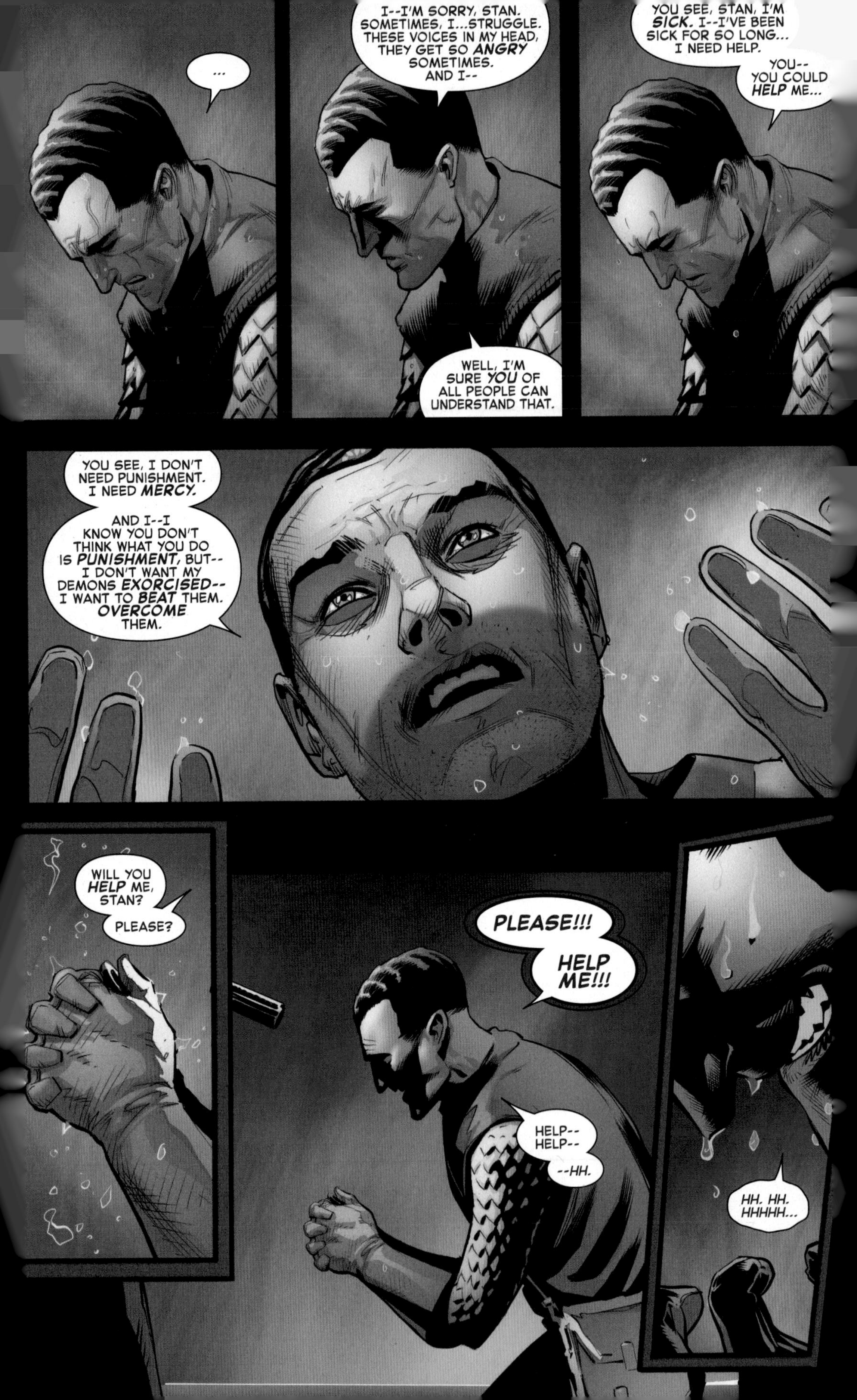
...
I--I'M SORRY, STAN. SOMETIMES, I...STRUGGLE. THESE VOICES IN MY HEAD, THEY GET SO ANGRY SOMETIMES. AND I--
WELL, I'M SURE YOU OF ALL PEOPLE CAN UNDERSTAND THAT.
YOU SEE, STAN, I'M SICK. I--I'VE BEEN SICK FOR SO LONG... I NEED HELP.
YOU-- YOU COULD HELP ME...
YOU SEE, I DON'T NEED PUNISHMENT. I NEED MERCY.
AND I--I KNOW YOU DON'T THINK WHAT YOU DO IS PUNISHMENT, BUT-- I DON'T WANT MY DEMONS EXORCISED-- I WANT TO BEAT THEM. OVERCOME THEM.
WILL YOU HELP ME, STAN?
PLEASE?
PLEASE!!!
HELP ME!!!
HELP-- HELP--
--HH.
HH. HH. HHHHH...

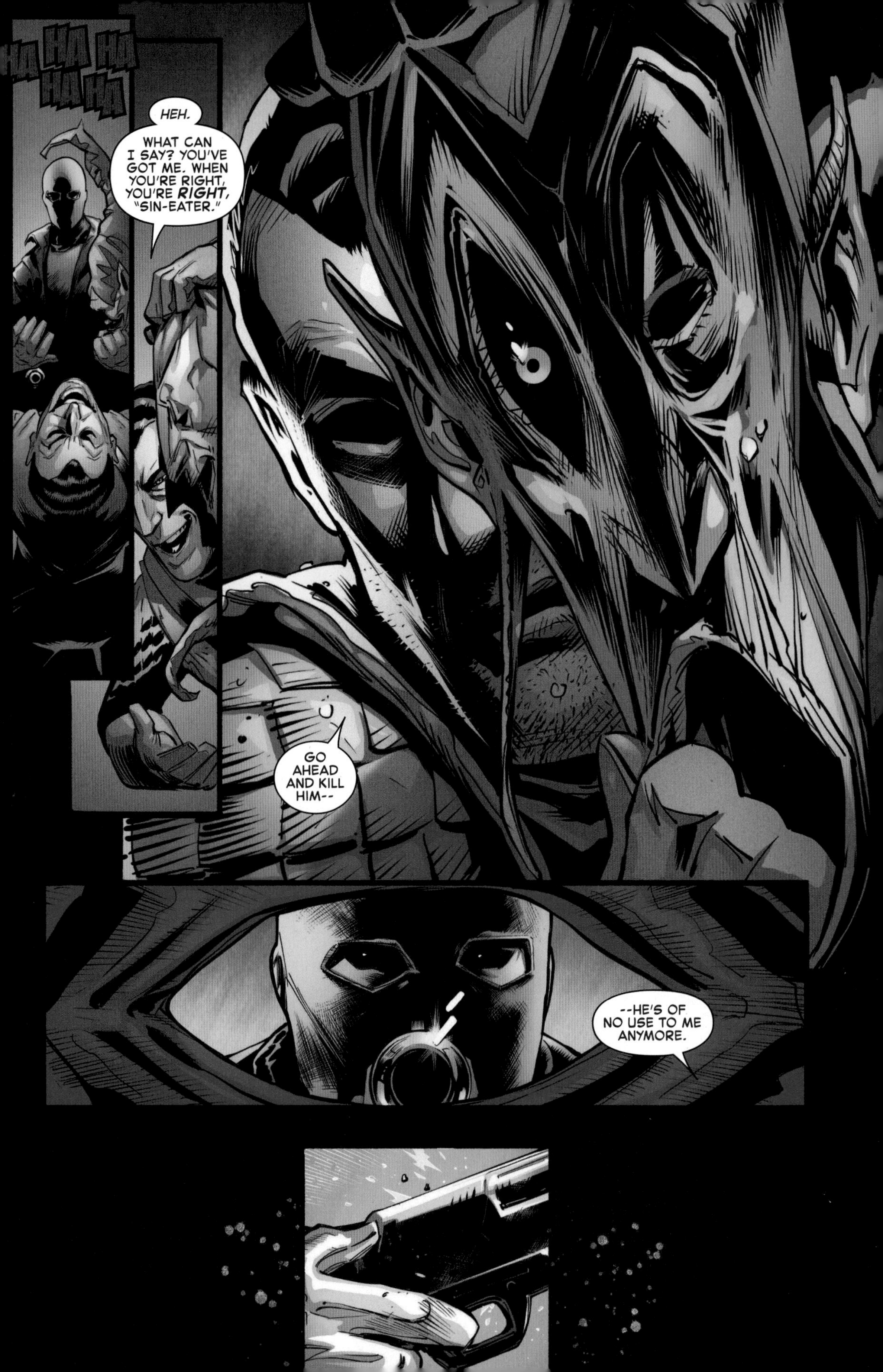
HA HA HA
HA HA
HEH.
WHAT CAN I SAY? YOU'VE GOT ME. WHEN YOU'RE RIGHT, YOU'RE **RIGHT,** "SIN-EATER."
GO AHEAD AND KILL HIM--
--HE'S OF NO USE TO ME ANYMORE.

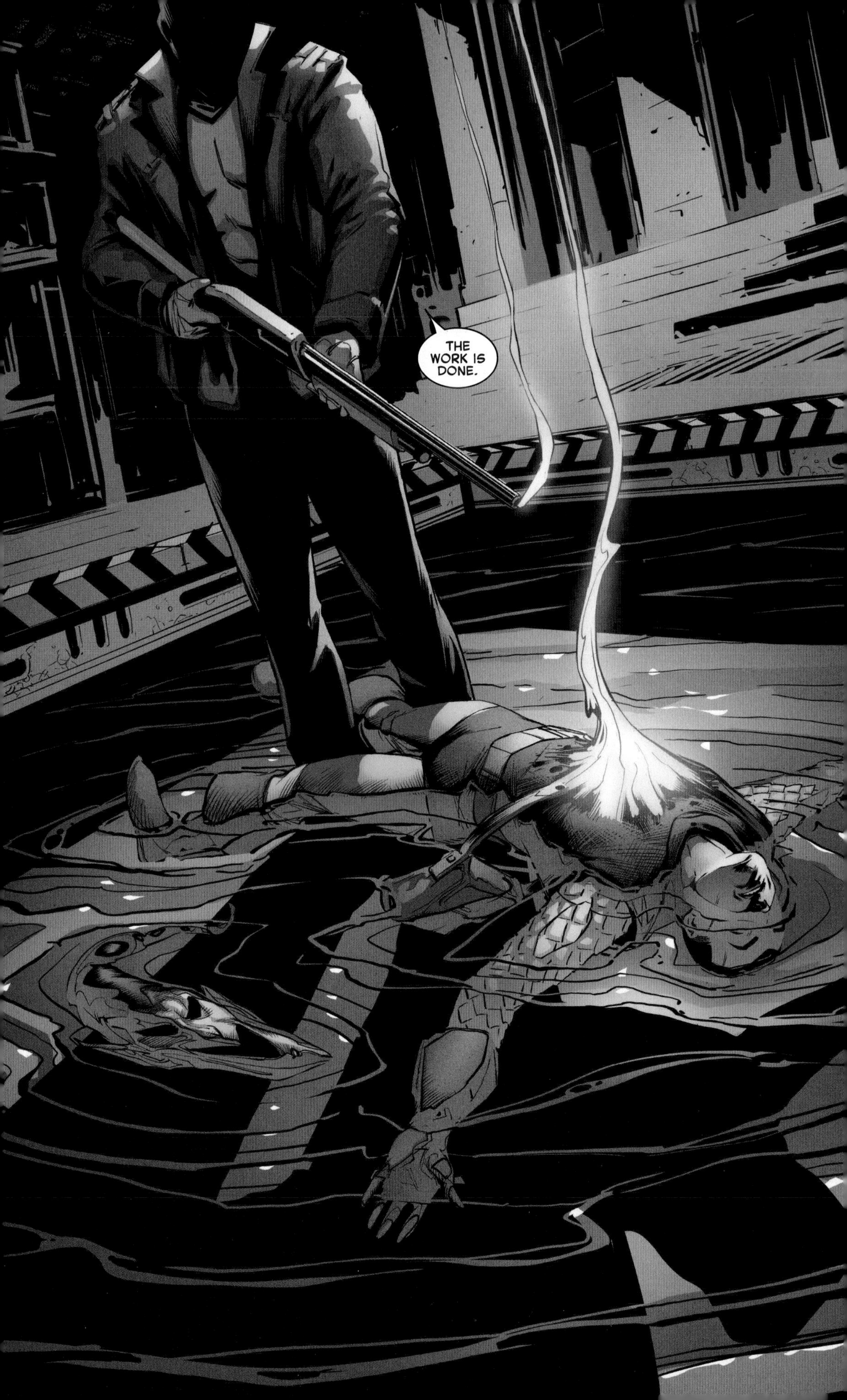
THE WORK IS DONE.

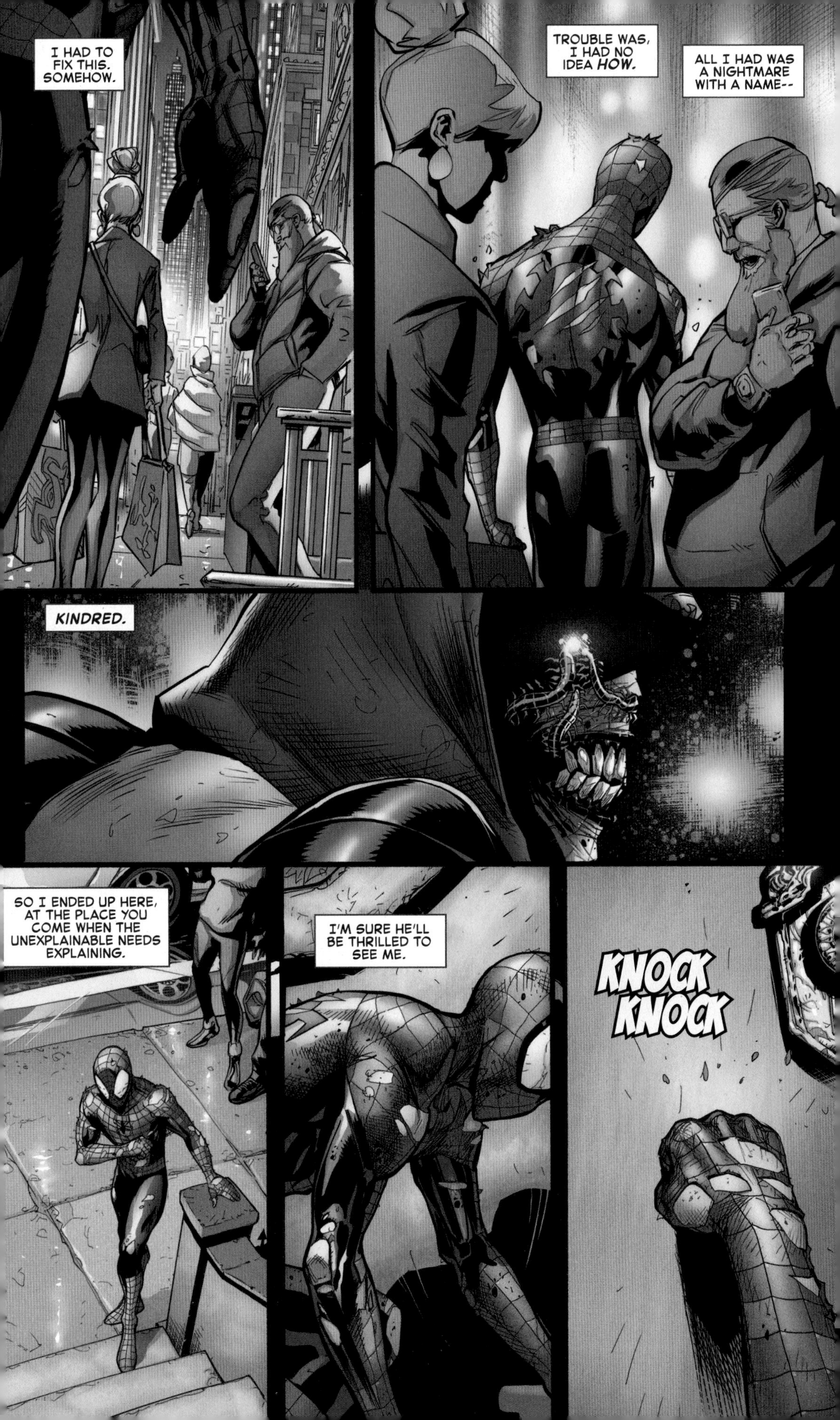

I HAD TO FIX THIS. SOMEHOW.
TROUBLE WAS, I HAD NO IDEA *HOW.*
ALL I HAD WAS A NIGHTMARE WITH A NAME--
KINDRED.
SO I ENDED UP HERE, AT THE PLACE YOU COME WHEN THE UNEXPLAINABLE NEEDS EXPLAINING.
I'M SURE HE'LL BE THRILLED TO SEE ME.
KNOCK KNOCK

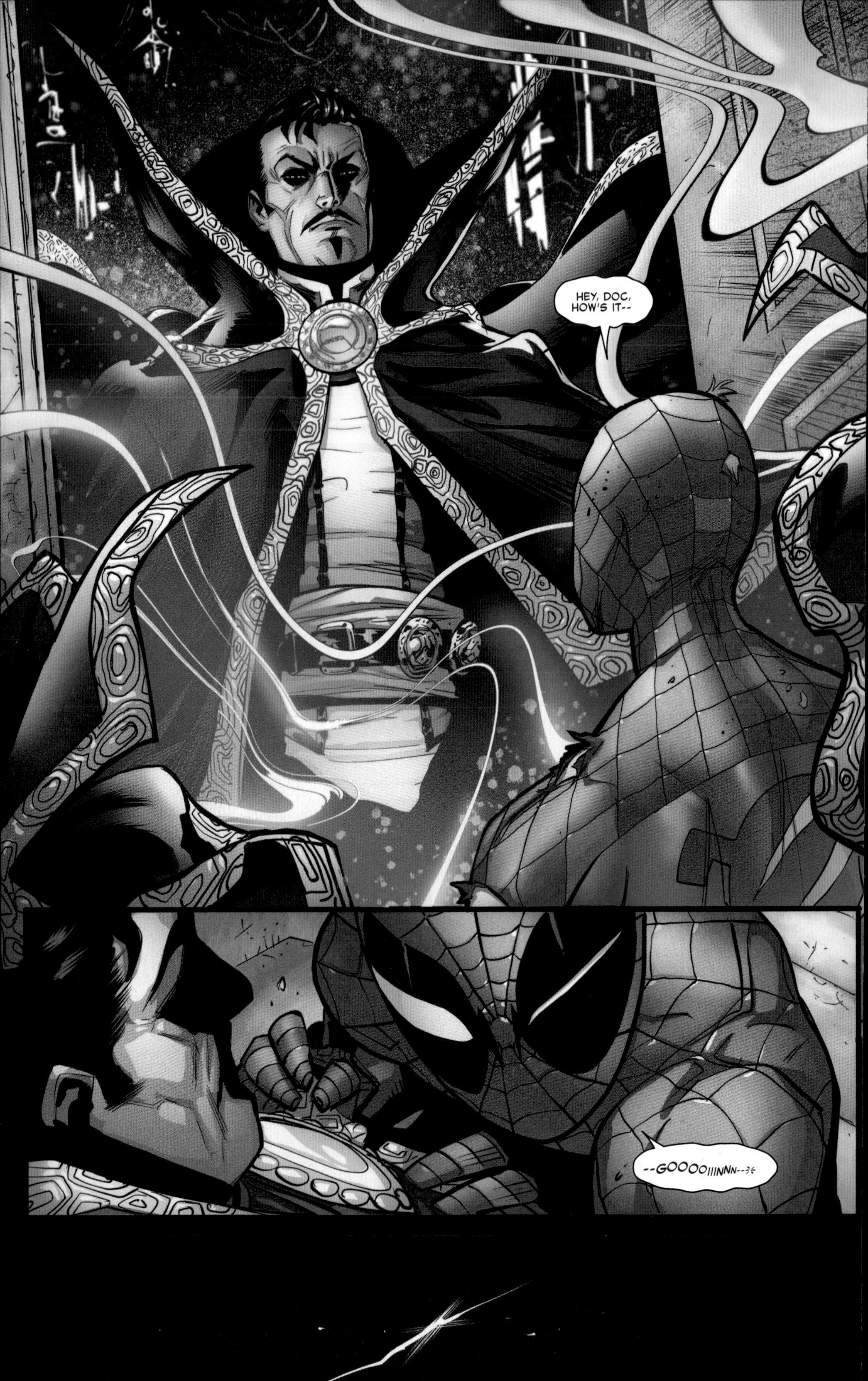
HEY, DOC, HOW'S IT--
--GOOOOIIIINNN--?!

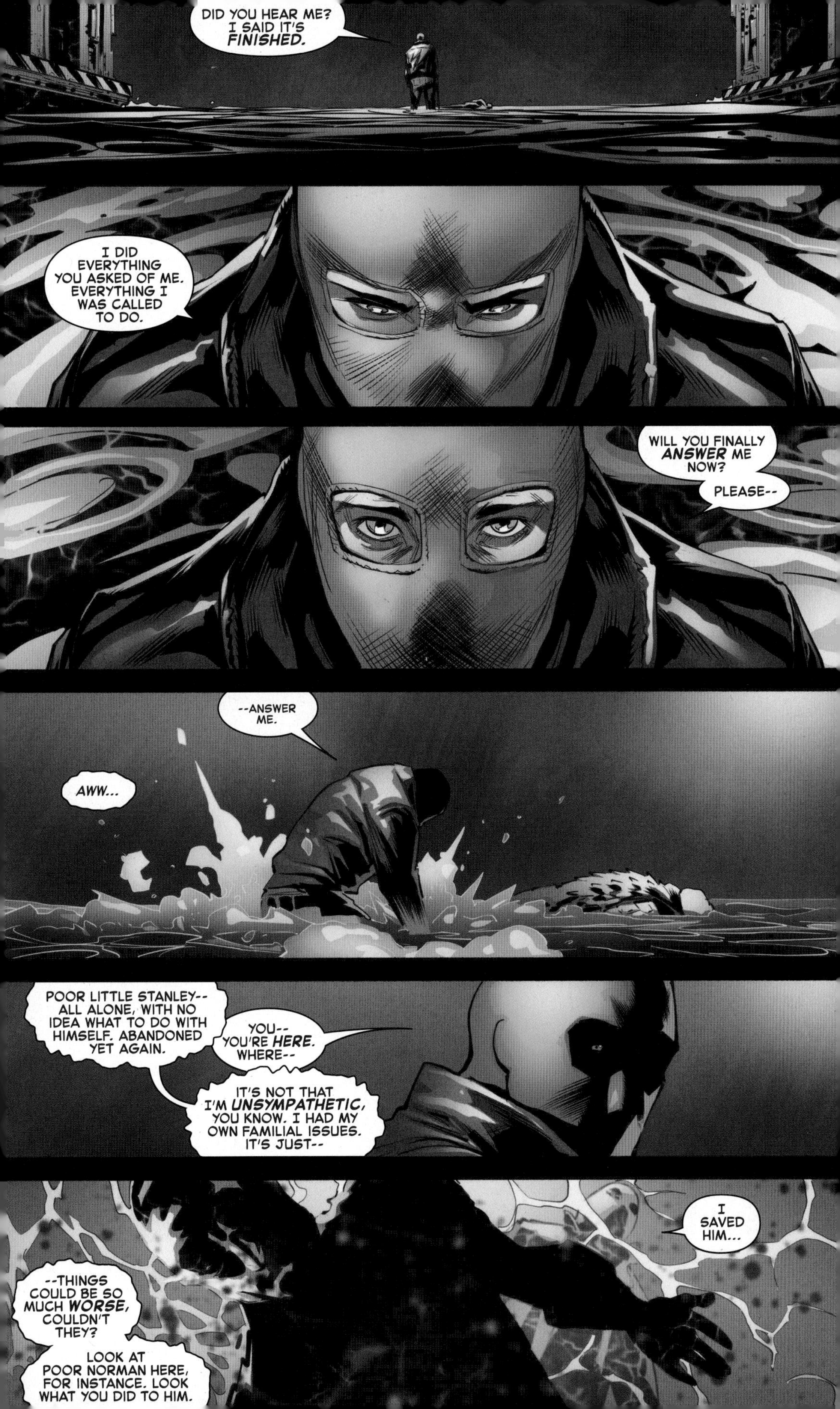
DID YOU HEAR ME? I SAID IT'S FINISHED.
I DID EVERYTHING YOU ASKED OF ME. EVERYTHING I WAS CALLED TO DO.
WILL YOU FINALLY ANSWER ME NOW?
PLEASE--
--ANSWER ME.
AWW...
POOR LITTLE STANLEY-- ALL ALONE, WITH NO IDEA WHAT TO DO WITH HIMSELF. ABANDONED YET AGAIN.
YOU-- YOU'RE HERE. WHERE--
IT'S NOT THAT I'M UNSYMPATHETIC, YOU KNOW. I HAD MY OWN FAMILIAL ISSUES. IT'S JUST--
I SAVED HIM...
--THINGS COULD BE SO MUCH WORSE, COULDN'T THEY?
LOOK AT POOR NORMAN HERE, FOR INSTANCE. LOOK WHAT YOU DID TO HIM.

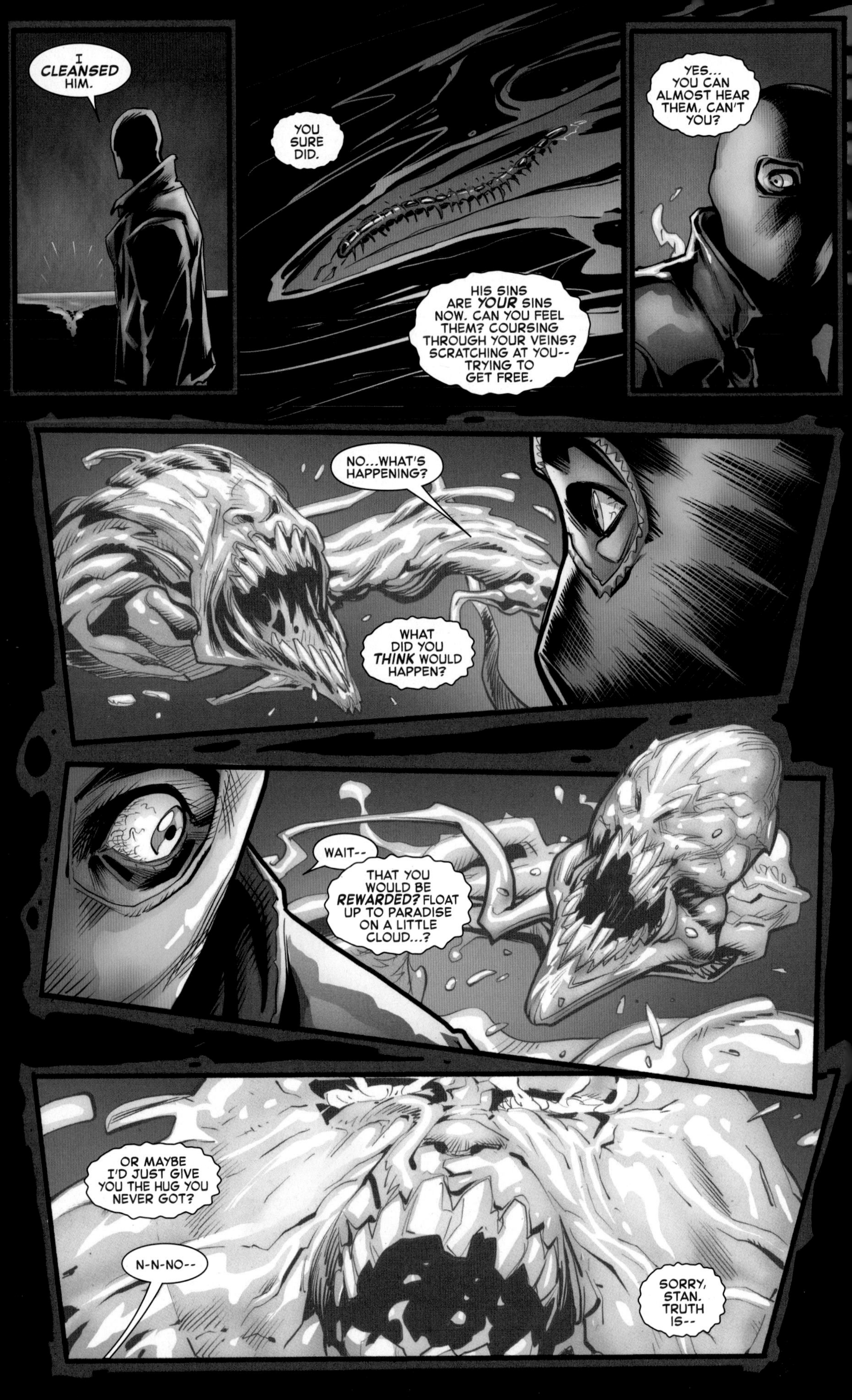
I CLEANSED HIM.
YOU SURE DID.
HIS SINS ARE YOUR SINS NOW. CAN YOU FEEL THEM? COURSING THROUGH YOUR VEINS? SCRATCHING AT YOU--TRYING TO GET FREE.
YES... YOU CAN ALMOST HEAR THEM, CAN'T YOU?
NO...WHAT'S HAPPENING?
WHAT DID YOU THINK WOULD HAPPEN?
WAIT--
THAT YOU WOULD BE REWARDED? FLOAT UP TO PARADISE ON A LITTLE CLOUD...?
OR MAYBE I'D JUST GIVE YOU THE HUG YOU NEVER GOT?
N-N-NO--
SORRY, STAN. TRUTH IS--

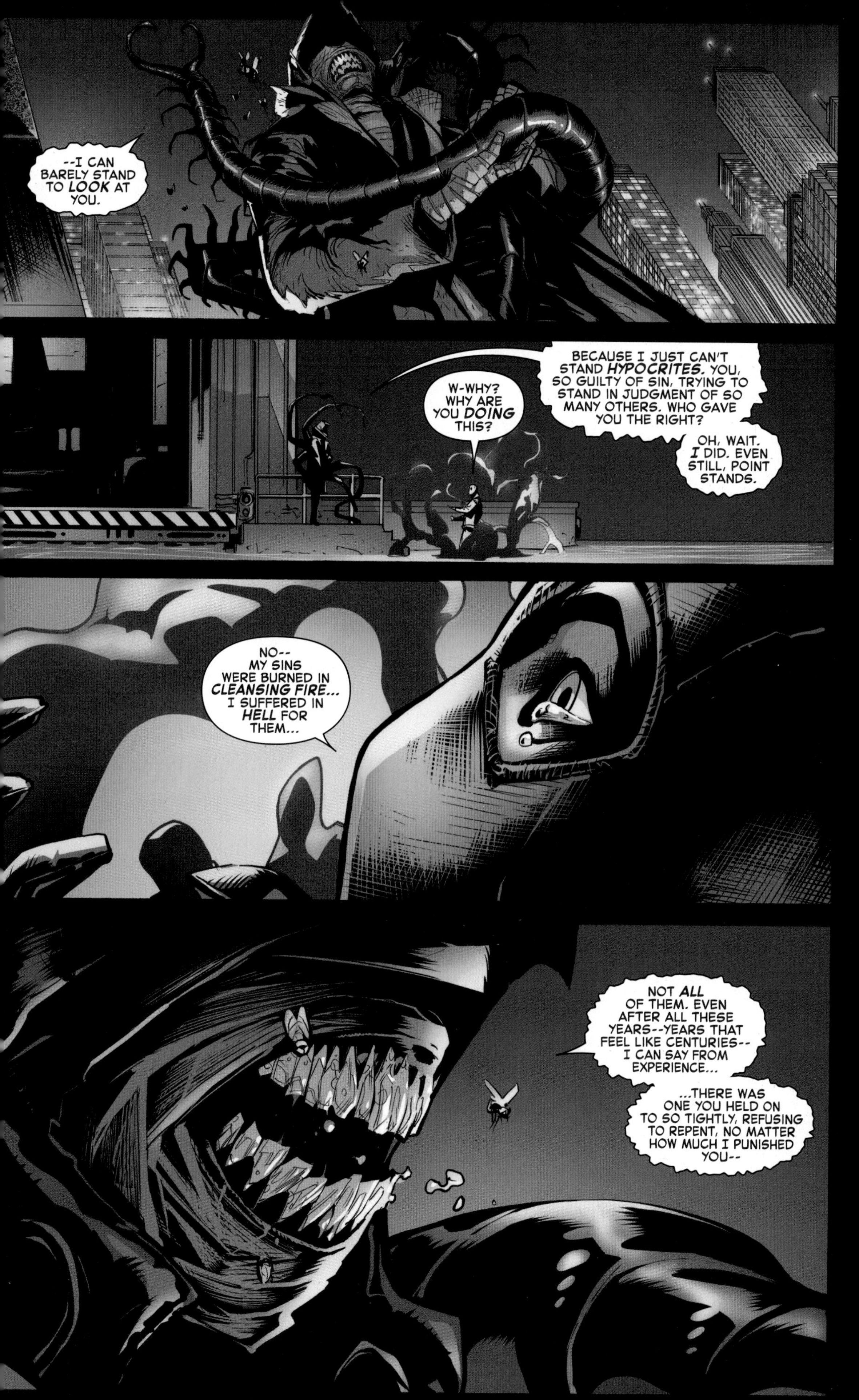
--I CAN BARELY STAND TO LOOK AT YOU.
W-WHY? WHY ARE YOU DOING THIS?
BECAUSE I JUST CAN'T STAND HYPOCRITES. YOU, SO GUILTY OF SIN, TRYING TO STAND IN JUDGMENT OF SO MANY OTHERS. WHO GAVE YOU THE RIGHT?
OH, WAIT. I DID. EVEN STILL, POINT STANDS.
NO-- MY SINS WERE BURNED IN CLEANSING FIRE... I SUFFERED IN HELL FOR THEM...
NOT ALL OF THEM. EVEN AFTER ALL THESE YEARS--YEARS THAT FEEL LIKE CENTURIES-- I CAN SAY FROM EXPERIENCE...
...THERE WAS ONE YOU HELD ON TO SO TIGHTLY, REFUSING TO REPENT, NO MATTER HOW MUCH I PUNISHED YOU--

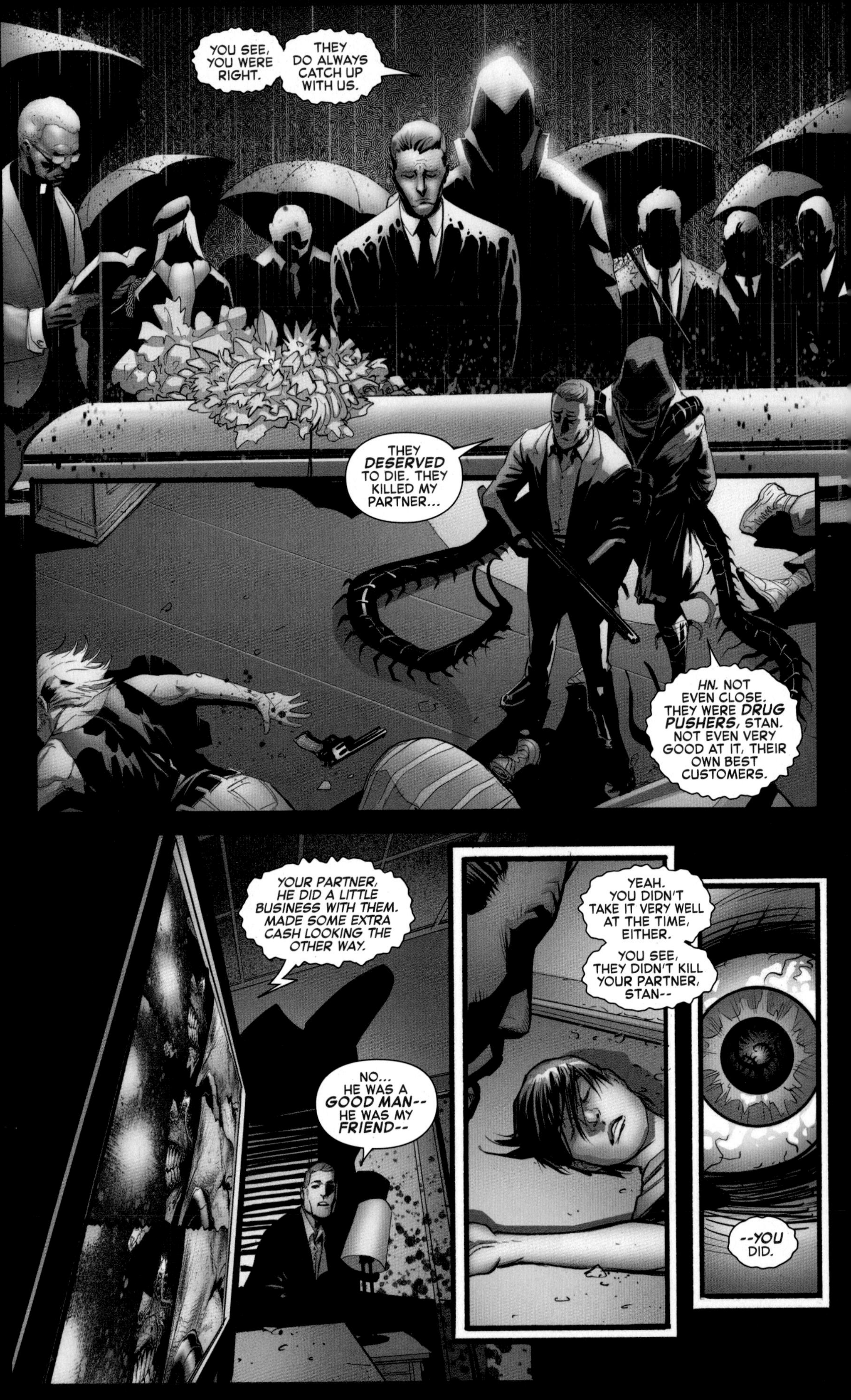
YOU SEE, YOU WERE RIGHT.
THEY DO ALWAYS CATCH UP WITH US.
THEY DESERVED TO DIE. THEY KILLED MY PARTNER...
HN. NOT EVEN CLOSE. THEY WERE DRUG PUSHERS, STAN. NOT EVEN VERY GOOD AT IT, THEIR OWN BEST CUSTOMERS.
YOUR PARTNER, HE DID A LITTLE BUSINESS WITH THEM. MADE SOME EXTRA CASH LOOKING THE OTHER WAY.
NO... HE WAS A GOOD MAN-- HE WAS MY FRIEND--
YEAH. YOU DIDN'T TAKE IT VERY WELL AT THE TIME, EITHER.
YOU SEE, THEY DIDN'T KILL YOUR PARTNER, STAN--
--YOU DID.

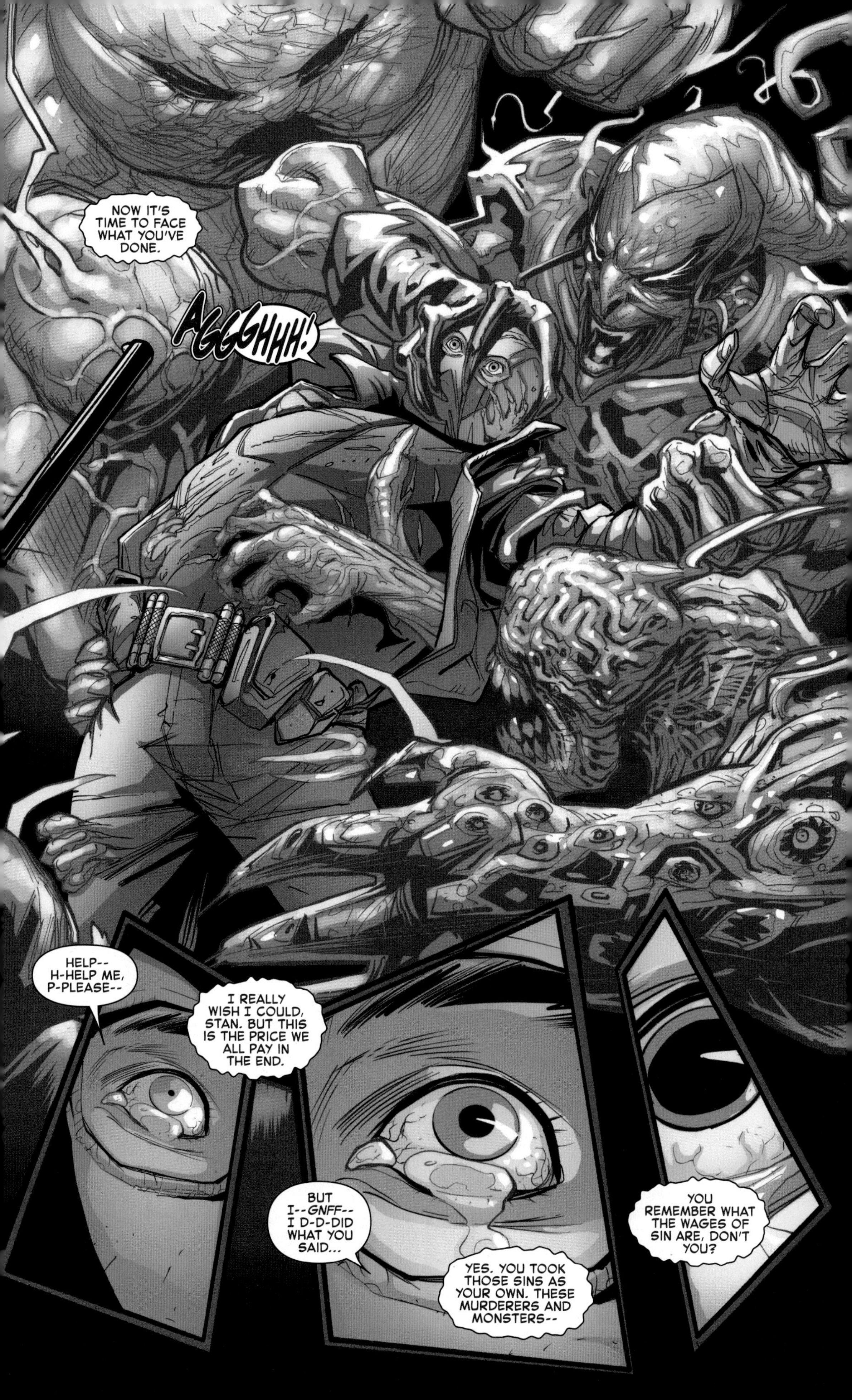
NOW IT'S TIME TO FACE WHAT YOU'VE DONE.
AGGGHHH!
HELP-- H-HELP ME, P-PLEASE--
I REALLY WISH I COULD, STAN. BUT THIS IS THE PRICE WE ALL PAY IN THE END.
BUT I--*GNFF*-- I D-D-DID WHAT YOU SAID...
YES. YOU TOOK THOSE SINS AS YOUR OWN. THESE MURDERERS AND MONSTERS--
YOU REMEMBER WHAT THE WAGES OF SIN ARE, DON'T YOU?

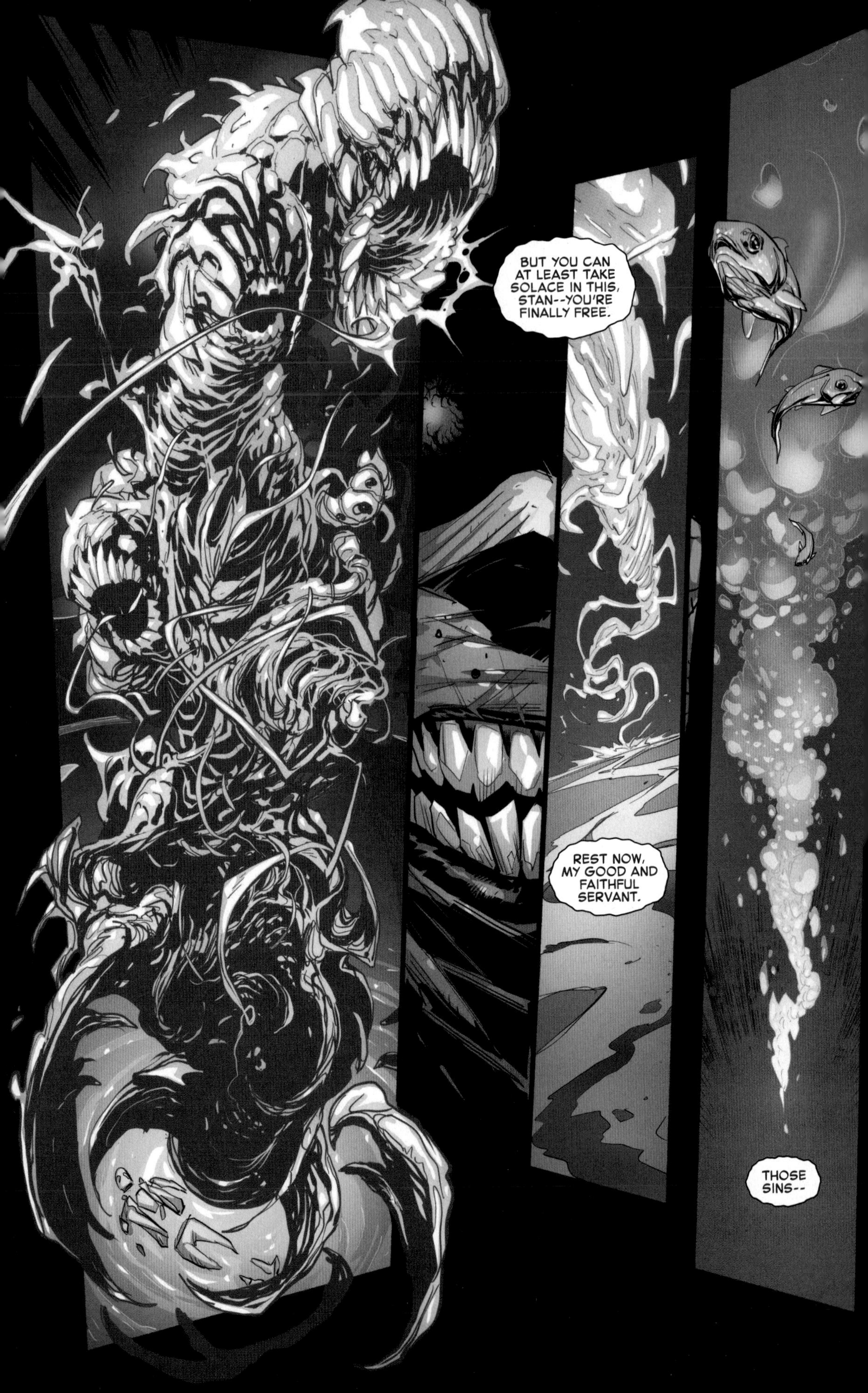
BUT YOU CAN AT LEAST TAKE SOLACE IN THIS, STAN--YOU'RE FINALLY FREE.
REST NOW, MY GOOD AND FAITHFUL SERVANT.
THOSE SINS--

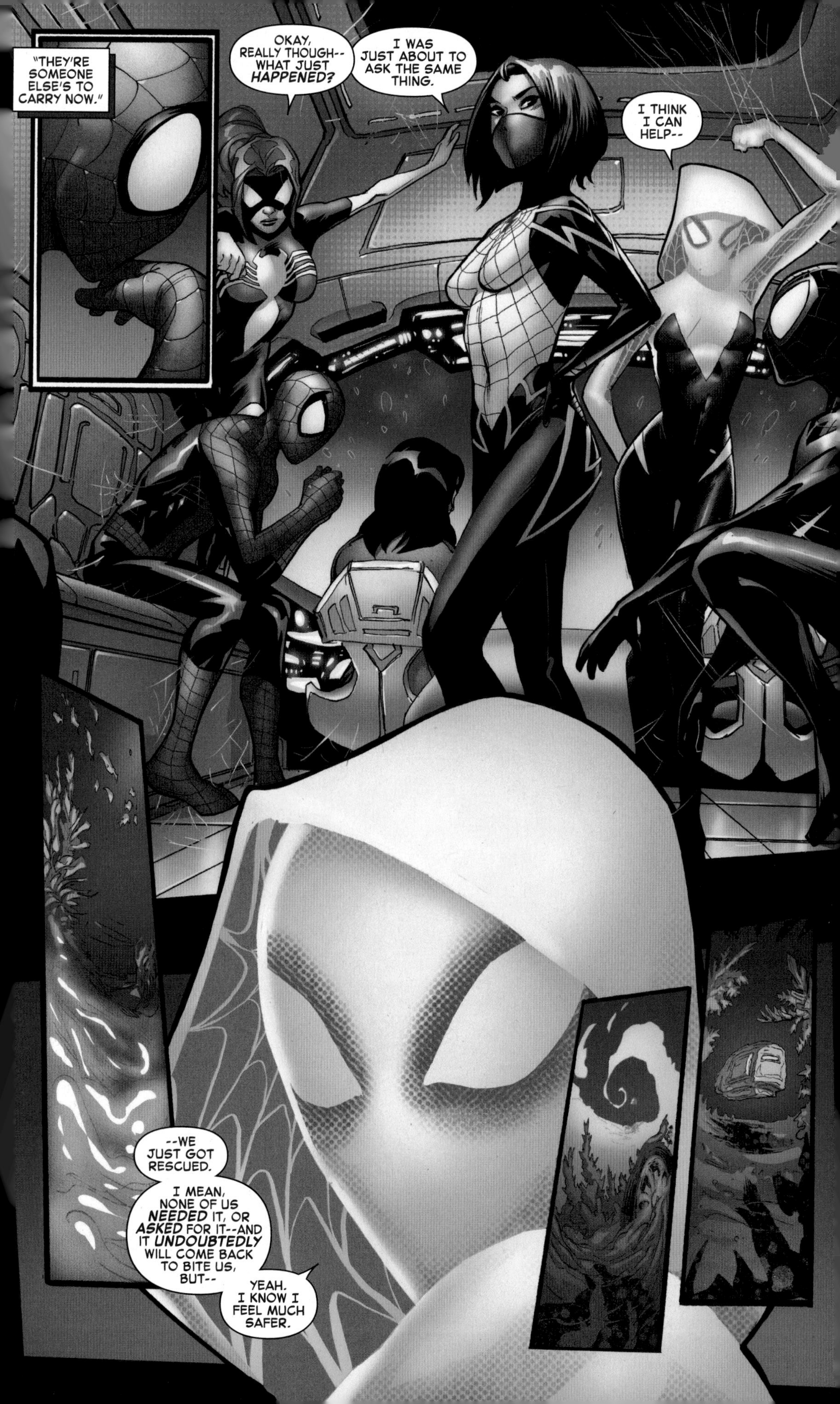
"THEY'RE SOMEONE ELSE'S TO CARRY NOW."
OKAY, REALLY THOUGH-- WHAT JUST *HAPPENED?*
I WAS JUST ABOUT TO ASK THE SAME THING.
I THINK I CAN HELP--
--WE JUST GOT RESCUED.
I MEAN, NONE OF US *NEEDED* IT, OR *ASKED* FOR IT--AND IT *UNDOUBTEDLY* WILL COME BACK TO BITE US, BUT--
YEAH. I KNOW I FEEL MUCH SAFER.

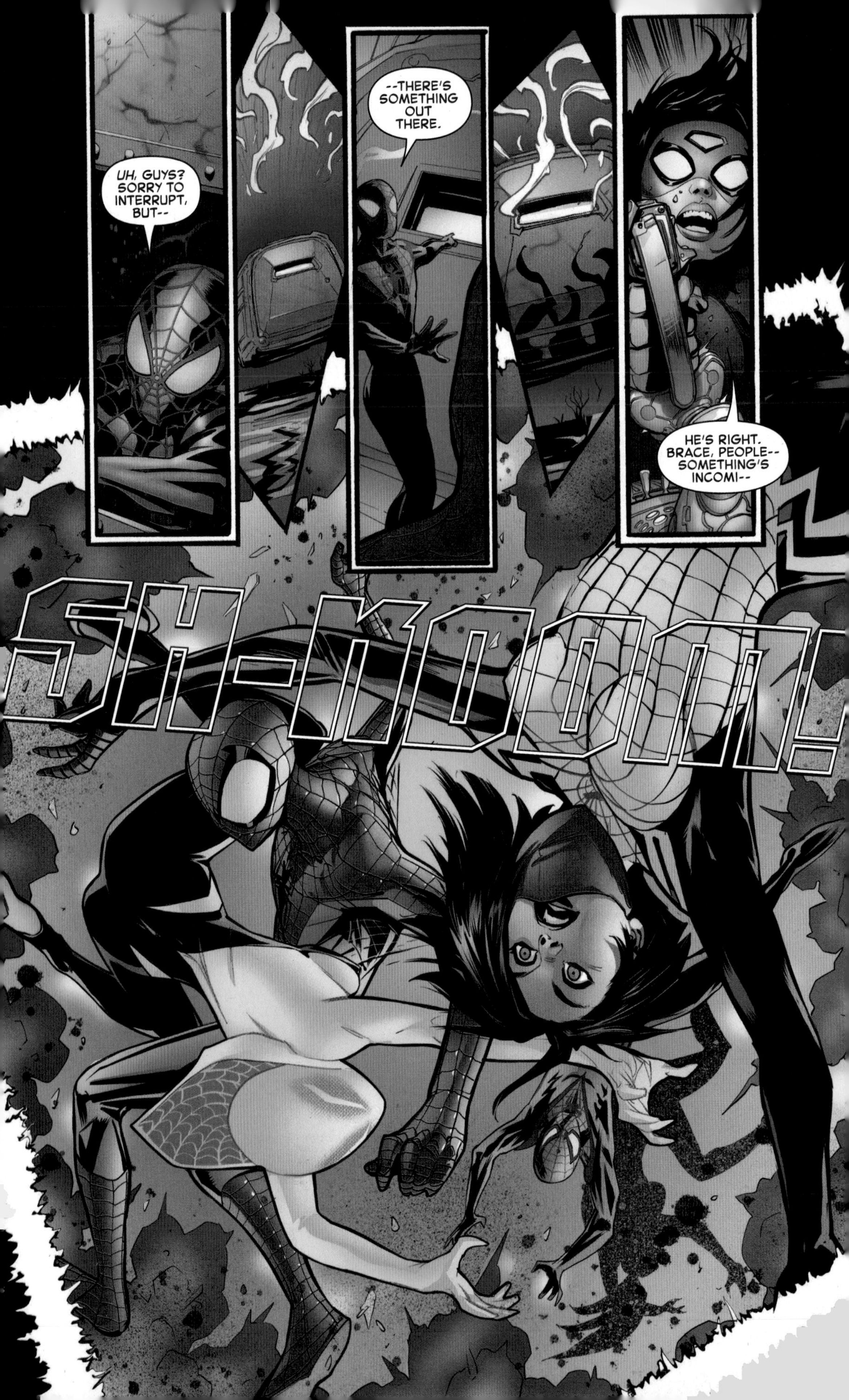
UH, GUYS? SORRY TO INTERRUPT, BUT--
--THERE'S SOMETHING OUT THERE.
HE'S RIGHT. BRACE, PEOPLE-- SOMETHING'S INCOMI--
SH-KOOM!

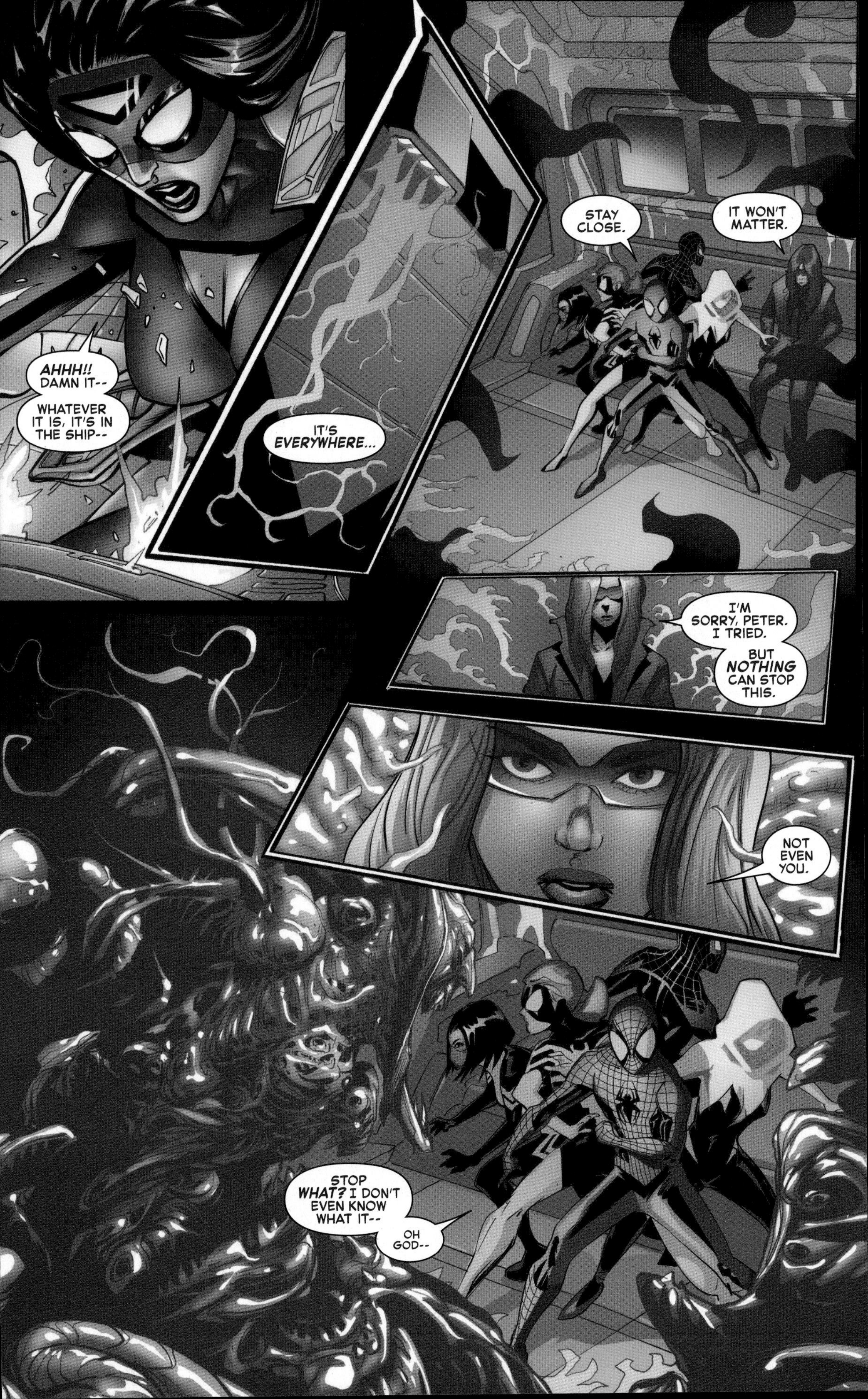
AHHH!! DAMN IT--
WHATEVER IT IS, IT'S IN THE SHIP--
IT'S EVERYWHERE...
STAY CLOSE.
IT WON'T MATTER.
I'M SORRY, PETER. I TRIED.
BUT NOTHING CAN STOP THIS.
NOT EVEN YOU.
STOP WHAT? I DON'T EVEN KNOW WHAT IT--
OH GOD--

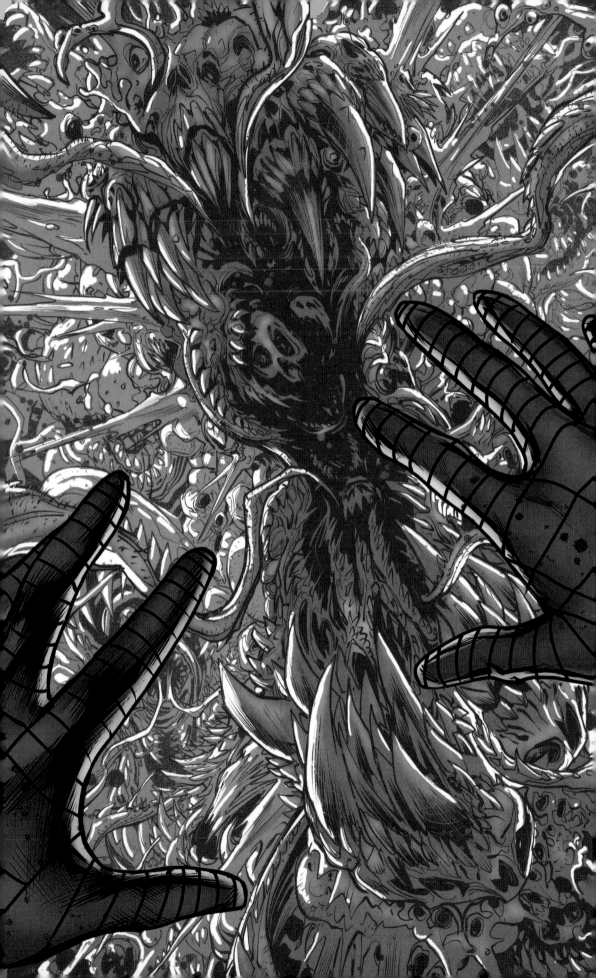

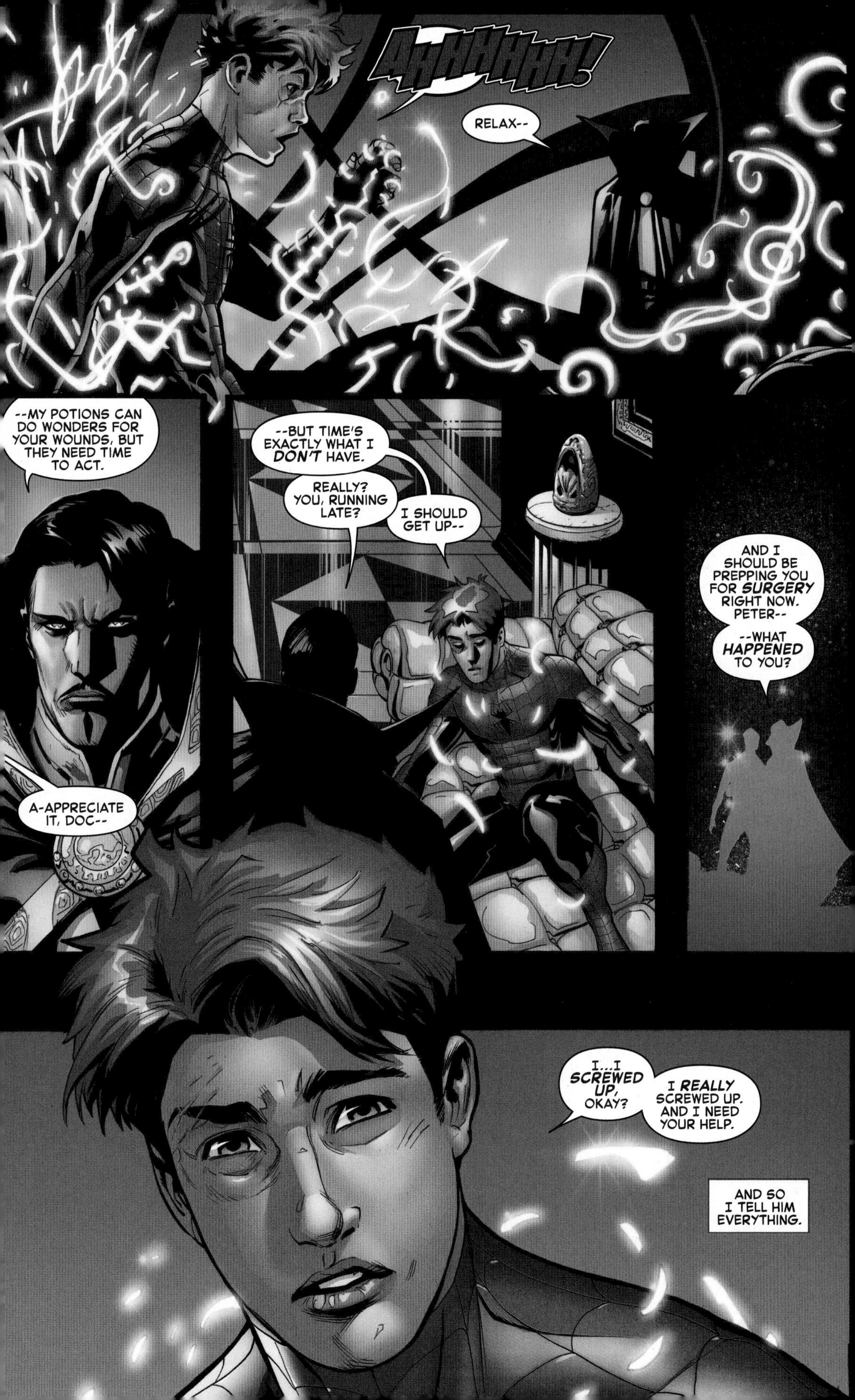
AHHHHHH!
RELAX--
--MY POTIONS CAN DO WONDERS FOR YOUR WOUNDS, BUT THEY NEED TIME TO ACT.
--BUT TIME'S EXACTLY WHAT I DON'T HAVE.
REALLY? YOU, RUNNING LATE?
I SHOULD GET UP--
AND I SHOULD BE PREPPING YOU FOR SURGERY RIGHT NOW. PETER--
--WHAT HAPPENED TO YOU?
A-APPRECIATE IT, DOC--
I...I SCREWED UP, OKAY?
I REALLY SCREWED UP. AND I NEED YOUR HELP.
AND SO I TELL HIM EVERYTHING.

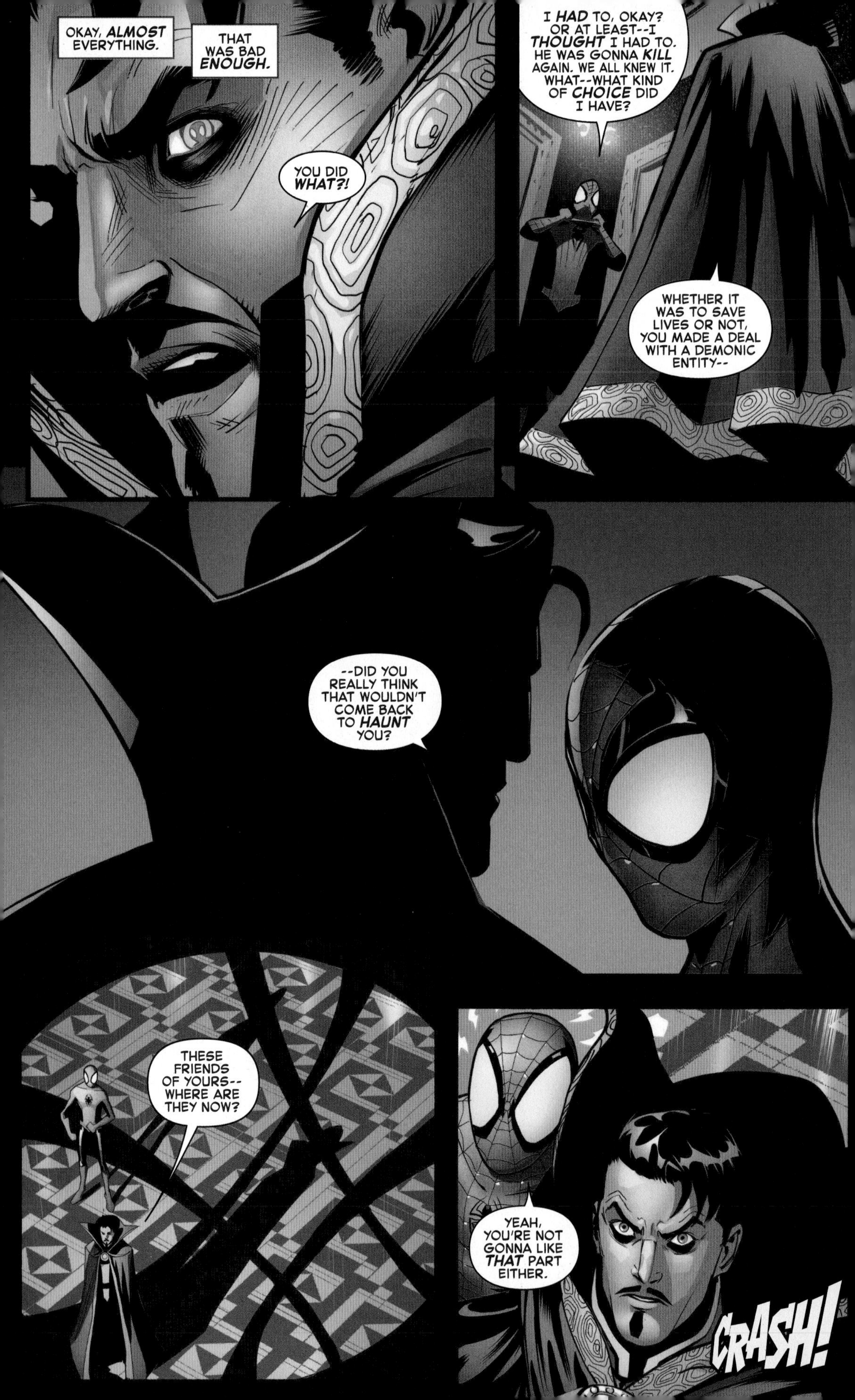
OKAY, ALMOST EVERYTHING.
THAT WAS BAD ENOUGH.
YOU DID WHAT?!
I HAD TO, OKAY? OR AT LEAST--I THOUGHT I HAD TO. HE WAS GONNA KILL AGAIN. WE ALL KNEW IT. WHAT--WHAT KIND OF CHOICE DID I HAVE?
WHETHER IT WAS TO SAVE LIVES OR NOT, YOU MADE A DEAL WITH A DEMONIC ENTITY--
--DID YOU REALLY THINK THAT WOULDN'T COME BACK TO HAUNT YOU?
THESE FRIENDS OF YOURS-- WHERE ARE THEY NOW?
YEAH, YOU'RE NOT GONNA LIKE THAT PART EITHER.
CRASH!

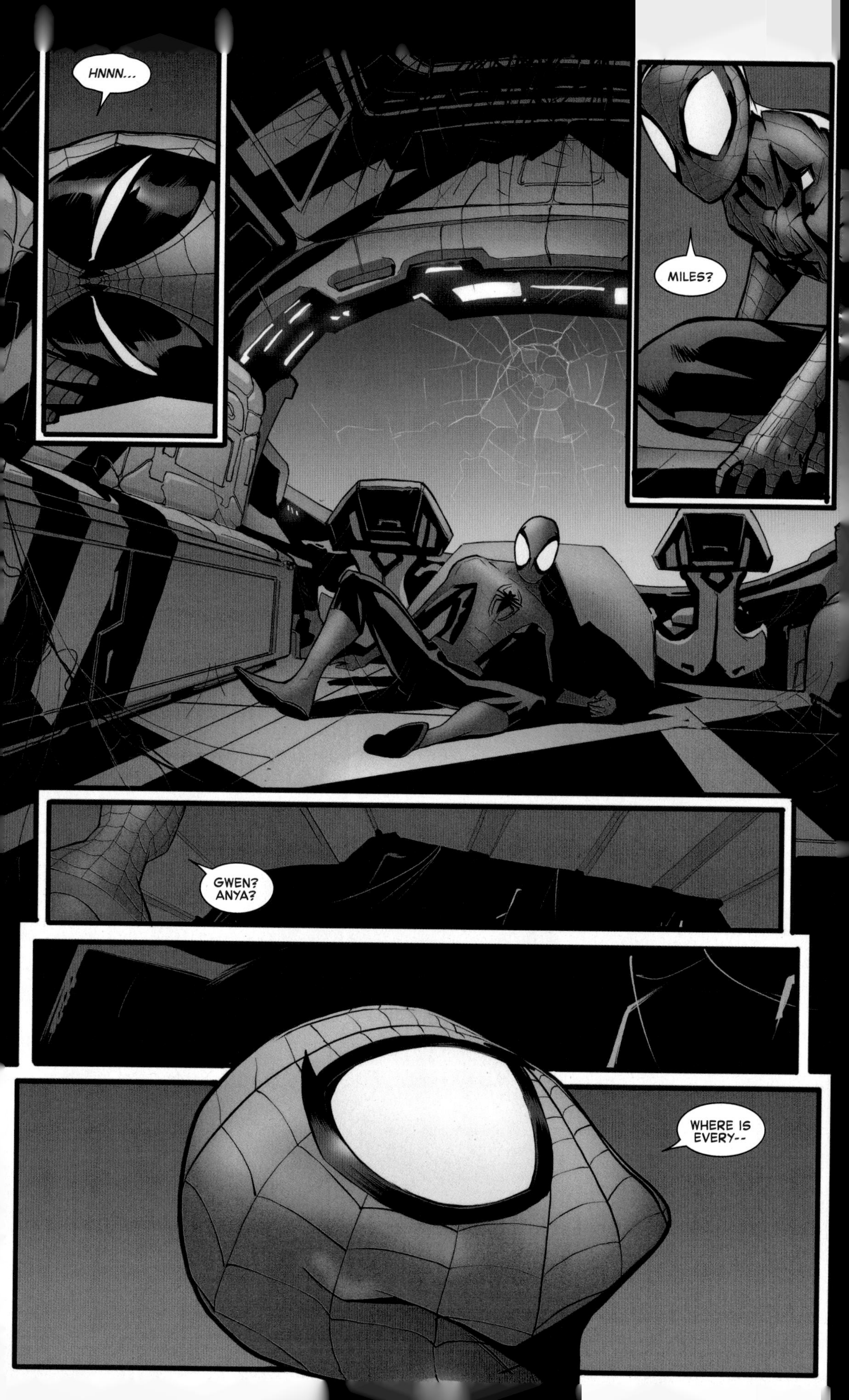
HNNN...
MILES?
GWEN? ANYA?
WHERE IS EVERY--

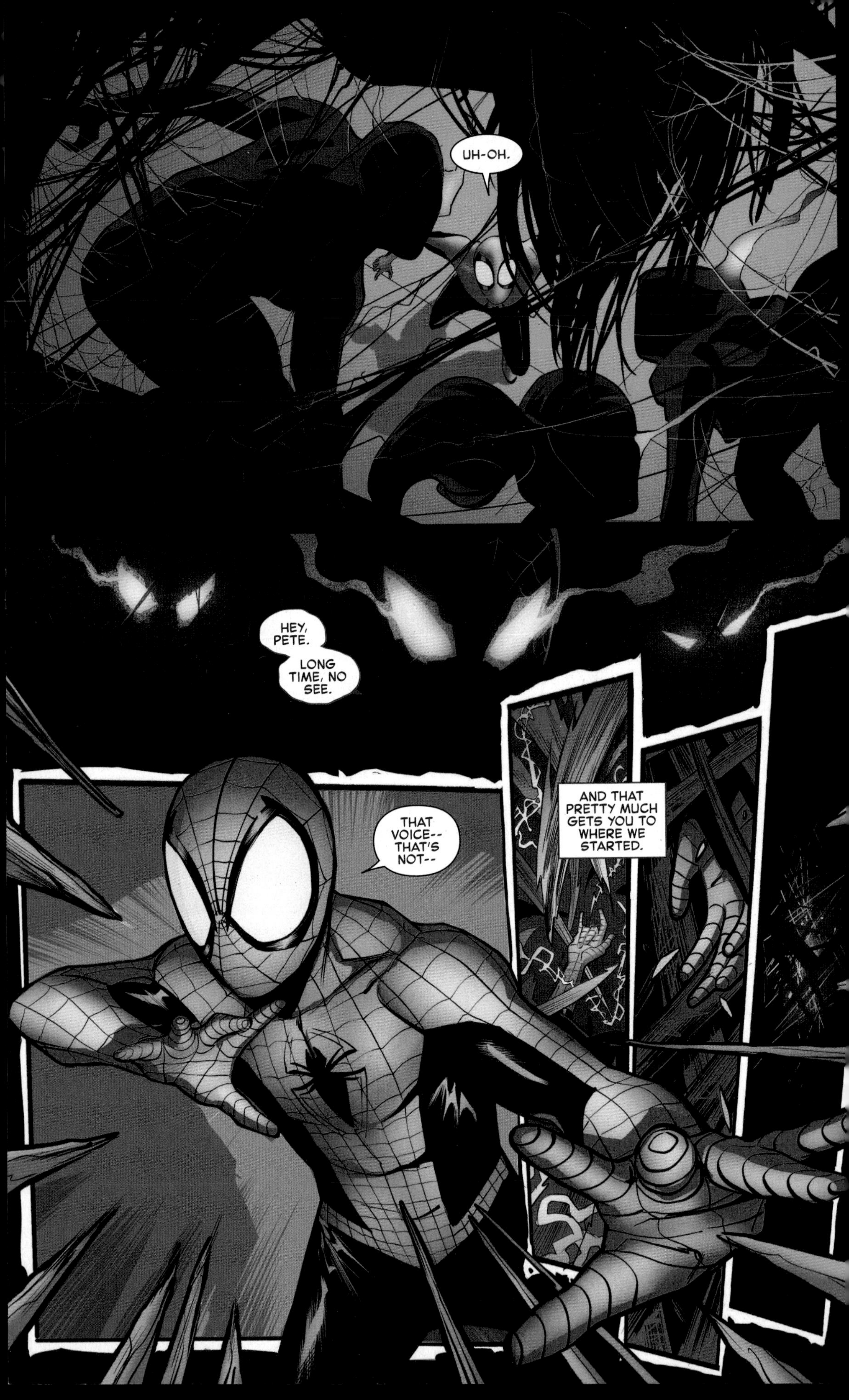
UH-OH.
HEY, PETE.
LONG TIME, NO SEE.
THAT VOICE-- THAT'S NOT--
AND THAT PRETTY MUCH GETS YOU TO WHERE WE STARTED.

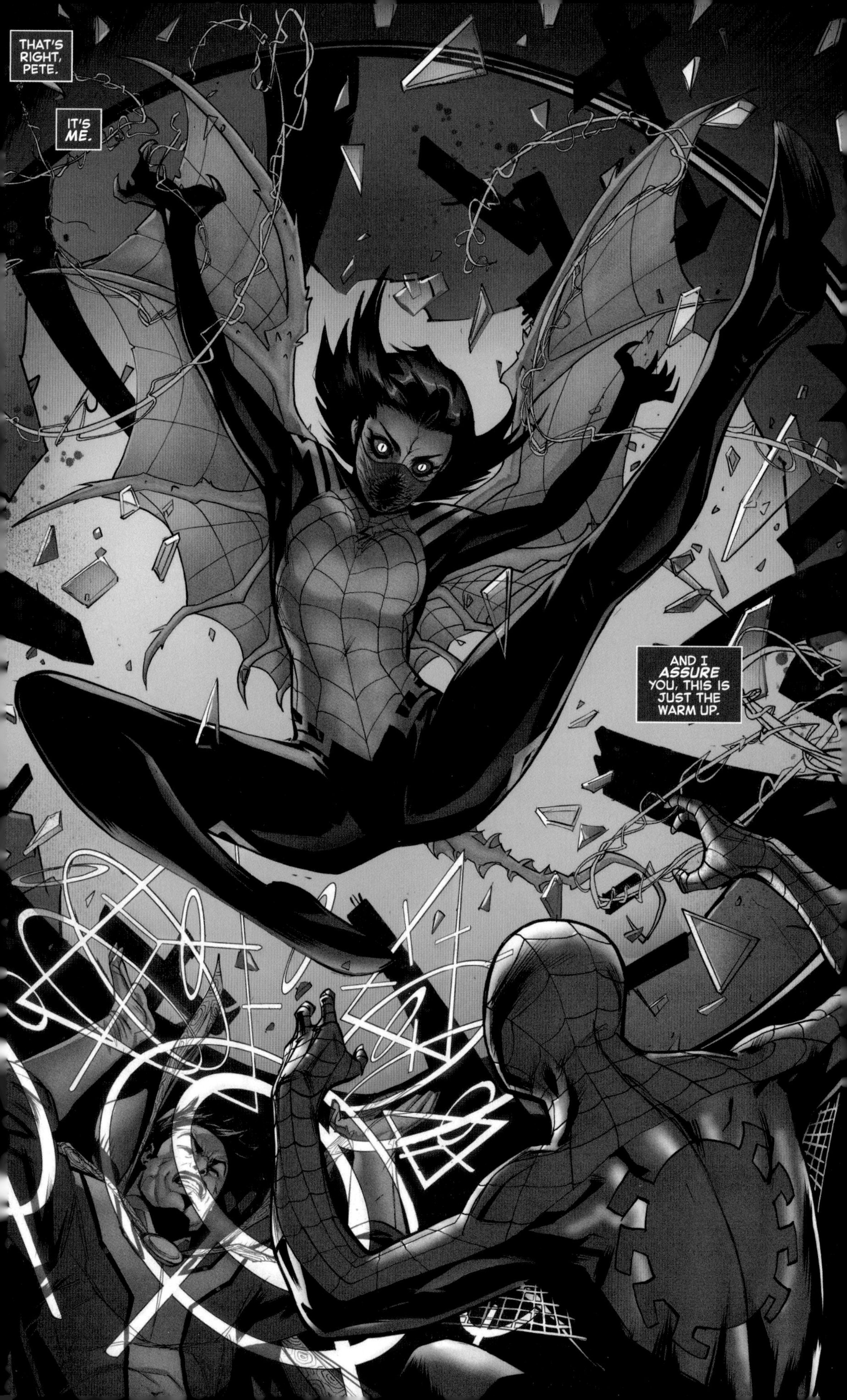
THAT'S RIGHT, PETE.
IT'S *ME.*
AND I *ASSURE* YOU, THIS IS JUST THE WARM UP.

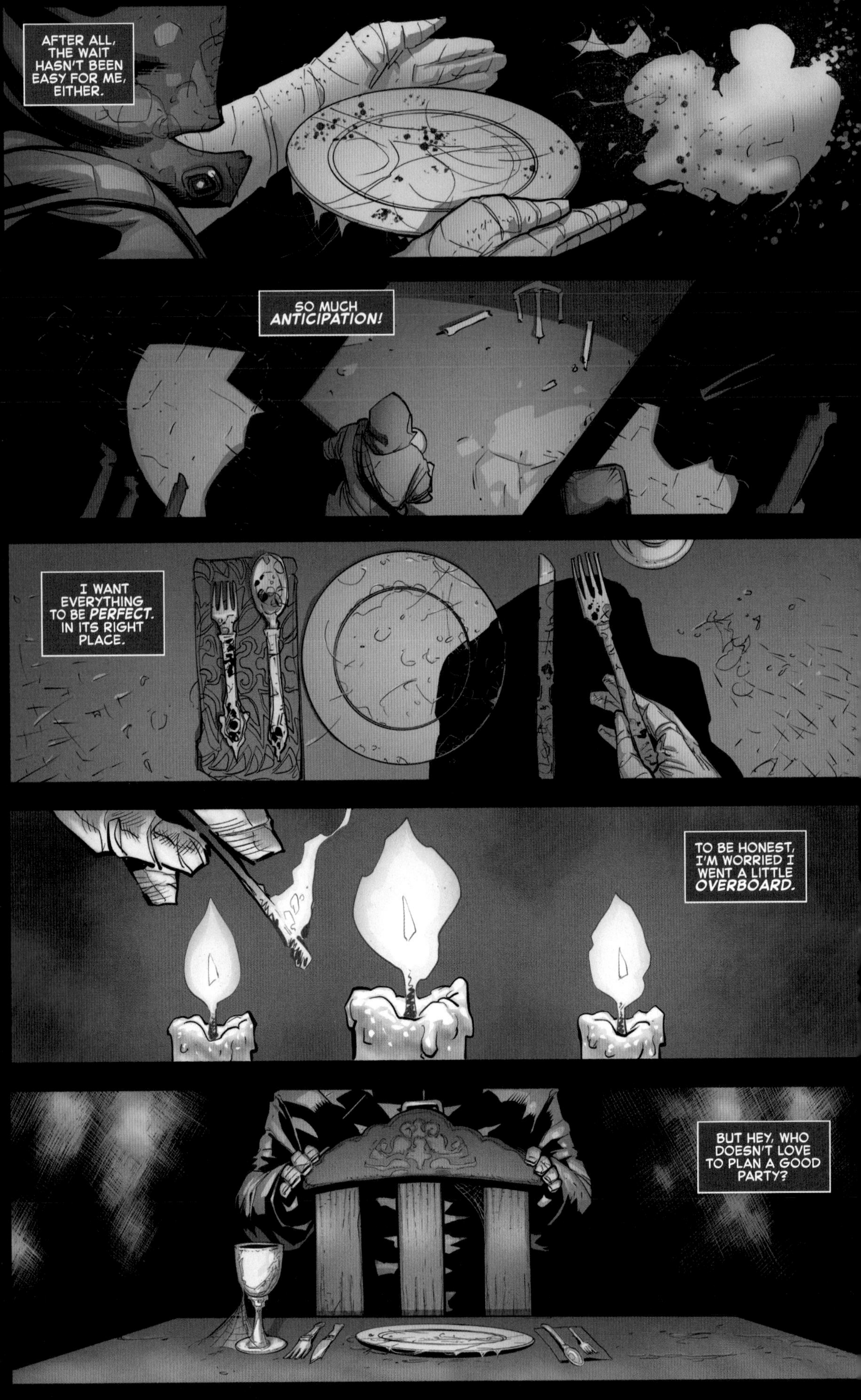
AFTER ALL, THE WAIT HASN'T BEEN EASY FOR ME, EITHER.
SO MUCH *ANTICIPATION!*
I WANT EVERYTHING TO BE *PERFECT*. IN ITS RIGHT PLACE.
TO BE HONEST, I'M WORRIED I WENT A LITTLE *OVERBOARD.*
BUT HEY, WHO DOESN'T LOVE TO PLAN A GOOD PARTY?

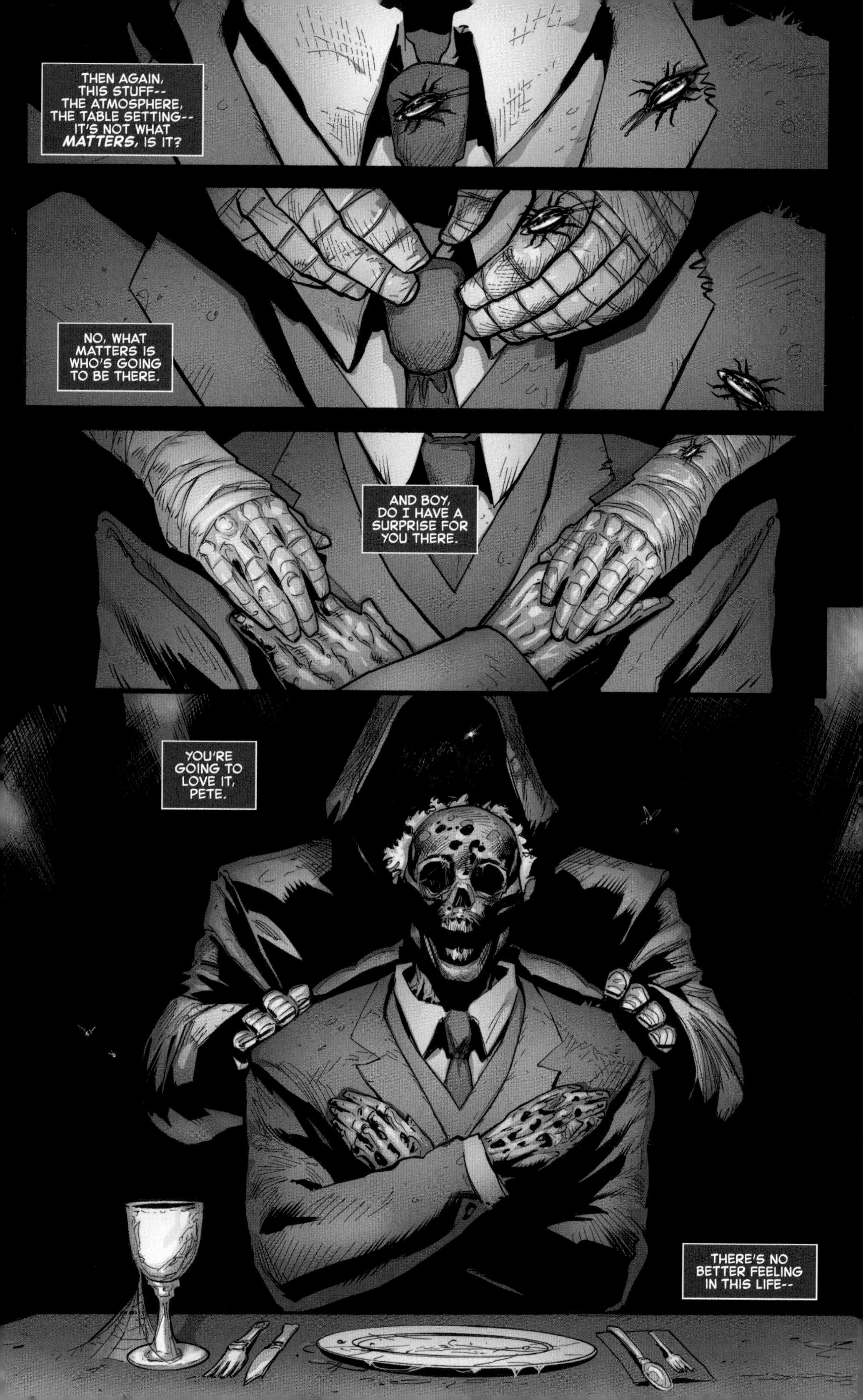
THEN AGAIN, THIS STUFF-- THE ATMOSPHERE, THE TABLE SETTING-- IT'S NOT WHAT *MATTERS,* IS IT?
NO, WHAT MATTERS IS WHO'S GOING TO BE THERE.
AND BOY, DO I HAVE A SURPRISE FOR YOU THERE.
YOU'RE GOING TO LOVE IT, PETE.
THERE'S NO BETTER FEELING IN THIS LIFE--

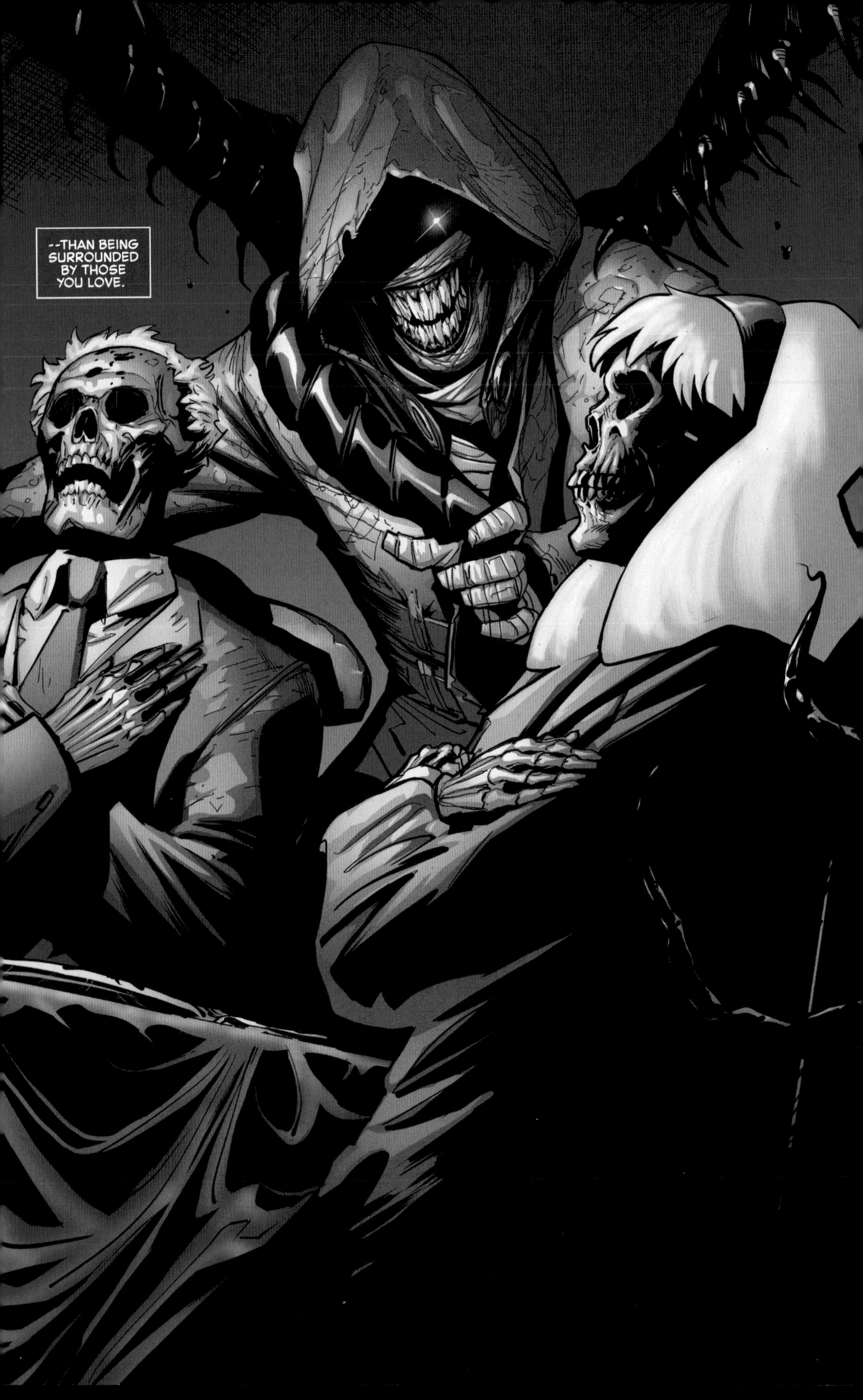
--THAN BEING SURROUNDED BY THOSE YOU LOVE.

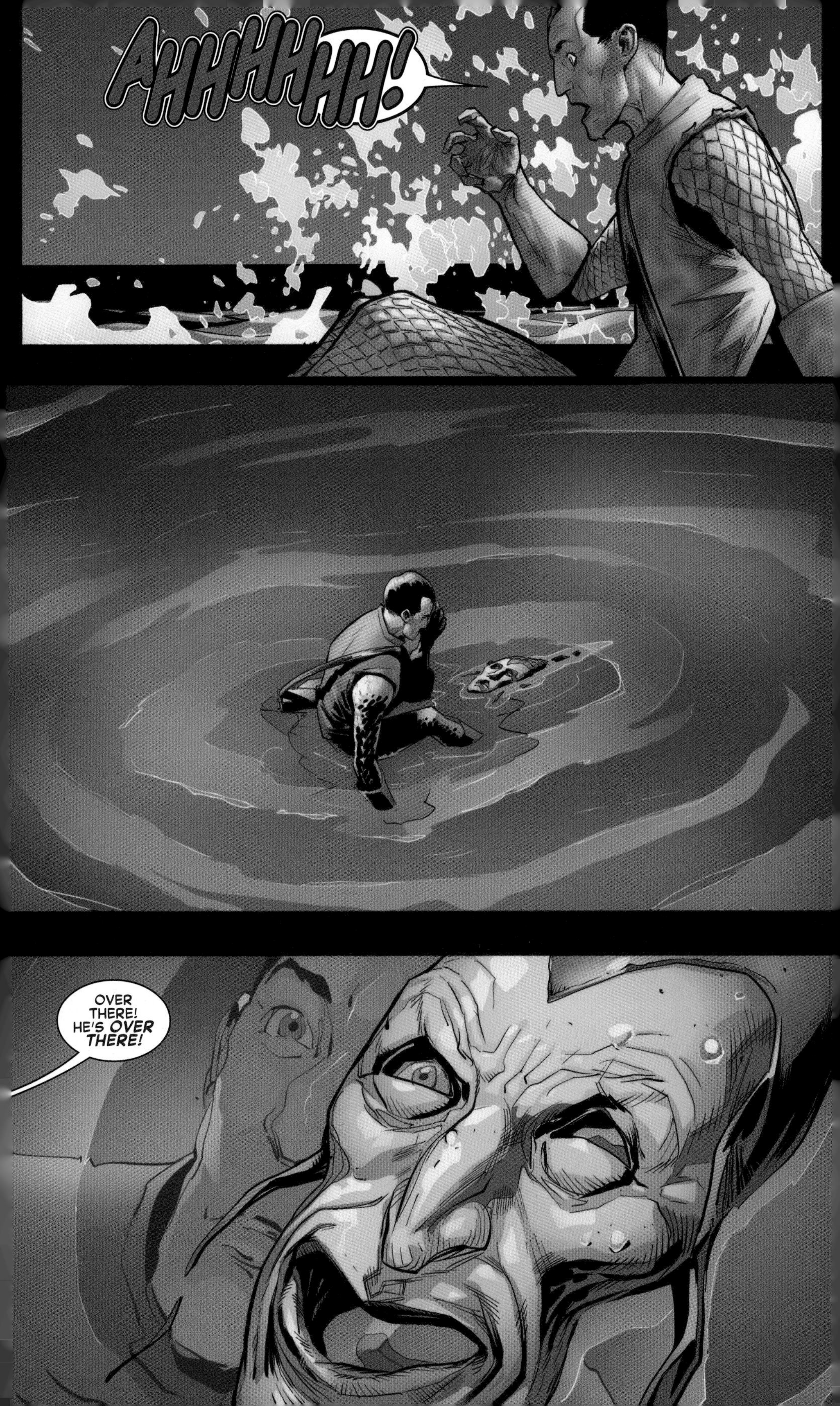
AHHHHHHH!
OVER THERE! HE'S OVER THERE!

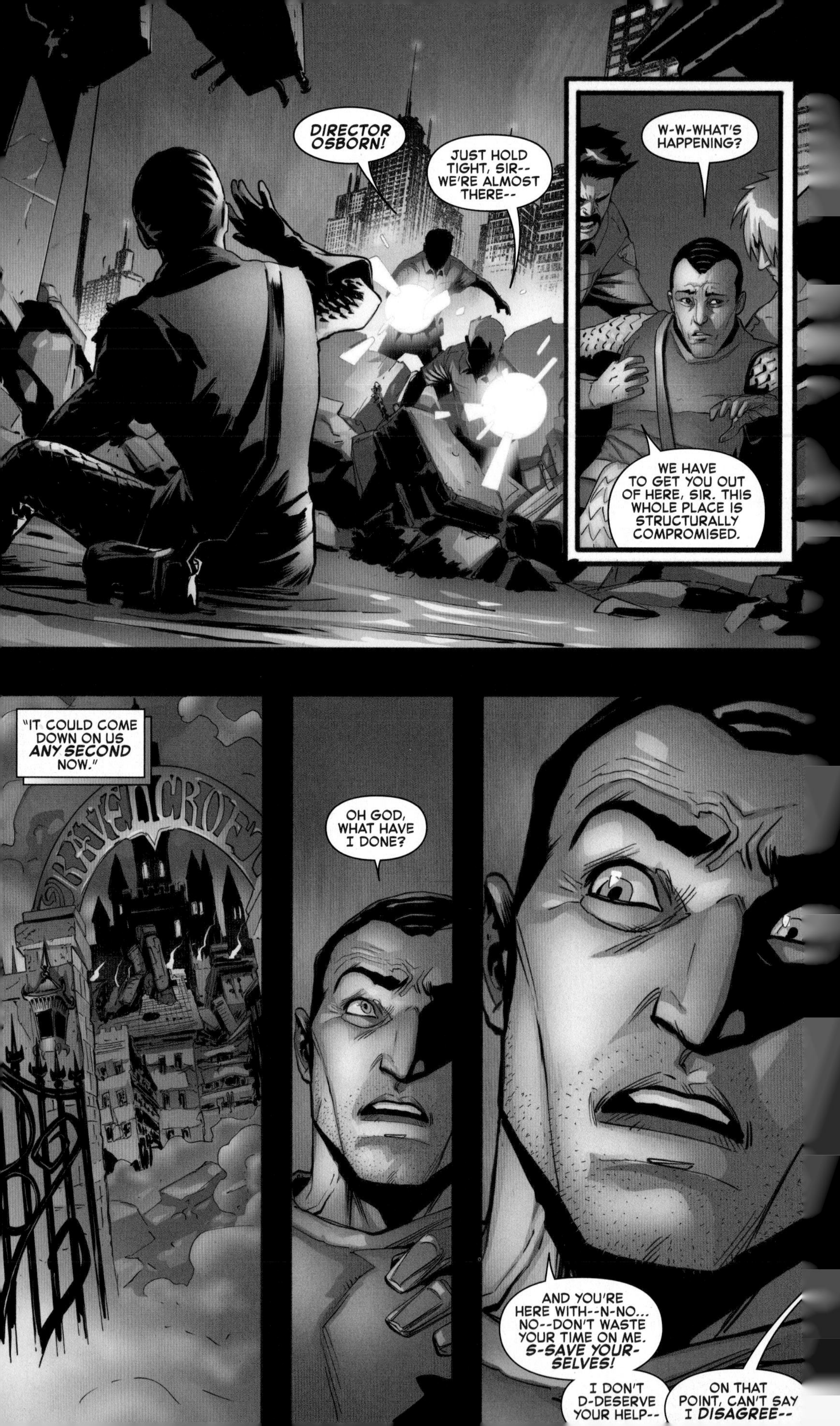
DIRECTOR OSBORN!
JUST HOLD TIGHT, SIR-- WE'RE ALMOST THERE--
W-W-WHAT'S HAPPENING?
WE HAVE TO GET YOU OUT OF HERE, SIR. THIS WHOLE PLACE IS STRUCTURALLY COMPROMISED.
"IT COULD COME DOWN ON US ANY SECOND NOW."
OH GOD, WHAT HAVE I DONE?
AND YOU'RE HERE WITH--N-NO... NO--DON'T WASTE YOUR TIME ON ME. S-SAVE YOUR-SELVES!
I DON'T D-DESERVE YOUR HELP--
ON THAT POINT, CAN'T SAY I DISAGREE--

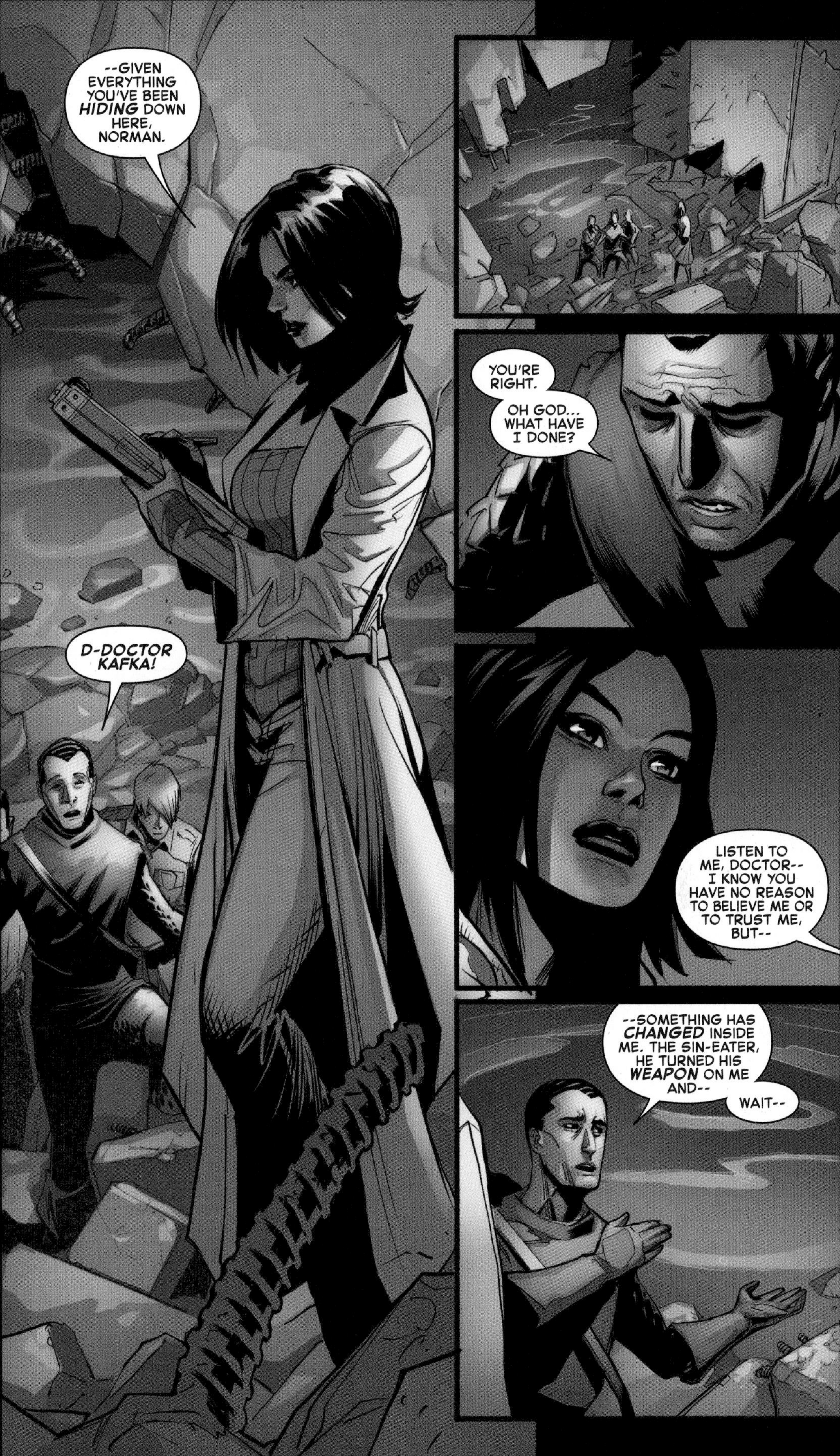
--GIVEN EVERYTHING YOU'VE BEEN HIDING DOWN HERE, NORMAN.
D-DOCTOR KAFKA!
YOU'RE RIGHT.
OH GOD... WHAT HAVE I DONE?
LISTEN TO ME, DOCTOR-- I KNOW YOU HAVE NO REASON TO BELIEVE ME OR TO TRUST ME, BUT--
--SOMETHING HAS CHANGED INSIDE ME. THE SIN-EATER, HE TURNED HIS WEAPON ON ME AND--
WAIT--

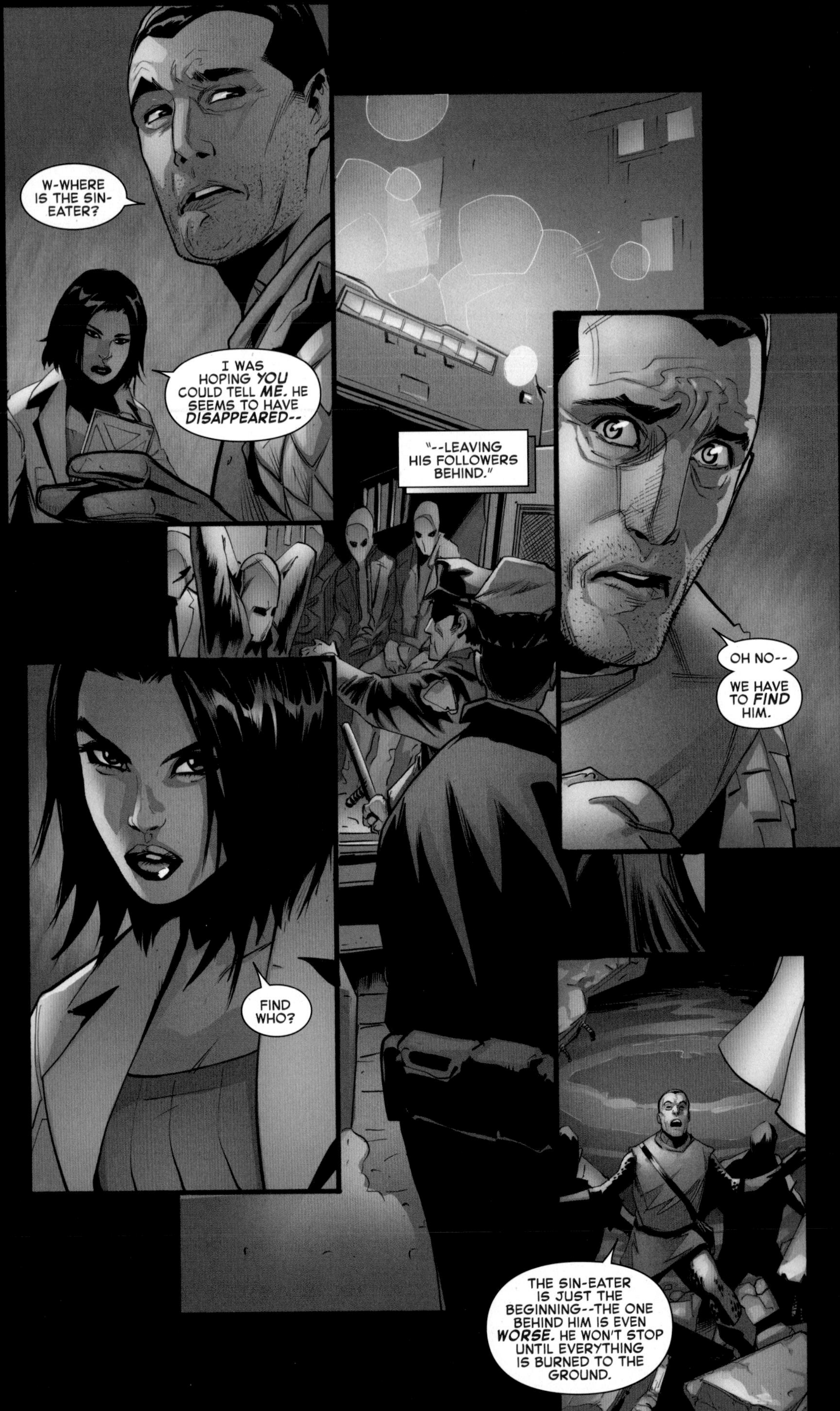
W-WHERE IS THE SIN-EATER?
I WAS HOPING YOU COULD TELL ME. HE SEEMS TO HAVE DISAPPEARED--
"--LEAVING HIS FOLLOWERS BEHIND."
OH NO--
WE HAVE TO FIND HIM.
FIND WHO?
THE SIN-EATER IS JUST THE BEGINNING--THE ONE BEHIND HIM IS EVEN WORSE. HE WON'T STOP UNTIL EVERYTHING IS BURNED TO THE GROUND.

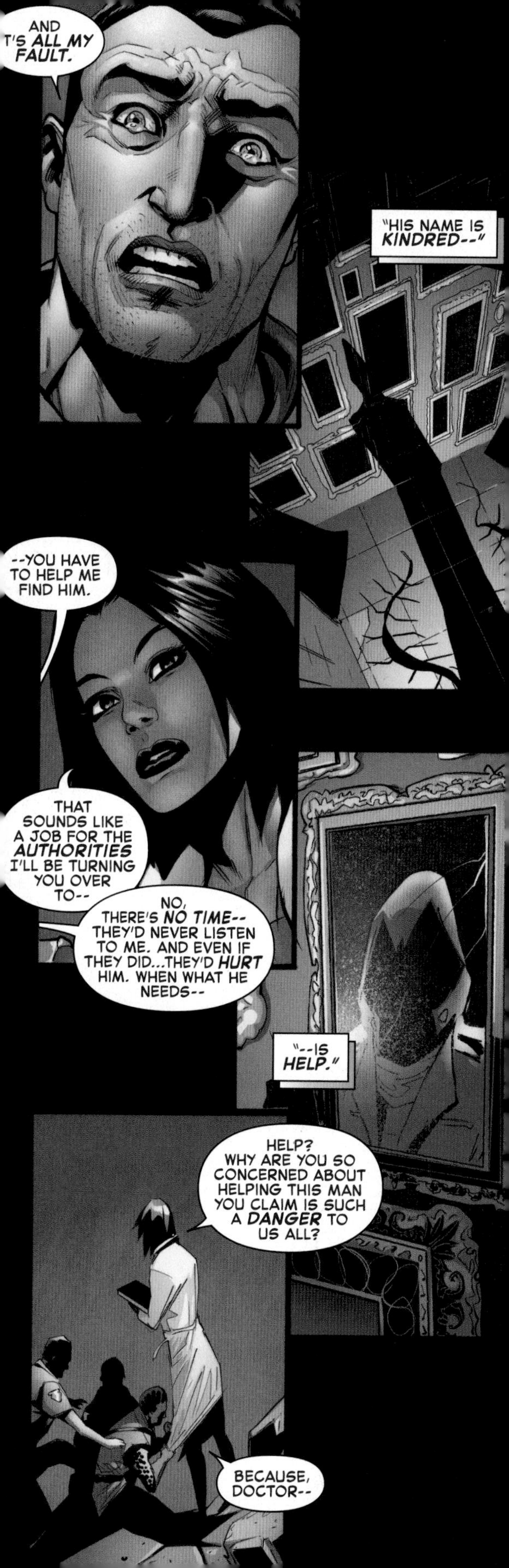
AND IT'S ALL MY FAULT.
"HIS NAME IS KINDRED--"
--YOU HAVE TO HELP ME FIND HIM.
THAT SOUNDS LIKE A JOB FOR THE AUTHORITIES I'LL BE TURNING YOU OVER TO--
NO, THERE'S NO TIME-- THEY'D NEVER LISTEN TO ME. AND EVEN IF THEY DID...THEY'D HURT HIM. WHEN WHAT HE NEEDS--
"--IS HELP."
HELP? WHY ARE YOU SO CONCERNED ABOUT HELPING THIS MAN YOU CLAIM IS SUCH A DANGER TO US ALL?
BECAUSE, DOCTOR--

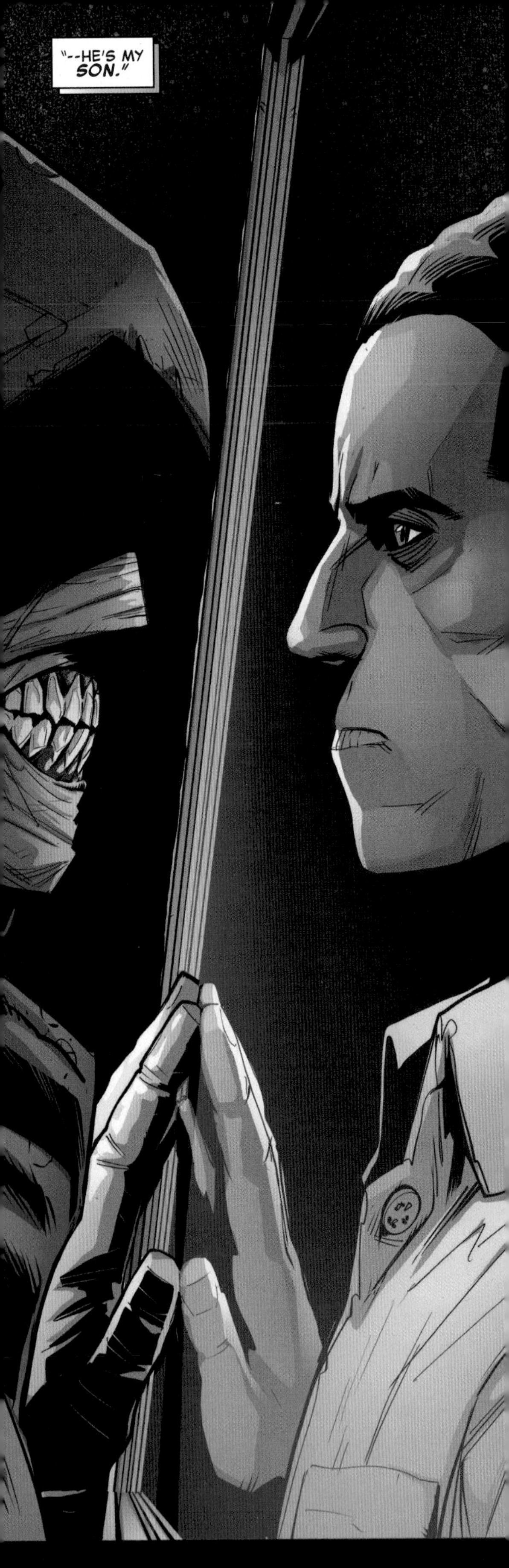
"--HE'S MY SON."

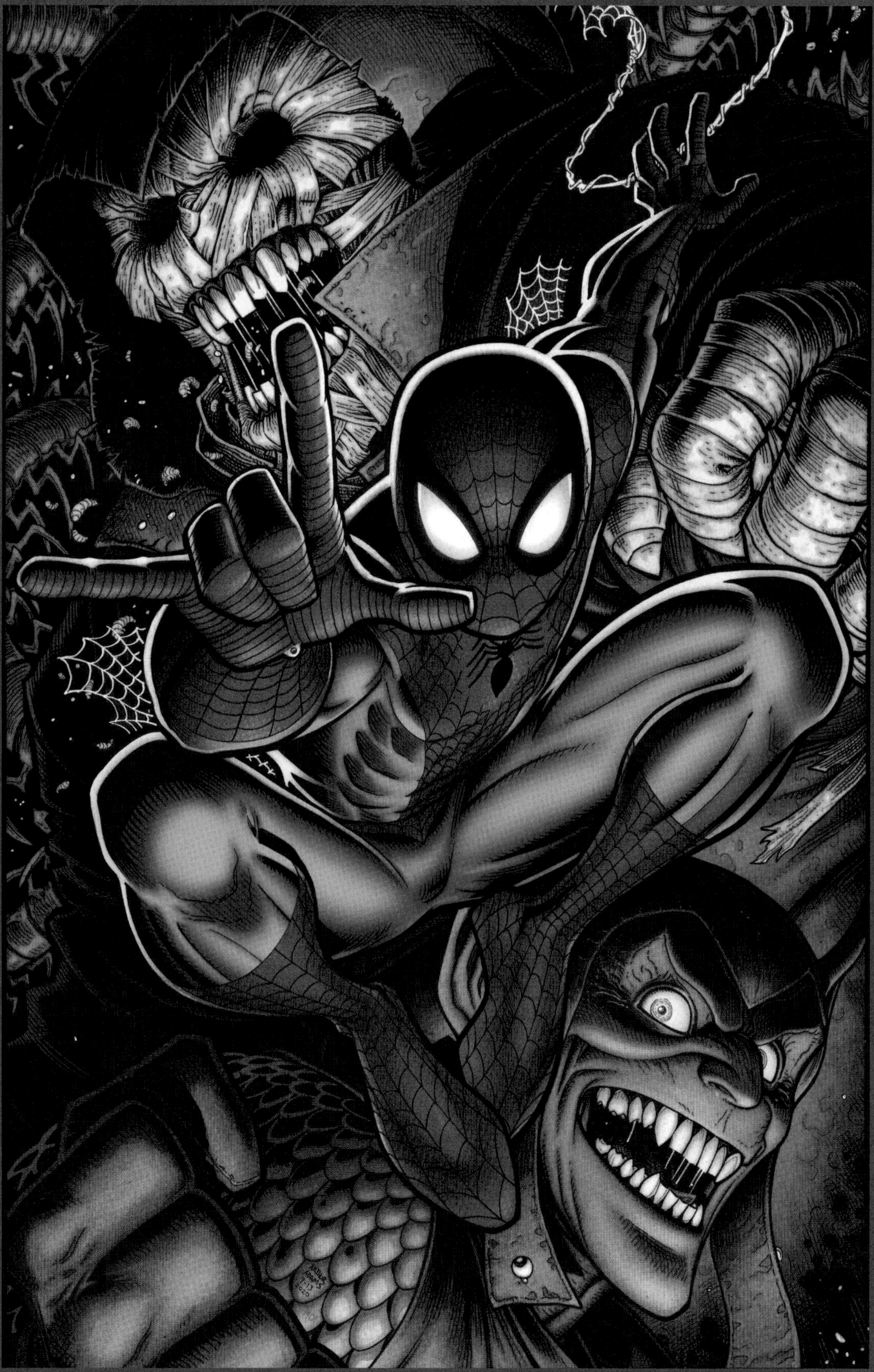

#50 VARIANT BY ARTHUR ADAMS & MORRY HOLLOWELL

51

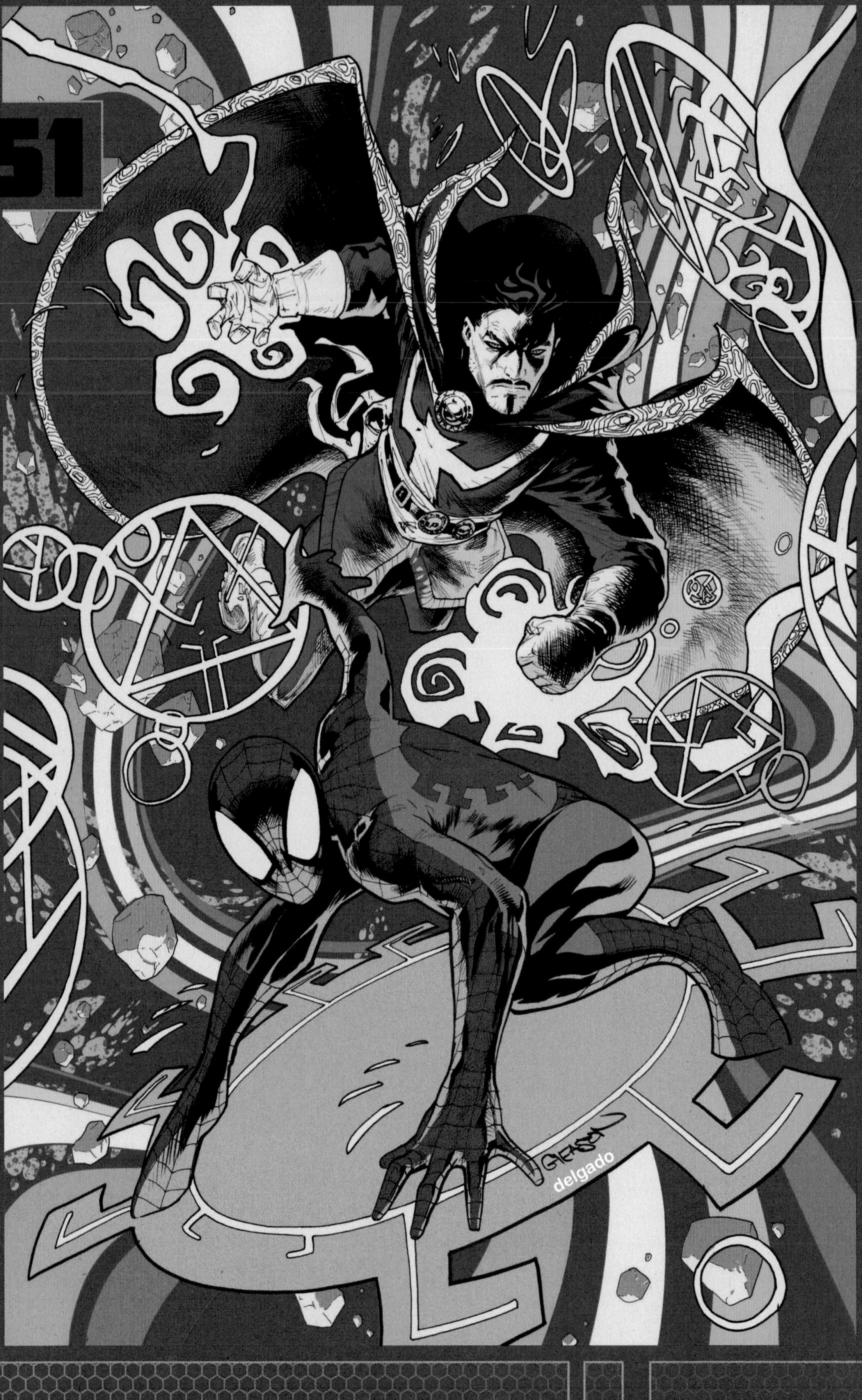
delgado

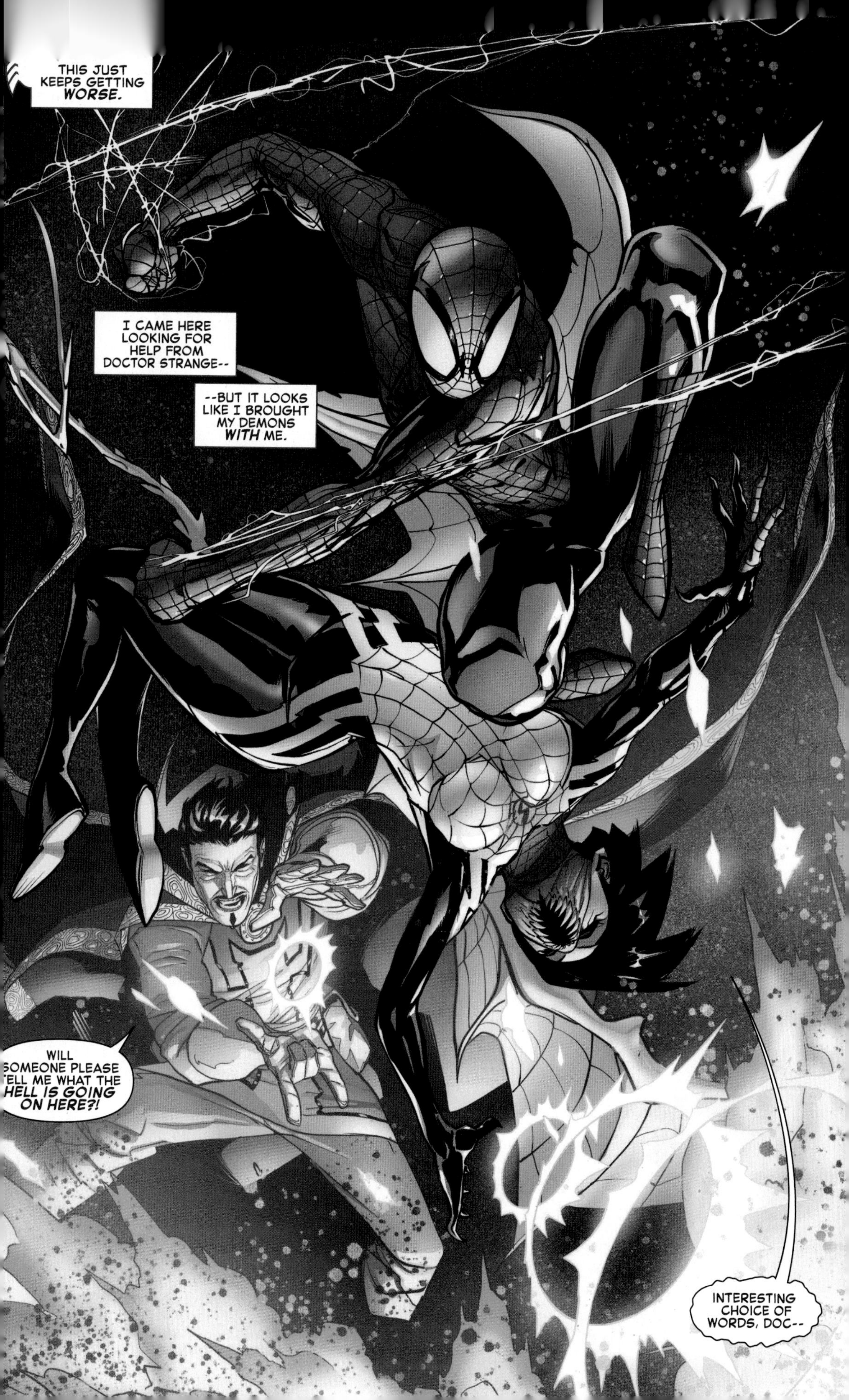

THIS JUST KEEPS GETTING WORSE.
I CAME HERE LOOKING FOR HELP FROM DOCTOR STRANGE--
--BUT IT LOOKS LIKE I BROUGHT MY DEMONS WITH ME.
WILL SOMEONE PLEASE TELL ME WHAT THE HELL IS GOING ON HERE?!
INTERESTING CHOICE OF WORDS, DOC--

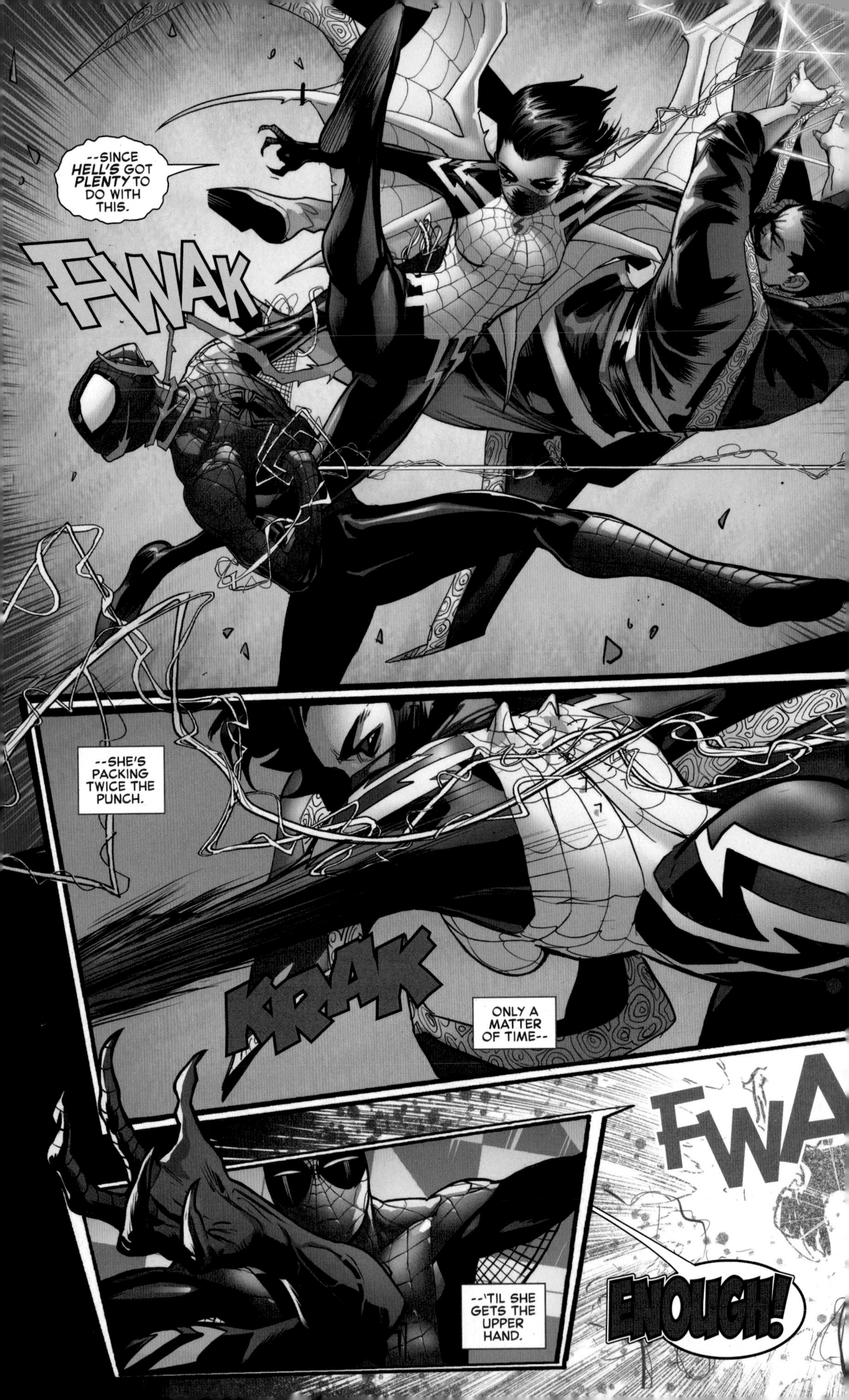
--SINCE HELL'S GOT PLENTY TO DO WITH THIS.
FWAK
--SHE'S PACKING TWICE THE PUNCH.
KRAK
ONLY A MATTER OF TIME--
FWA
--'TIL SHE GETS THE UPPER HAND.
ENOUGH!

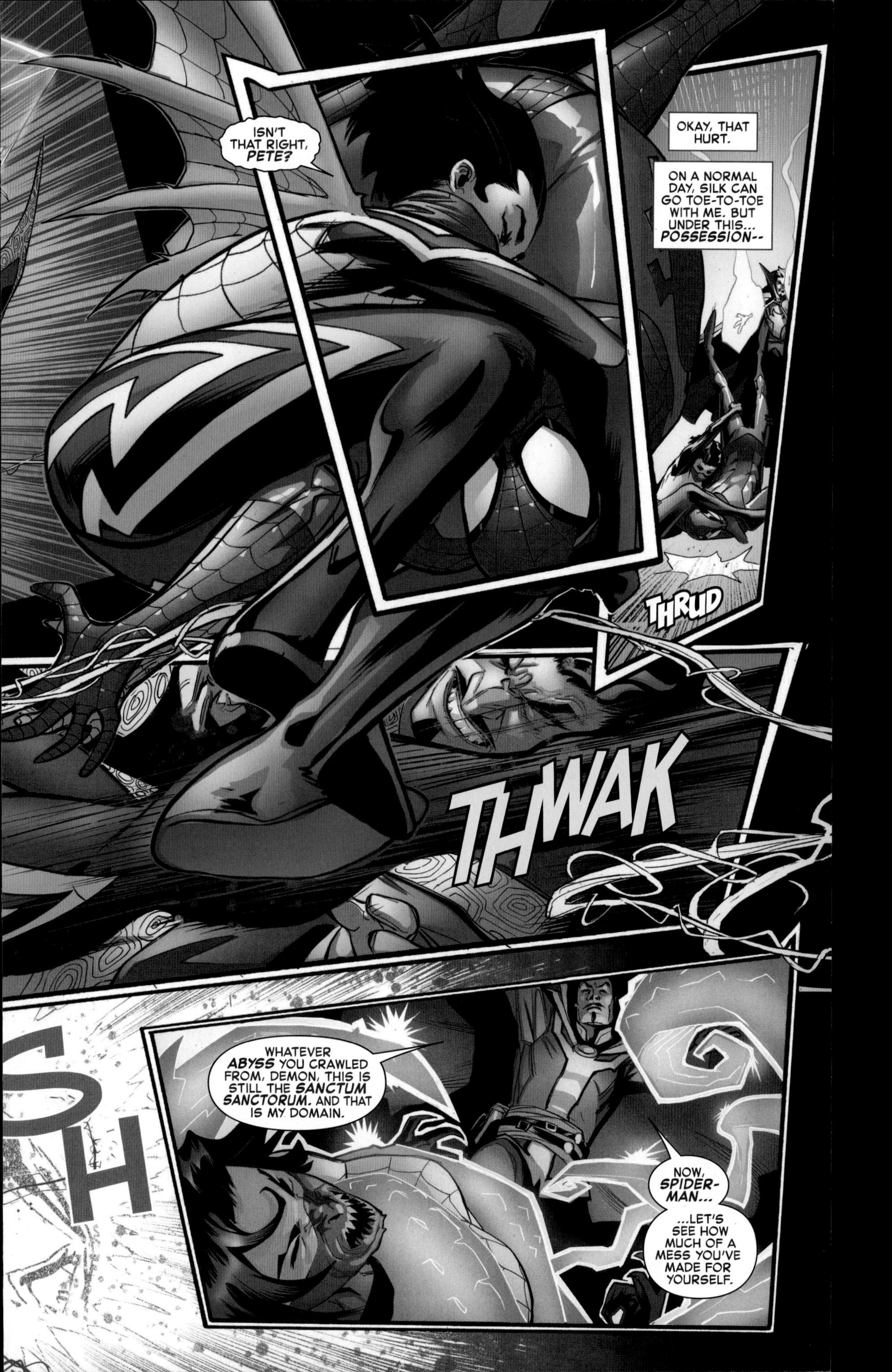
ISN'T THAT RIGHT, PETE?
OKAY, THAT HURT.
ON A NORMAL DAY, SILK CAN GO TOE-TO-TOE WITH ME. BUT UNDER THIS... POSSESSION--
THRUD
THWAK
WHATEVER ABYSS YOU CRAWLED FROM, DEMON, THIS IS STILL THE SANCTUM SANCTORUM. AND THAT IS MY DOMAIN.
NOW, SPIDER-MAN...
...LET'S SEE HOW MUCH OF A MESS YOU'VE MADE FOR YOURSELF.

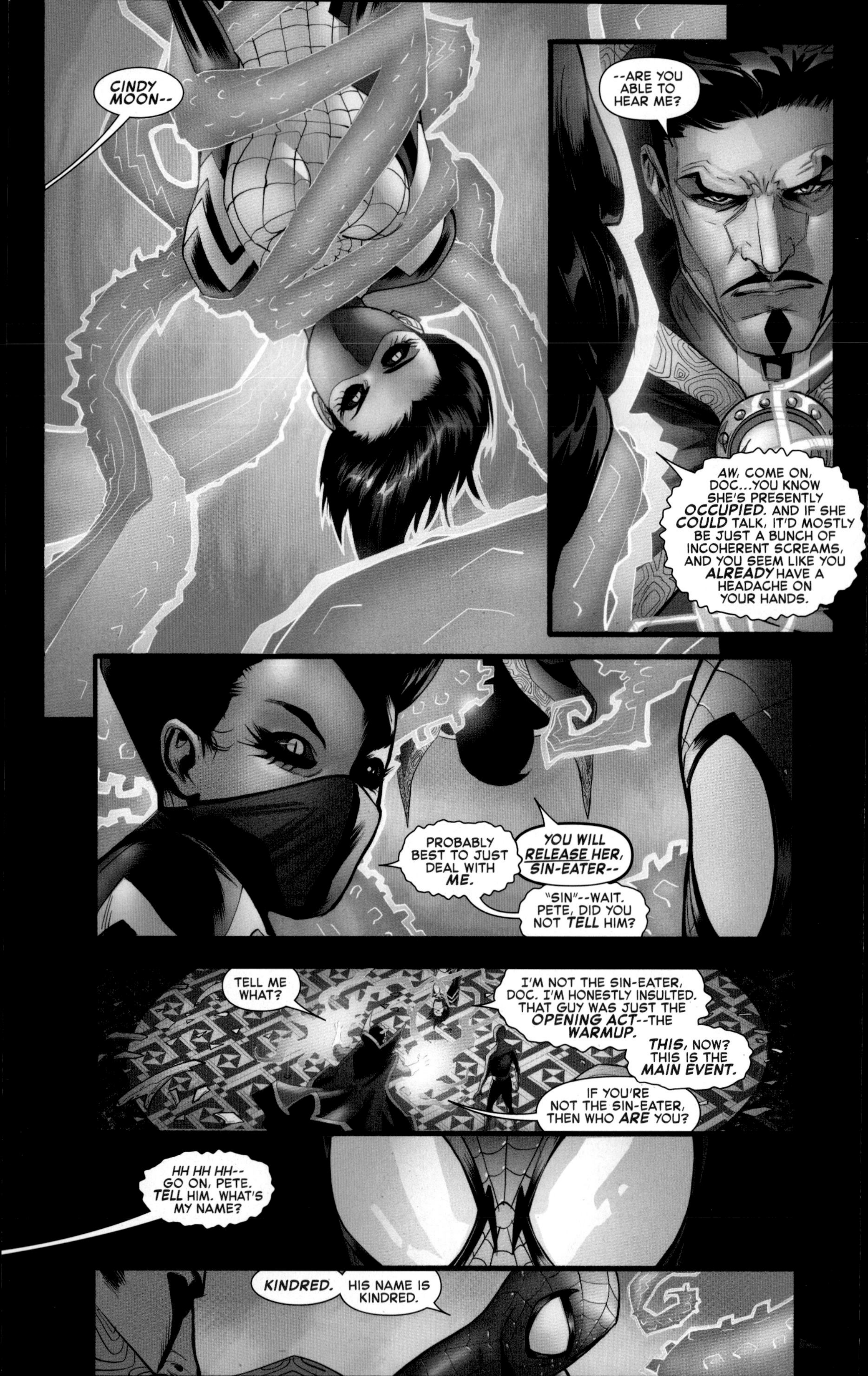
CINDY MOON--
--ARE YOU ABLE TO HEAR ME?
AW, COME ON, DOC...YOU KNOW SHE'S PRESENTLY OCCUPIED. AND IF SHE COULD TALK, IT'D MOSTLY BE JUST A BUNCH OF INCOHERENT SCREAMS, AND YOU SEEM LIKE YOU ALREADY HAVE A HEADACHE ON YOUR HANDS.
YOU WILL RELEASE HER, SIN-EATER--
PROBABLY BEST TO JUST DEAL WITH ME.
"SIN"--WAIT. PETE, DID YOU NOT TELL HIM?
TELL ME WHAT?
I'M NOT THE SIN-EATER, DOC. I'M HONESTLY INSULTED. THAT GUY WAS JUST THE OPENING ACT--THE WARMUP.
THIS, NOW? THIS IS THE MAIN EVENT.
IF YOU'RE NOT THE SIN-EATER, THEN WHO ARE YOU?
HH HH HH-- GO ON, PETE. TELL HIM. WHAT'S MY NAME?
KINDRED.
HIS NAME IS KINDRED.

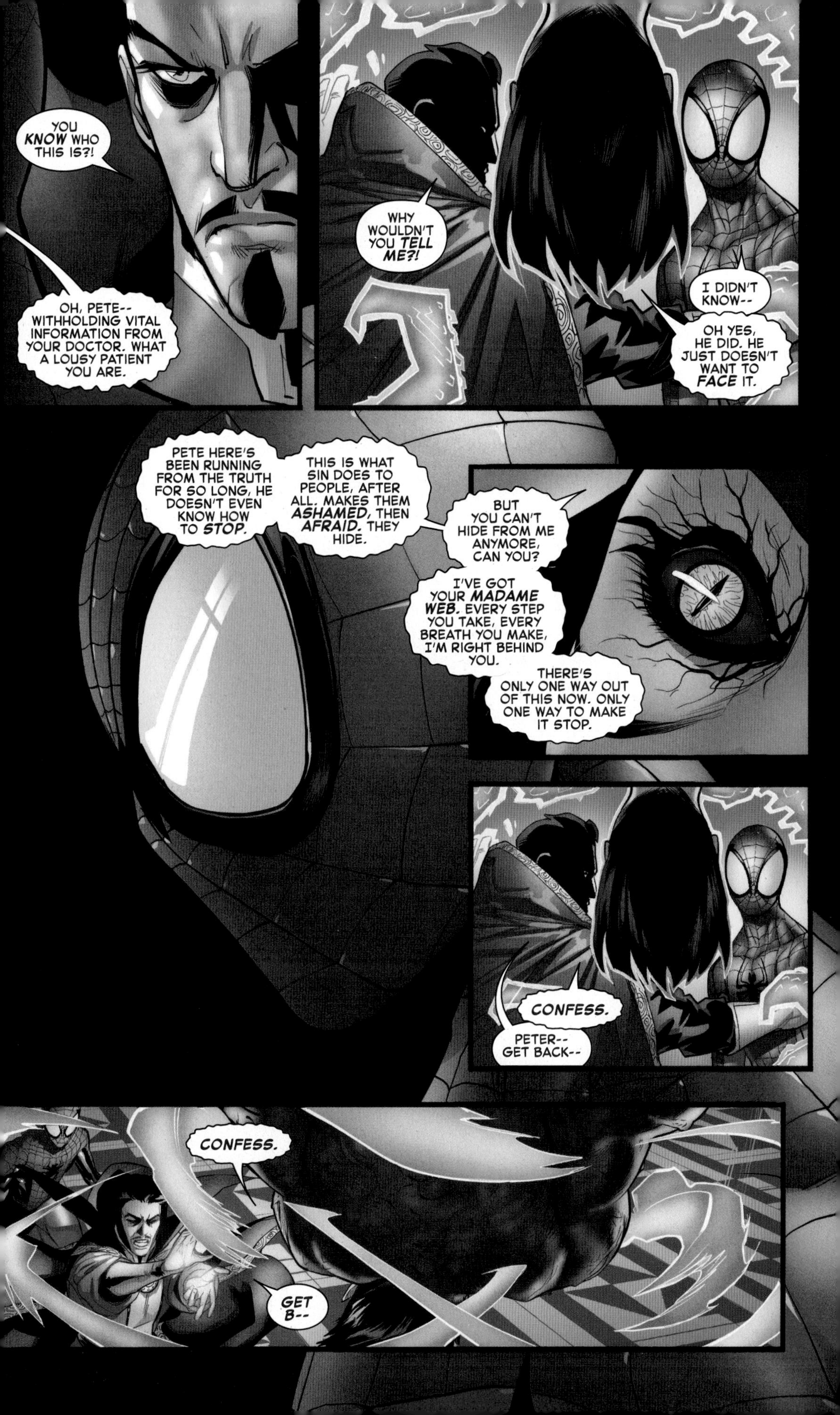
YOU KNOW WHO THIS IS?!
OH, PETE-- WITHHOLDING VITAL INFORMATION FROM YOUR DOCTOR. WHAT A LOUSY PATIENT YOU ARE.
WHY WOULDN'T YOU TELL ME?!
I DIDN'T KNOW--
OH YES, HE DID. HE JUST DOESN'T WANT TO FACE IT.
PETE HERE'S BEEN RUNNING FROM THE TRUTH FOR SO LONG, HE DOESN'T EVEN KNOW HOW TO STOP.
THIS IS WHAT SIN DOES TO PEOPLE, AFTER ALL. MAKES THEM ASHAMED, THEN AFRAID. THEY HIDE.
BUT YOU CAN'T HIDE FROM ME ANYMORE, CAN YOU?
I'VE GOT YOUR MADAME WEB. EVERY STEP YOU TAKE, EVERY BREATH YOU MAKE, I'M RIGHT BEHIND YOU.
THERE'S ONLY ONE WAY OUT OF THIS NOW. ONLY ONE WAY TO MAKE IT STOP.
CONFESS.
PETER-- GET BACK--
CONFESS.
GET B--

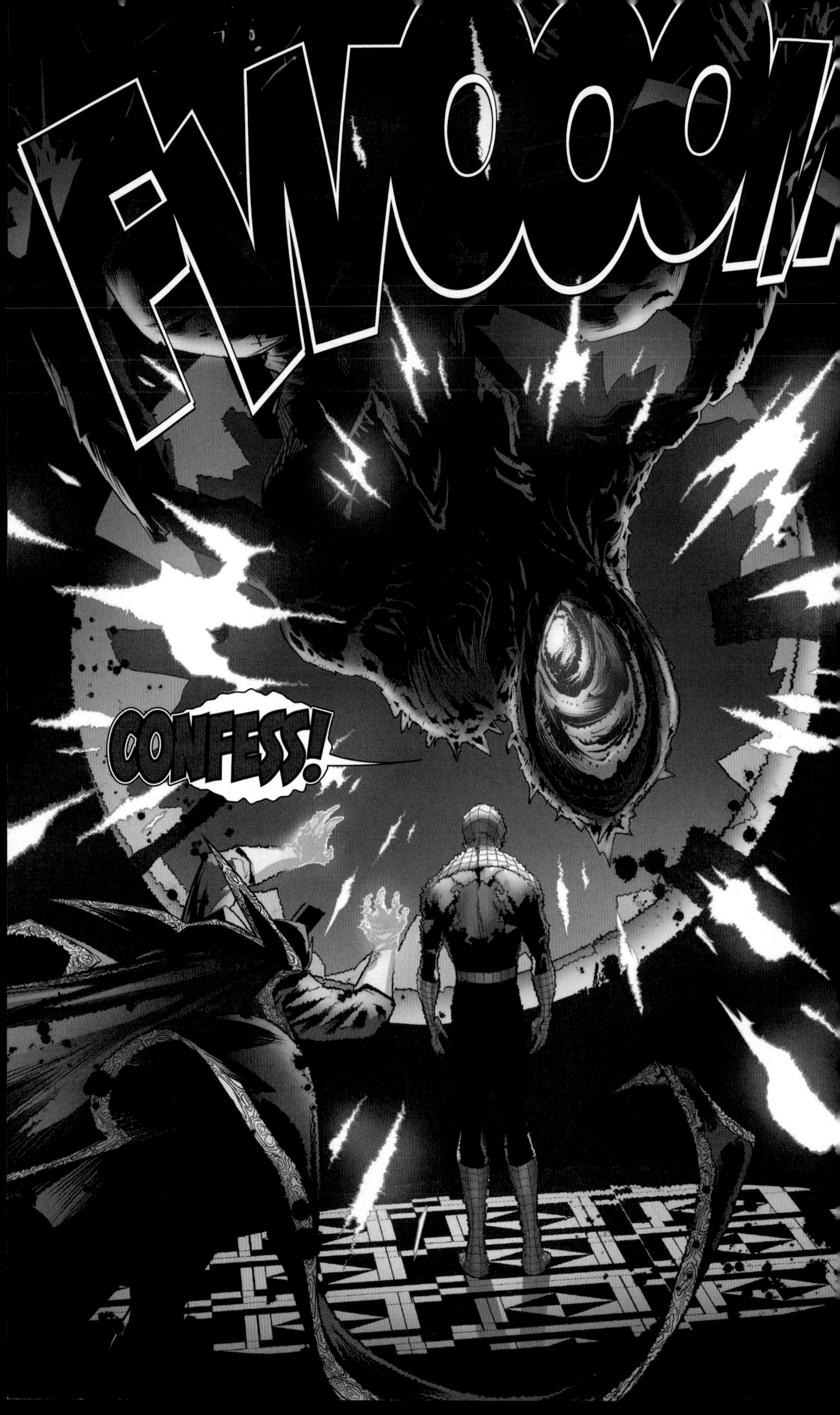
FWOOOM!
CONFESS!

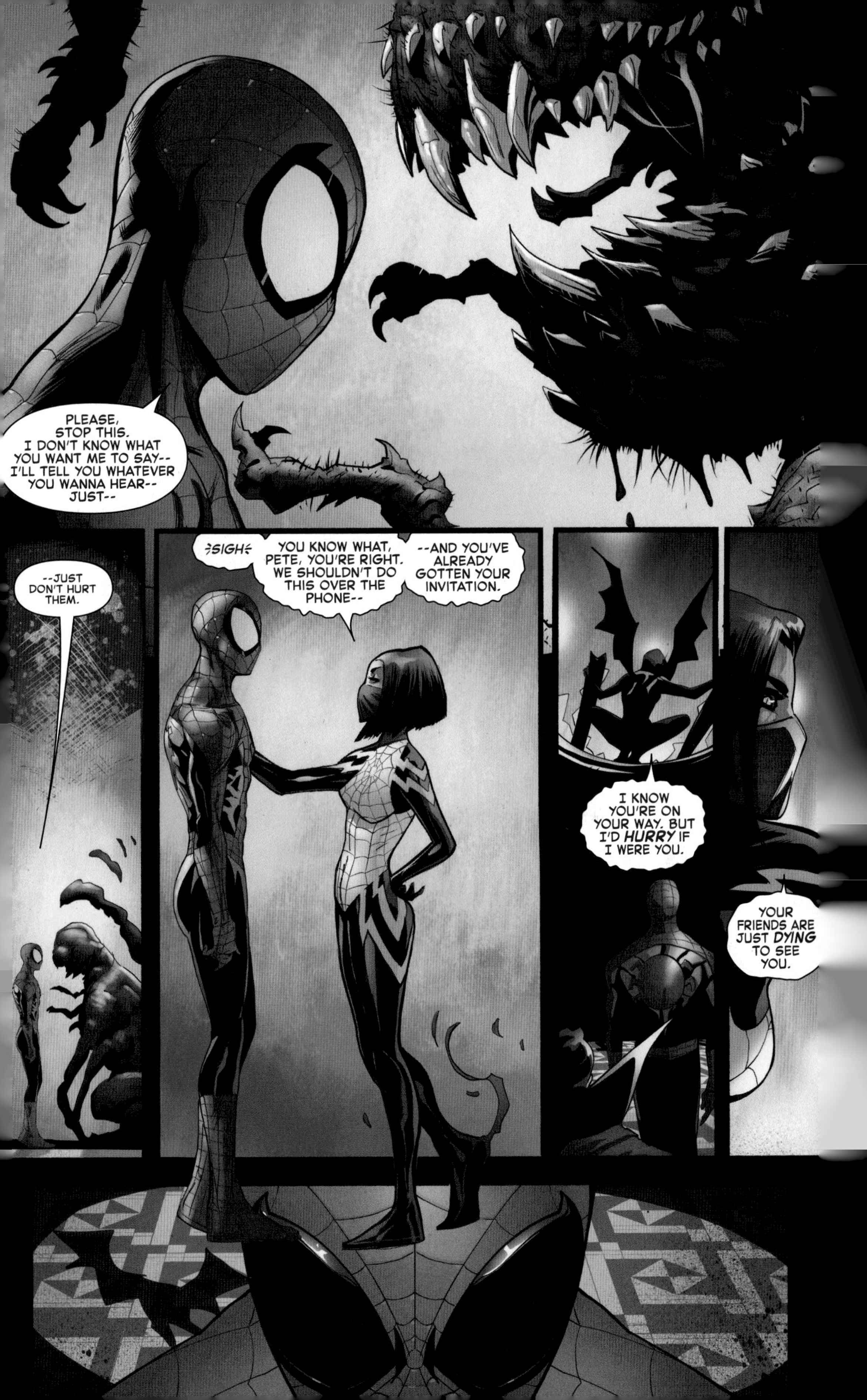
PLEASE, STOP THIS. I DON'T KNOW WHAT YOU WANT ME TO SAY-- I'LL TELL YOU WHATEVER YOU WANNA HEAR-- JUST--
--JUST DON'T HURT THEM.
SIGH
YOU KNOW WHAT, PETE, YOU'RE RIGHT. WE SHOULDN'T DO THIS OVER THE PHONE--
--AND YOU'VE ALREADY GOTTEN YOUR INVITATION.
I KNOW YOU'RE ON YOUR WAY. BUT I'D HURRY IF I WERE YOU.
YOUR FRIENDS ARE JUST DYING TO SEE YOU.

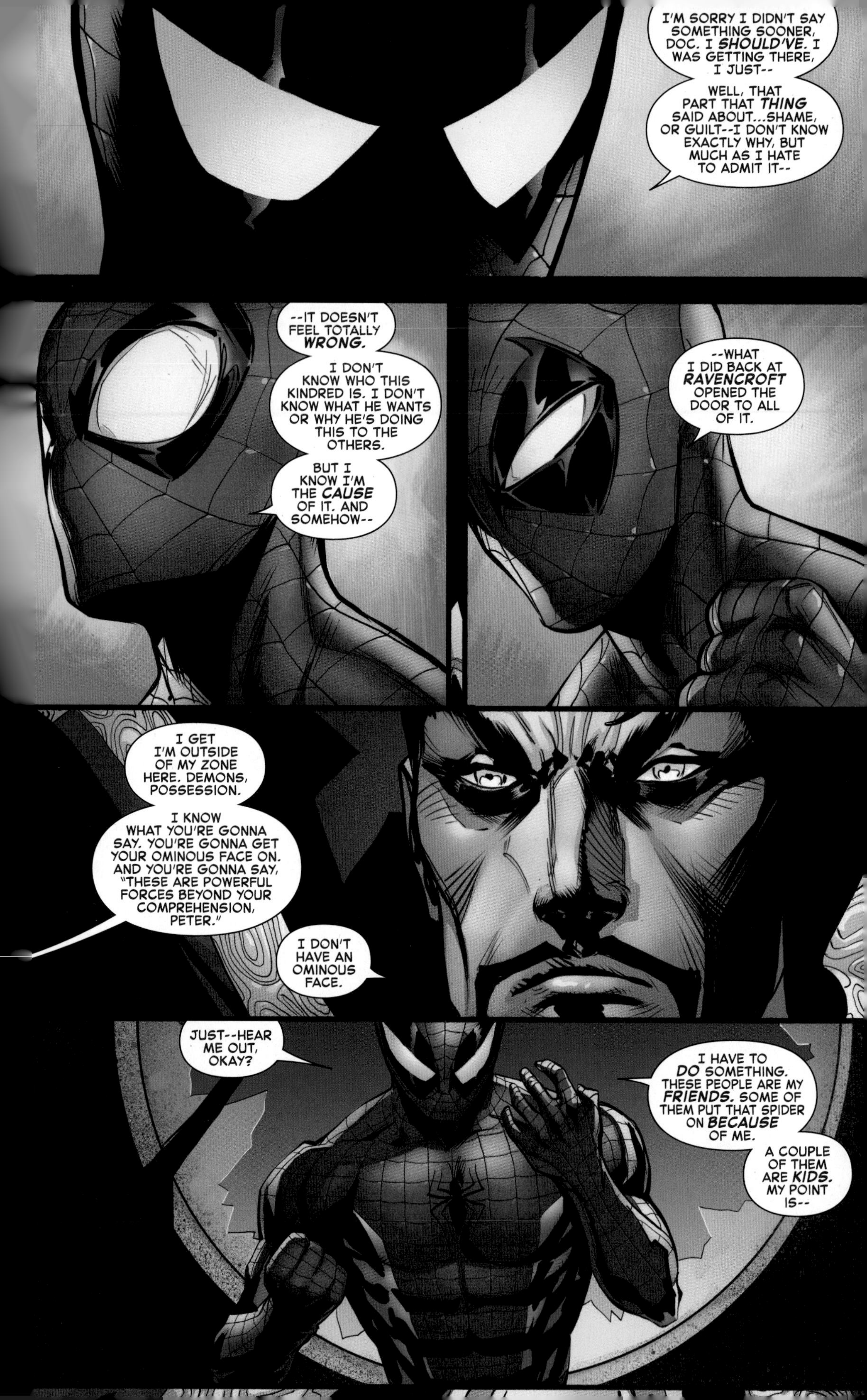
I'M SORRY I DIDN'T SAY SOMETHING SOONER, DOC. I SHOULD'VE. I WAS GETTING THERE, I JUST--
WELL, THAT PART THAT THING SAID ABOUT...SHAME, OR GUILT--I DON'T KNOW EXACTLY WHY, BUT MUCH AS I HATE TO ADMIT IT--
--IT DOESN'T FEEL TOTALLY WRONG.
I DON'T KNOW WHO THIS KINDRED IS. I DON'T KNOW WHAT HE WANTS OR WHY HE'S DOING THIS TO THE OTHERS.
BUT I KNOW I'M THE CAUSE OF IT. AND SOMEHOW--
--WHAT I DID BACK AT RAVENCROFT OPENED THE DOOR TO ALL OF IT.
I GET I'M OUTSIDE OF MY ZONE HERE. DEMONS, POSSESSION.
I KNOW WHAT YOU'RE GONNA SAY. YOU'RE GONNA GET YOUR OMINOUS FACE ON. AND YOU'RE GONNA SAY, "THESE ARE POWERFUL FORCES BEYOND YOUR COMPREHENSION, PETER."
I DON'T HAVE AN OMINOUS FACE.
JUST--HEAR ME OUT, OKAY?
I HAVE TO DO SOMETHING. THESE PEOPLE ARE MY FRIENDS. SOME OF THEM PUT THAT SPIDER ON BECAUSE OF ME.
A COUPLE OF THEM ARE KIDS. MY POINT IS--

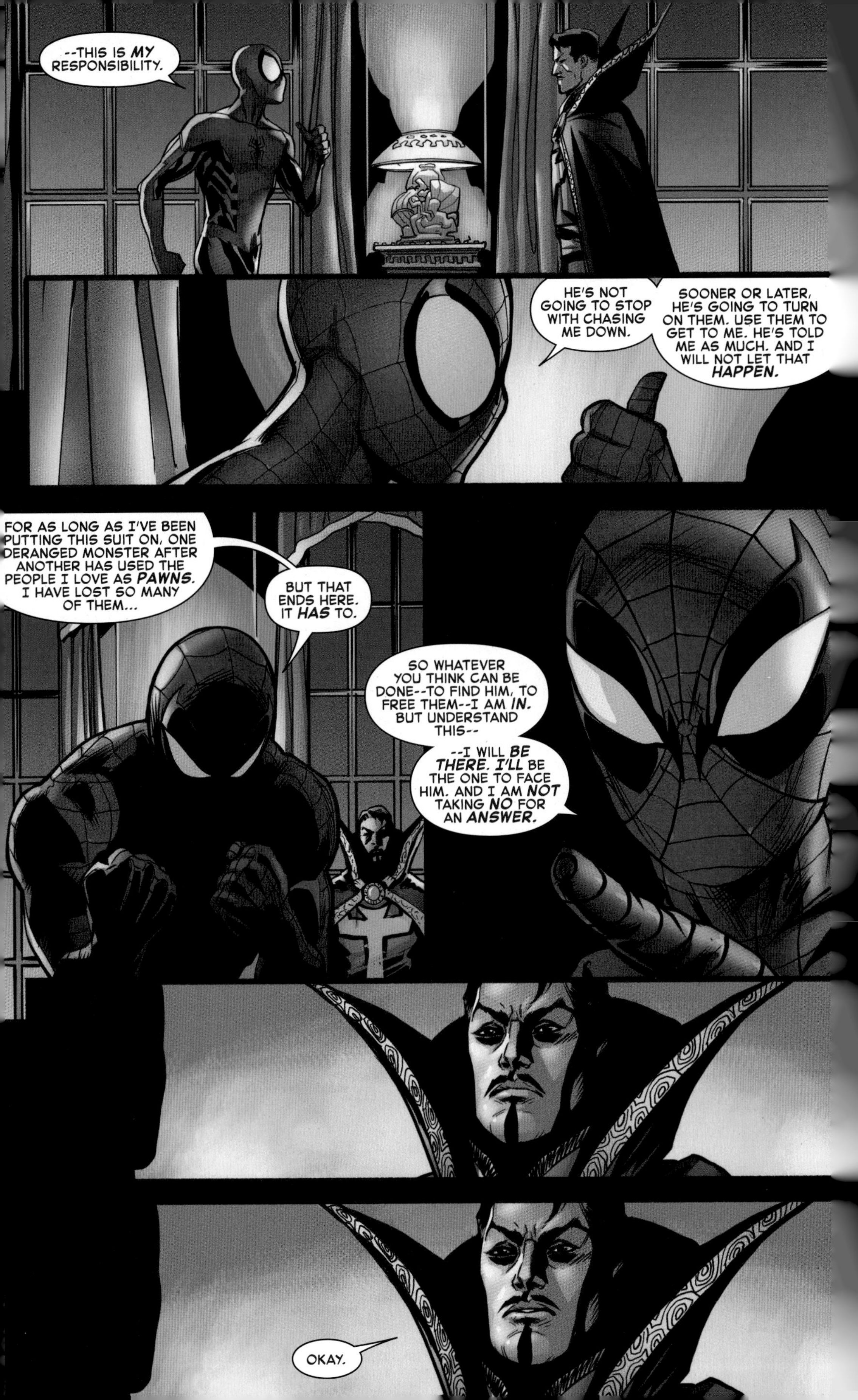
--THIS IS MY RESPONSIBILITY.
HE'S NOT GOING TO STOP WITH CHASING ME DOWN.
SOONER OR LATER, HE'S GOING TO TURN ON THEM. USE THEM TO GET TO ME. HE'S TOLD ME AS MUCH. AND I WILL NOT LET THAT HAPPEN.
FOR AS LONG AS I'VE BEEN PUTTING THIS SUIT ON, ONE DERANGED MONSTER AFTER ANOTHER HAS USED THE PEOPLE I LOVE AS PAWNS. I HAVE LOST SO MANY OF THEM...
BUT THAT ENDS HERE. IT HAS TO.
SO WHATEVER YOU THINK CAN BE DONE--TO FIND HIM, TO FREE THEM--I AM IN. BUT UNDERSTAND THIS--
--I WILL BE THERE. I'LL BE THE ONE TO FACE HIM. AND I AM NOT TAKING NO FOR AN ANSWER.
OKAY.

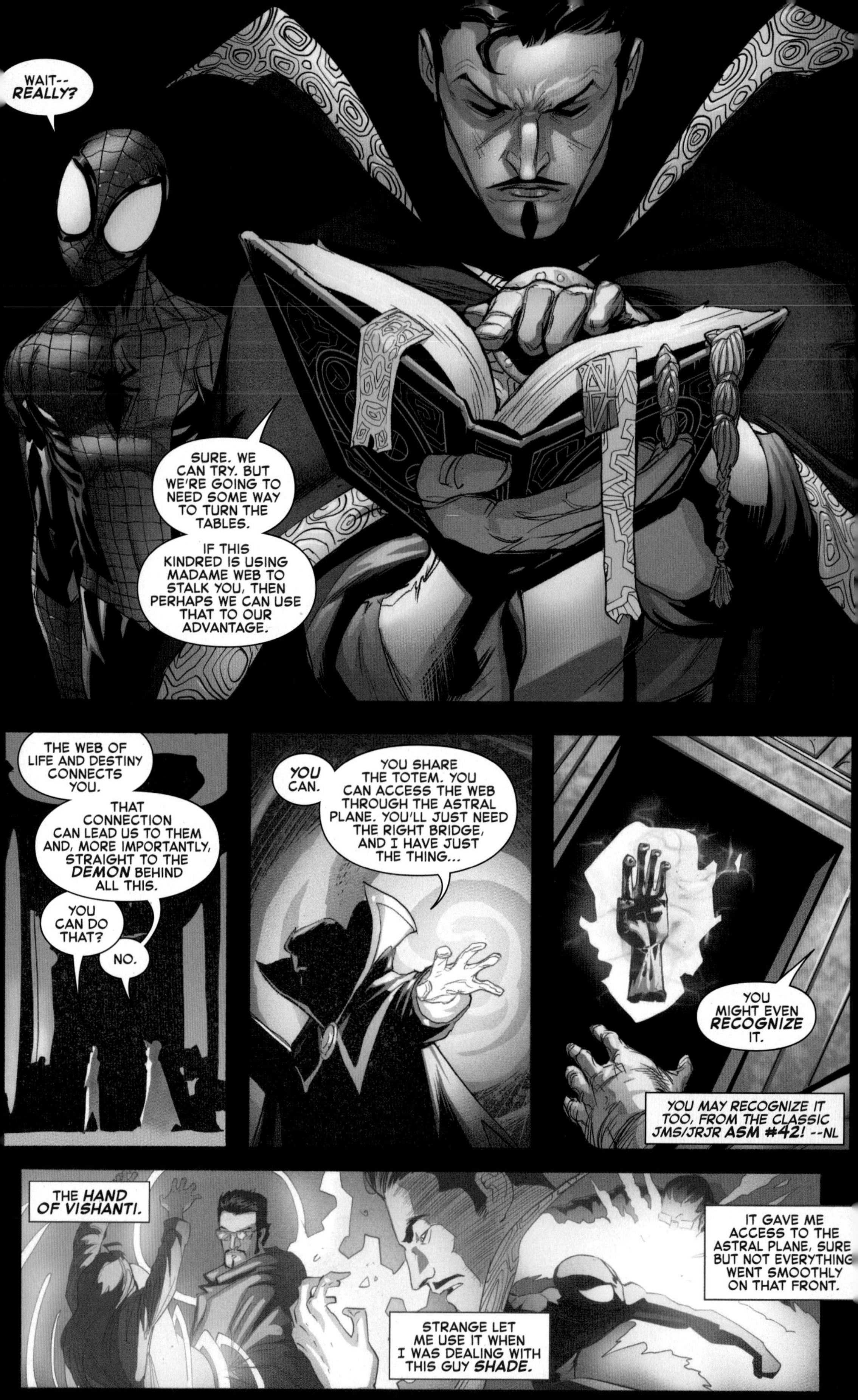
WAIT-- REALLY?
SURE. WE CAN TRY. BUT WE'RE GOING TO NEED SOME WAY TO TURN THE TABLES.
IF THIS KINDRED IS USING MADAME WEB TO STALK YOU, THEN PERHAPS WE CAN USE THAT TO OUR ADVANTAGE.
THE WEB OF LIFE AND DESTINY CONNECTS YOU.
THAT CONNECTION CAN LEAD US TO THEM AND, MORE IMPORTANTLY, STRAIGHT TO THE DEMON BEHIND ALL THIS.
YOU CAN DO THAT?
NO.
YOU CAN.
YOU SHARE THE TOTEM. YOU CAN ACCESS THE WEB THROUGH THE ASTRAL PLANE. YOU'LL JUST NEED THE RIGHT BRIDGE, AND I HAVE JUST THE THING...
YOU MIGHT EVEN RECOGNIZE IT.
YOU MAY RECOGNIZE IT TOO, FROM THE CLASSIC JMS/JRJR ASM #42! --NL
THE HAND OF VISHANTI.
STRANGE LET ME USE IT WHEN I WAS DEALING WITH THIS GUY SHADE.
IT GAVE ME ACCESS TO THE ASTRAL PLANE, SURE BUT NOT EVERYTHING WENT SMOOTHLY ON THAT FRONT.

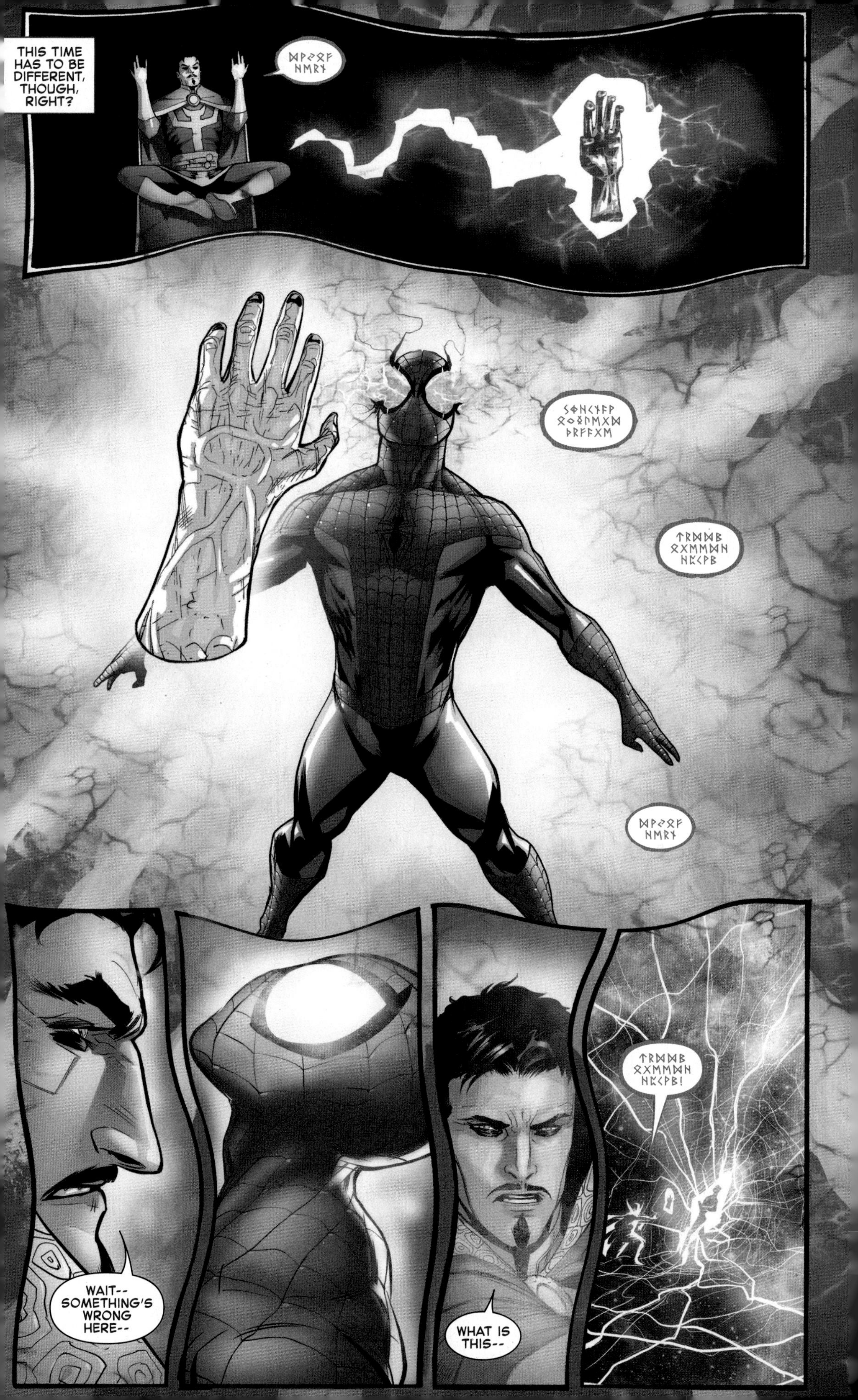
THIS TIME HAS TO BE DIFFERENT, THOUGH, RIGHT?
WAIT-- SOMETHING'S WRONG HERE--
WHAT IS THIS--

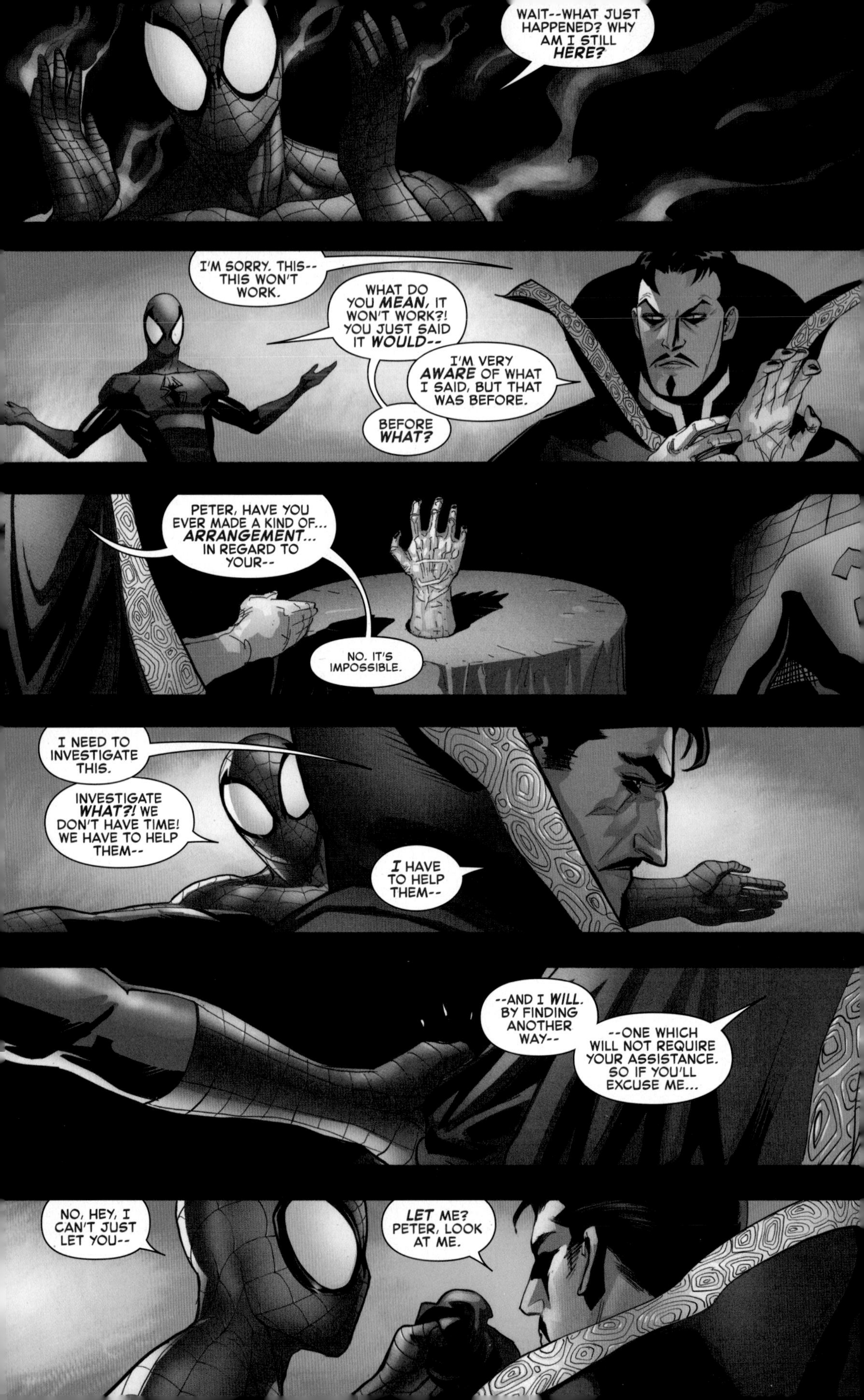
WAIT--WHAT JUST HAPPENED? WHY AM I STILL HERE?
I'M SORRY. THIS-- THIS WON'T WORK.
WHAT DO YOU MEAN, IT WON'T WORK?! YOU JUST SAID IT WOULD--
I'M VERY AWARE OF WHAT I SAID, BUT THAT WAS BEFORE.
BEFORE WHAT?
PETER, HAVE YOU EVER MADE A KIND OF... ARRANGEMENT... IN REGARD TO YOUR--
NO. IT'S IMPOSSIBLE.
I NEED TO INVESTIGATE THIS.
INVESTIGATE WHAT?! WE DON'T HAVE TIME! WE HAVE TO HELP THEM--
I HAVE TO HELP THEM--
--AND I WILL. BY FINDING ANOTHER WAY--
--ONE WHICH WILL NOT REQUIRE YOUR ASSISTANCE. SO IF YOU'LL EXCUSE ME...
NO, HEY, I CAN'T JUST LET YOU--
LET ME? PETER, LOOK AT ME.

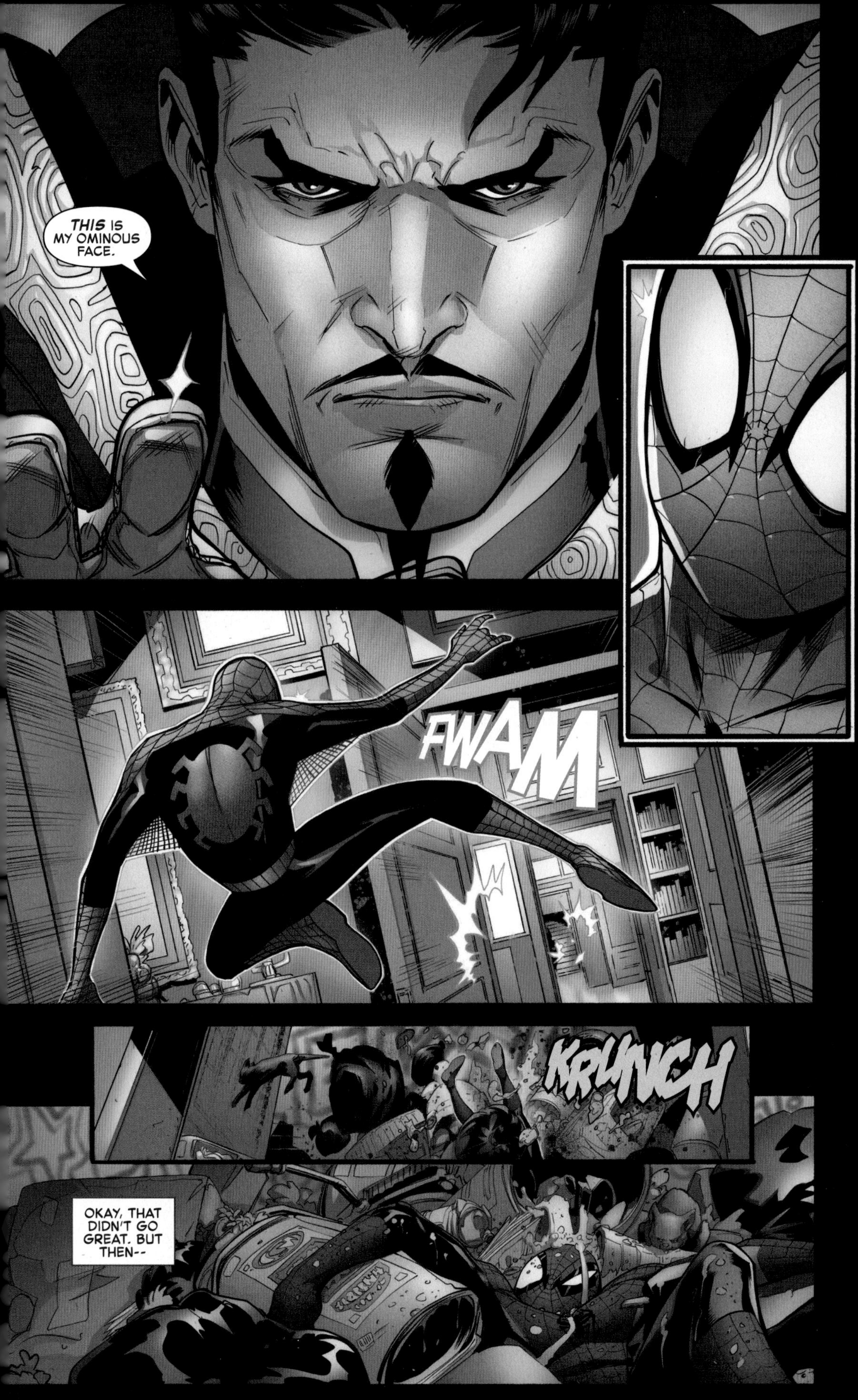
THIS IS MY OMINOUS FACE.
FWAM
KRUNCH
OKAY, THAT DIDN'T GO GREAT. BUT THEN--

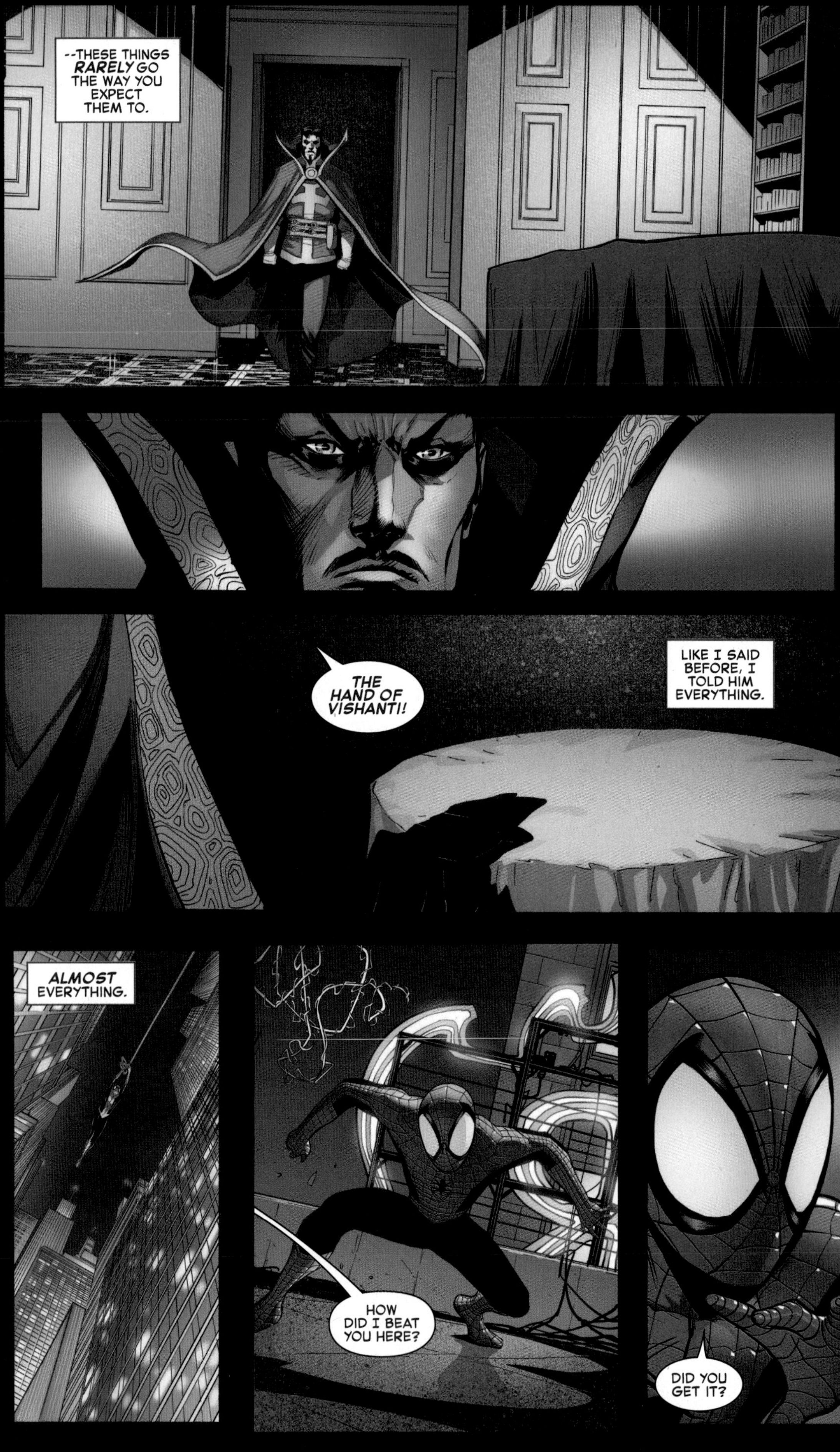
--THESE THINGS RARELY GO THE WAY YOU EXPECT THEM TO.
THE HAND OF VISHANTI!
LIKE I SAID BEFORE, I TOLD HIM EVERYTHING.
ALMOST EVERYTHING.
HOW DID I BEAT YOU HERE?
DID YOU GET IT?

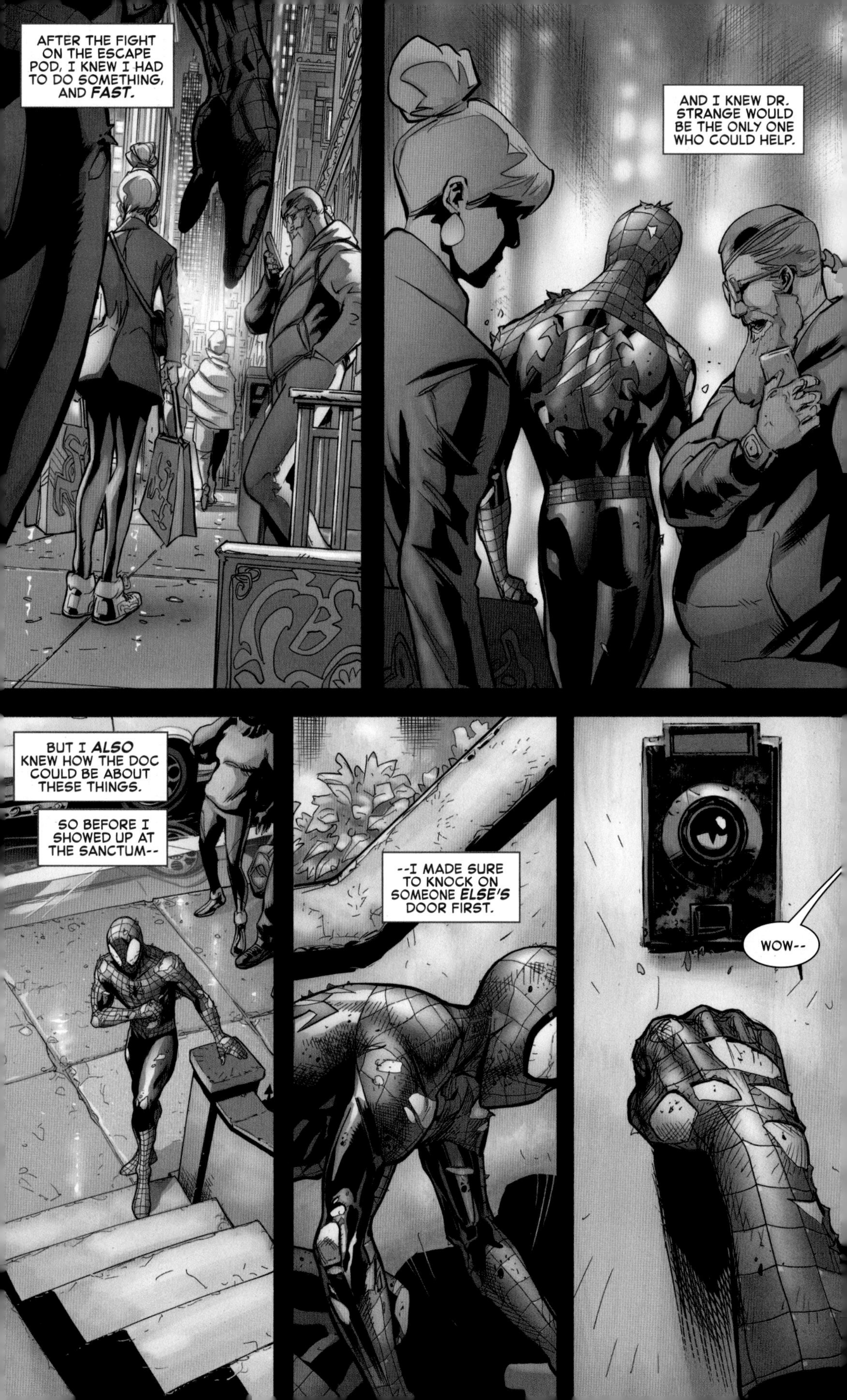
AFTER THE FIGHT ON THE ESCAPE POD, I KNEW I HAD TO DO SOMETHING, AND FAST.
AND I KNEW DR. STRANGE WOULD BE THE ONLY ONE WHO COULD HELP.
BUT I ALSO KNEW HOW THE DOC COULD BE ABOUT THESE THINGS.
SO BEFORE I SHOWED UP AT THE SANCTUM--
--I MADE SURE TO KNOCK ON SOMEONE ELSE'S DOOR FIRST.
WOW--

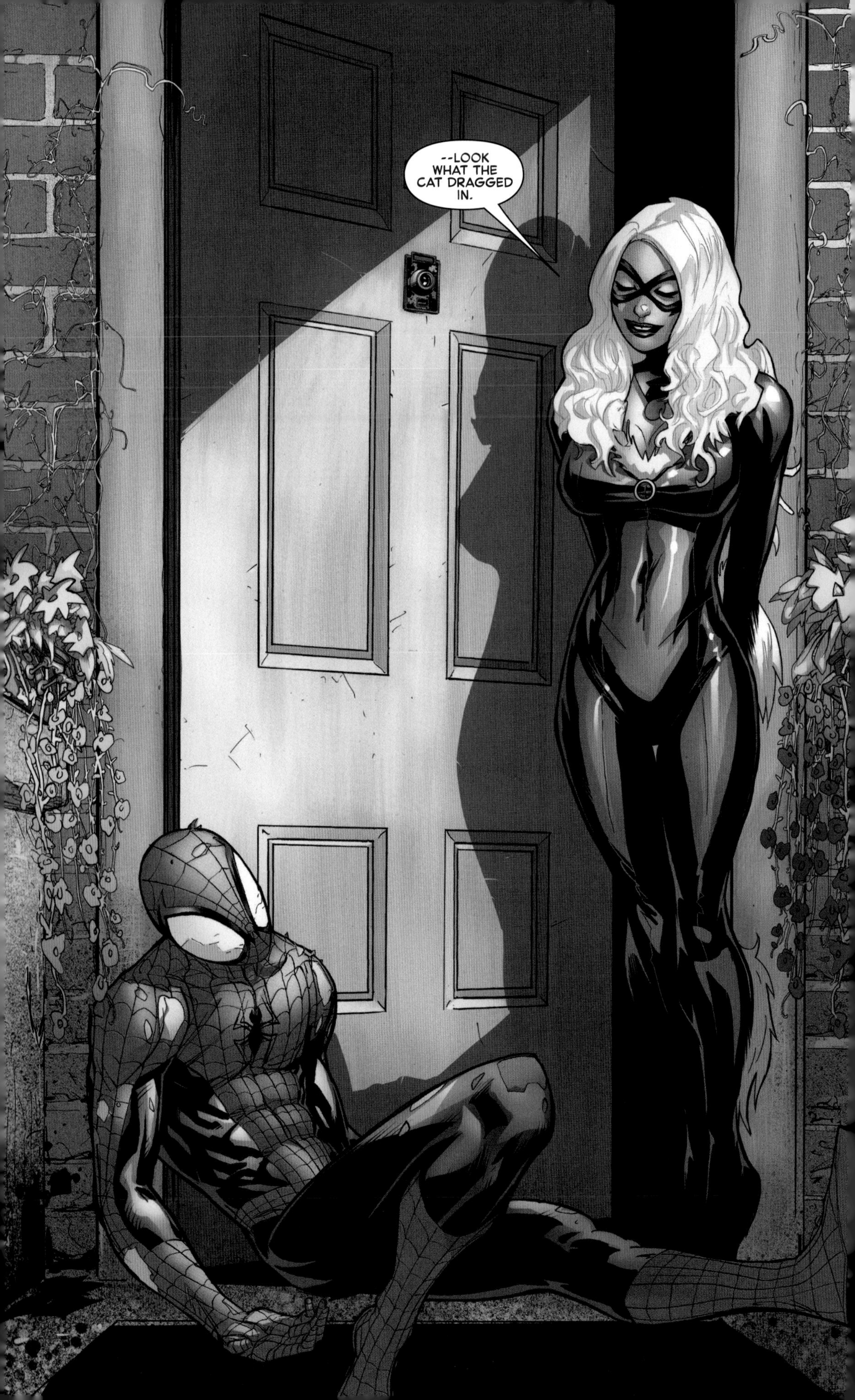
--LOOK WHAT THE CAT DRAGGED IN.

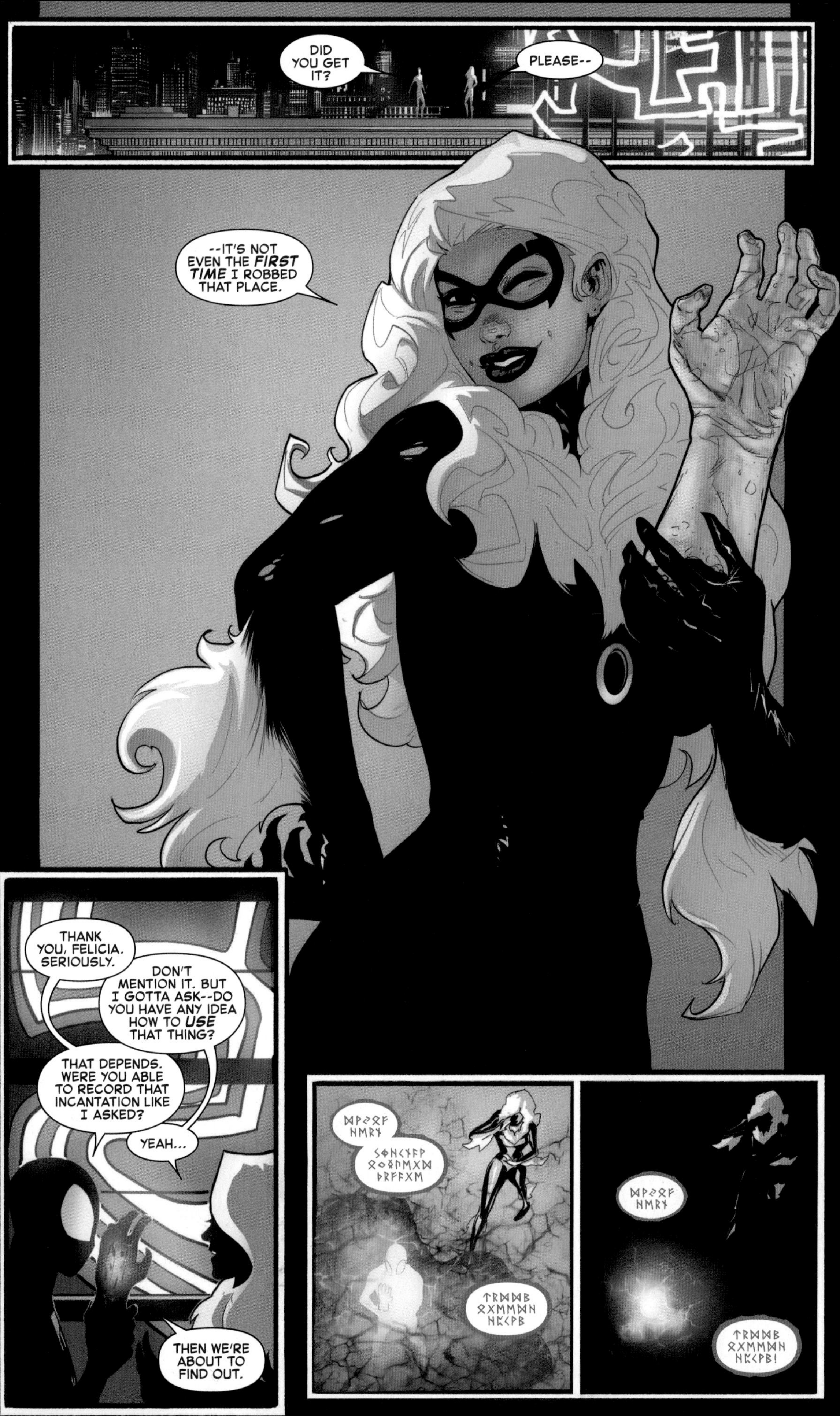
DID YOU GET IT?
PLEASE--
--IT'S NOT EVEN THE *FIRST TIME* I ROBBED THAT PLACE.
THANK YOU, FELICIA. SERIOUSLY.
DON'T MENTION IT. BUT I GOTTA ASK--DO YOU HAVE ANY IDEA HOW TO *USE* THAT THING?
THAT DEPENDS. WERE YOU ABLE TO RECORD THAT INCANTATION LIKE I ASKED?
YEAH...
THEN WE'RE ABOUT TO FIND OUT.

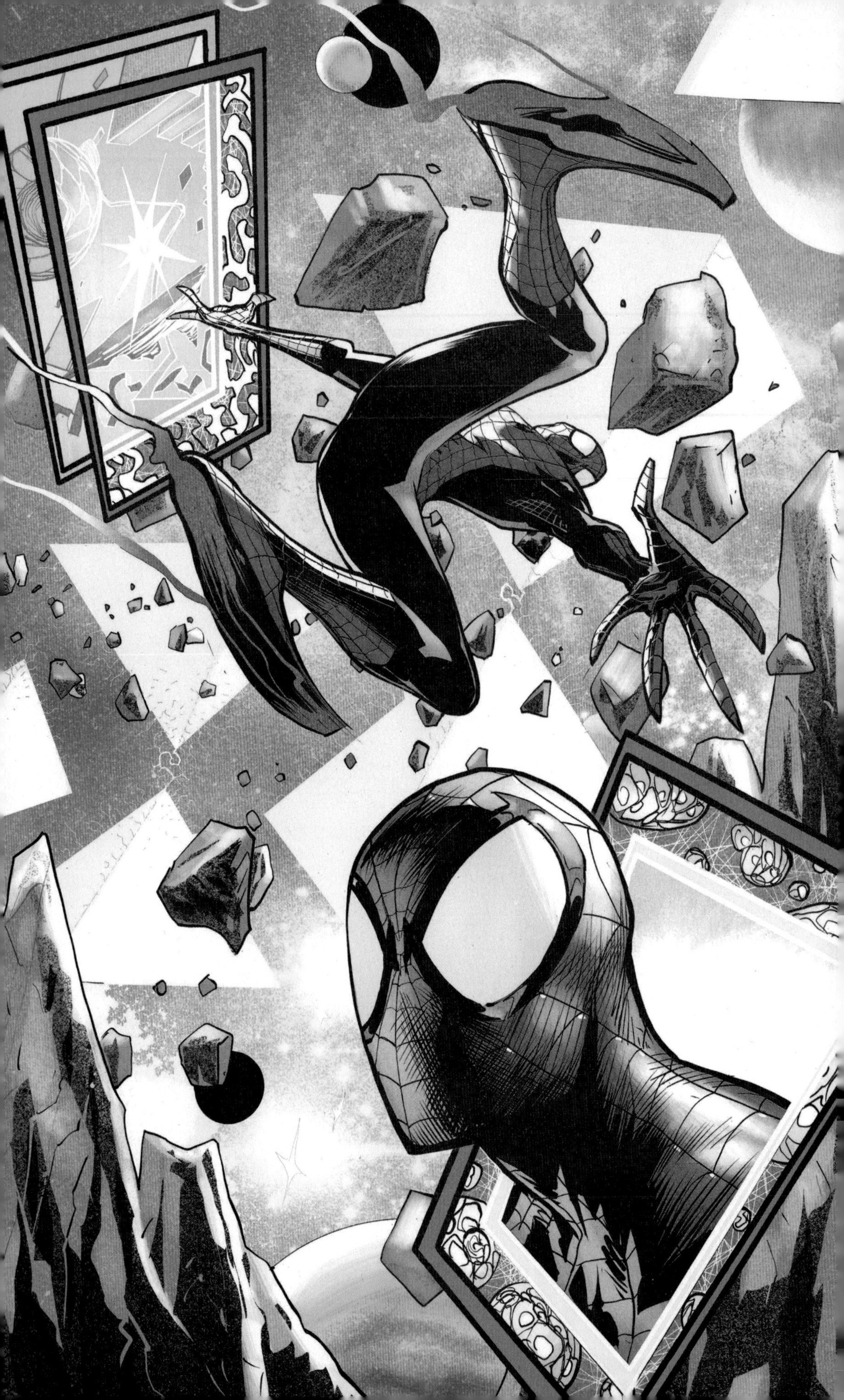

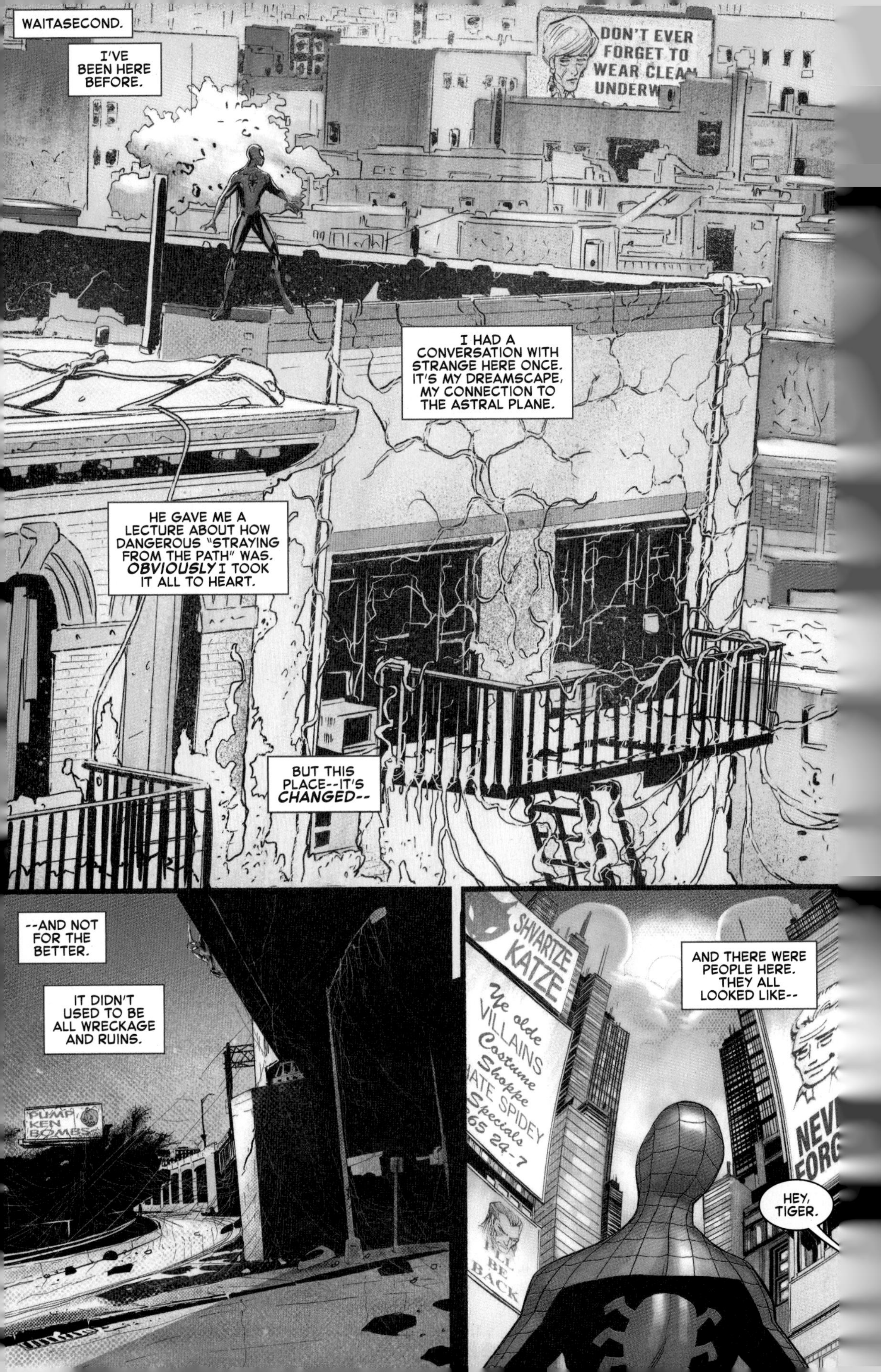
WAITASECOND.
I'VE BEEN HERE BEFORE.
DON'T EVER FORGET TO WEAR CLEAN UNDERW
I HAD A CONVERSATION WITH STRANGE HERE ONCE. IT'S MY DREAMSCAPE, MY CONNECTION TO THE ASTRAL PLANE.
HE GAVE ME A LECTURE ABOUT HOW DANGEROUS "STRAYING FROM THE PATH" WAS. OBVIOUSLY I TOOK IT ALL TO HEART.
BUT THIS PLACE--IT'S CHANGED--
--AND NOT FOR THE BETTER.
IT DIDN'T USED TO BE ALL WRECKAGE AND RUINS.
PUMP KEN BOMBS
SHVARTZE KATZE
Ye olde VILLAINS Costume Shoppe HATE SPIDEY Specials 65 24-7
I'LL BE BACK
AND THERE WERE PEOPLE HERE. THEY ALL LOOKED LIKE--
NEV FORG
HEY, TIGER.

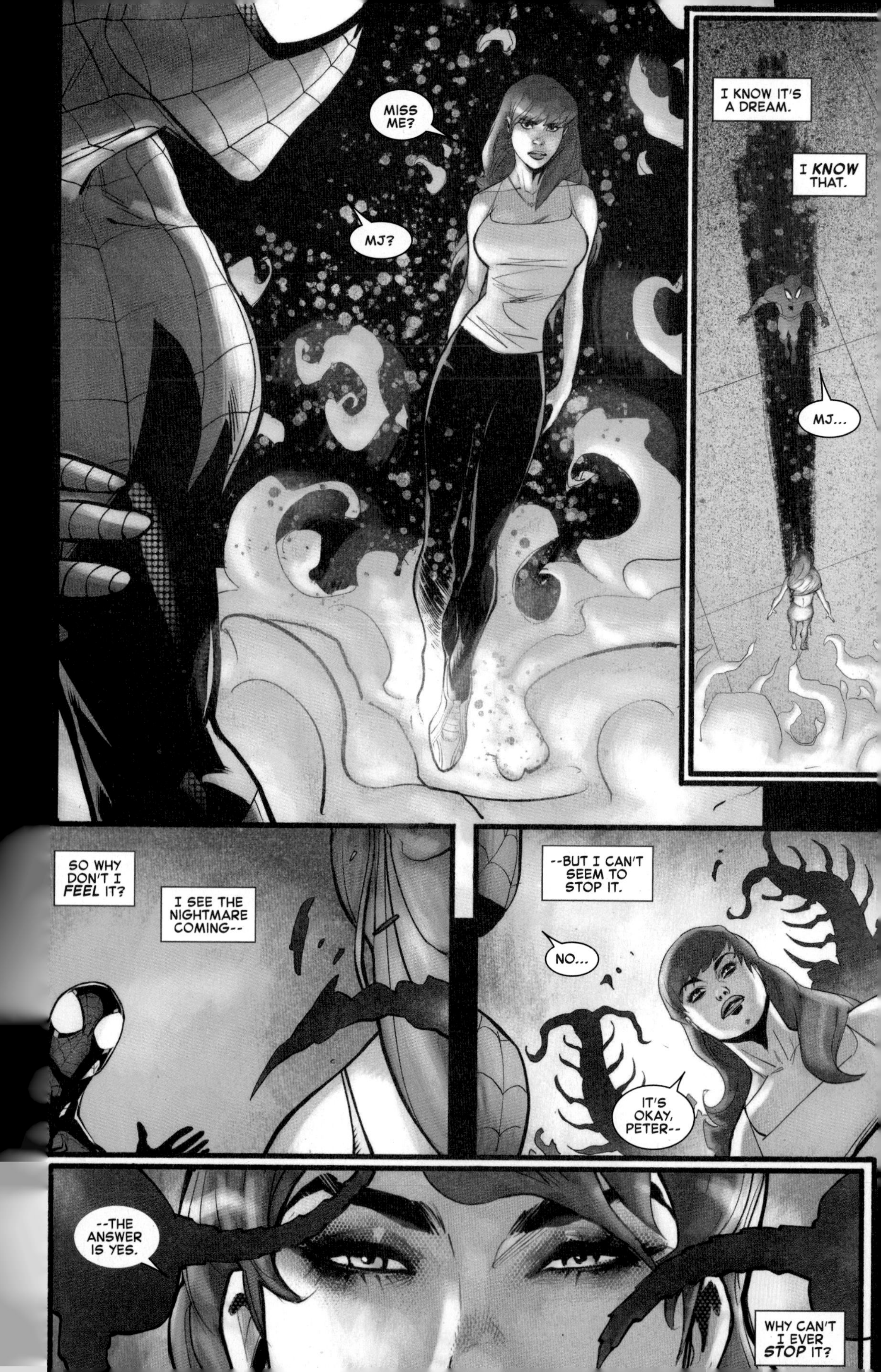
MISS ME?
MJ?
I KNOW IT'S A DREAM.
I KNOW THAT.
MJ...
SO WHY DON'T I FEEL IT?
I SEE THE NIGHTMARE COMING--
--BUT I CAN'T SEEM TO STOP IT.
NO...
IT'S OKAY, PETER--
--THE ANSWER IS YES.
WHY CAN'T I EVER STOP IT?

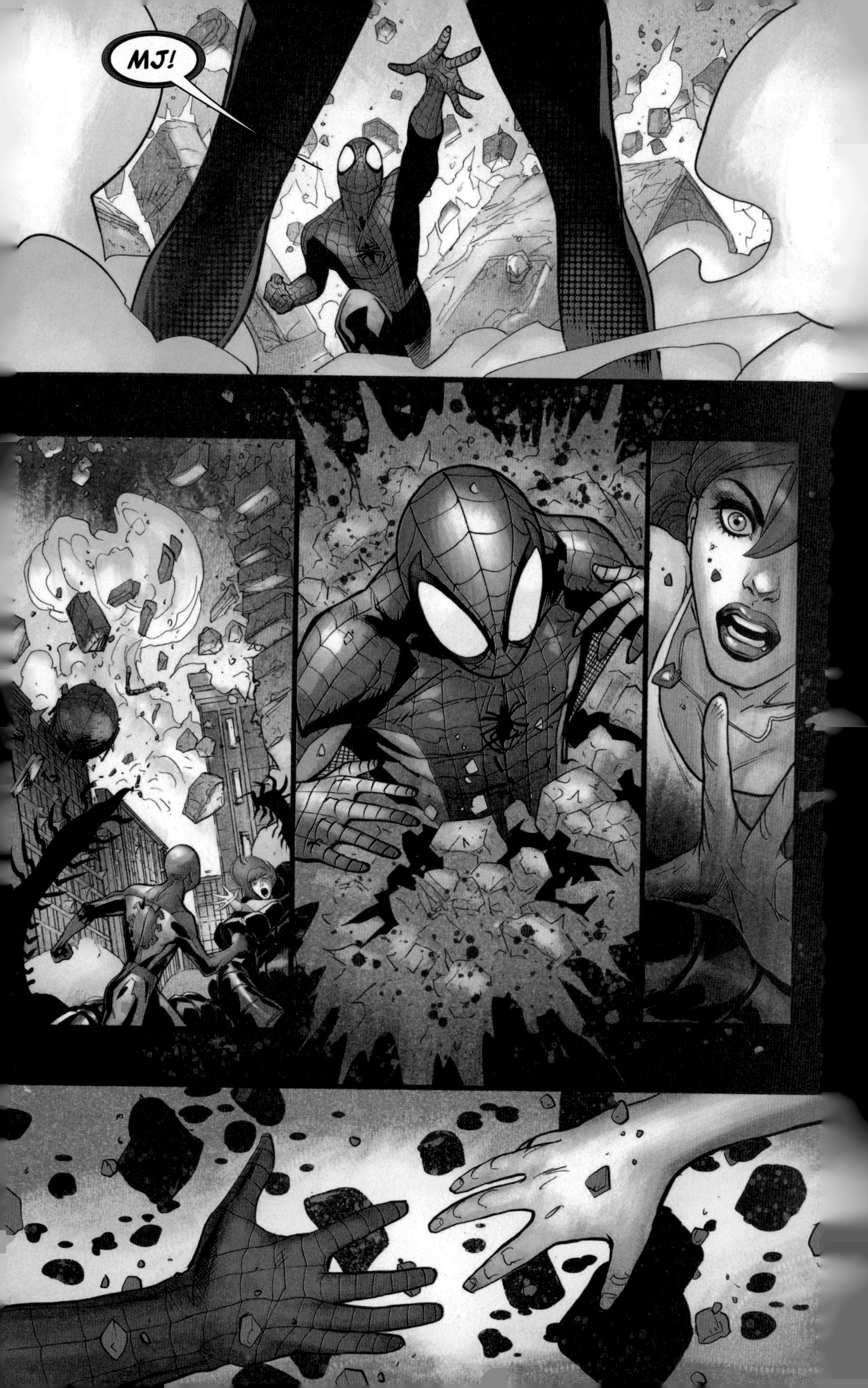
MJ!

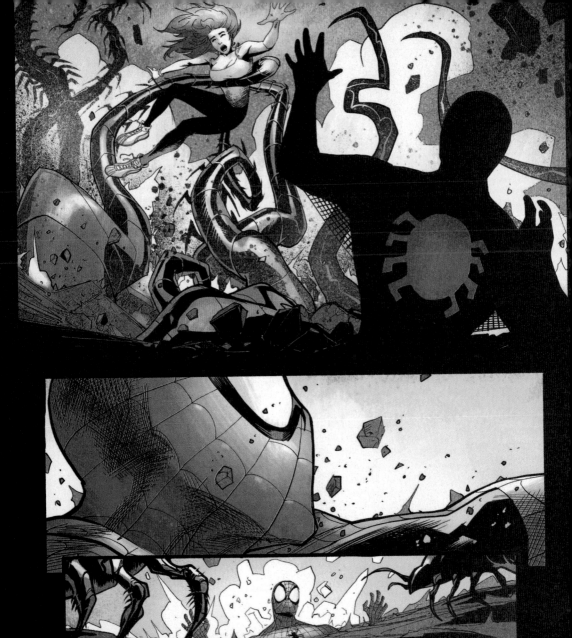

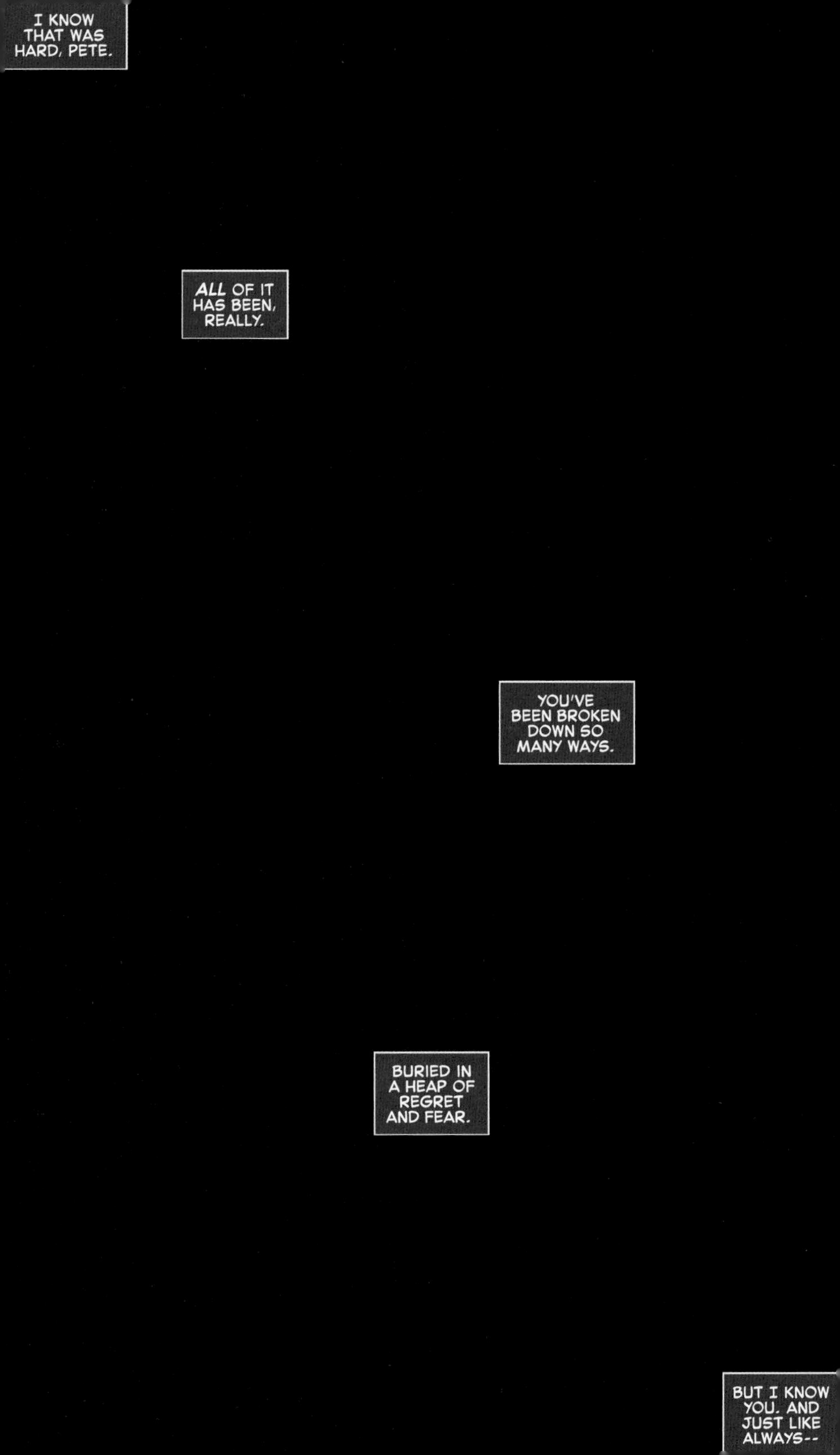
I KNOW THAT WAS HARD, PETE.
ALL OF IT HAS BEEN, REALLY.
YOU'VE BEEN BROKEN DOWN SO MANY WAYS.
BURIED IN A HEAP OF REGRET AND FEAR.
BUT I KNOW YOU. AND JUST LIKE ALWAYS--

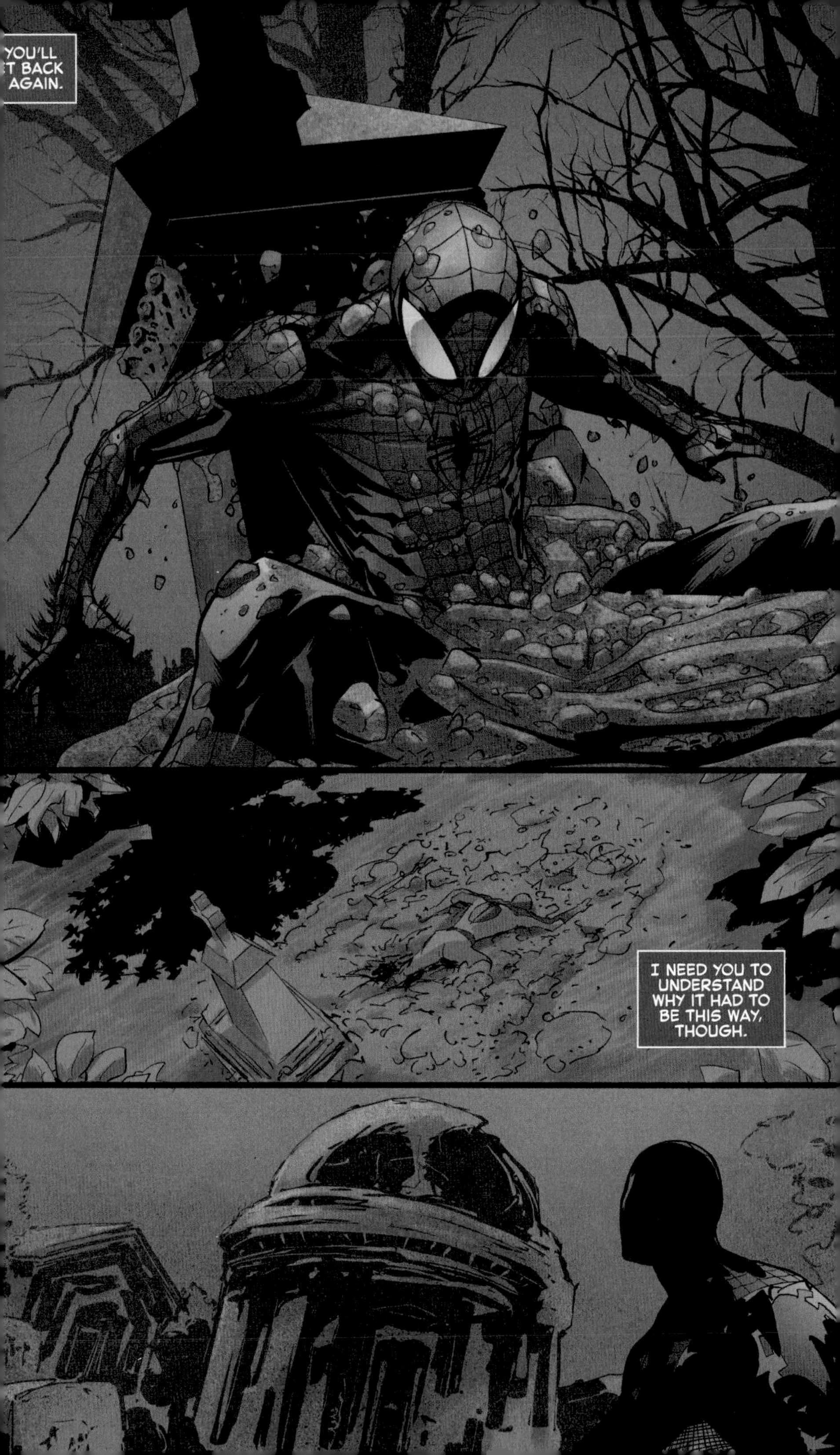
YOU'LL
T BACK
AGAIN.
I NEED YOU TO UNDERSTAND WHY IT HAD TO BE THIS WAY, THOUGH.

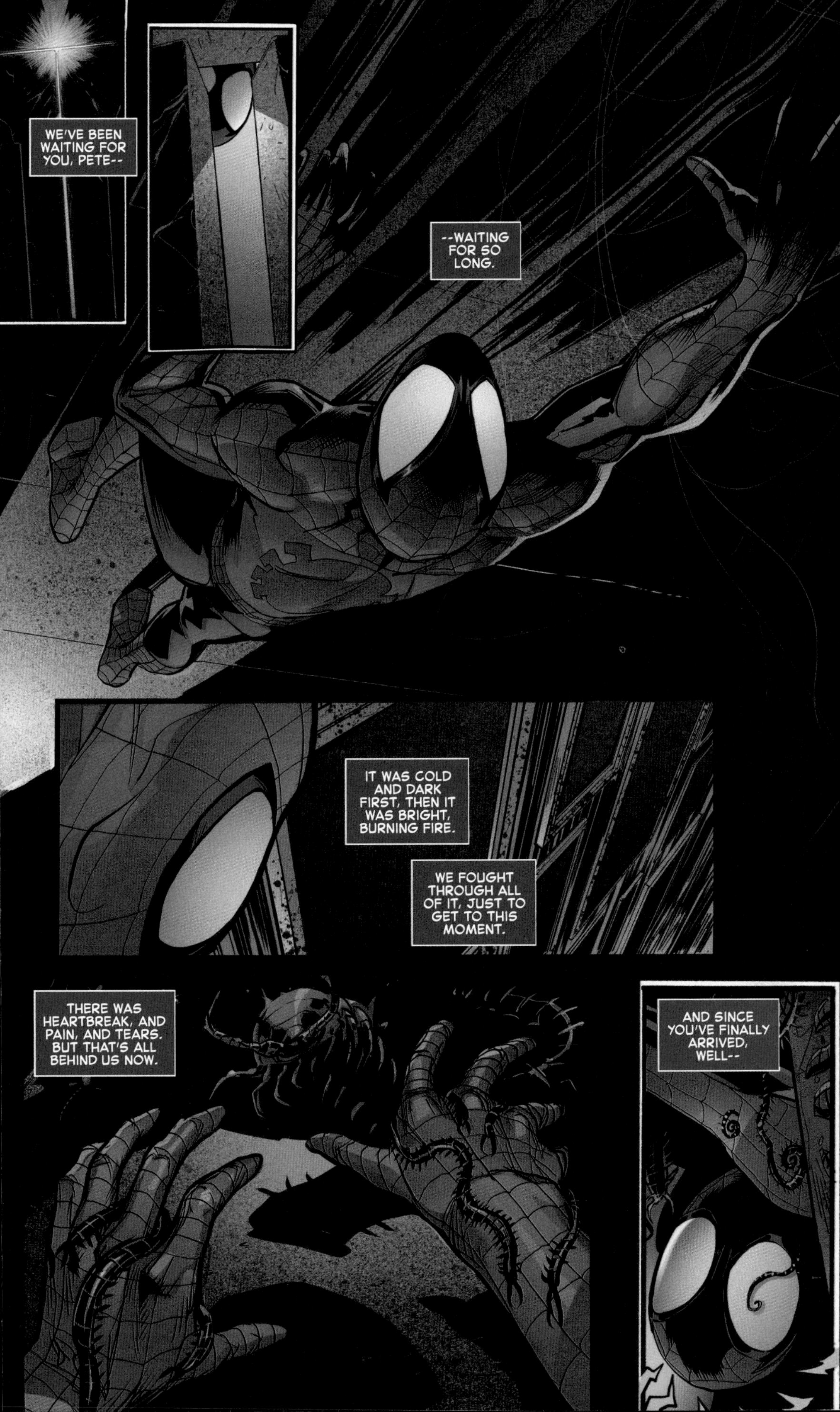

WE'VE BEEN WAITING FOR YOU, PETE--
--WAITING FOR SO LONG.
IT WAS COLD AND DARK FIRST, THEN IT WAS BRIGHT, BURNING FIRE.
WE FOUGHT THROUGH ALL OF IT, JUST TO GET TO THIS MOMENT.
THERE WAS HEARTBREAK, AND PAIN, AND TEARS. BUT THAT'S ALL BEHIND US NOW.
AND SINCE YOU'VE FINALLY ARRIVED, WELL--

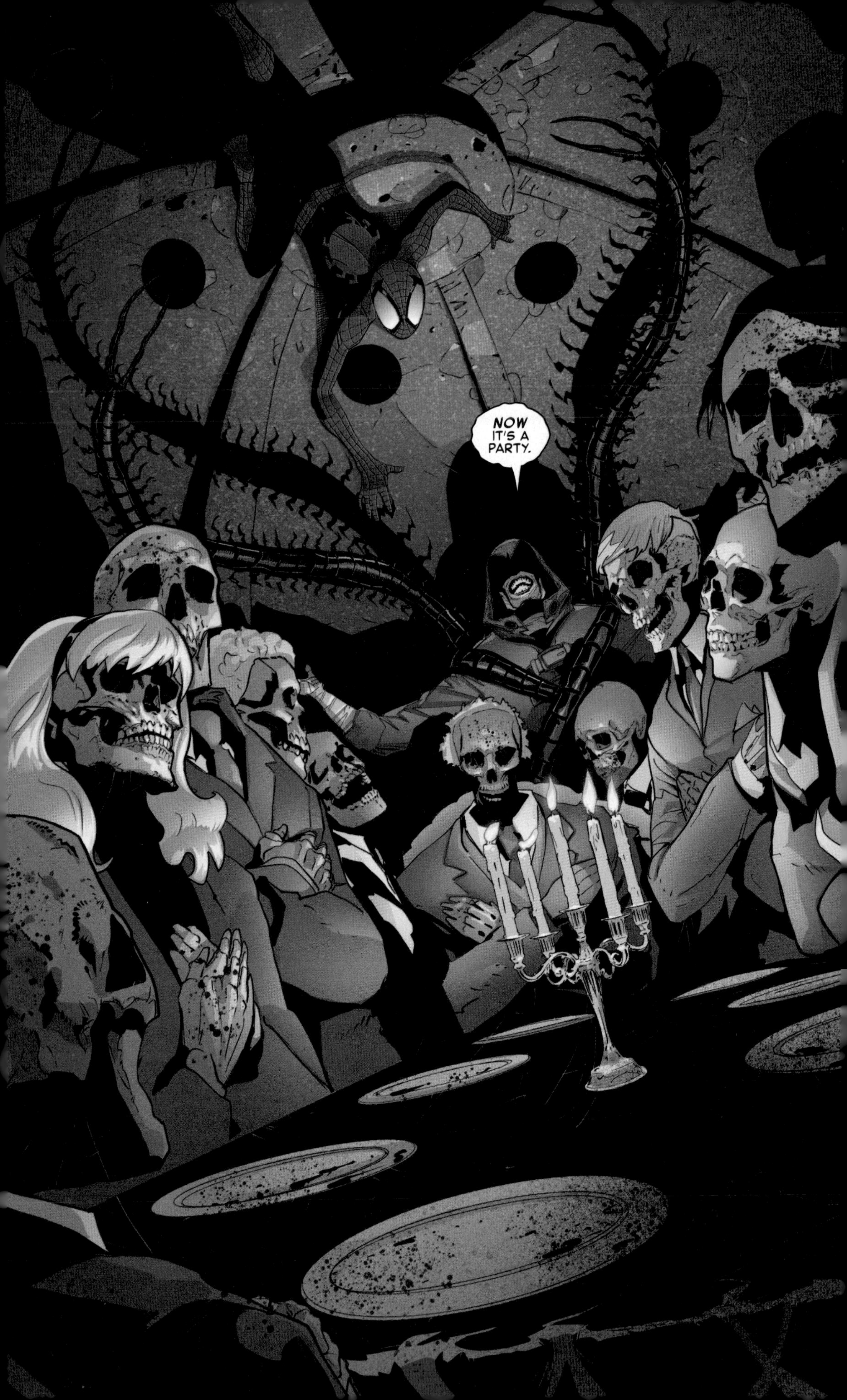
NOW IT'S A PARTY.

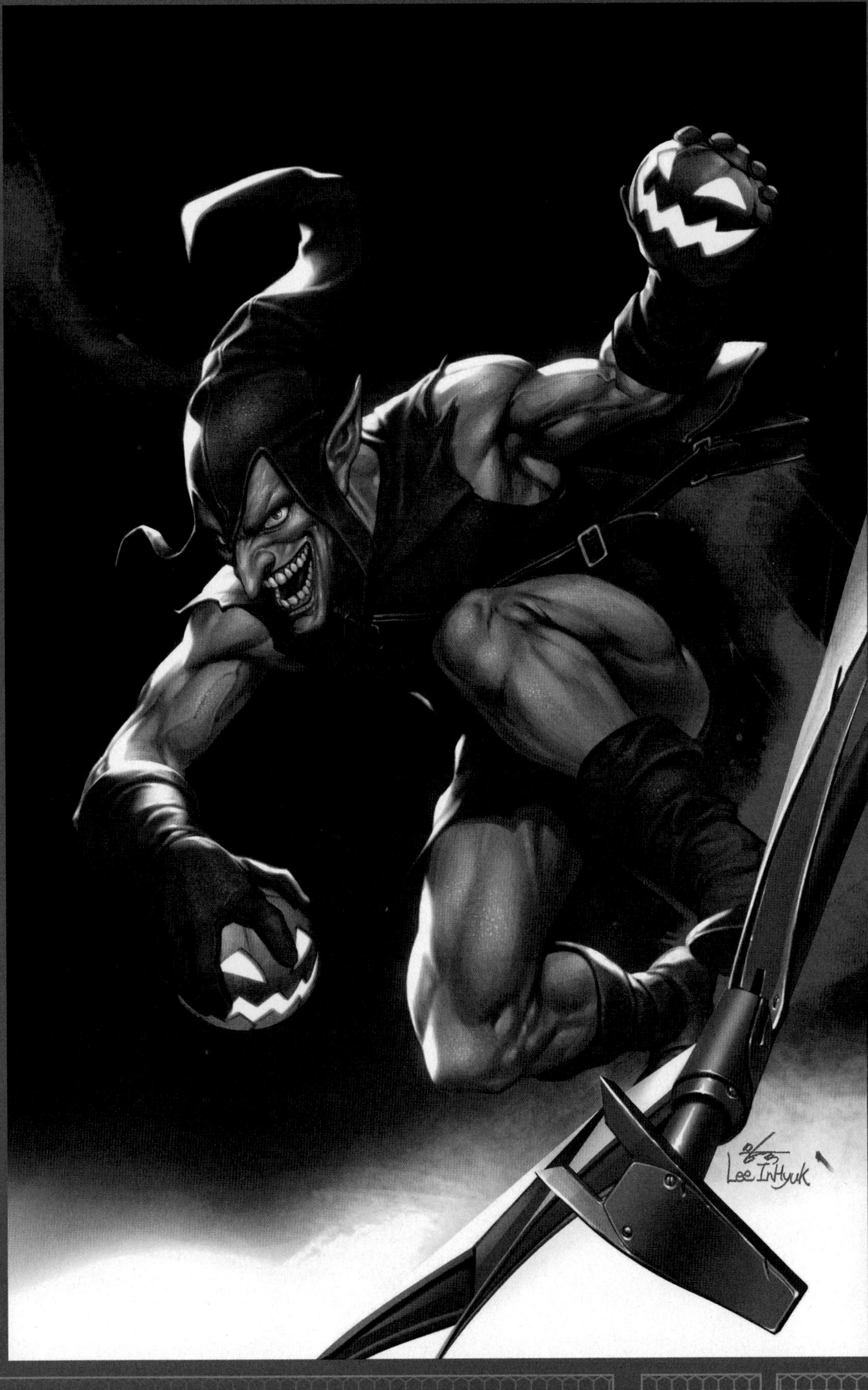
Lee InHyuk

#50 VARIANT BY INHYUK LEE

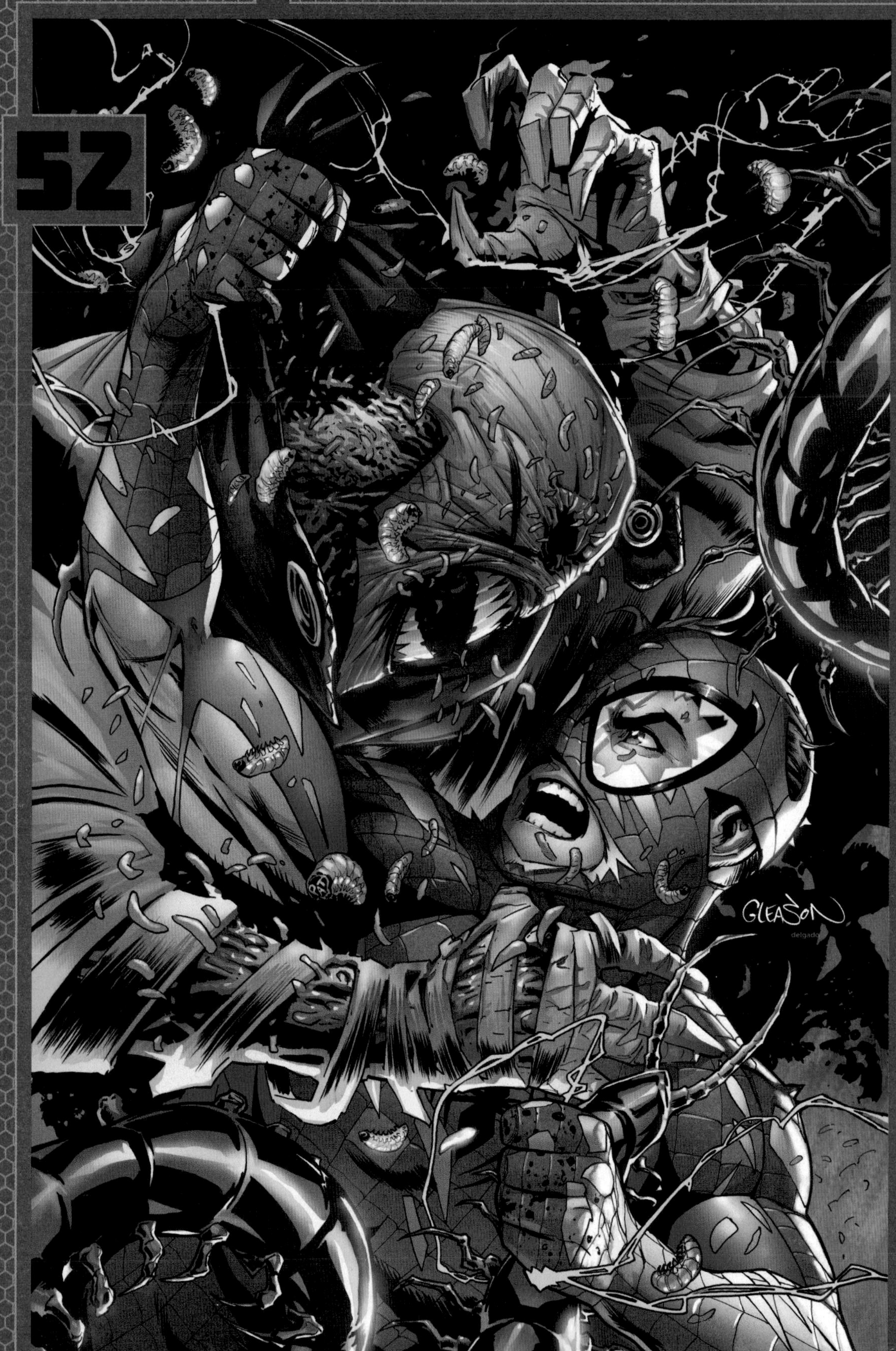
52
GLEASON
delgado

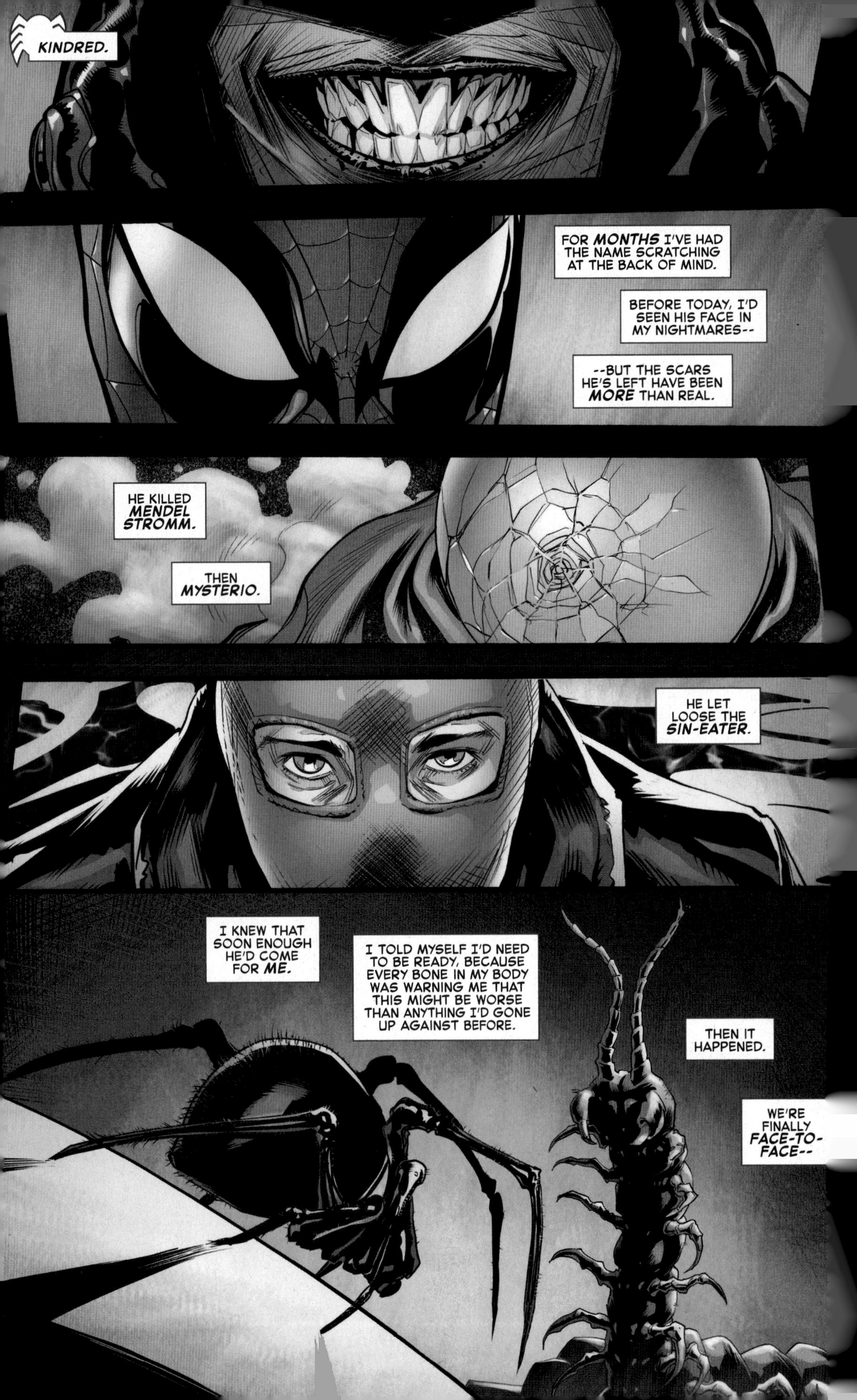
KINDRED.
FOR MONTHS I'VE HAD THE NAME SCRATCHING AT THE BACK OF MIND.
BEFORE TODAY, I'D SEEN HIS FACE IN MY NIGHTMARES--
--BUT THE SCARS HE'S LEFT HAVE BEEN MORE THAN REAL.
HE KILLED MENDEL STROMM.
THEN MYSTERIO.
HE LET LOOSE THE SIN-EATER.
I KNEW THAT SOON ENOUGH HE'D COME FOR ME.
I TOLD MYSELF I'D NEED TO BE READY, BECAUSE EVERY BONE IN MY BODY WAS WARNING ME THAT THIS MIGHT BE WORSE THAN ANYTHING I'D GONE UP AGAINST BEFORE.
THEN IT HAPPENED.
WE'RE FINALLY FACE-TO-FACE--

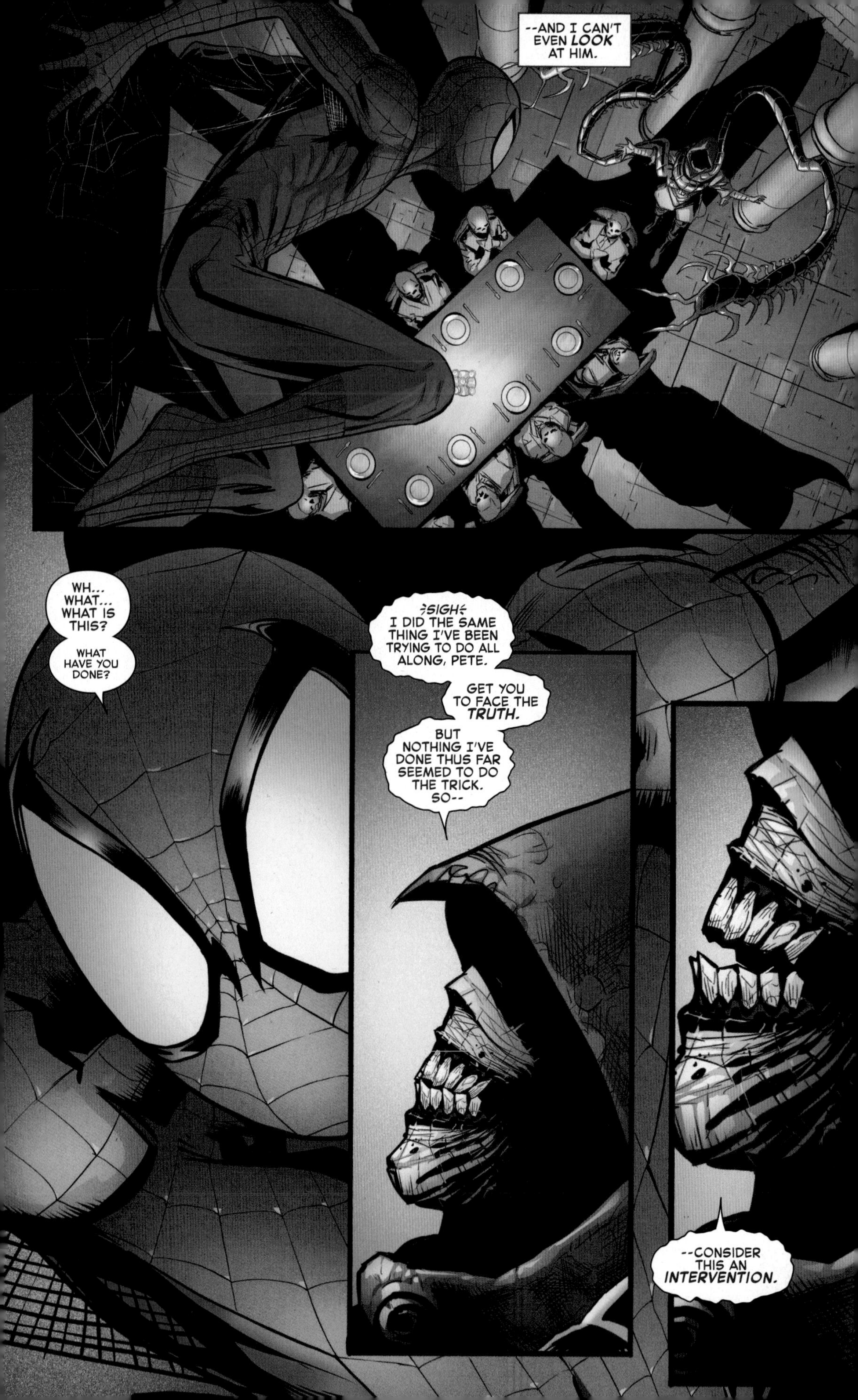
--AND I CAN'T EVEN LOOK AT HIM.
WH... WHAT... WHAT IS THIS?
WHAT HAVE YOU DONE?
SIGH I DID THE SAME THING I'VE BEEN TRYING TO DO ALL ALONG, PETE.
GET YOU TO FACE THE TRUTH.
BUT NOTHING I'VE DONE THUS FAR SEEMED TO DO THE TRICK. SO--
--CONSIDER THIS AN INTERVENTION.

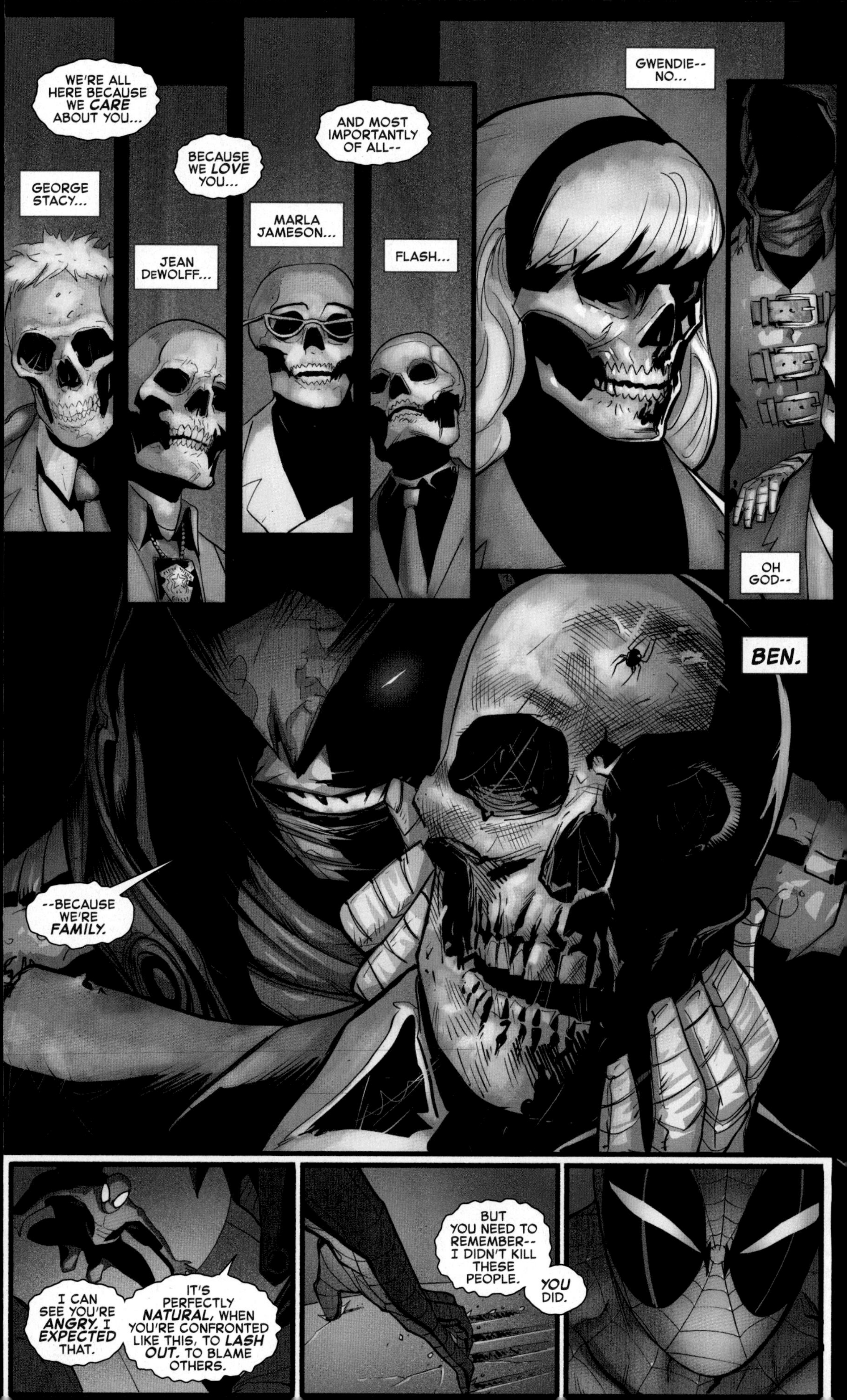
WE'RE ALL HERE BECAUSE WE CARE ABOUT YOU...
GEORGE STACY...
BECAUSE WE LOVE YOU...
JEAN DEWOLFF...
MARLA JAMESON...
AND MOST IMPORTANTLY OF ALL--
FLASH...
GWENDIE-- NO...
OH GOD--
BEN.
--BECAUSE WE'RE FAMILY.
I CAN SEE YOU'RE ANGRY. I EXPECTED THAT.
IT'S PERFECTLY NATURAL, WHEN YOU'RE CONFRONTED LIKE THIS, TO LASH OUT. TO BLAME OTHERS.
BUT YOU NEED TO REMEMBER-- I DIDN'T KILL THESE PEOPLE.
YOU DID.

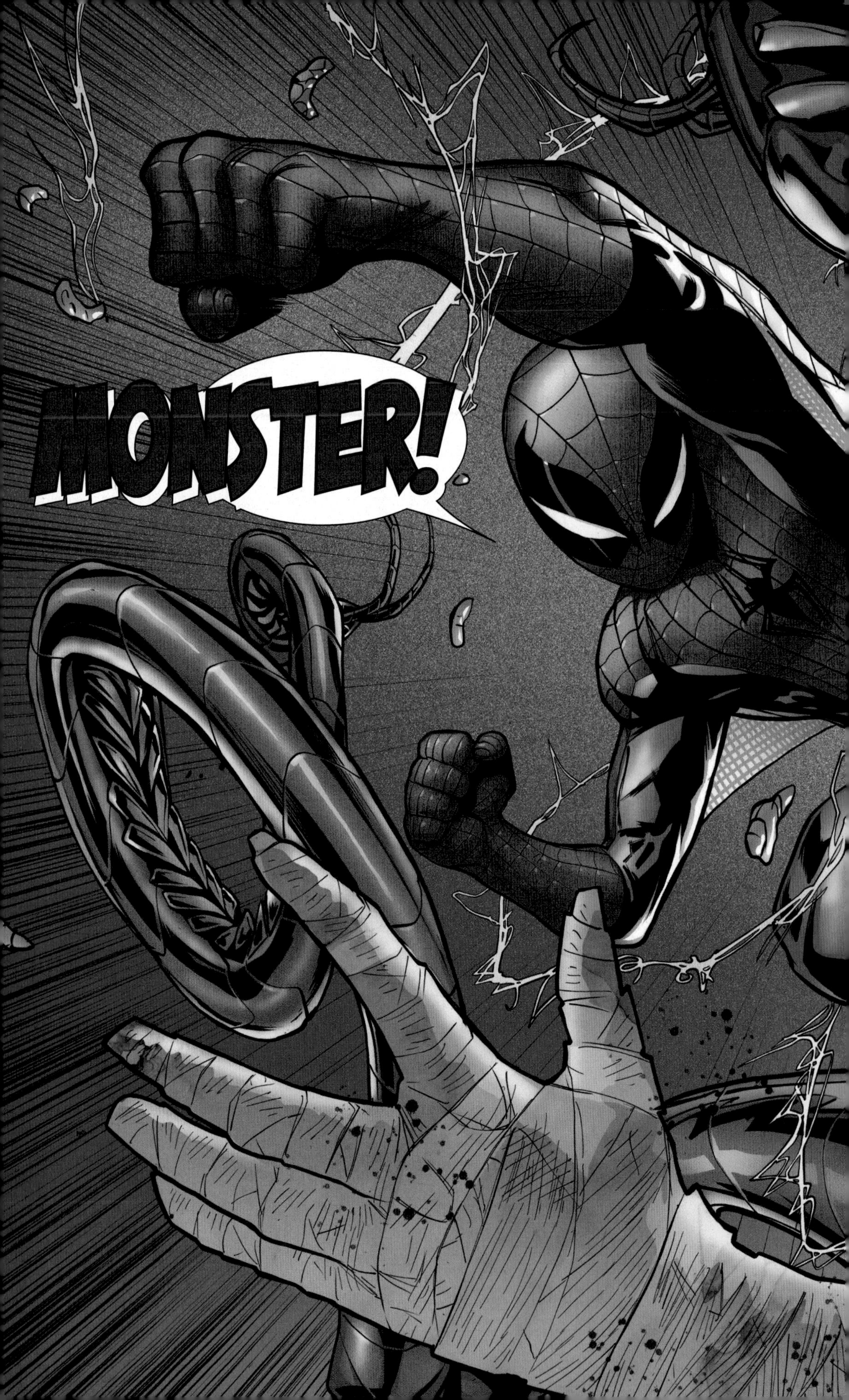
MONSTER!

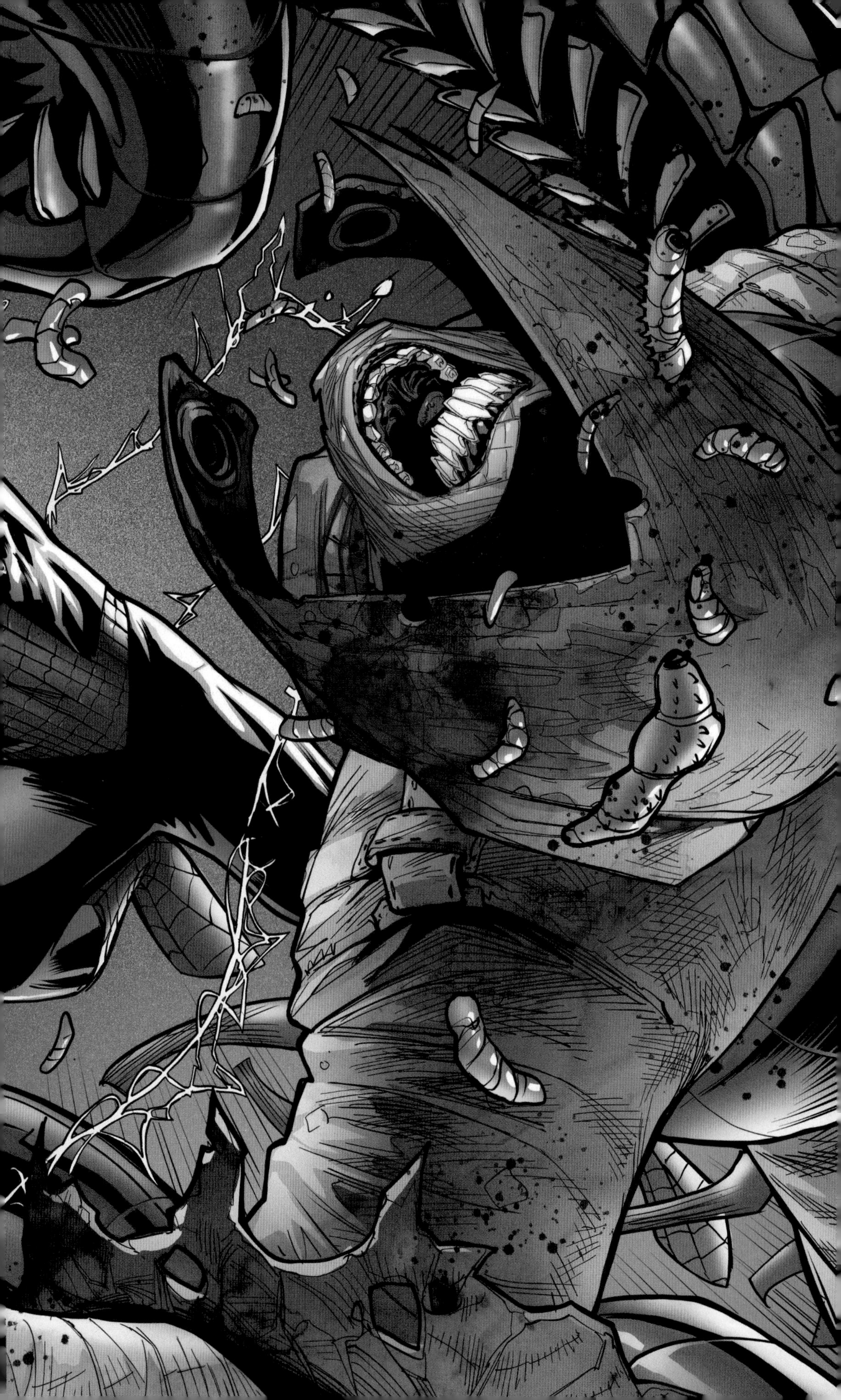

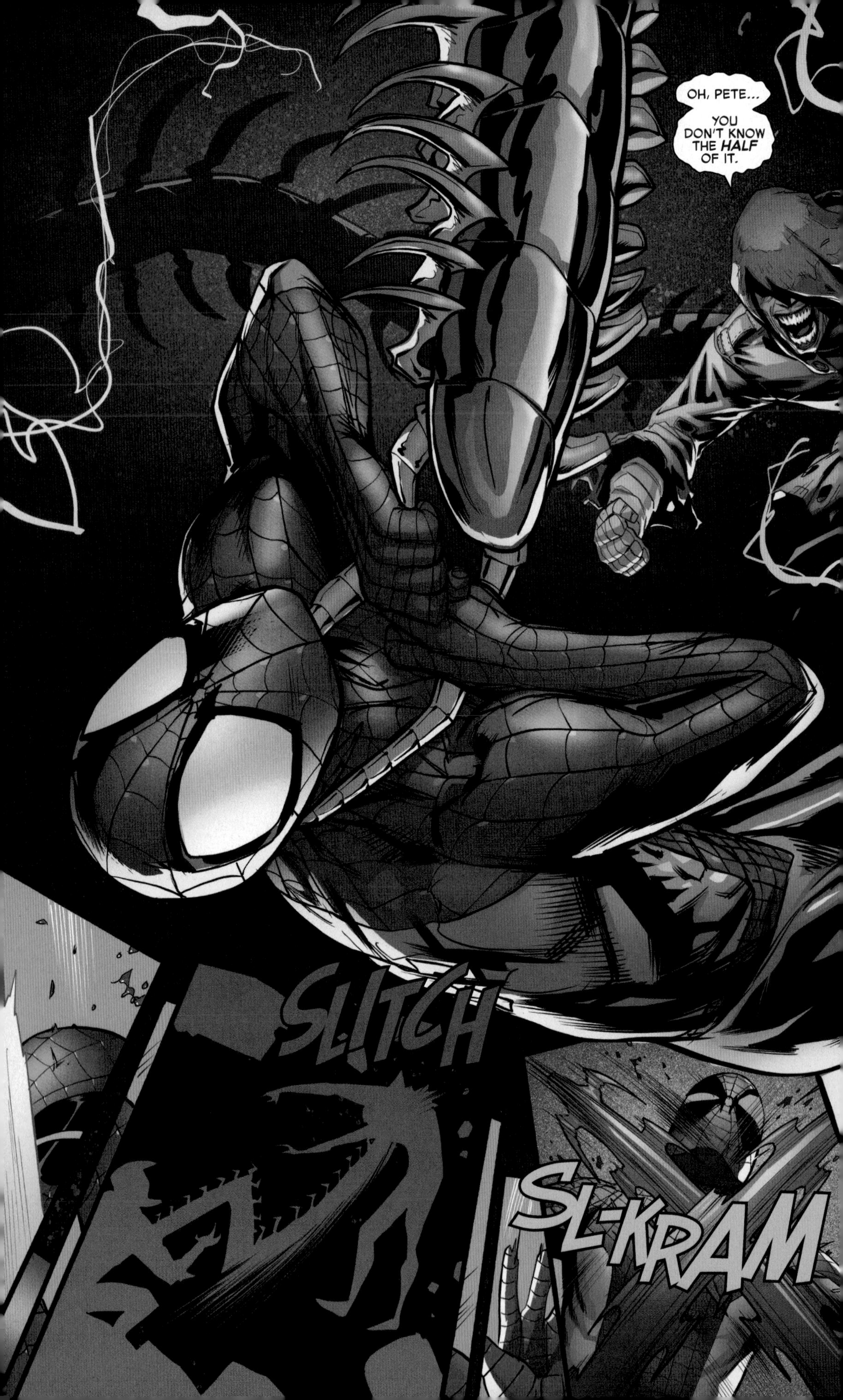
OH, PETE...
YOU DON'T KNOW THE HALF OF IT.
SLITCH
SL-KRAM

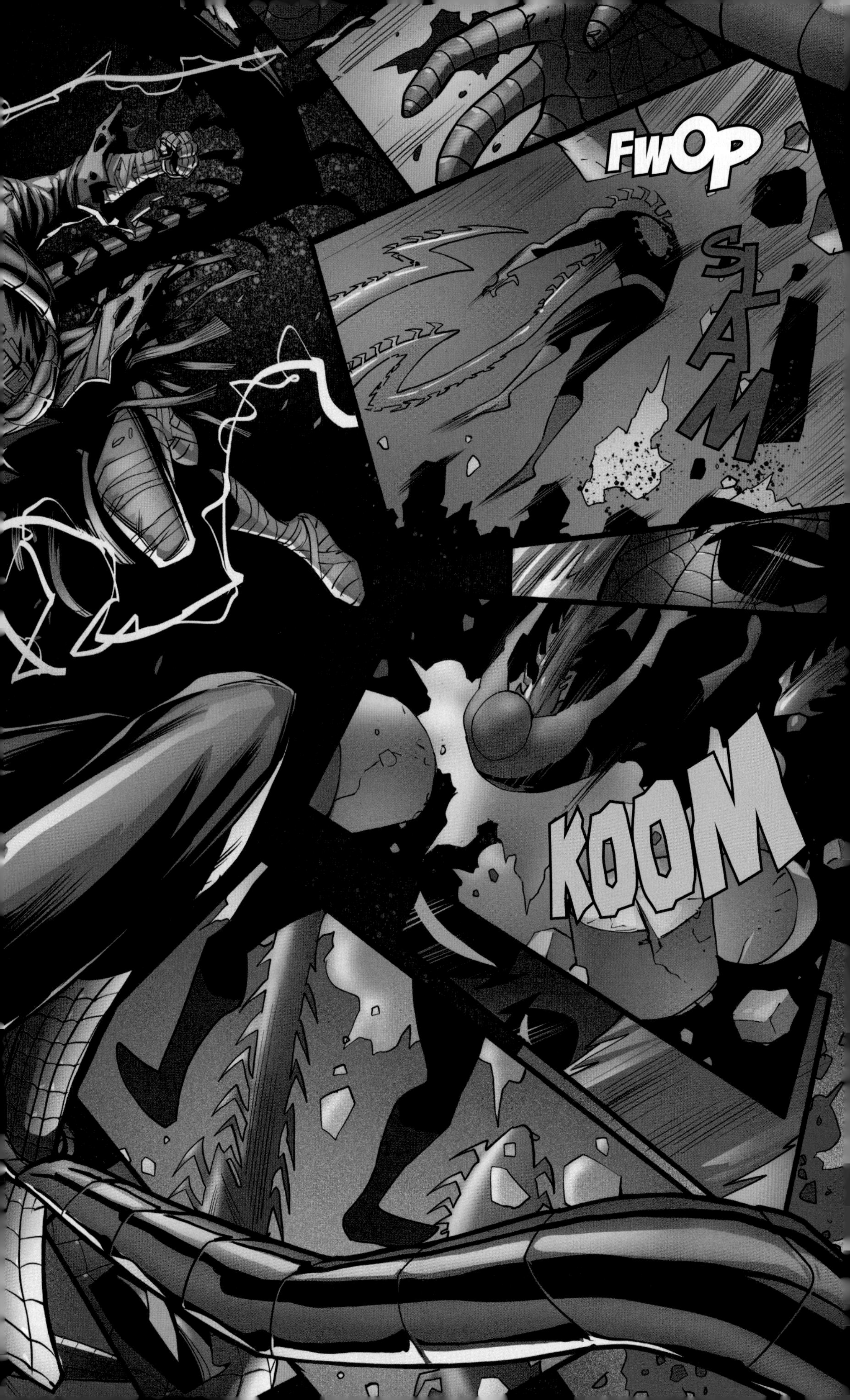
FWOP
SLAM
KOOM

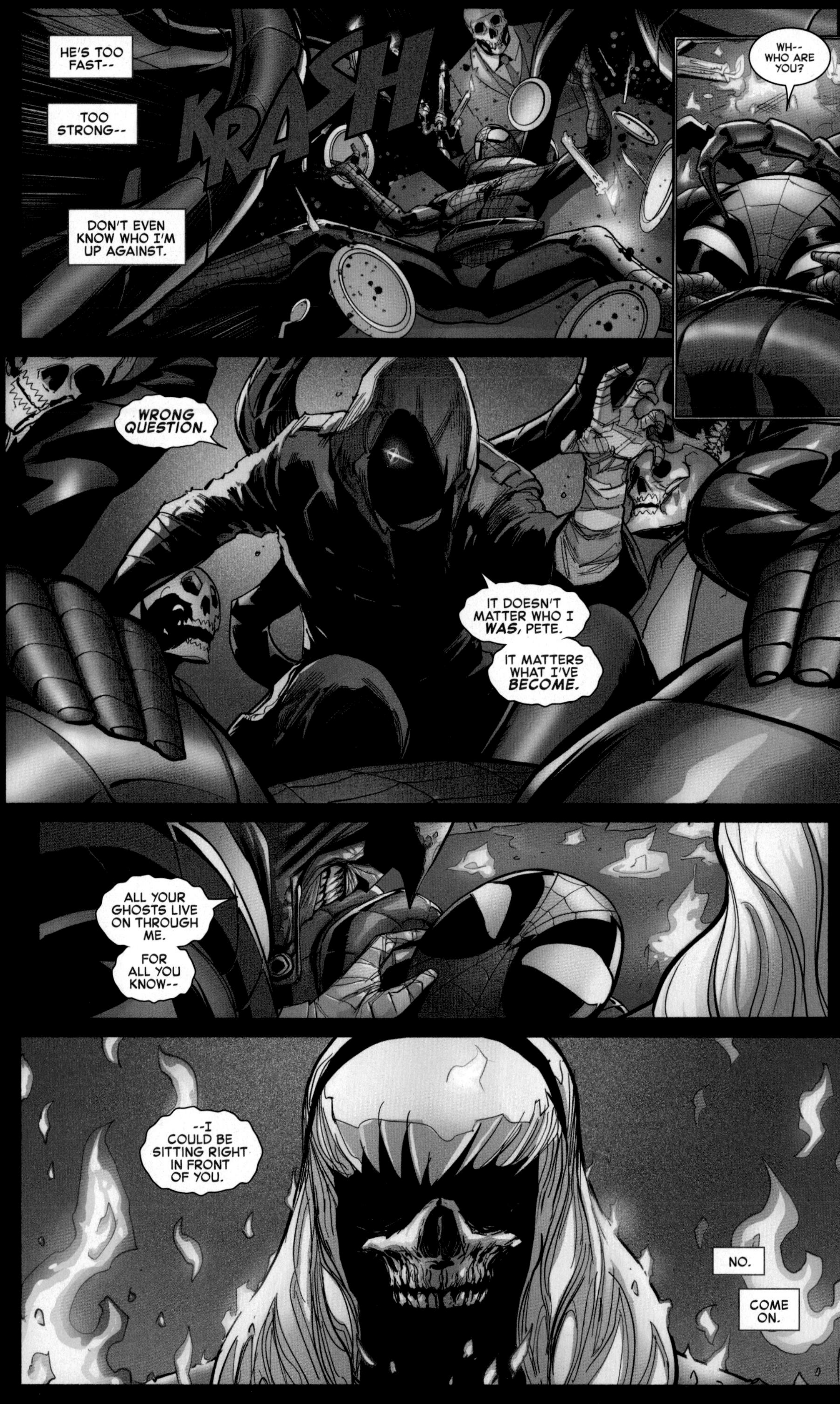
HE'S TOO FAST--
TOO STRONG--
KRASH
DON'T EVEN KNOW WHO I'M UP AGAINST.
WH-- WHO ARE YOU?
WRONG QUESTION.
IT DOESN'T MATTER WHO I WAS, PETE.
IT MATTERS WHAT I'VE BECOME.
ALL YOUR GHOSTS LIVE ON THROUGH ME.
FOR ALL YOU KNOW--
--I COULD BE SITTING RIGHT IN FRONT OF YOU.
NO.
COME ON.

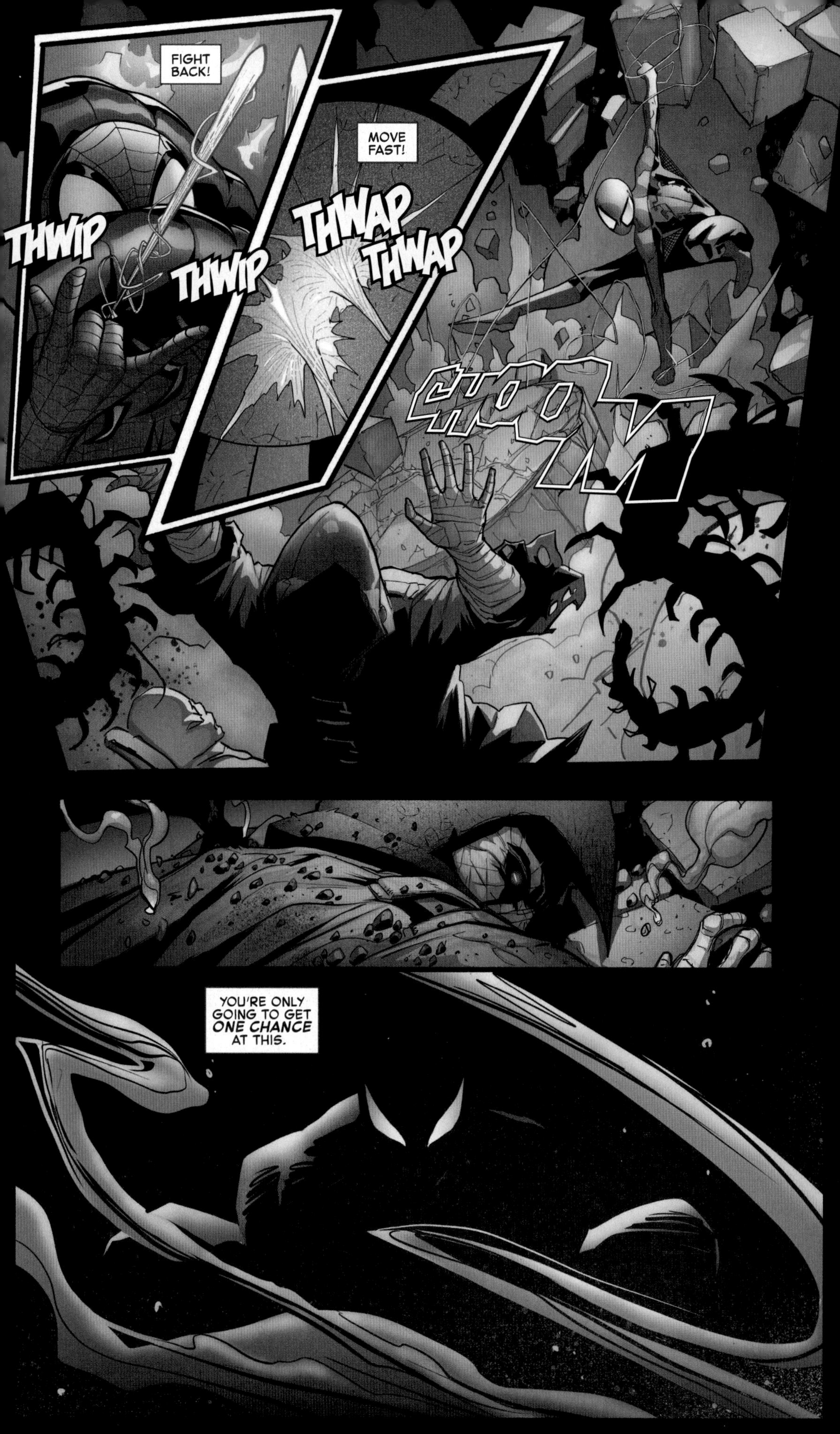

FIGHT BACK!
THWIP
THWIP
MOVE FAST!
THWAP THWAP
CHOOM
YOU'RE ONLY GOING TO GET ONE CHANCE AT THIS.

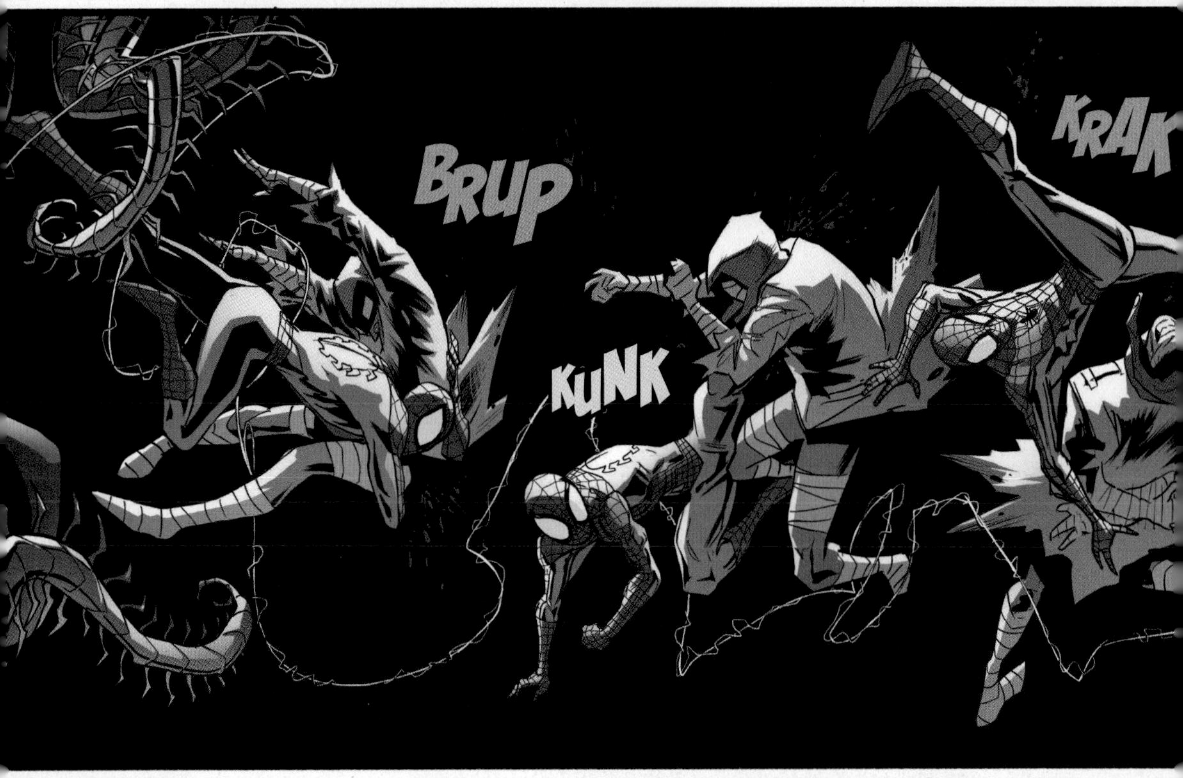
BRUP
KUNK
KRAK

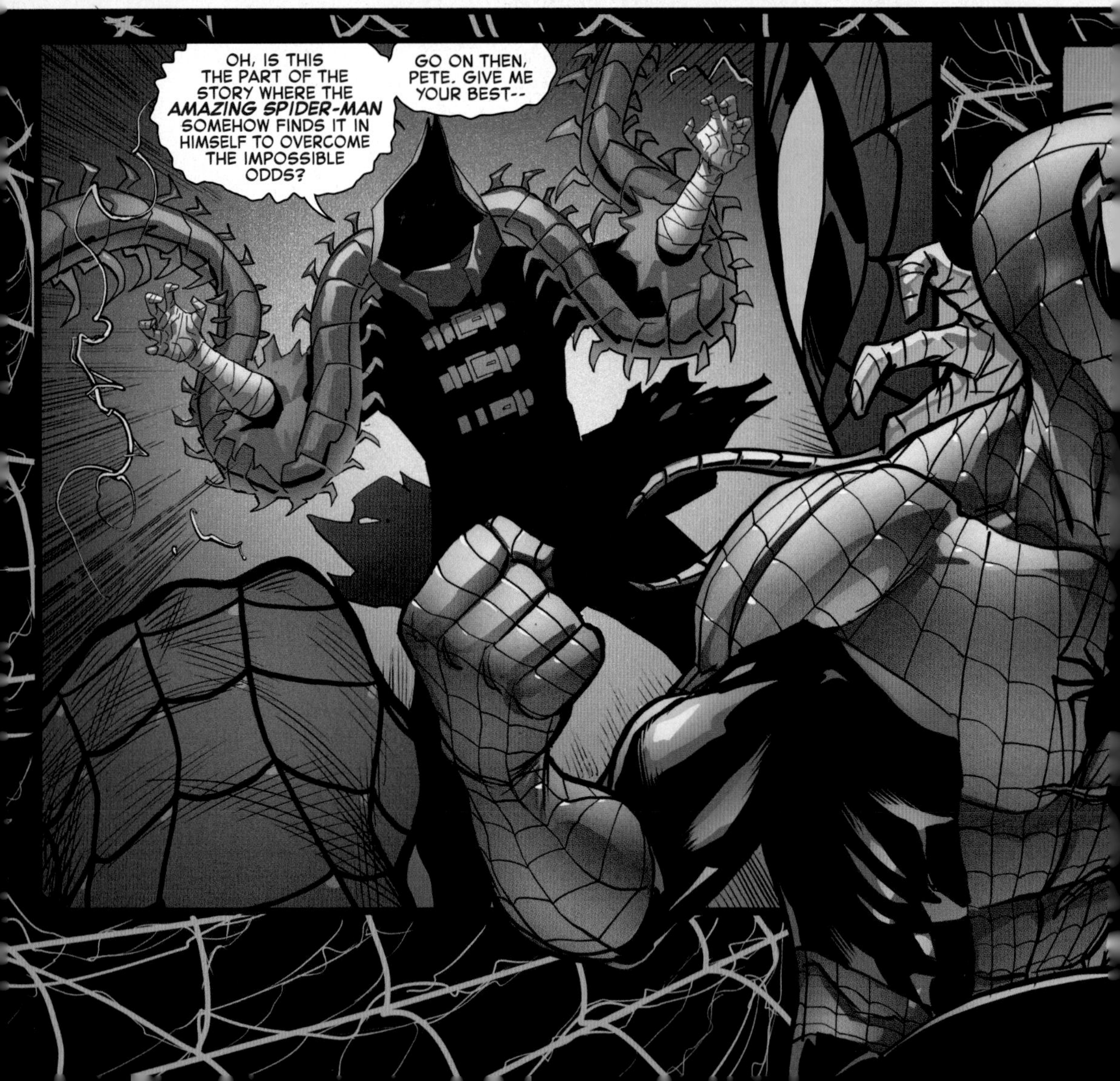
OH, IS THIS THE PART OF THE STORY WHERE THE *AMAZING SPIDER-MAN* SOMEHOW FINDS IT IN HIMSELF TO OVERCOME THE IMPOSSIBLE ODDS?
GO ON THEN, PETE. GIVE ME YOUR BEST--

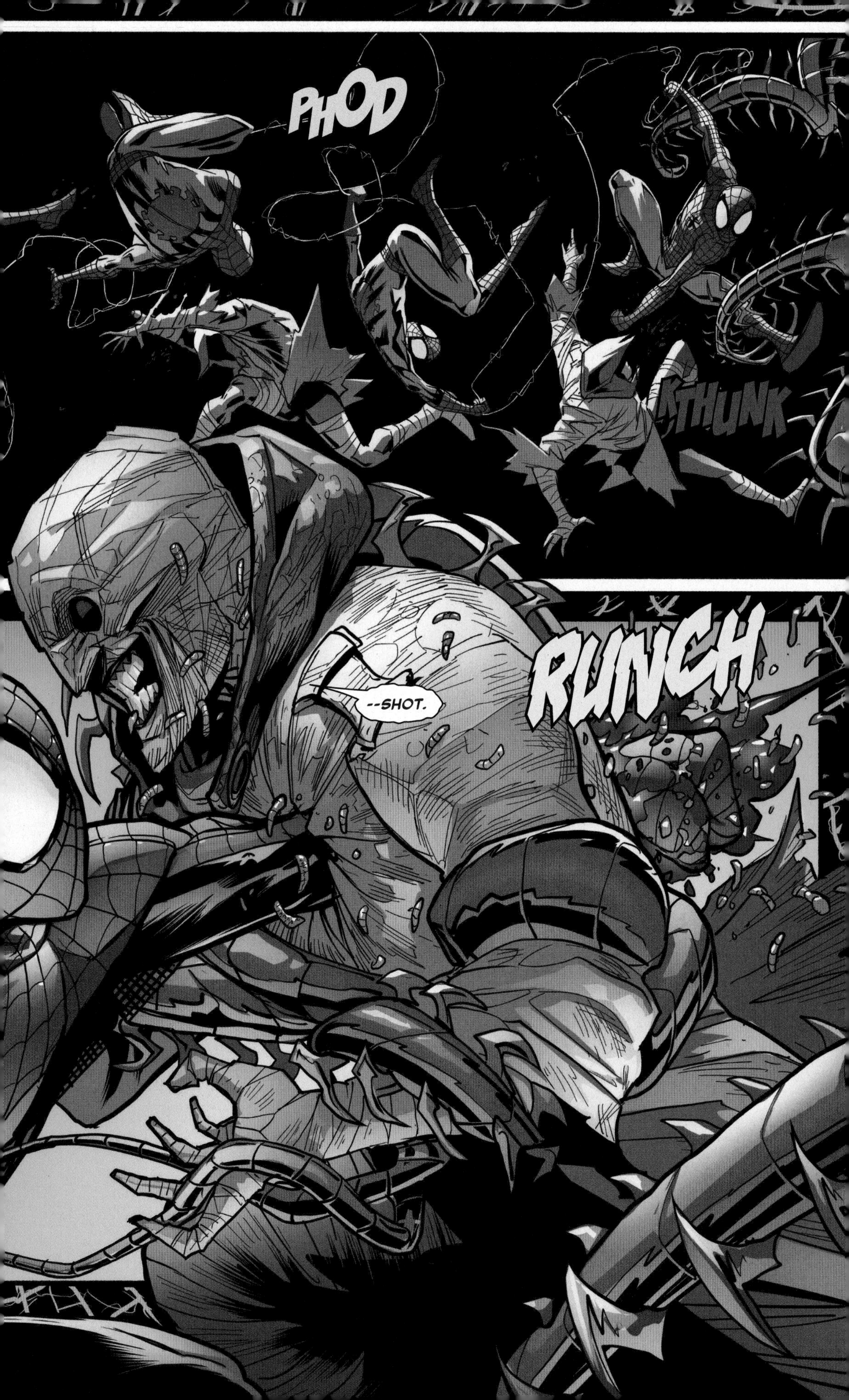
PHOD
KTHUNK
RUNCH
--SHOT.

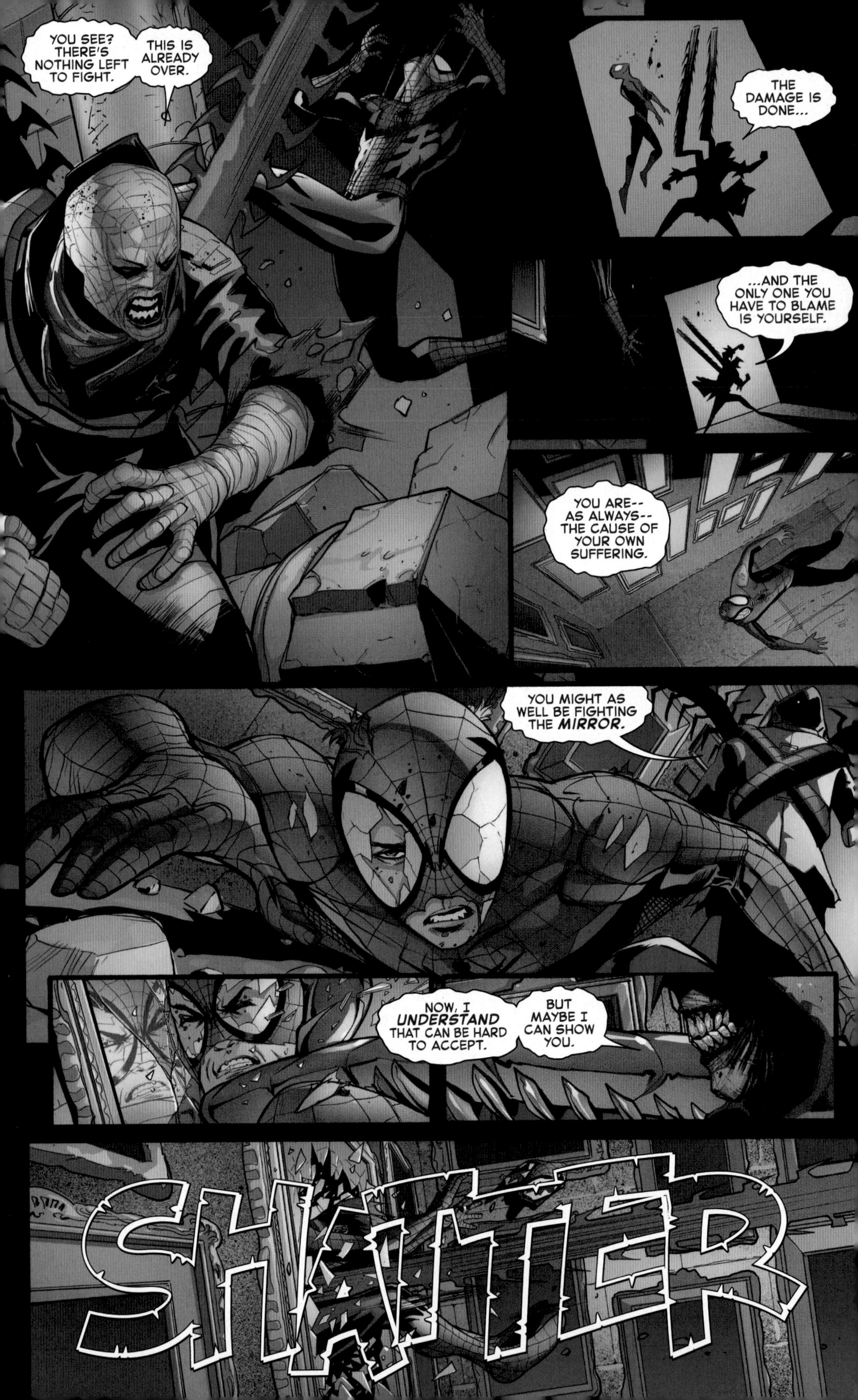
YOU SEE? THERE'S NOTHING LEFT TO FIGHT.
THIS IS ALREADY OVER.
THE DAMAGE IS DONE...
...AND THE ONLY ONE YOU HAVE TO BLAME IS YOURSELF.
YOU ARE-- AS ALWAYS-- THE CAUSE OF YOUR OWN SUFFERING.
YOU MIGHT AS WELL BE FIGHTING THE MIRROR.
NOW, I UNDERSTAND THAT CAN BE HARD TO ACCEPT.
BUT MAYBE I CAN SHOW YOU.
SHATTER

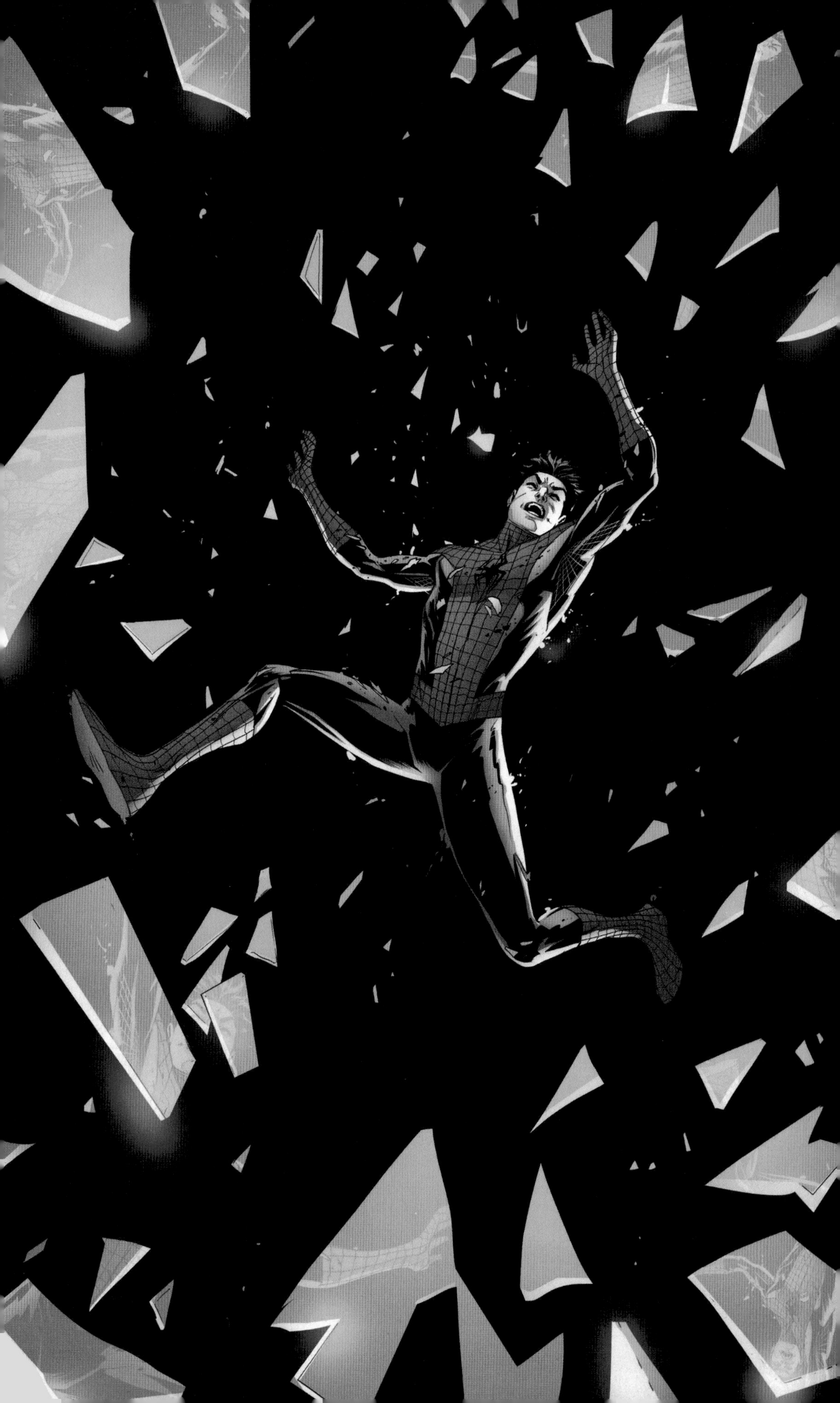

WHERE AM I?

SHUD

OUTSIDE...

PEOPLE RUNNING...

WHAT IS--

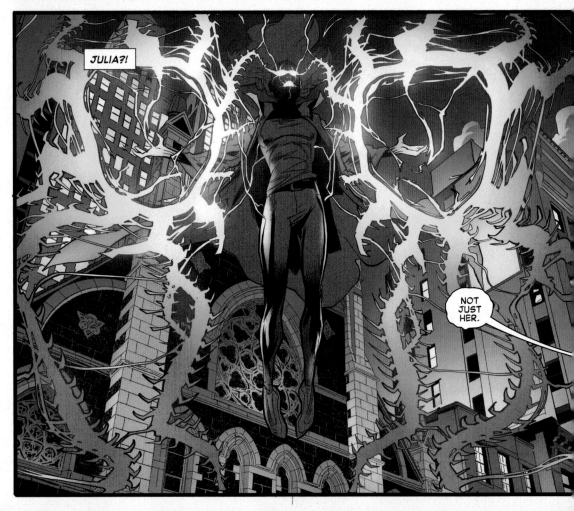

JULIA?!

NOT JUST HER.

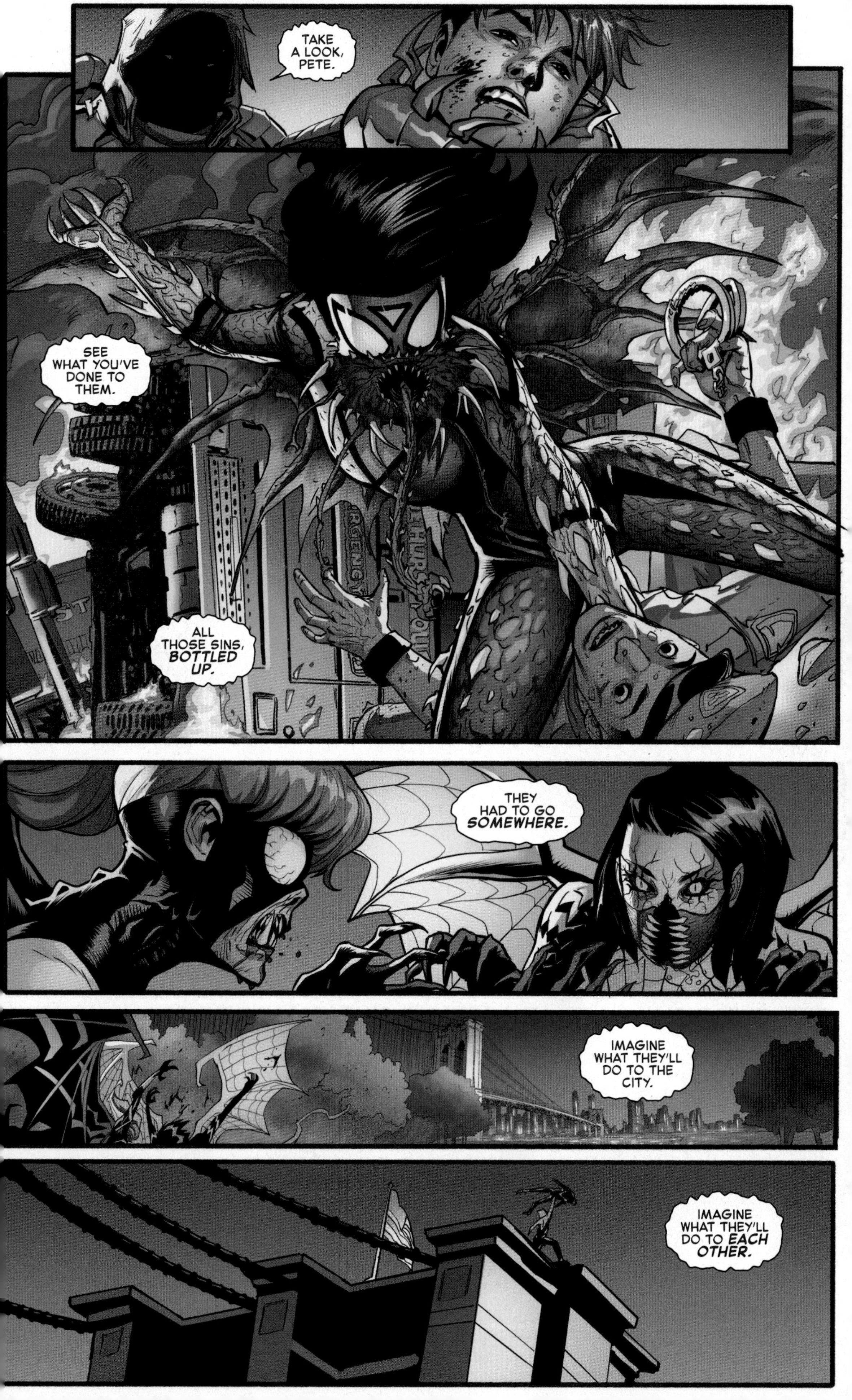
TAKE A LOOK, PETE.
SEE WHAT YOU'VE DONE TO THEM.
ALL THOSE SINS, BOTTLED UP.
THEY HAD TO GO SOMEWHERE.
IMAGINE WHAT THEY'LL DO TO THE CITY.
IMAGINE WHAT THEY'LL DO TO EACH OTHER.

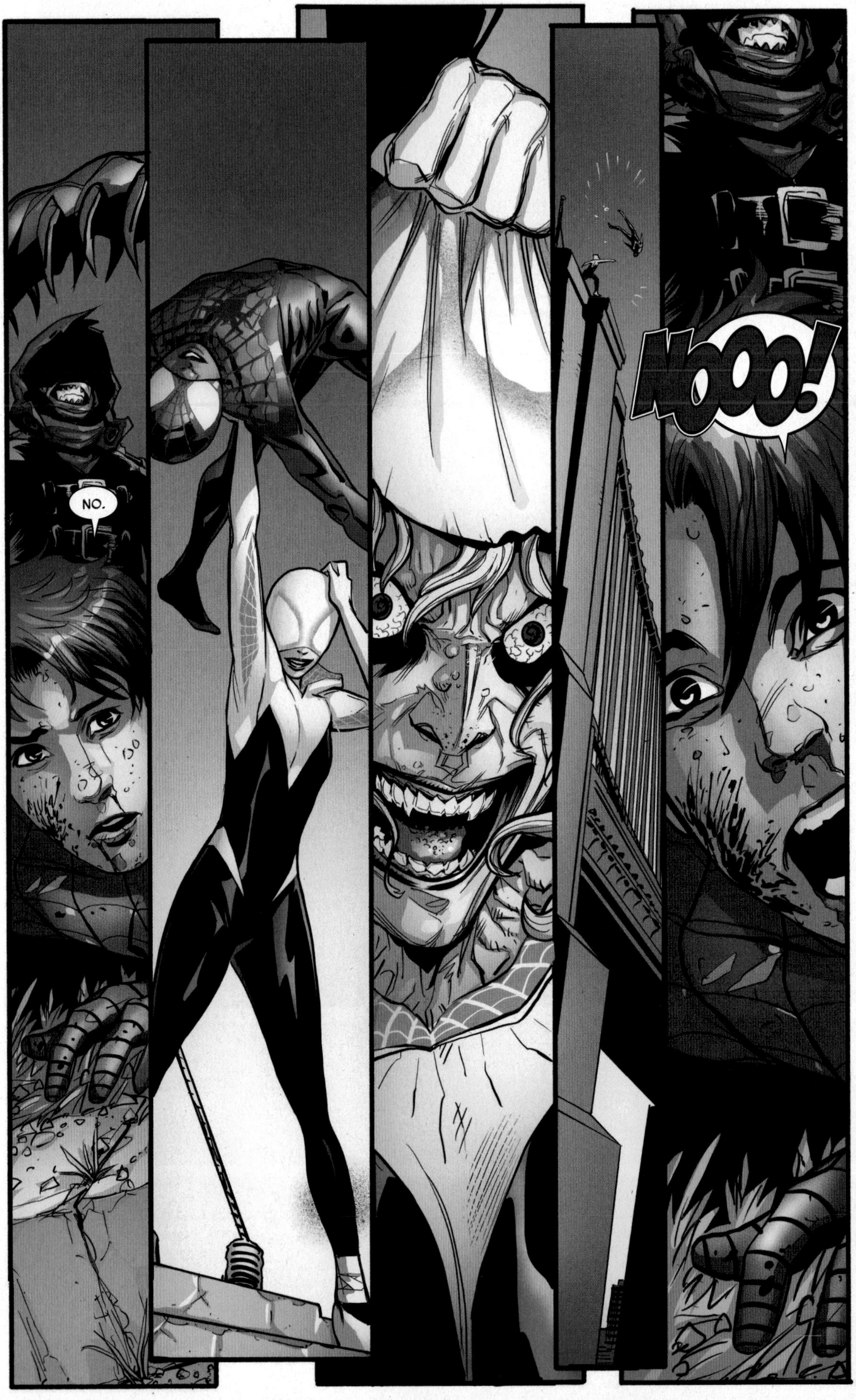
NO.
NOOO!

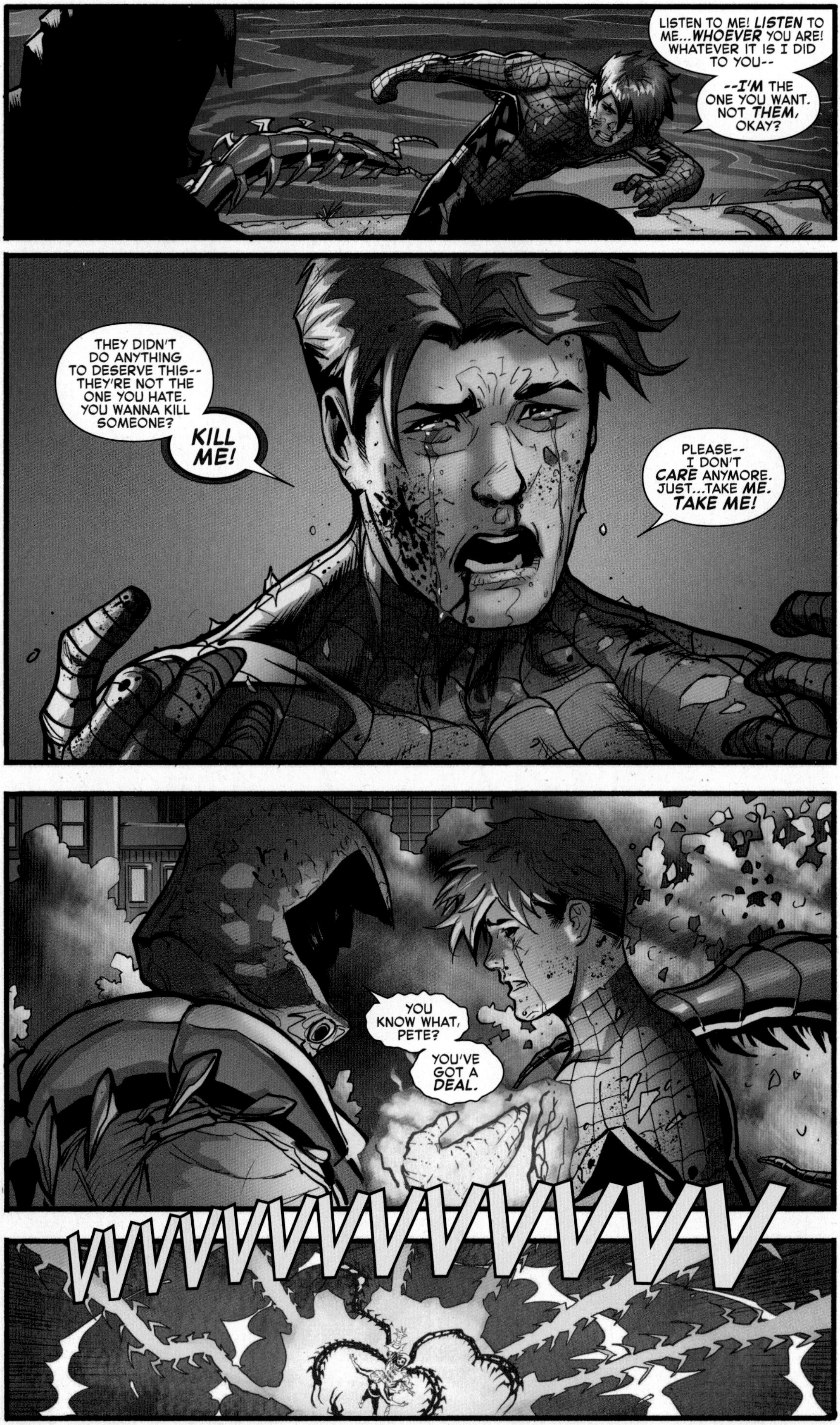
LISTEN TO ME! LISTEN TO ME...WHOEVER YOU ARE! WHATEVER IT IS I DID TO YOU--
--I'M THE ONE YOU WANT. NOT THEM, OKAY?
THEY DIDN'T DO ANYTHING TO DESERVE THIS--THEY'RE NOT THE ONE YOU HATE. YOU WANNA KILL SOMEONE? KILL ME!
PLEASE-- I DON'T CARE ANYMORE. JUST...TAKE ME. TAKE ME!
YOU KNOW WHAT, PETE?
YOU'VE GOT A DEAL.
VVVVVVVVVVVVVVVV

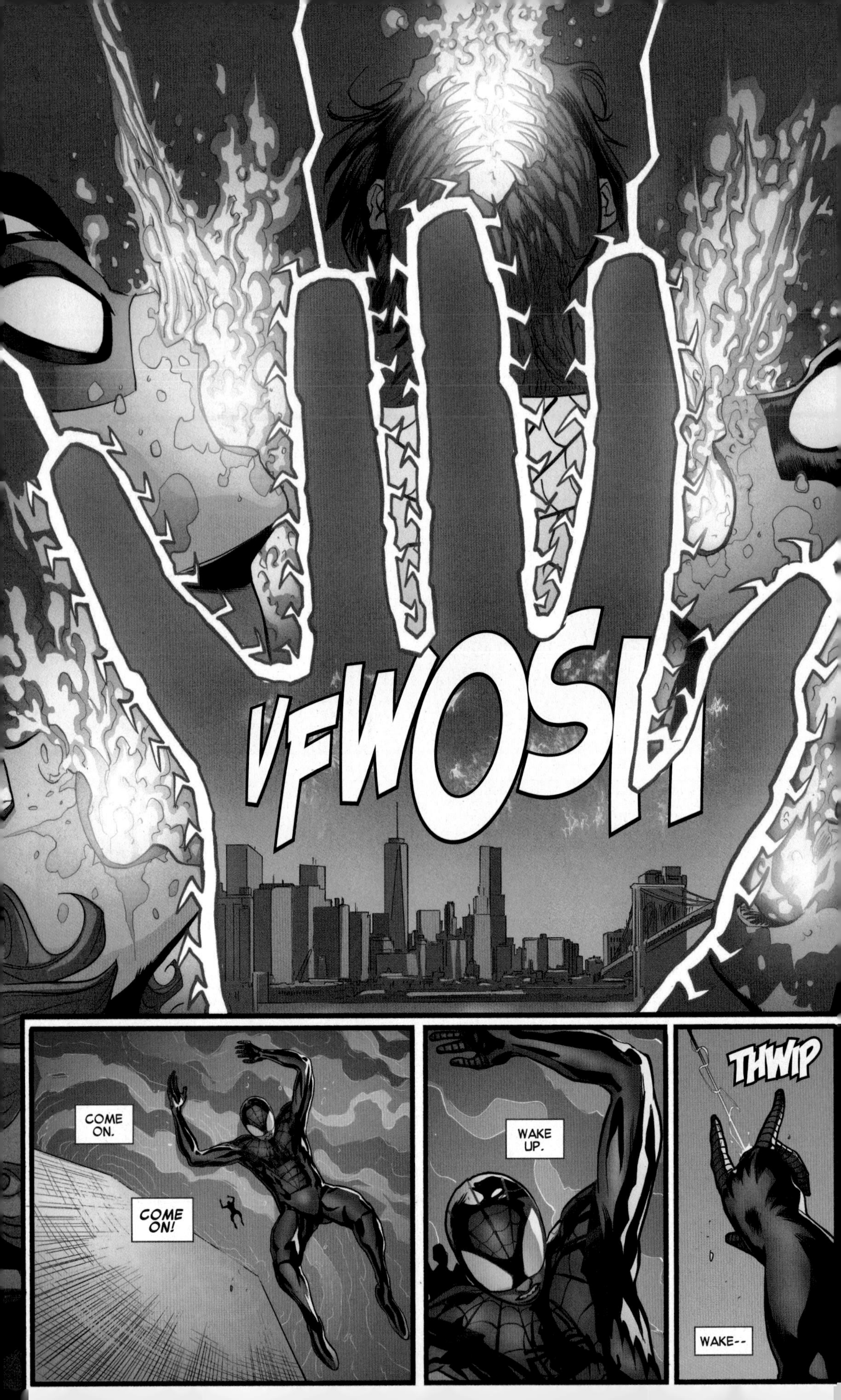
VFWOSH
COME ON.
COME ON!
WAKE UP.
THWIP
WAKE--

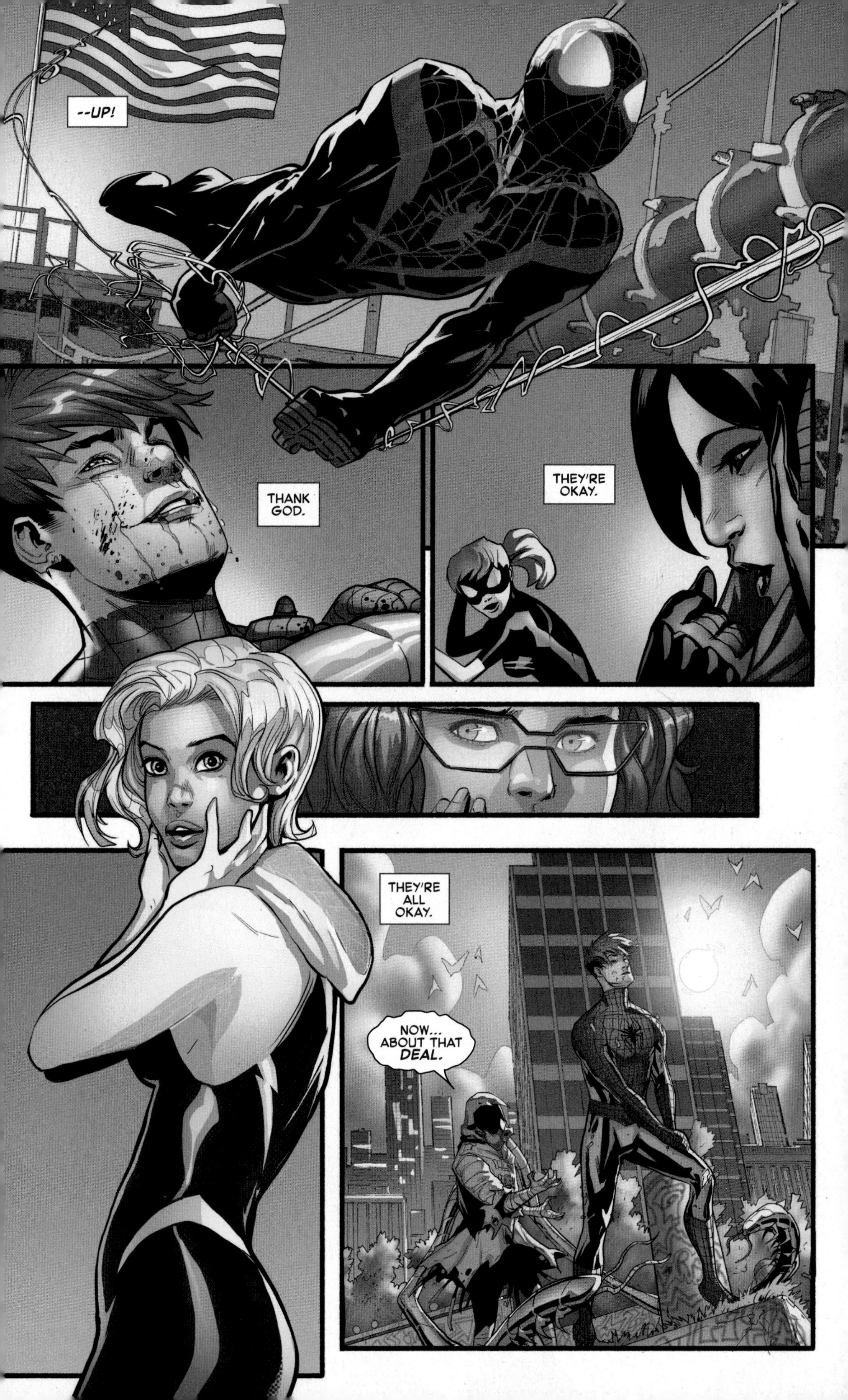
--UP!
THANK GOD.
THEY'RE OKAY.
THEY'RE ALL OKAY.
NOW... ABOUT THAT DEAL.

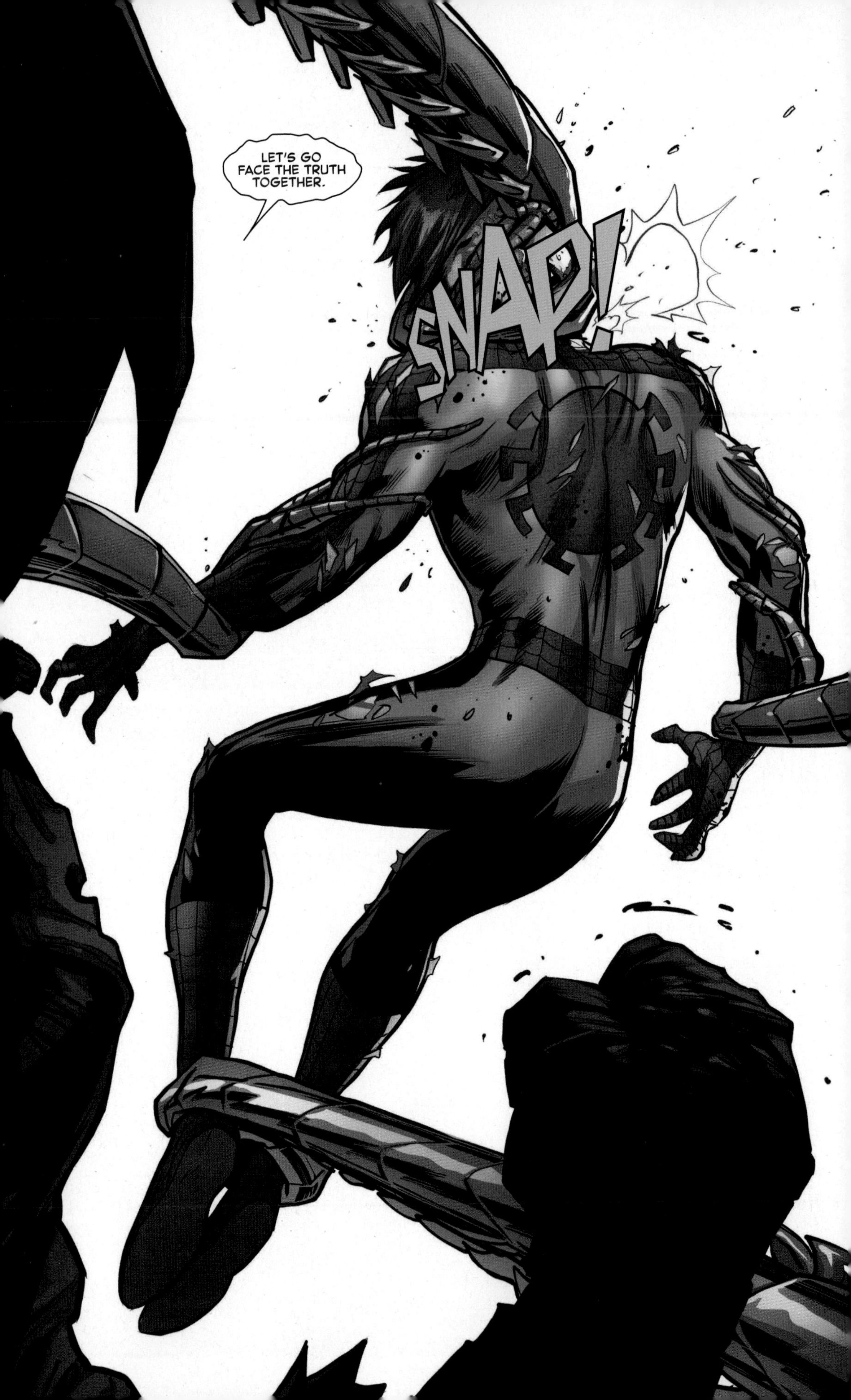
LET'S GO FACE THE TRUTH TOGETHER.
SNAP!

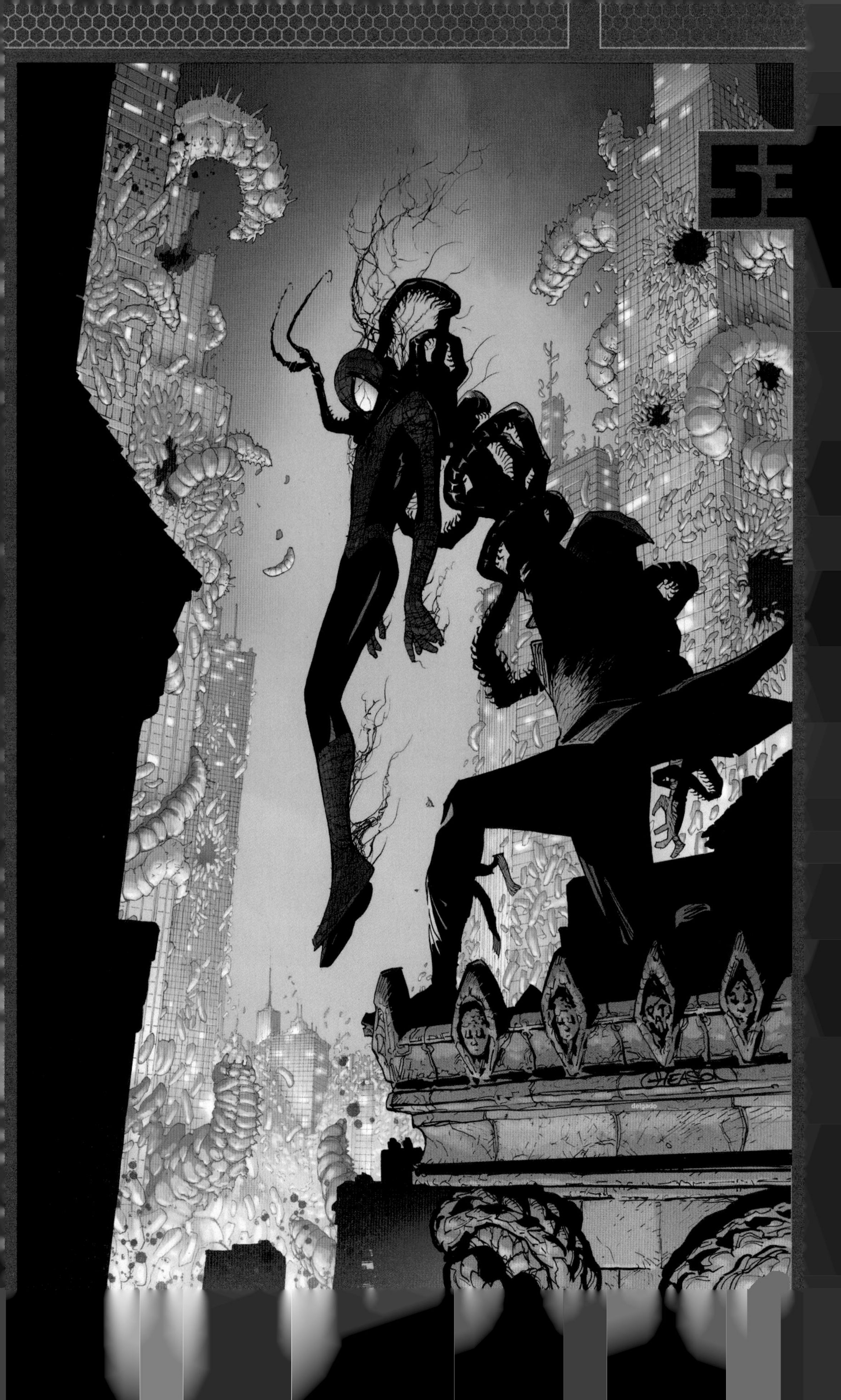
53
delgado

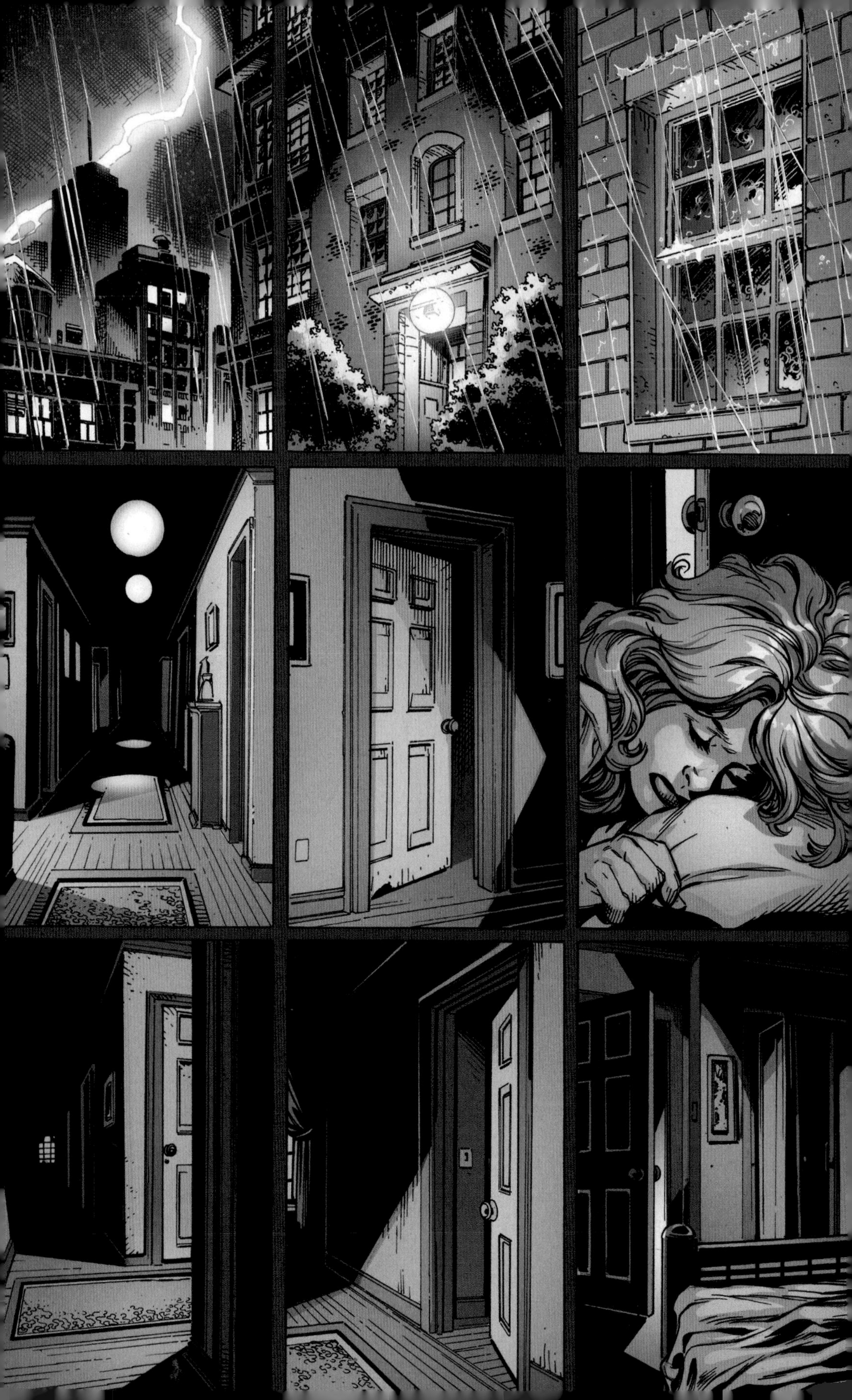

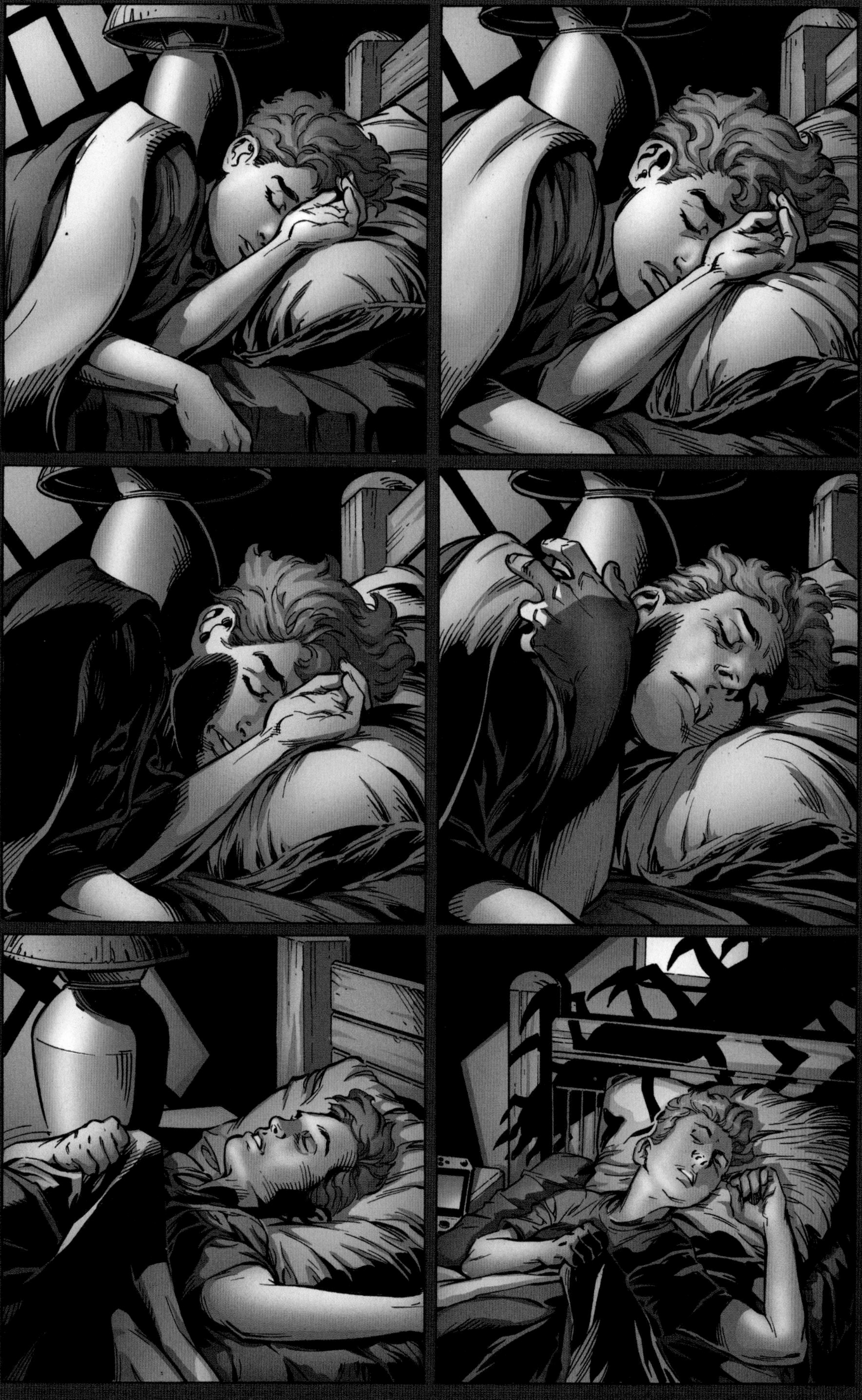

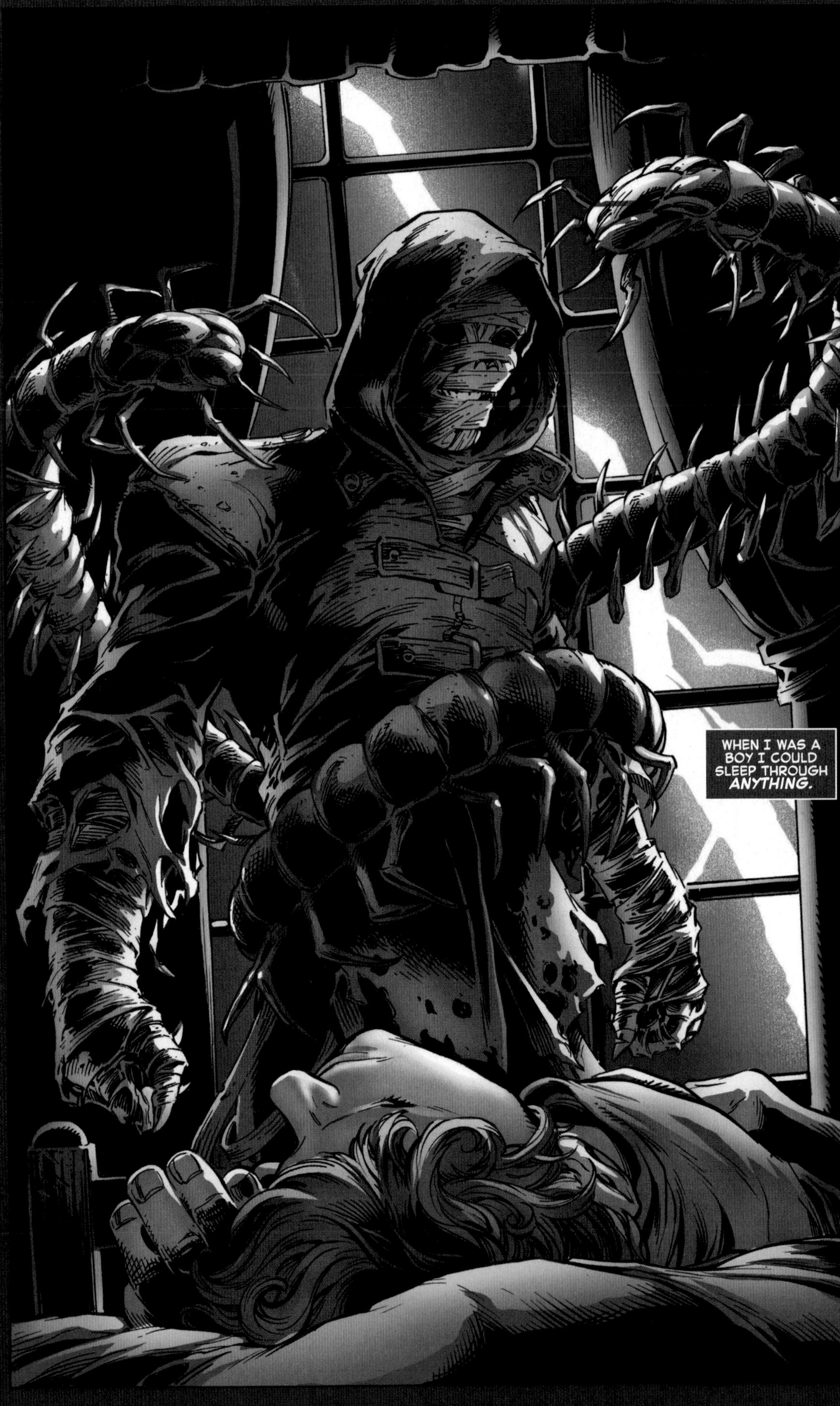
WHEN I WAS A BOY I COULD SLEEP THROUGH *ANYTHING.*

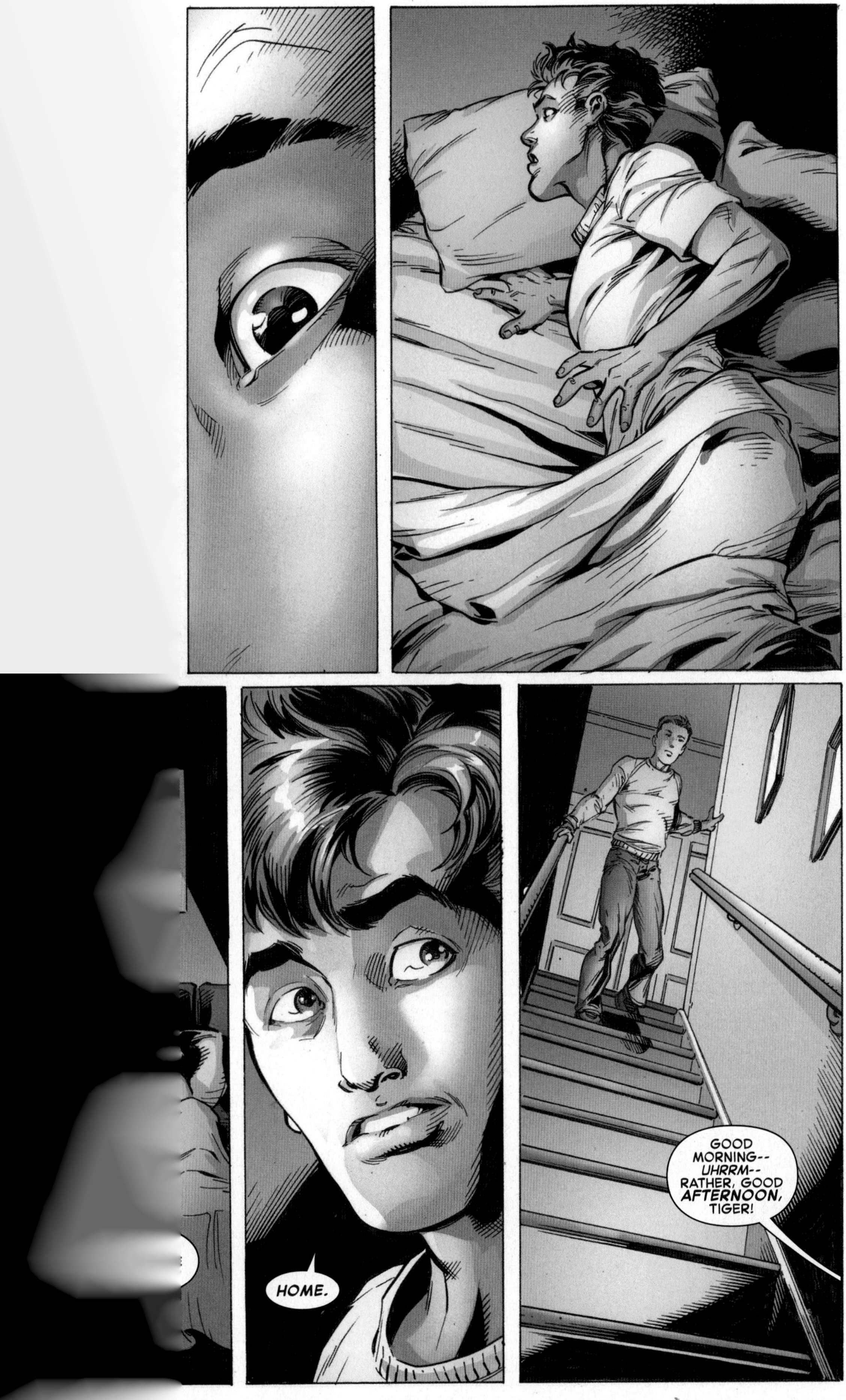
HOME.
GOOD MORNING-- UHRRM-- RATHER, GOOD AFTERNOON, TIGER!

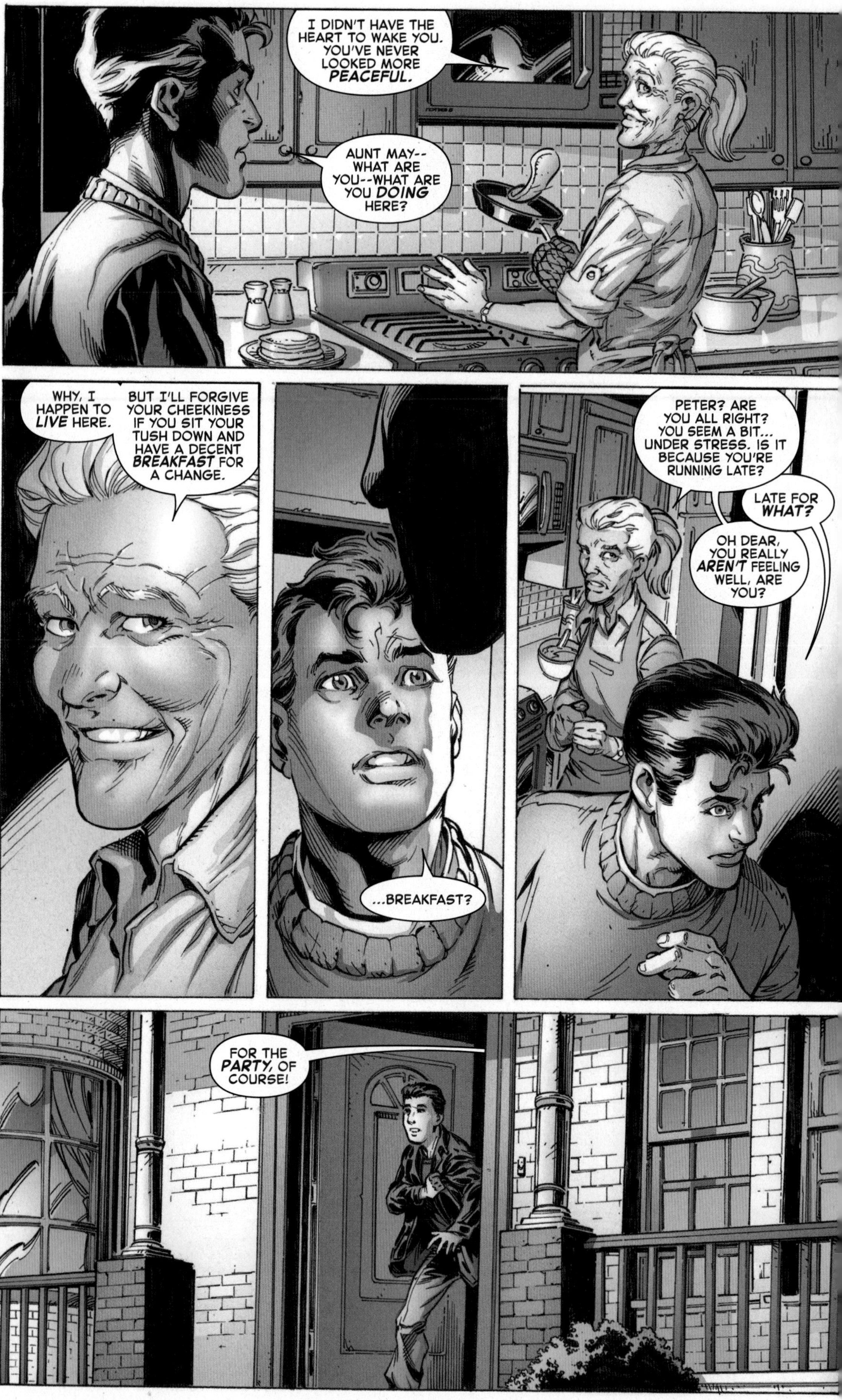
I DIDN'T HAVE THE HEART TO WAKE YOU. YOU'VE NEVER LOOKED MORE PEACEFUL.
AUNT MAY-- WHAT ARE YOU--WHAT ARE YOU DOING HERE?
WHY, I HAPPEN TO LIVE HERE.
BUT I'LL FORGIVE YOUR CHEEKINESS IF YOU SIT YOUR TUSH DOWN AND HAVE A DECENT BREAKFAST FOR A CHANGE.
...BREAKFAST?
PETER? ARE YOU ALL RIGHT? YOU SEEM A BIT... UNDER STRESS. IS IT BECAUSE YOU'RE RUNNING LATE?
LATE FOR WHAT?
OH DEAR, YOU REALLY AREN'T FEELING WELL, ARE YOU?
FOR THE PARTY, OF COURSE!

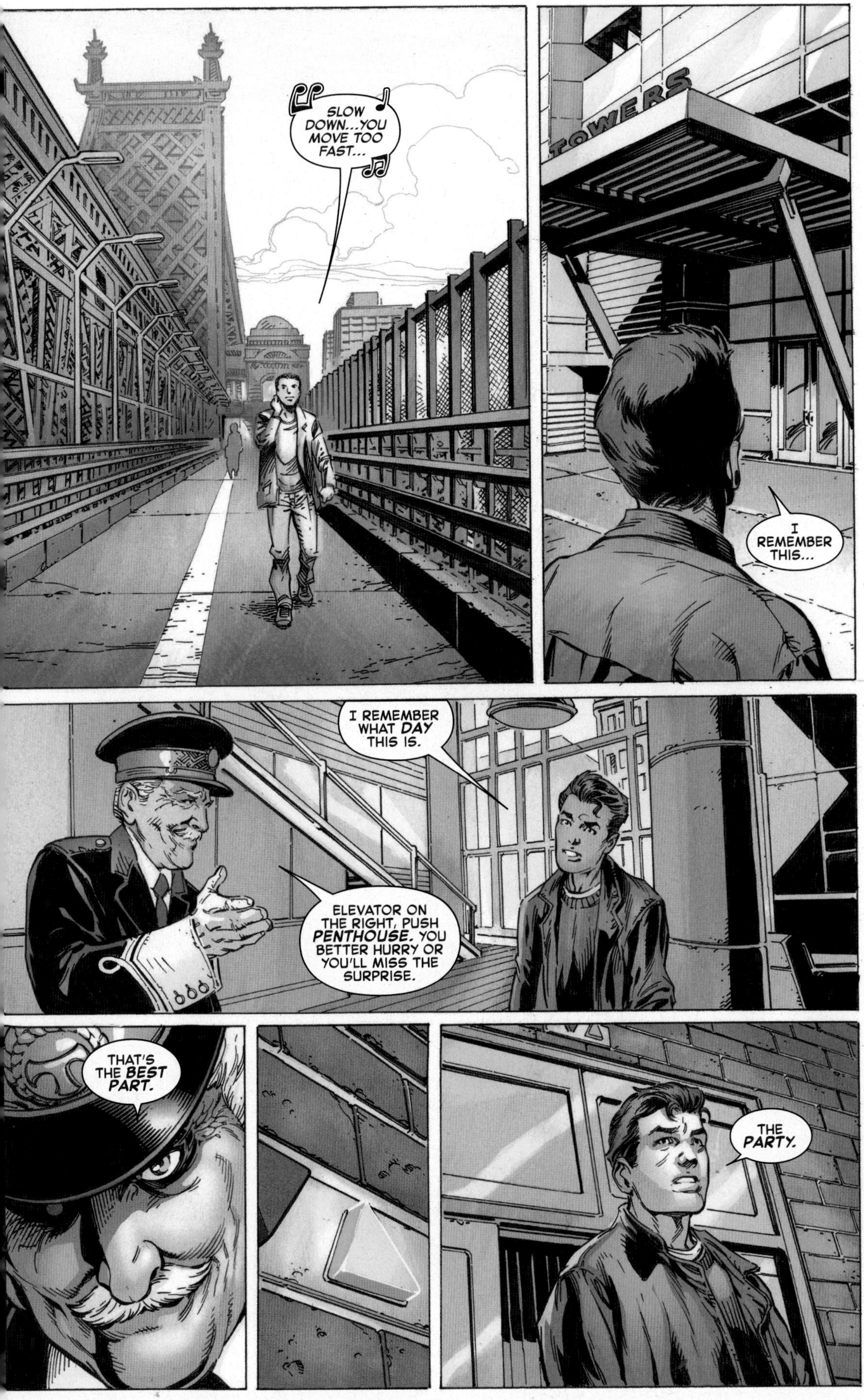
SLOW DOWN...YOU MOVE TOO FAST...
TOWERS
I REMEMBER THIS...
I REMEMBER WHAT DAY THIS IS.
ELEVATOR ON THE RIGHT, PUSH PENTHOUSE. YOU BETTER HURRY OR YOU'LL MISS THE SURPRISE.
THAT'S THE BEST PART.
THE PARTY.

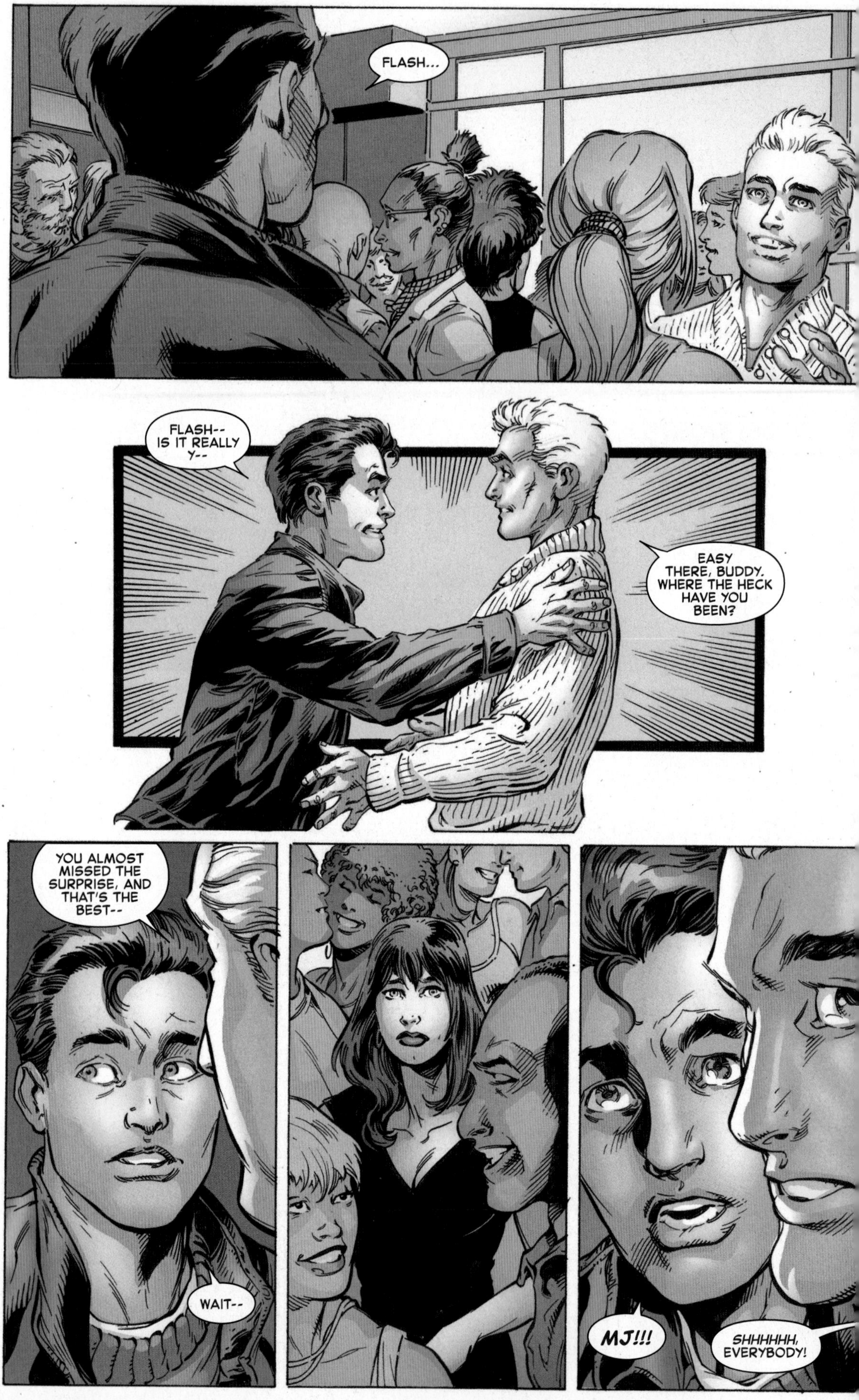
FLASH...
FLASH-- IS IT REALLY Y--
EASY THERE, BUDDY. WHERE THE HECK HAVE YOU BEEN?
YOU ALMOST MISSED THE SURPRISE, AND THAT'S THE BEST--
WAIT--
MJ!!!
SHHHHHH, EVERYBODY!

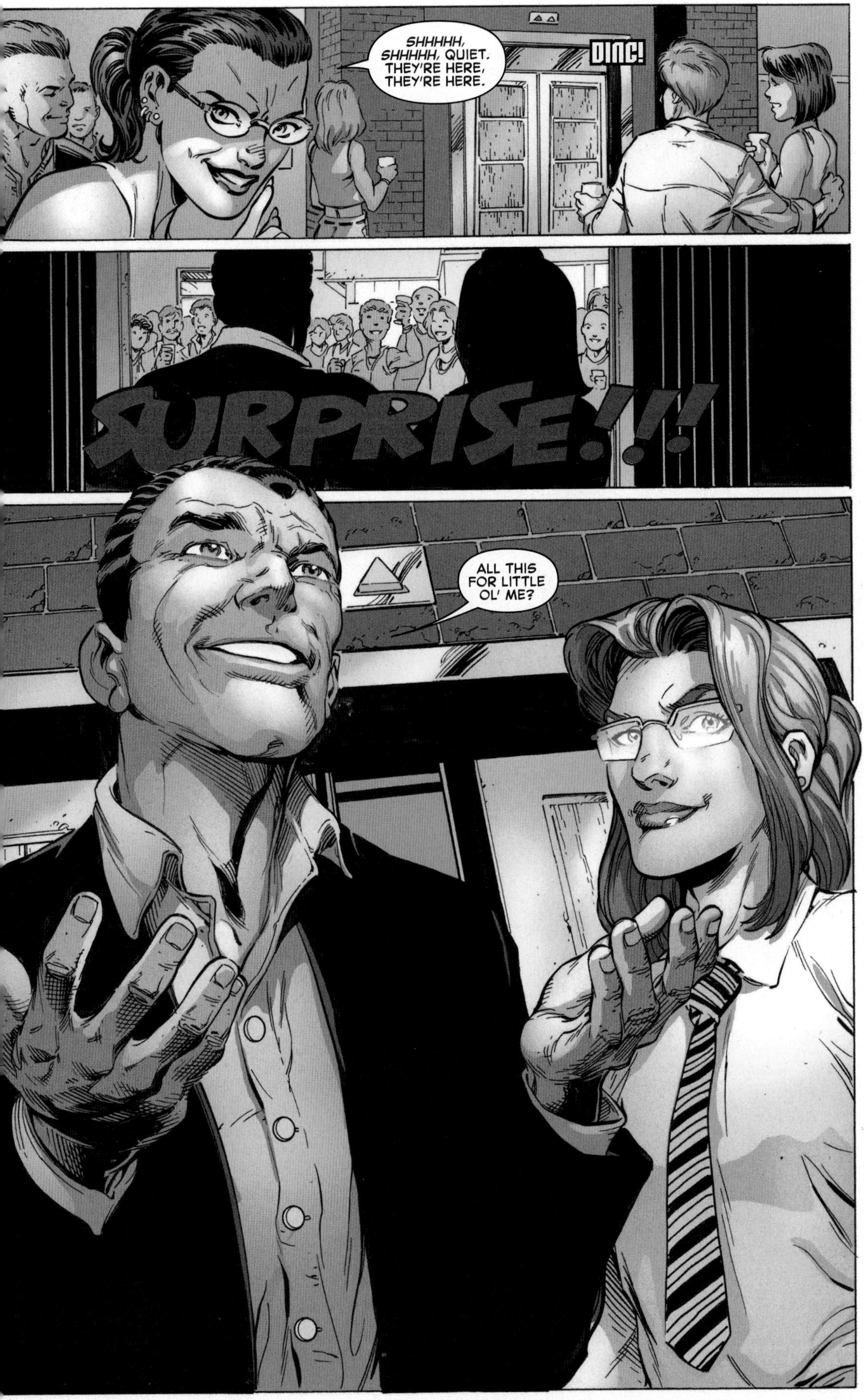
SHHHHH, SHHHHH, QUIET. THEY'RE HERE, THEY'RE HERE.
DING!
SURPRISE!!!
ALL THIS FOR LITTLE OL' ME?

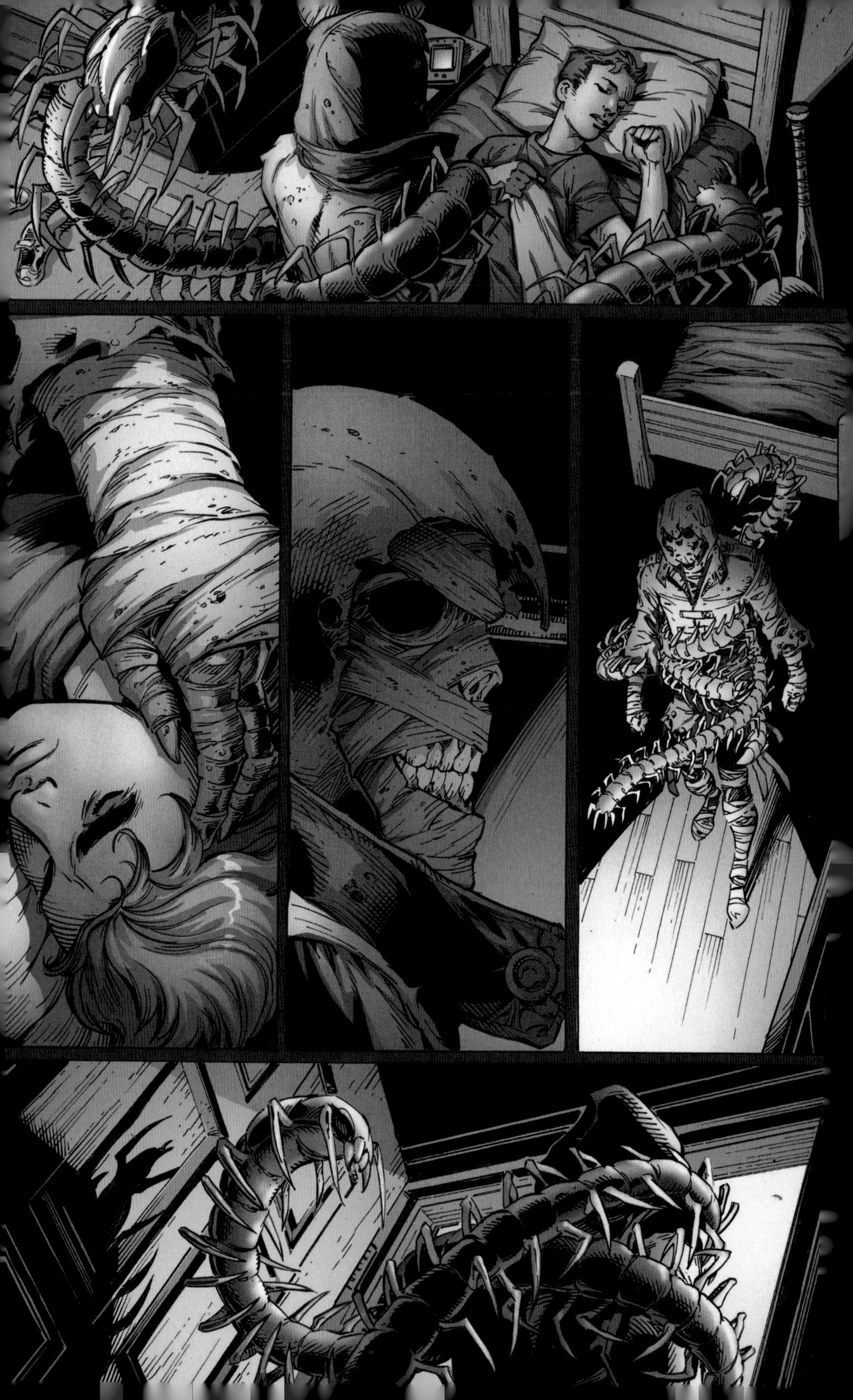

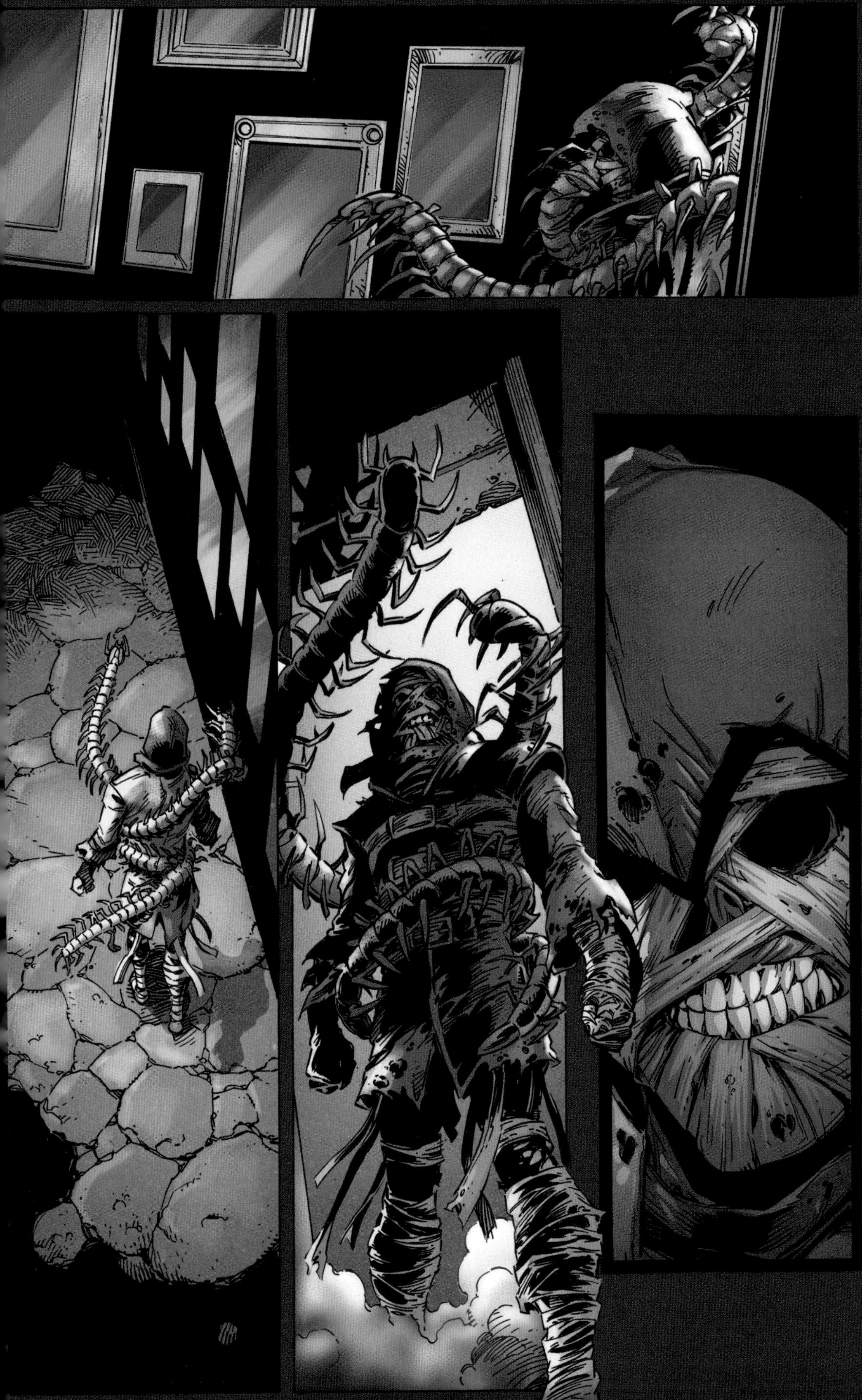

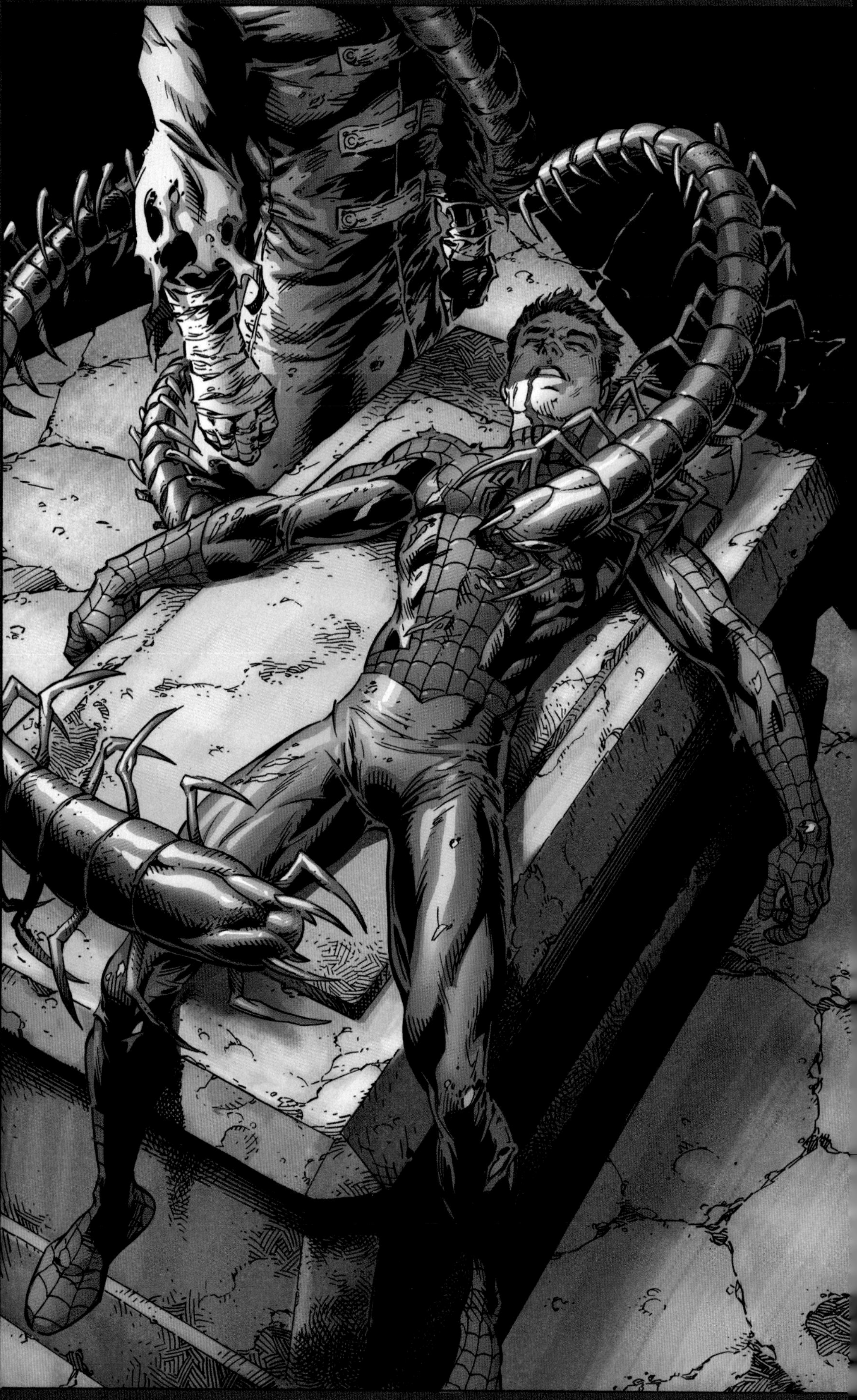

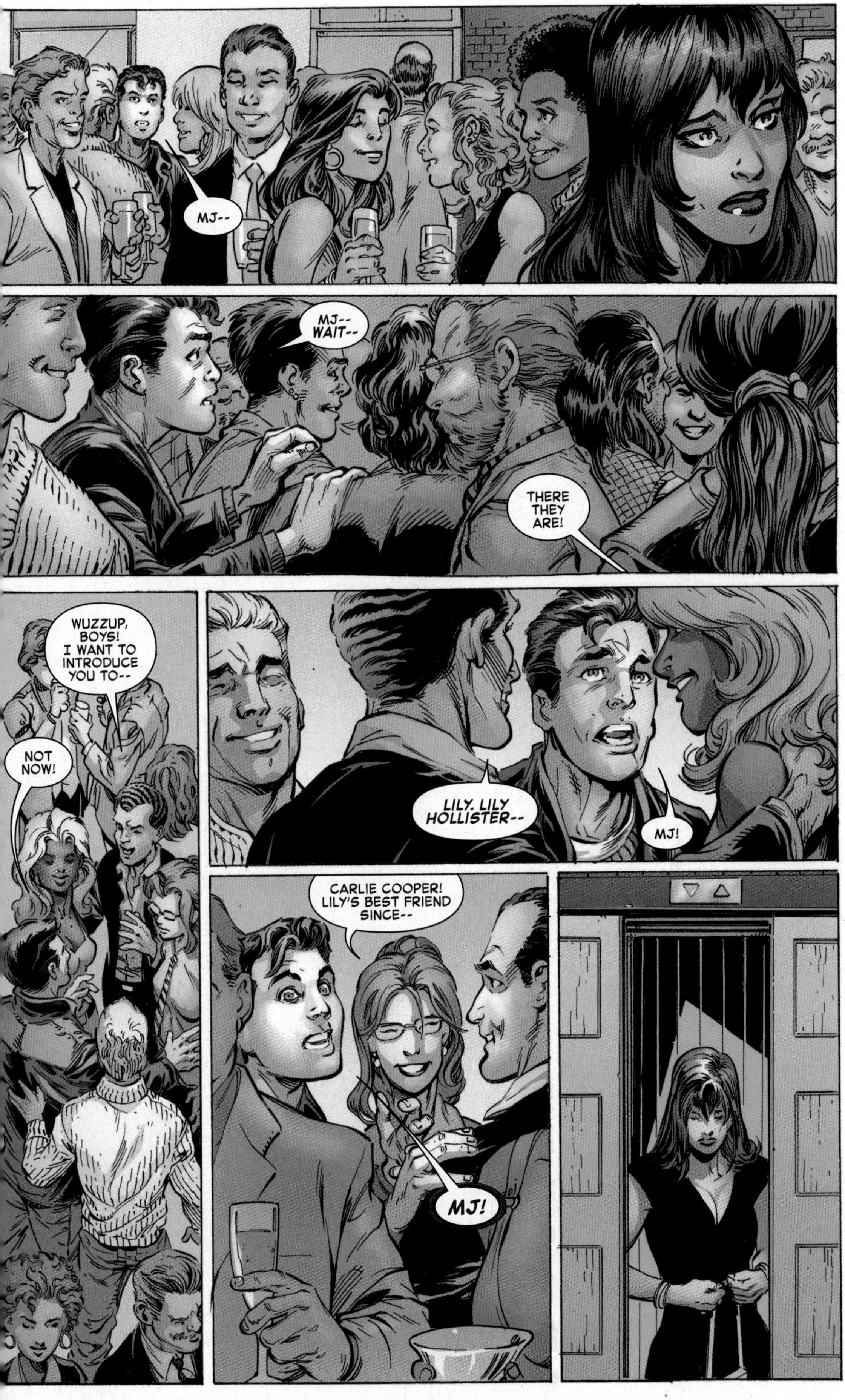
MJ--
MJ-- WAIT--
THERE THEY ARE!
WUZZUP, BOYS! I WANT TO INTRODUCE YOU TO--
NOT NOW!
LILY. LILY HOLLISTER--
MJ!
CARLIE COOPER! LILY'S BEST FRIEND SINCE--
MJ!

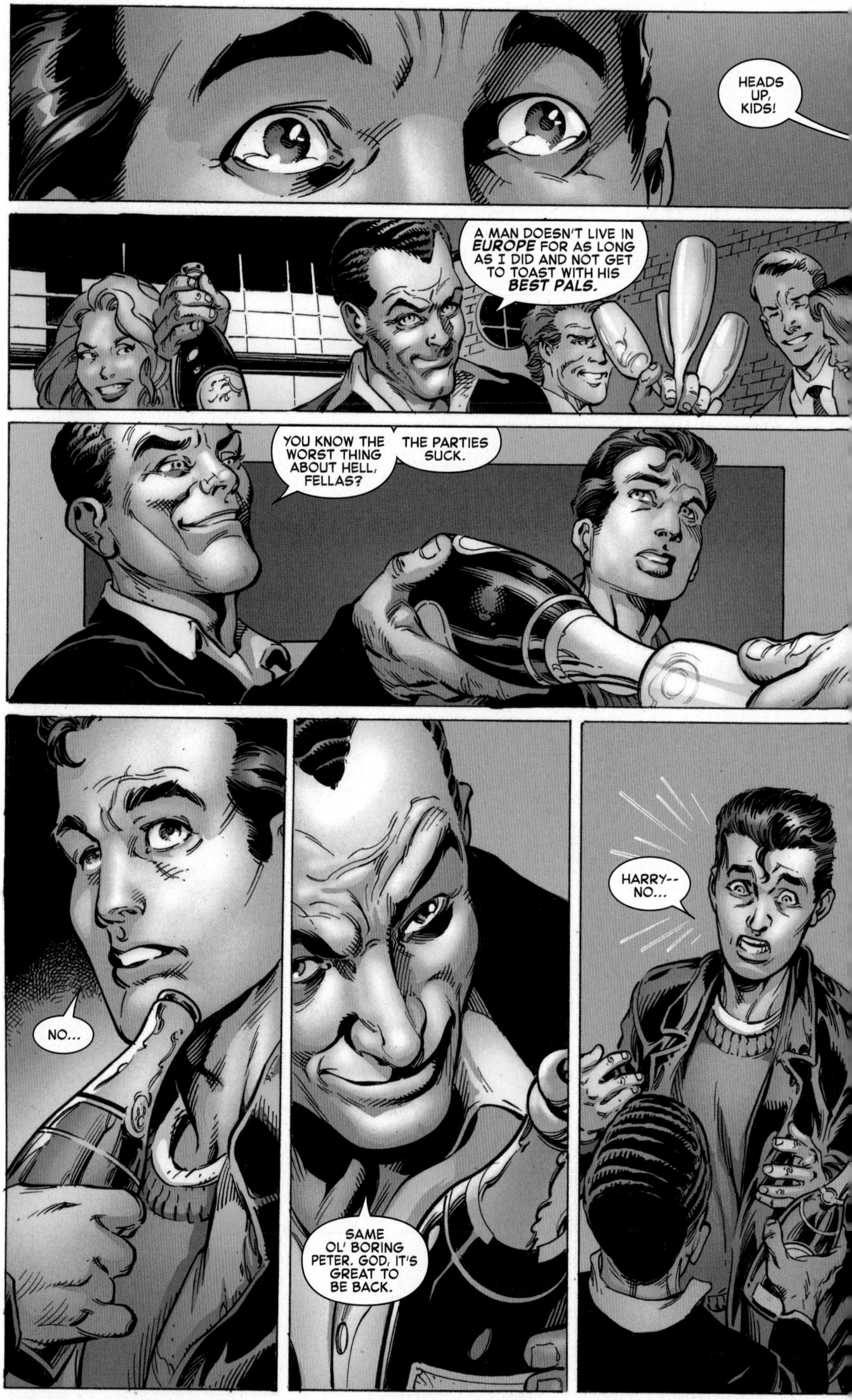
HEADS UP, KIDS!
A MAN DOESN'T LIVE IN EUROPE FOR AS LONG AS I DID AND NOT GET TO TOAST WITH HIS BEST PALS.
YOU KNOW THE WORST THING ABOUT HELL, FELLAS?
THE PARTIES SUCK.
NO...
SAME OL' BORING PETER. GOD, IT'S GREAT TO BE BACK.
HARRY-- NO...

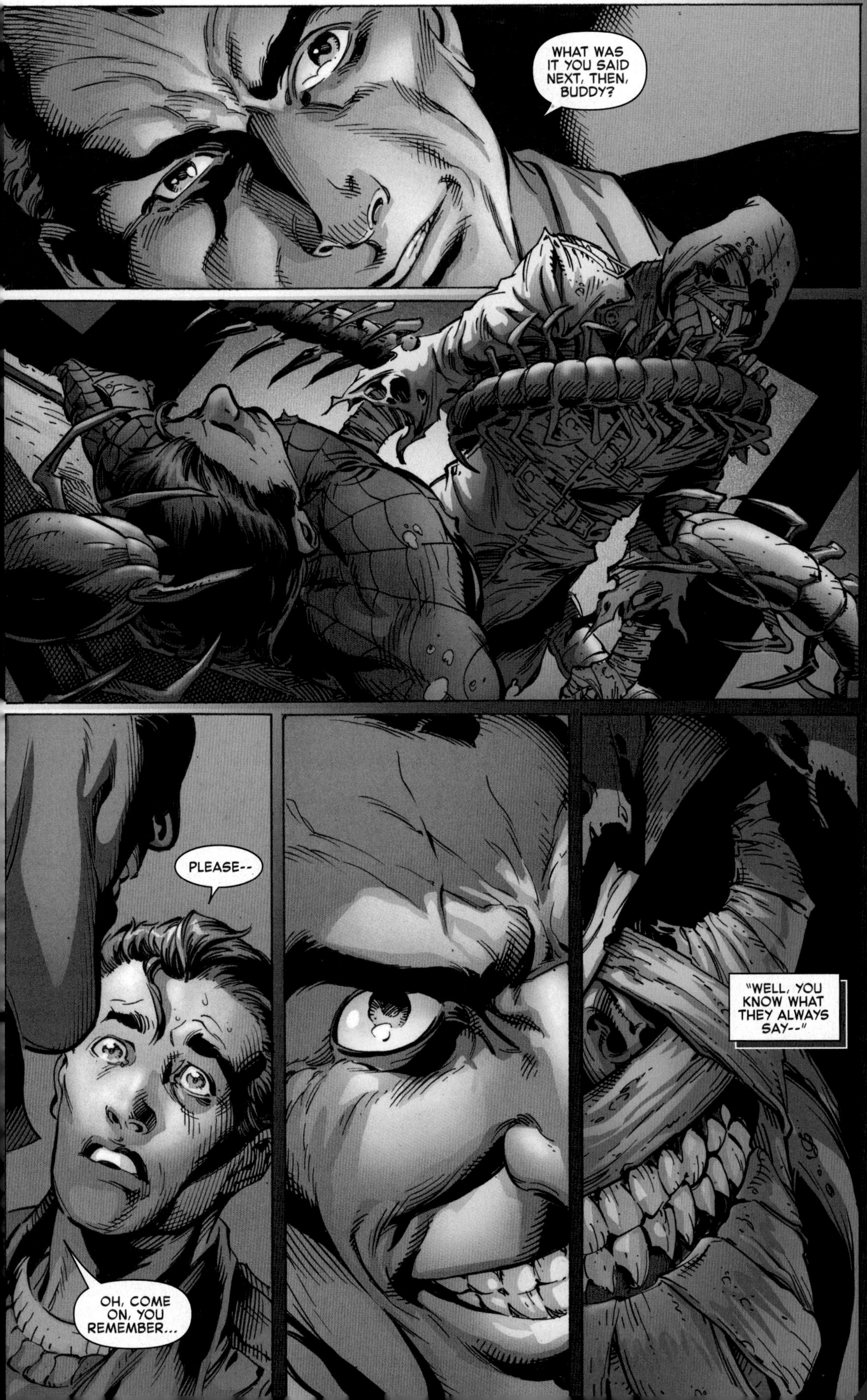
WHAT WAS IT YOU SAID NEXT, THEN, BUDDY?
PLEASE--
OH, COME ON, YOU REMEMBER...
"WELL, YOU KNOW WHAT THEY ALWAYS SAY--"

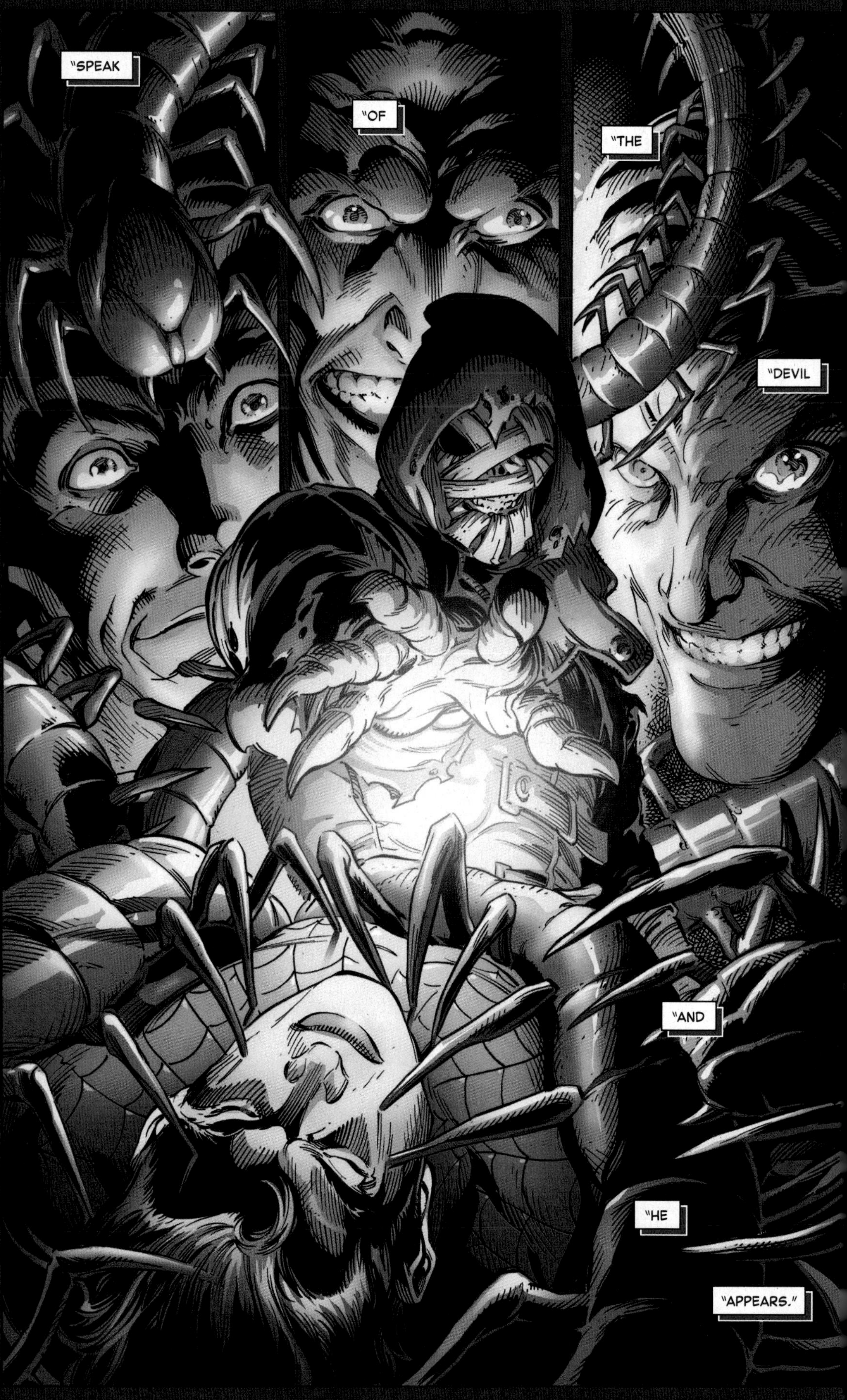
"SPEAK
"OF
"THE
"DEVIL
"AND
"HE
"APPEARS."

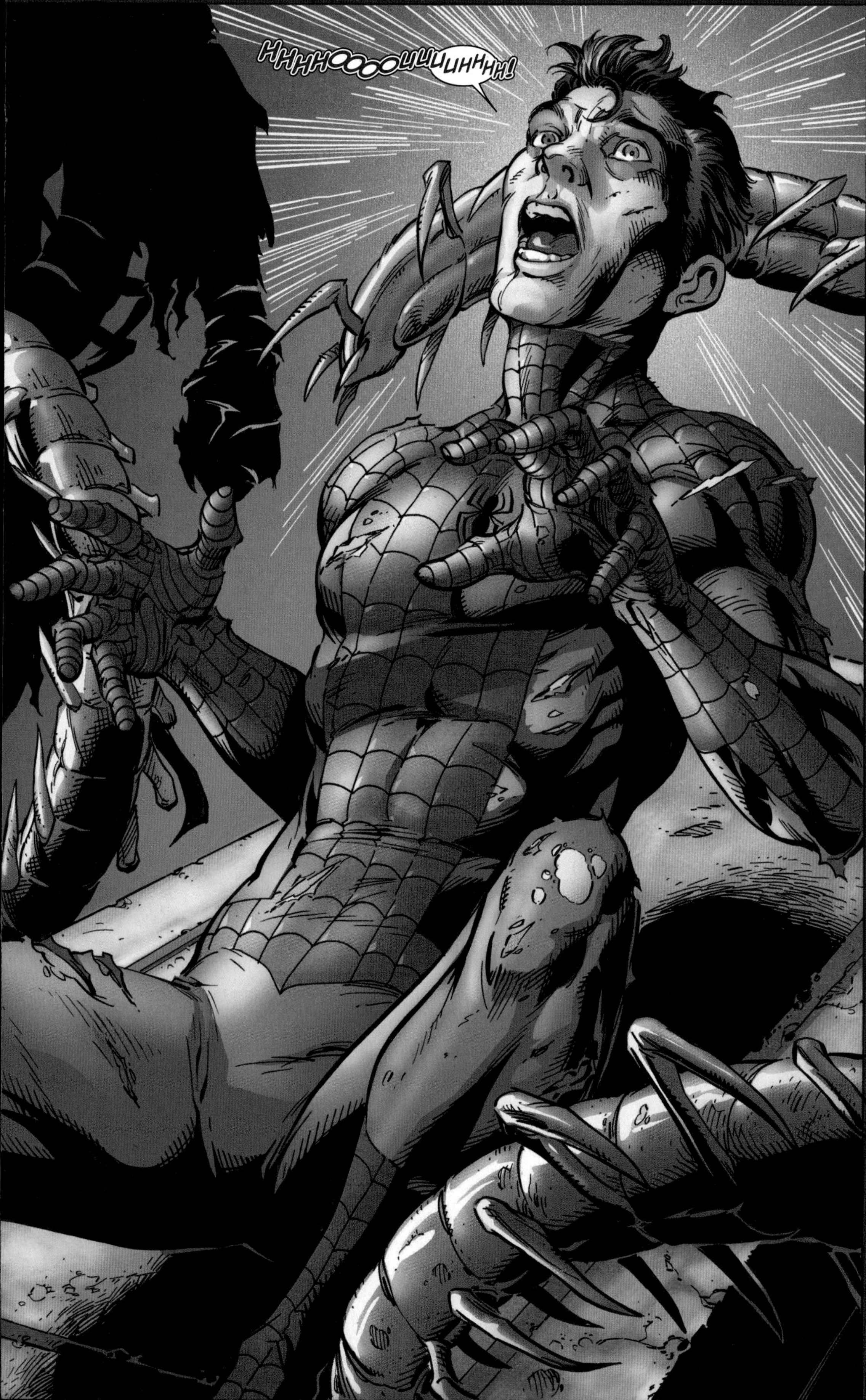
HHHHOOOOUUUUHHHHH!

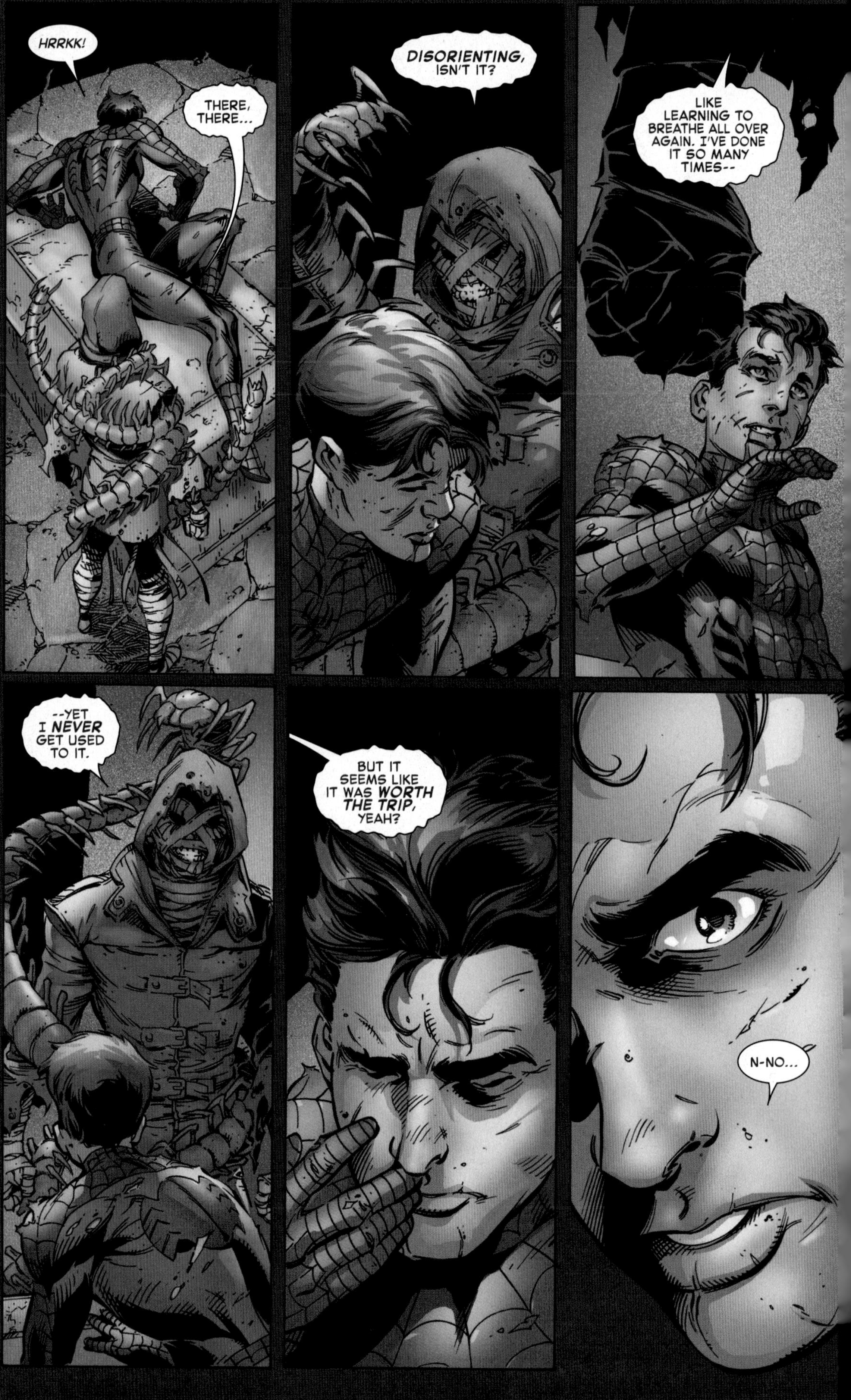
HRRKK!
THERE, THERE...
DISORIENTING, ISN'T IT?
LIKE LEARNING TO BREATHE ALL OVER AGAIN. I'VE DONE IT SO MANY TIMES--
--YET I NEVER GET USED TO IT.
BUT IT SEEMS LIKE IT WAS WORTH THE TRIP, YEAH?
N-NO...

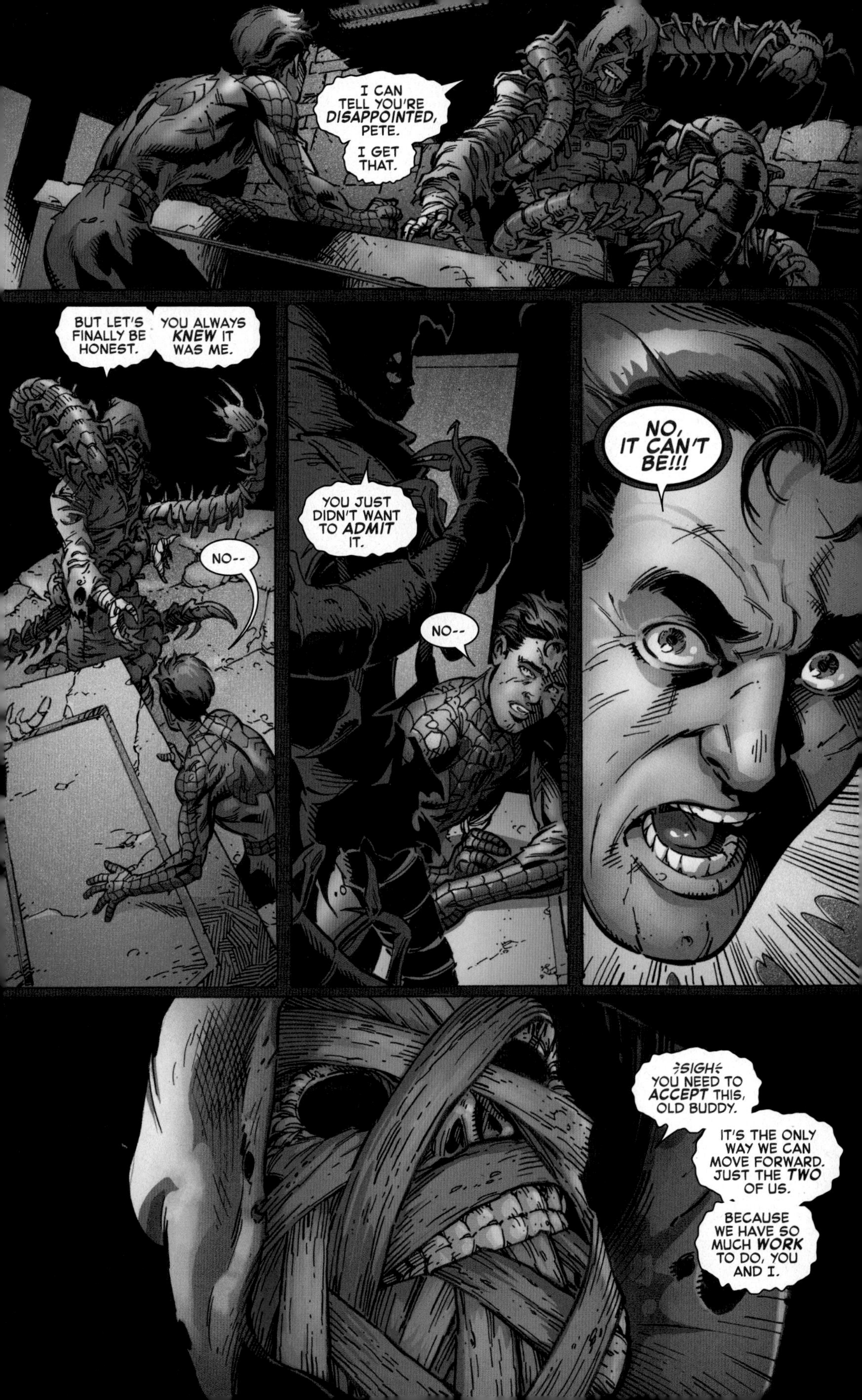

I CAN TELL YOU'RE DISAPPOINTED, PETE.
I GET THAT.
BUT LET'S FINALLY BE HONEST.
YOU ALWAYS KNEW IT WAS ME.
NO--
YOU JUST DIDN'T WANT TO ADMIT IT.
NO--
NO, IT CAN'T BE!!!
SIGH
YOU NEED TO ACCEPT THIS, OLD BUDDY.
IT'S THE ONLY WAY WE CAN MOVE FORWARD. JUST THE TWO OF US.
BECAUSE WE HAVE SO MUCH WORK TO DO, YOU AND I.

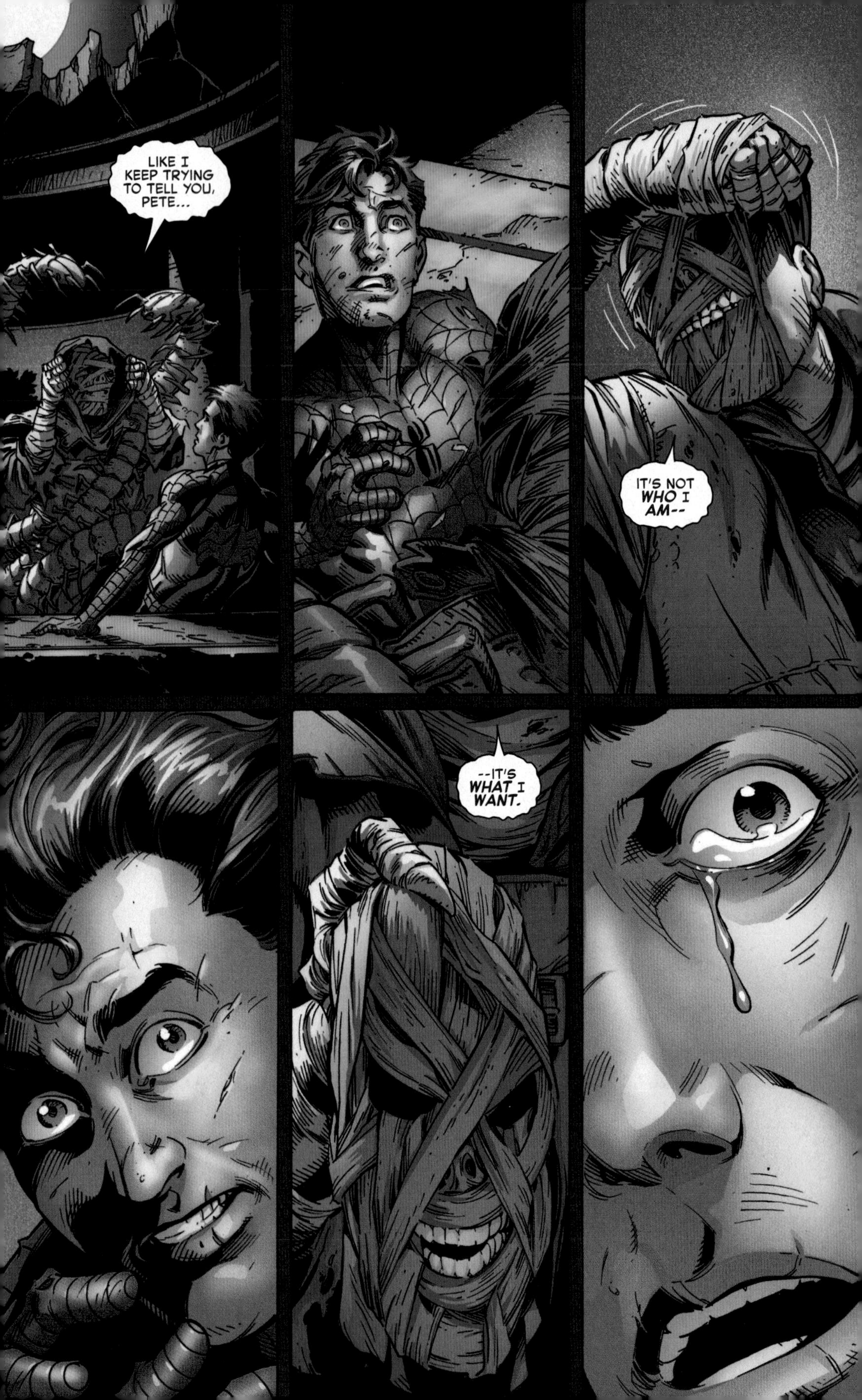
LIKE I KEEP TRYING TO TELL YOU, PETE...
IT'S NOT WHO I AM--
--IT'S WHAT I WANT.

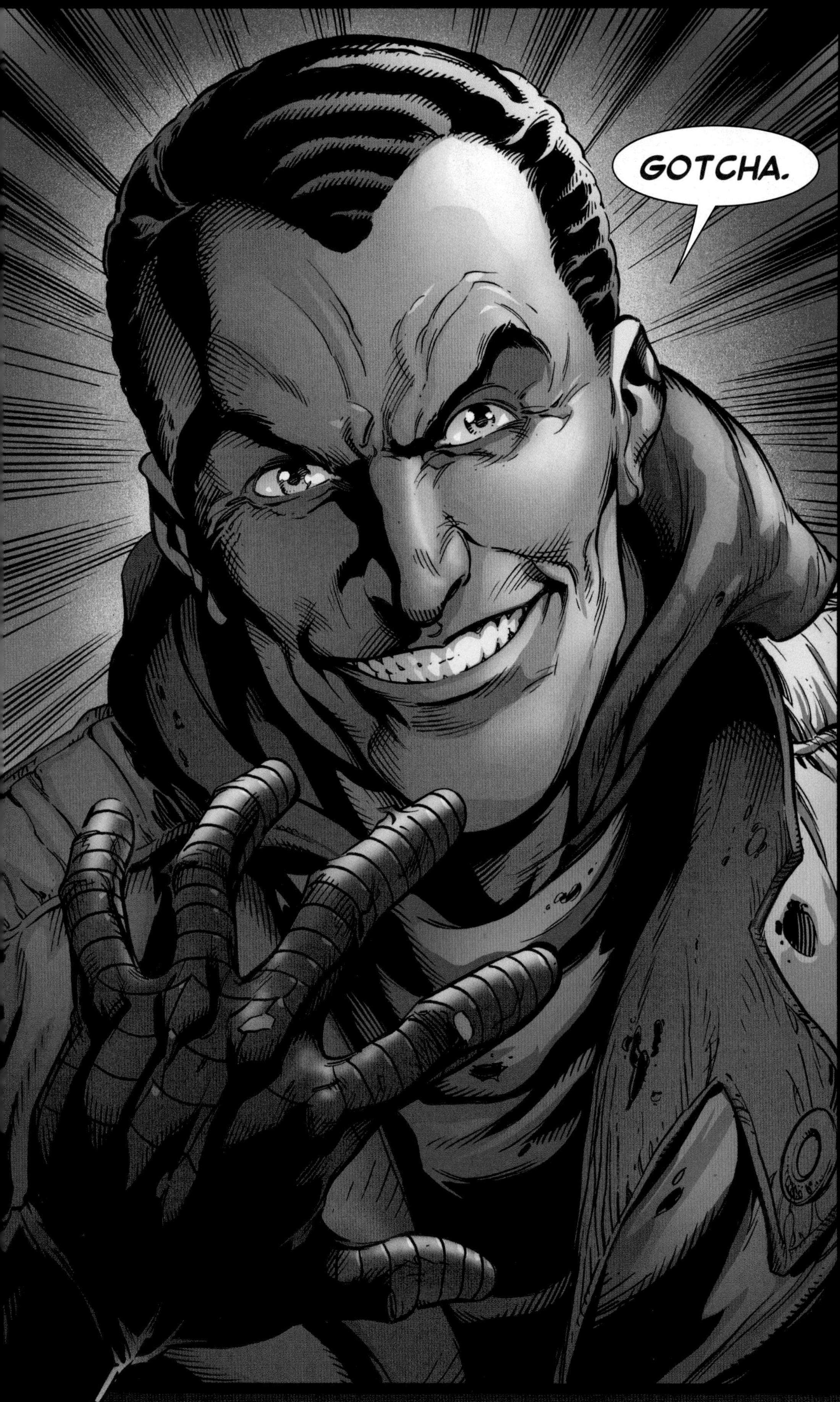
GOTCHA.

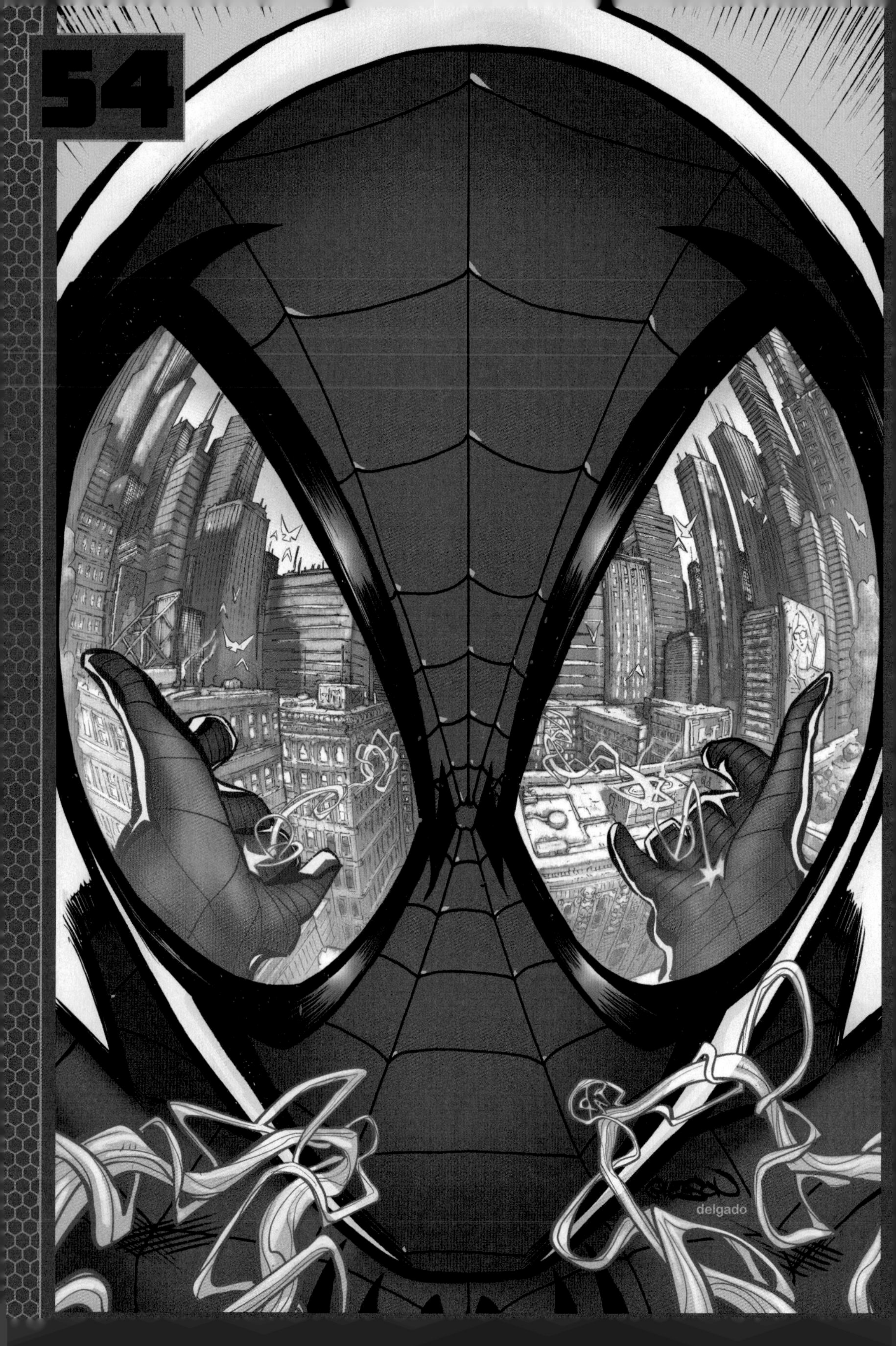
54
delgado

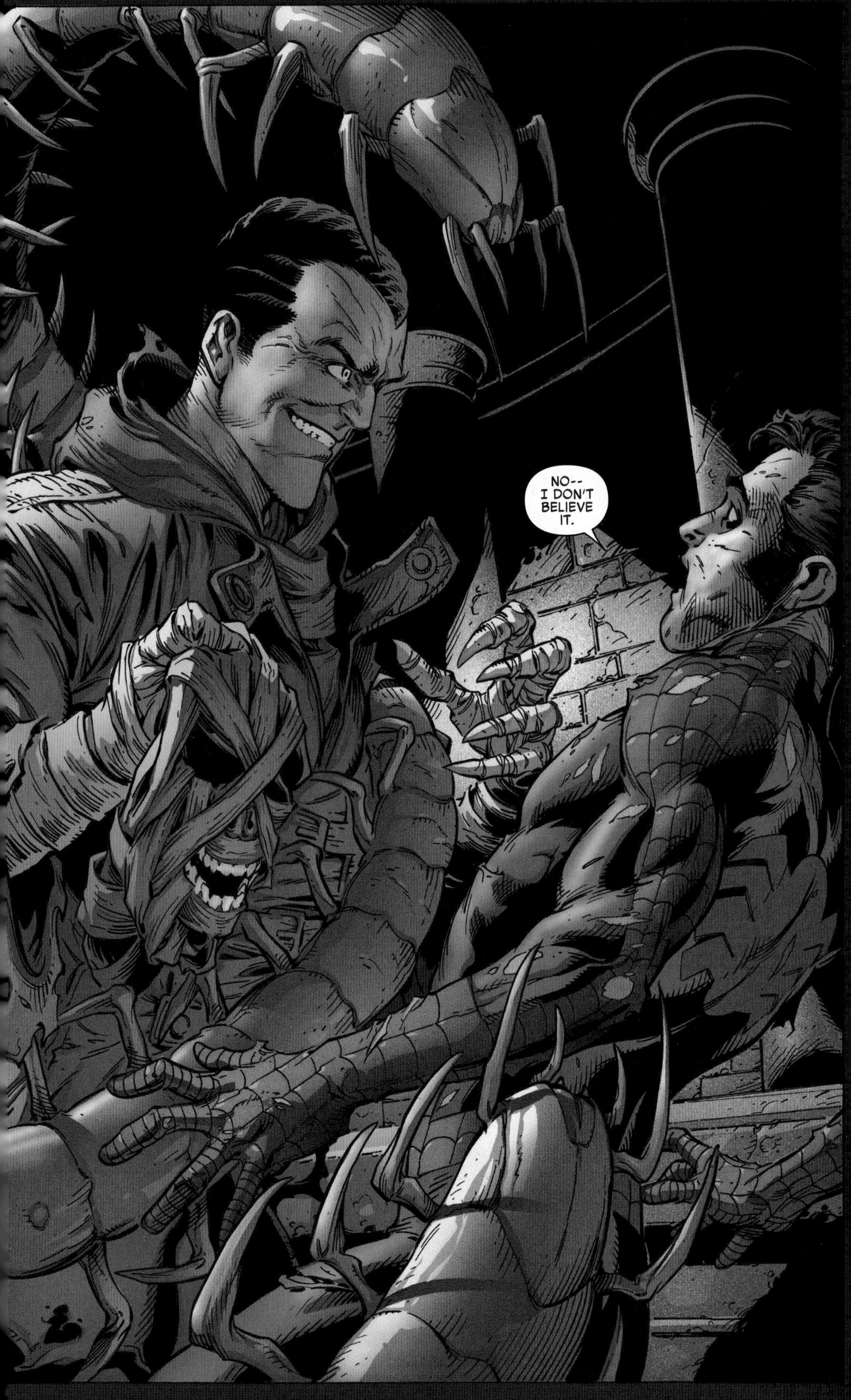
NO-- I DON'T BELIEVE IT.

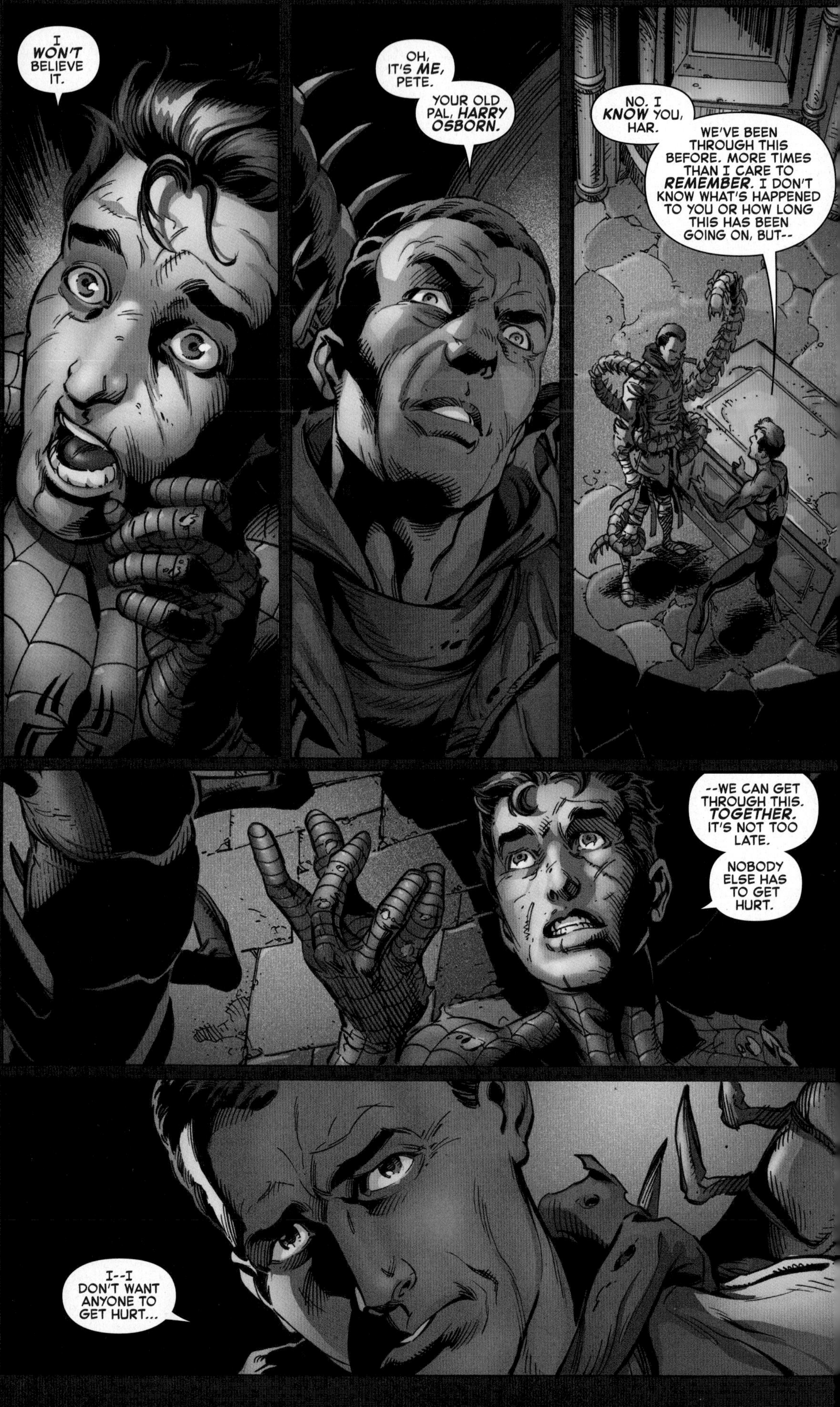

I WON'T BELIEVE IT.
OH, IT'S ME, PETE.
YOUR OLD PAL, HARRY OSBORN.
NO, I KNOW YOU, HAR.
WE'VE BEEN THROUGH THIS BEFORE. MORE TIMES THAN I CARE TO REMEMBER. I DON'T KNOW WHAT'S HAPPENED TO YOU OR HOW LONG THIS HAS BEEN GOING ON, BUT--
--WE CAN GET THROUGH THIS. TOGETHER. IT'S NOT TOO LATE.
NOBODY ELSE HAS TO GET HURT.
I--I DON'T WANT ANYONE TO GET HURT...

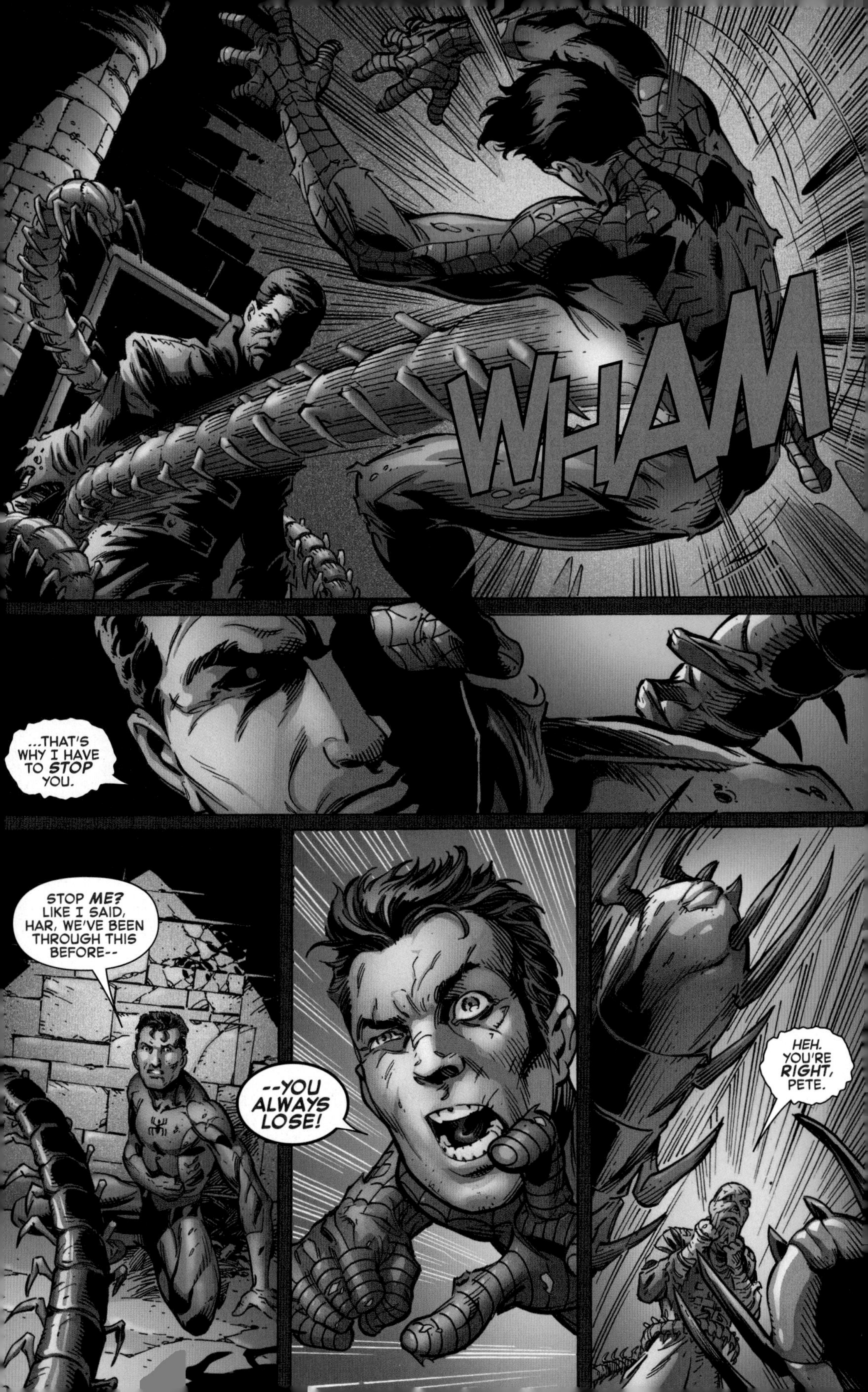
WHAM
...THAT'S WHY I HAVE TO STOP YOU.
STOP ME? LIKE I SAID, HAR, WE'VE BEEN THROUGH THIS BEFORE--
--YOU ALWAYS LOSE!
HEH. YOU'RE RIGHT, PETE.

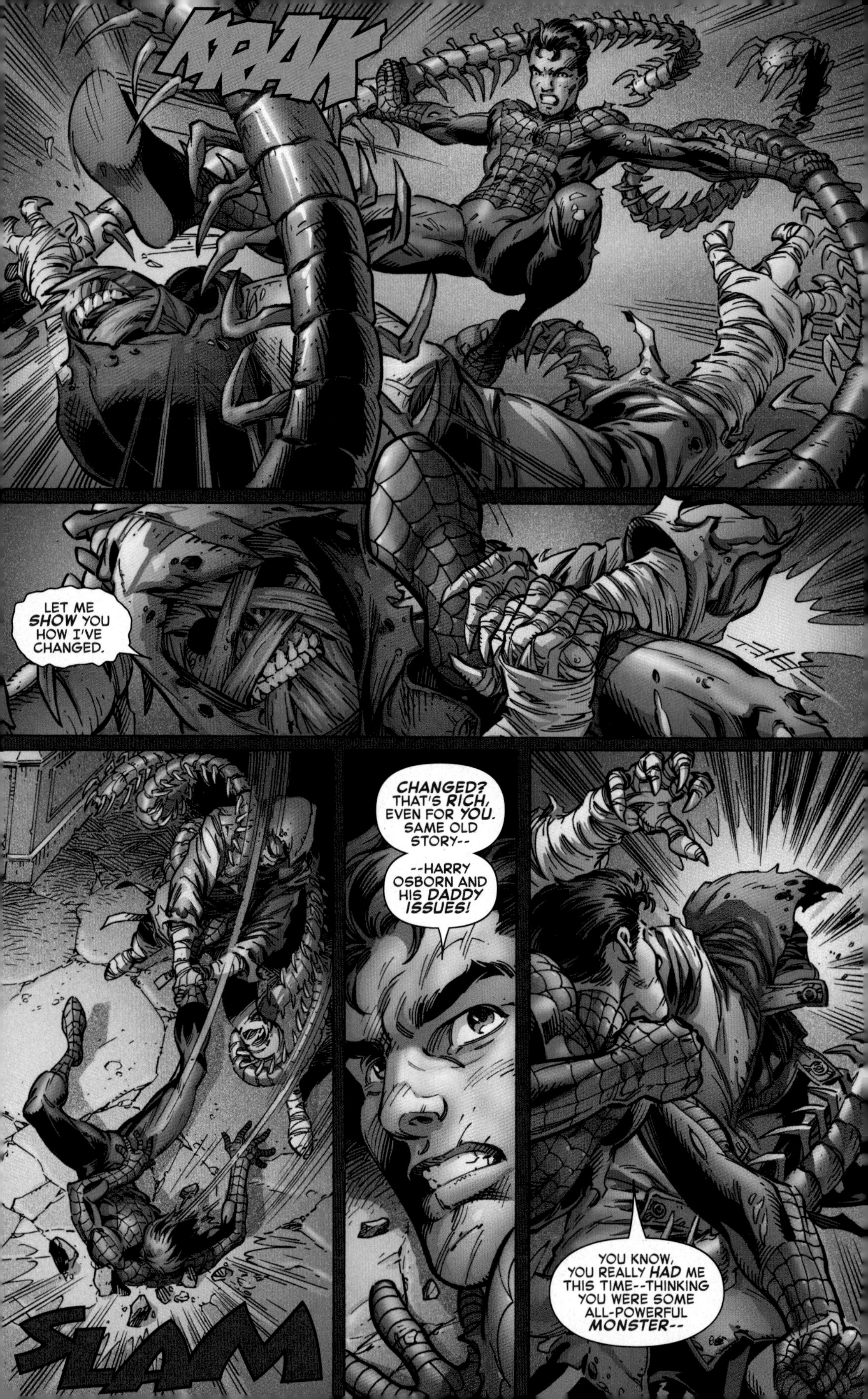
KRAAK
LET ME SHOW YOU HOW I'VE CHANGED.
SLAM
CHANGED? THAT'S RICH, EVEN FOR YOU. SAME OLD STORY--
--HARRY OSBORN AND HIS DADDY ISSUES!
YOU KNOW, YOU REALLY HAD ME THIS TIME--THINKING YOU WERE SOME ALL-POWERFUL MONSTER--

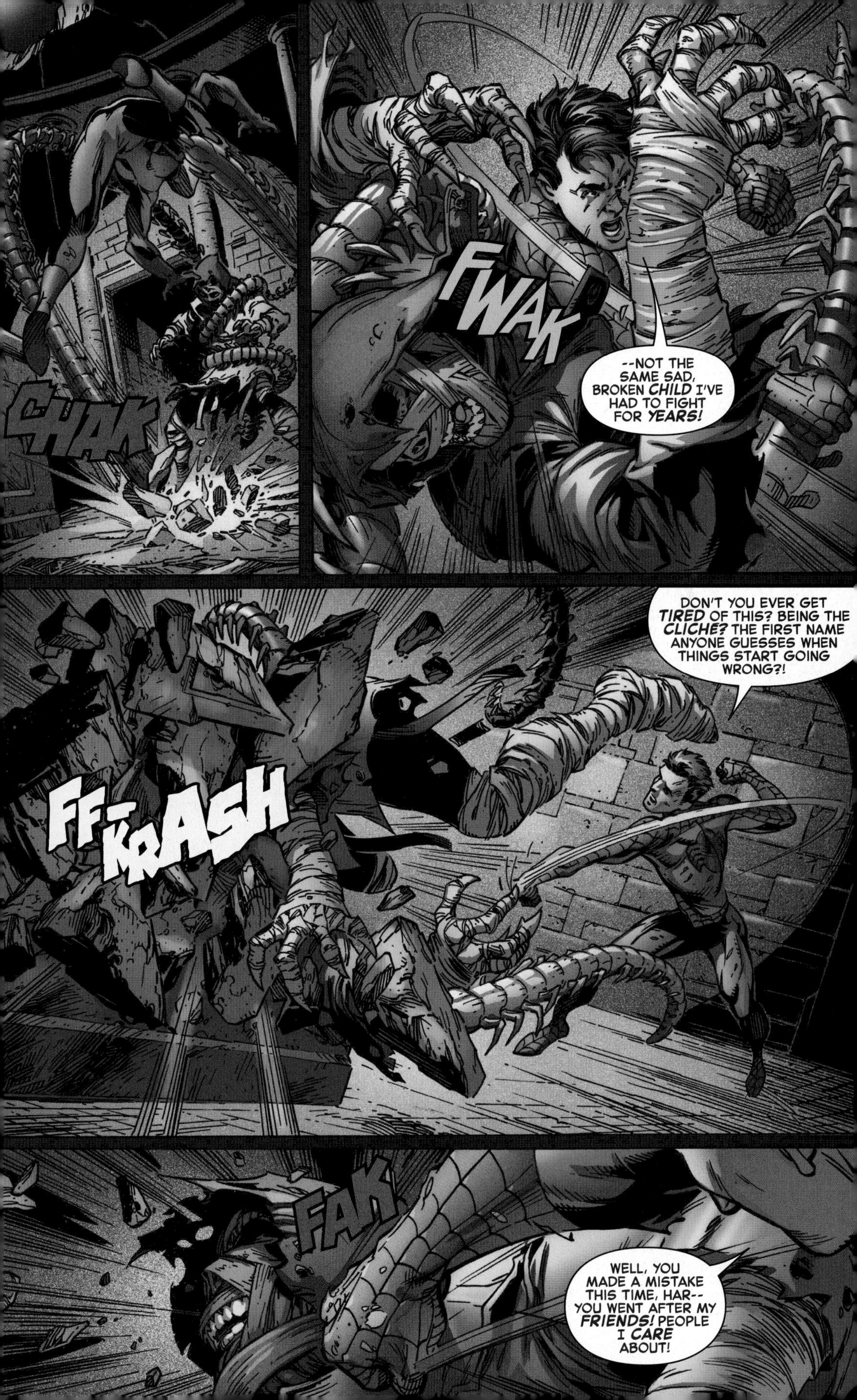
CHAK
FWAK
--NOT THE SAME SAD, BROKEN CHILD I'VE HAD TO FIGHT FOR YEARS!
DON'T YOU EVER GET TIRED OF THIS? BEING THE CLICHE? THE FIRST NAME ANYONE GUESSES WHEN THINGS START GOING WRONG?!
FF-KRASH
FAK
WELL, YOU MADE A MISTAKE THIS TIME, HAR--YOU WENT AFTER MY FRIENDS! PEOPLE I CARE ABOUT!

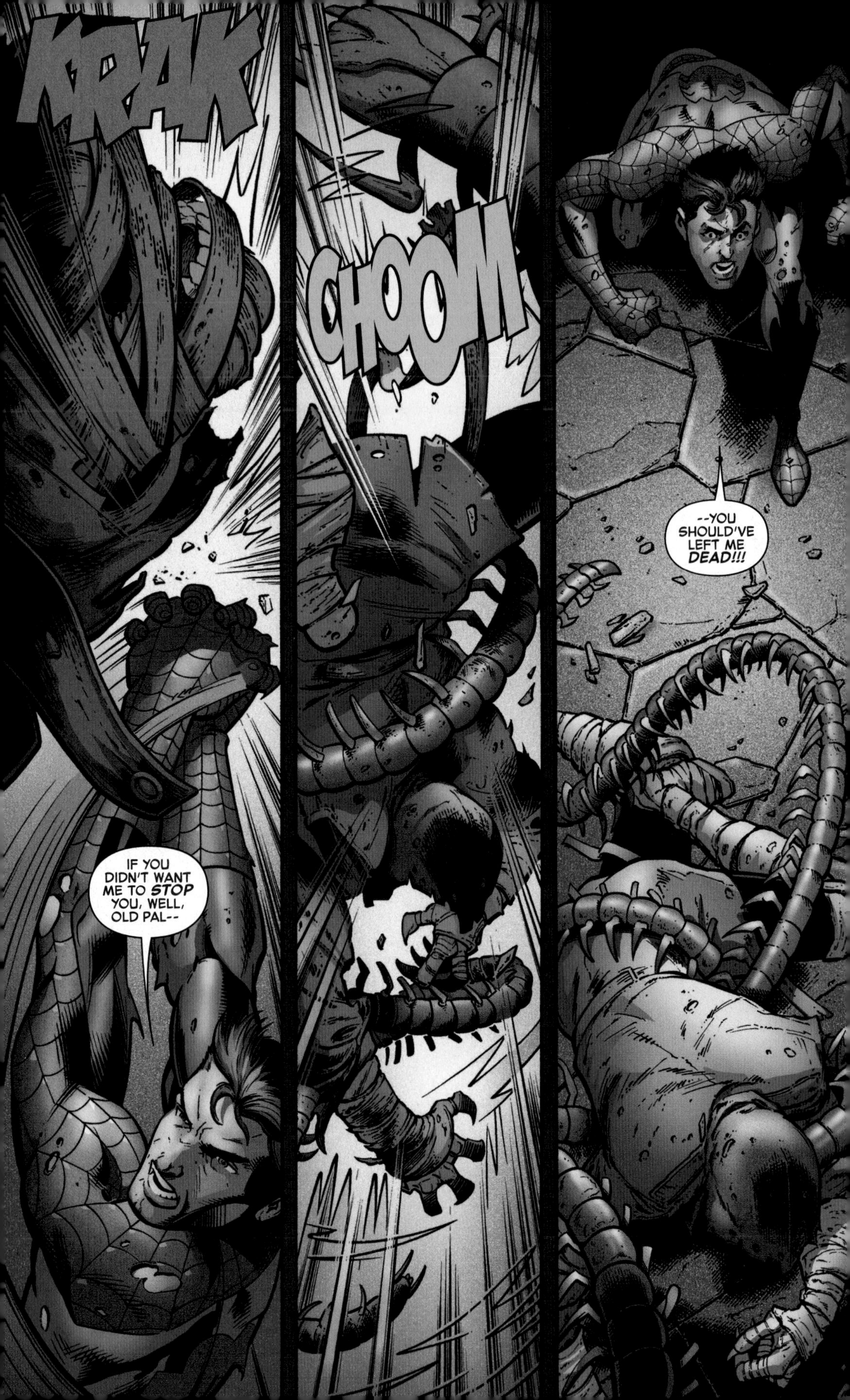
KRAK
IF YOU DIDN'T WANT ME TO STOP YOU, WELL, OLD PAL--
CHOOM
--YOU SHOULD'VE LEFT ME DEAD!!!

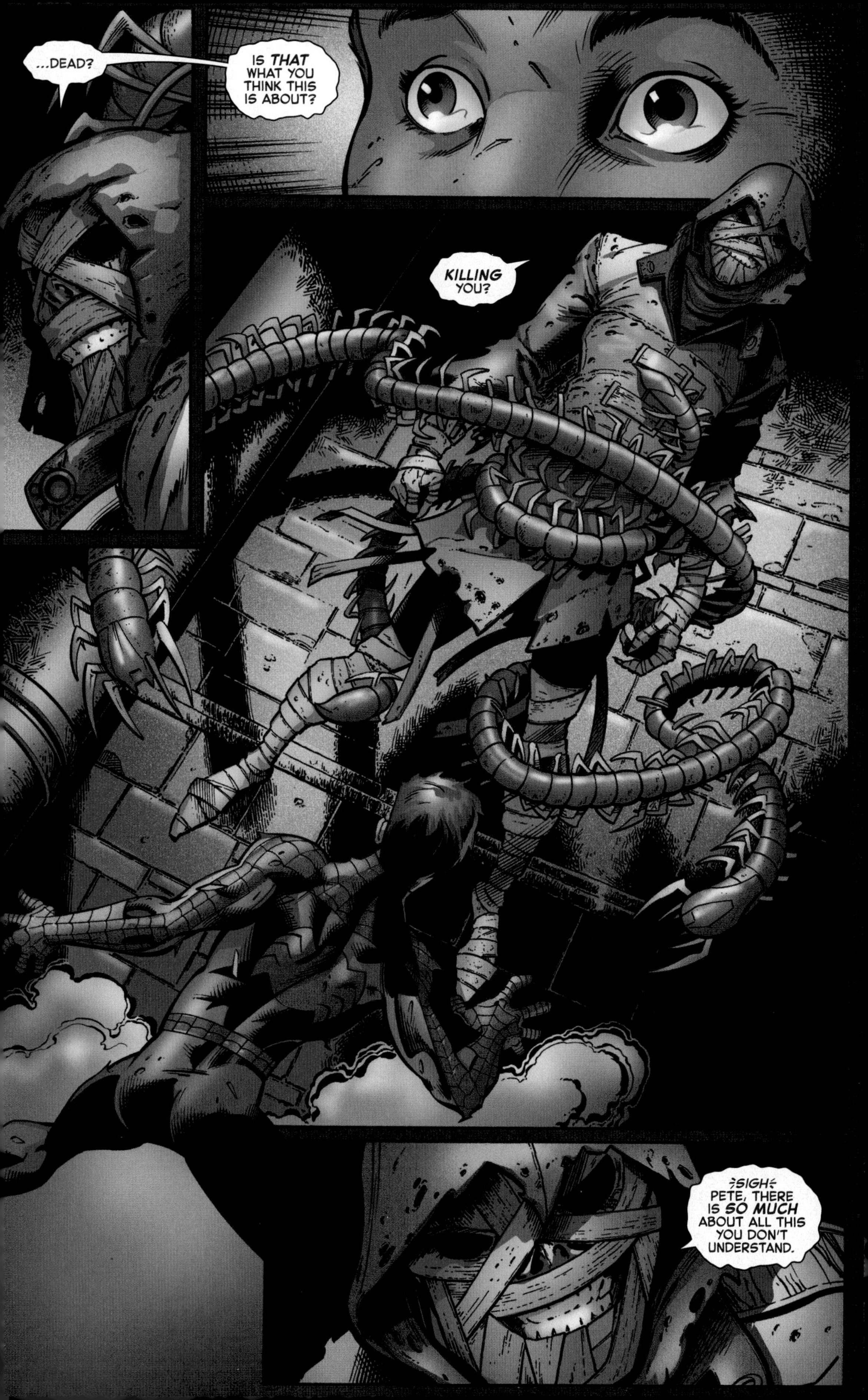
...DEAD?
IS THAT WHAT YOU THINK THIS IS ABOUT?
KILLING YOU?
SIGH
PETE, THERE IS SO MUCH ABOUT ALL THIS YOU DON'T UNDERSTAND.

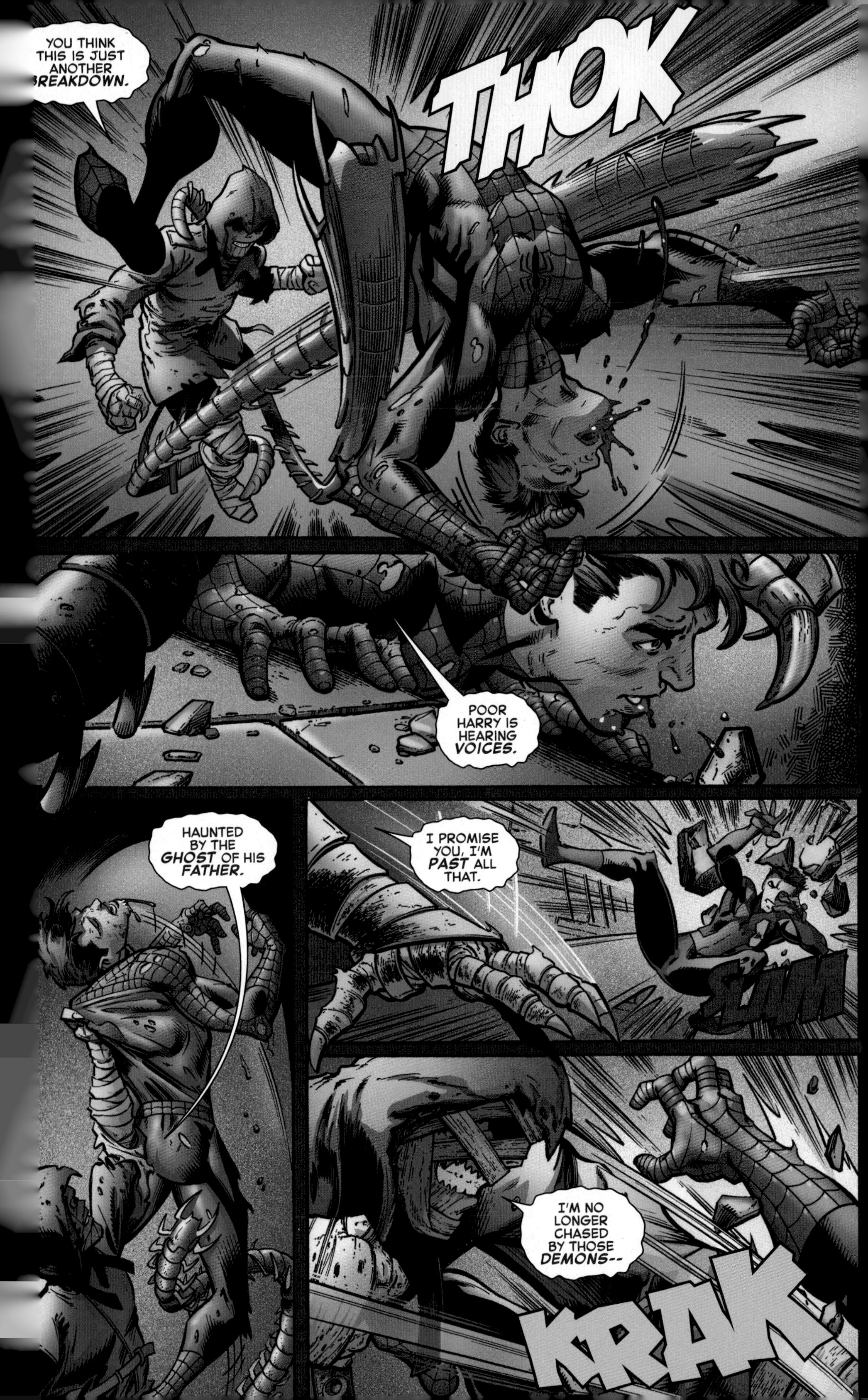
YOU THINK THIS IS JUST ANOTHER BREAKDOWN.
THOK
POOR HARRY IS HEARING VOICES.
HAUNTED BY THE GHOST OF HIS FATHER.
I PROMISE YOU, I'M PAST ALL THAT.
SLAM
I'M NO LONGER CHASED BY THOSE DEMONS--
KRAK

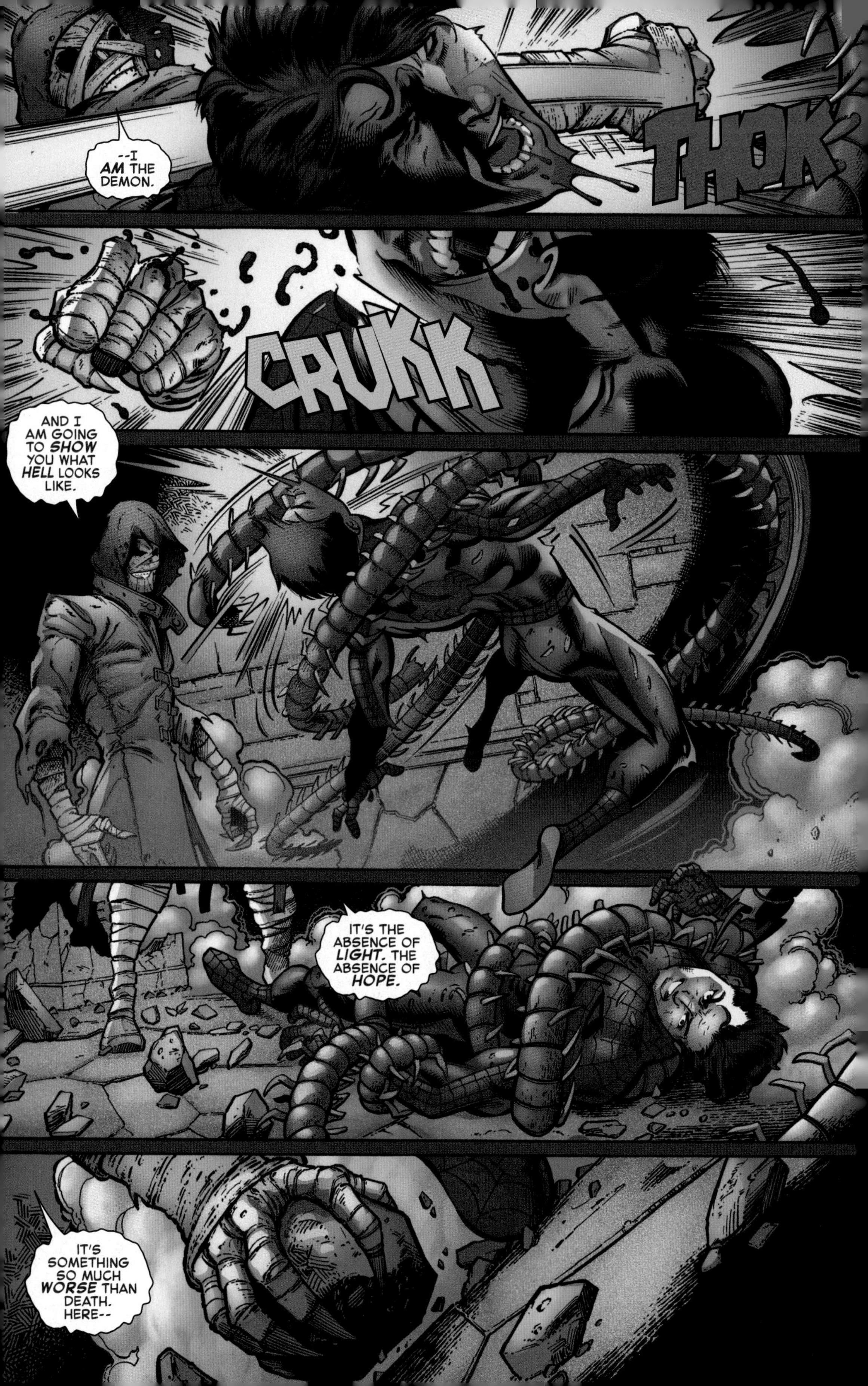

--I AM THE DEMON.
THOK
CRUKK
AND I AM GOING TO SHOW YOU WHAT HELL LOOKS LIKE.
IT'S THE ABSENCE OF LIGHT. THE ABSENCE OF HOPE.
IT'S SOMETHING SO MUCH WORSE THAN DEATH. HERE--

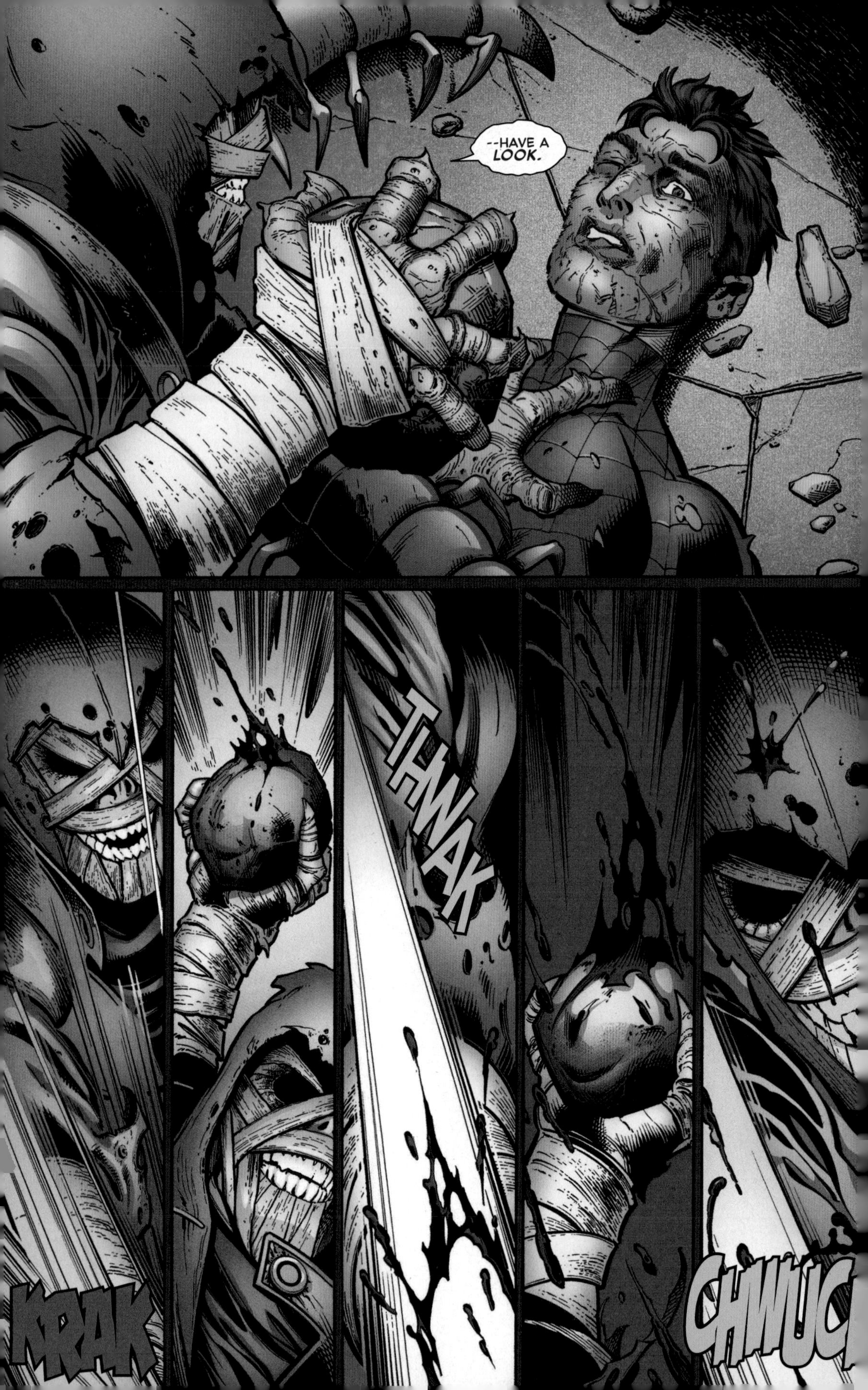
--HAVE A LOOK.
KRAK
THWAK
CHWUC

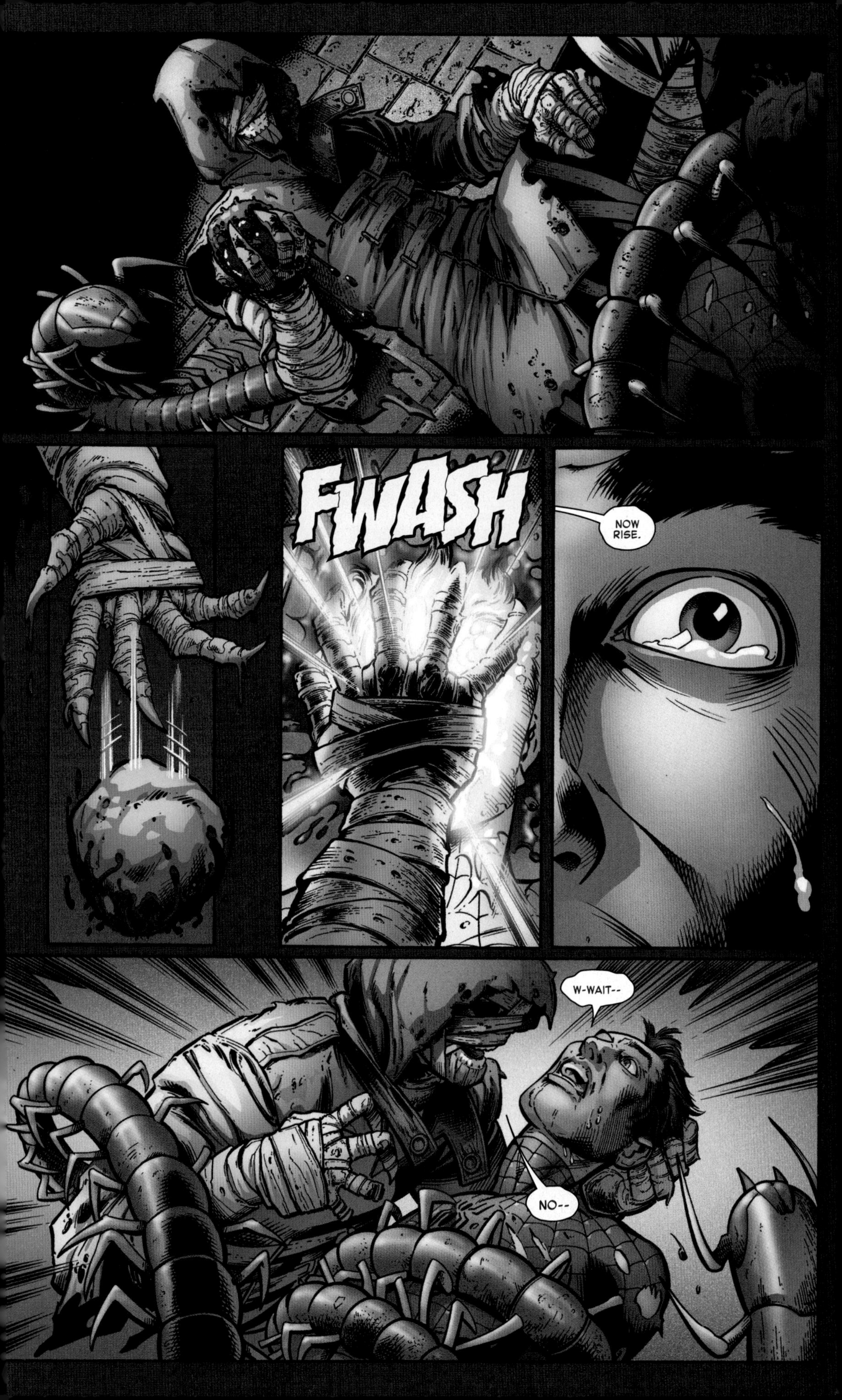
FWASH
NOW RISE.
W-WAIT--
NO--

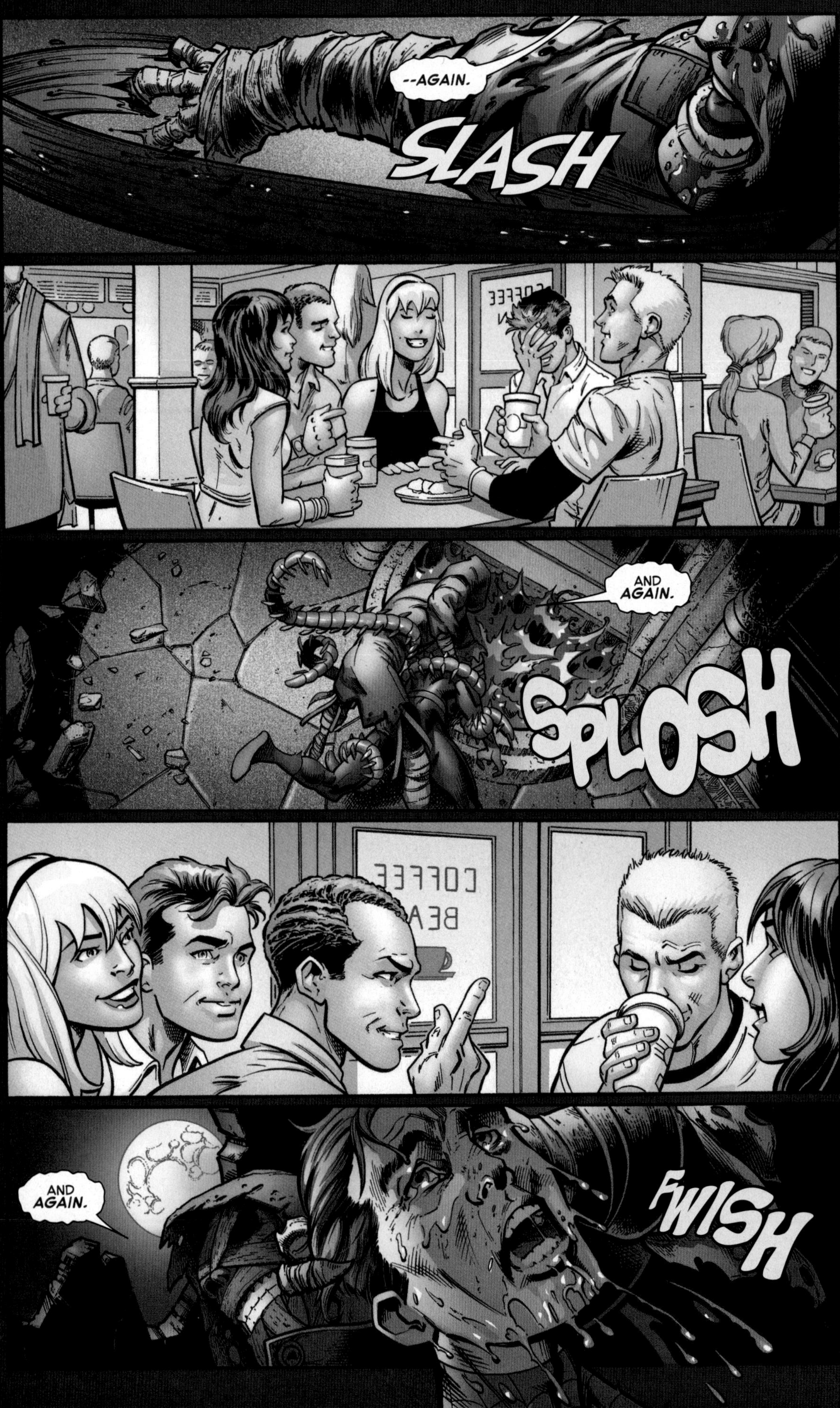
--AGAIN.
SLASH
AND AGAIN.
SPLOSH
AND AGAIN.
FWISH

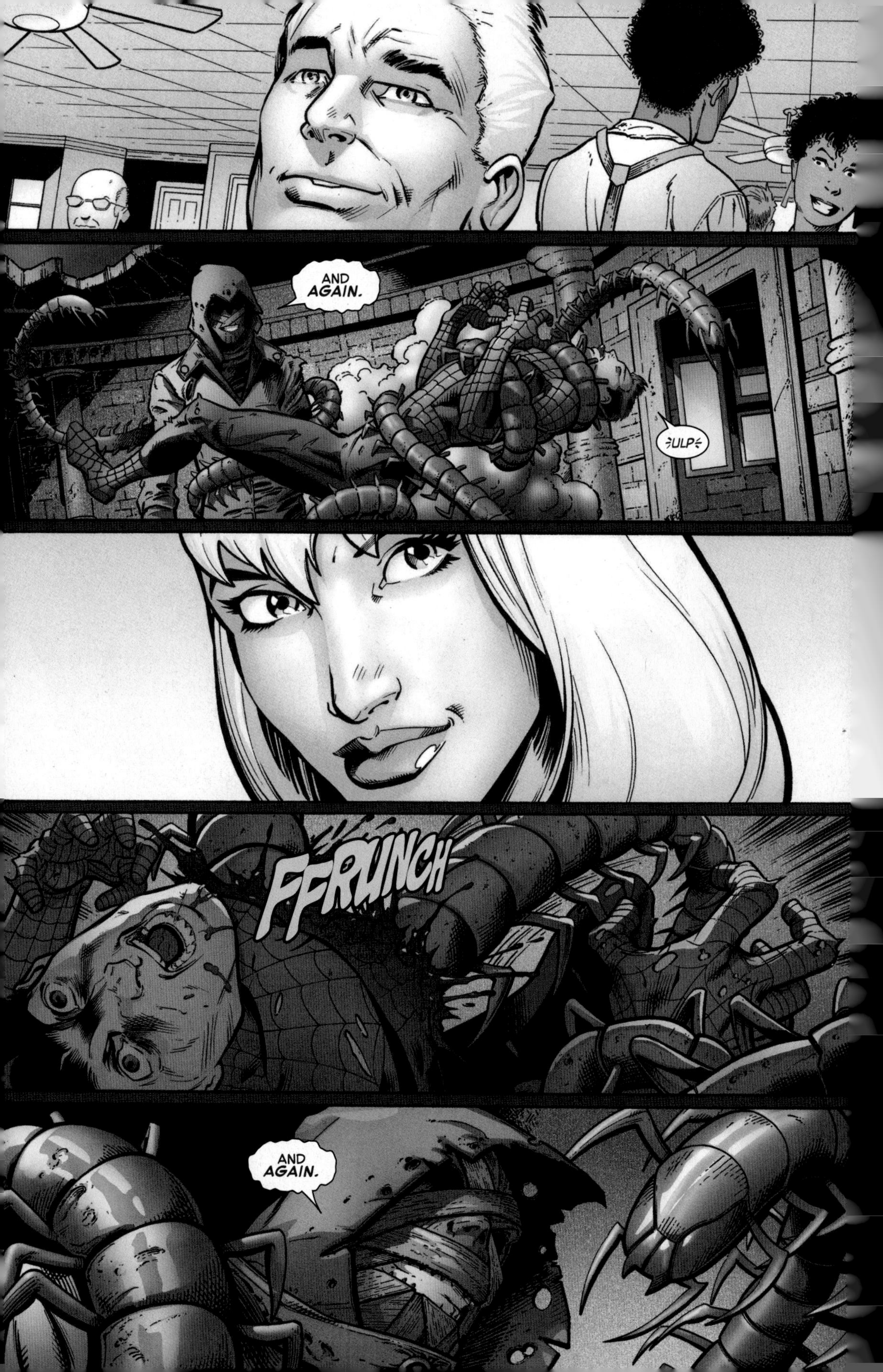
AND AGAIN.
ULP
FFRUNCH
AND AGAIN.

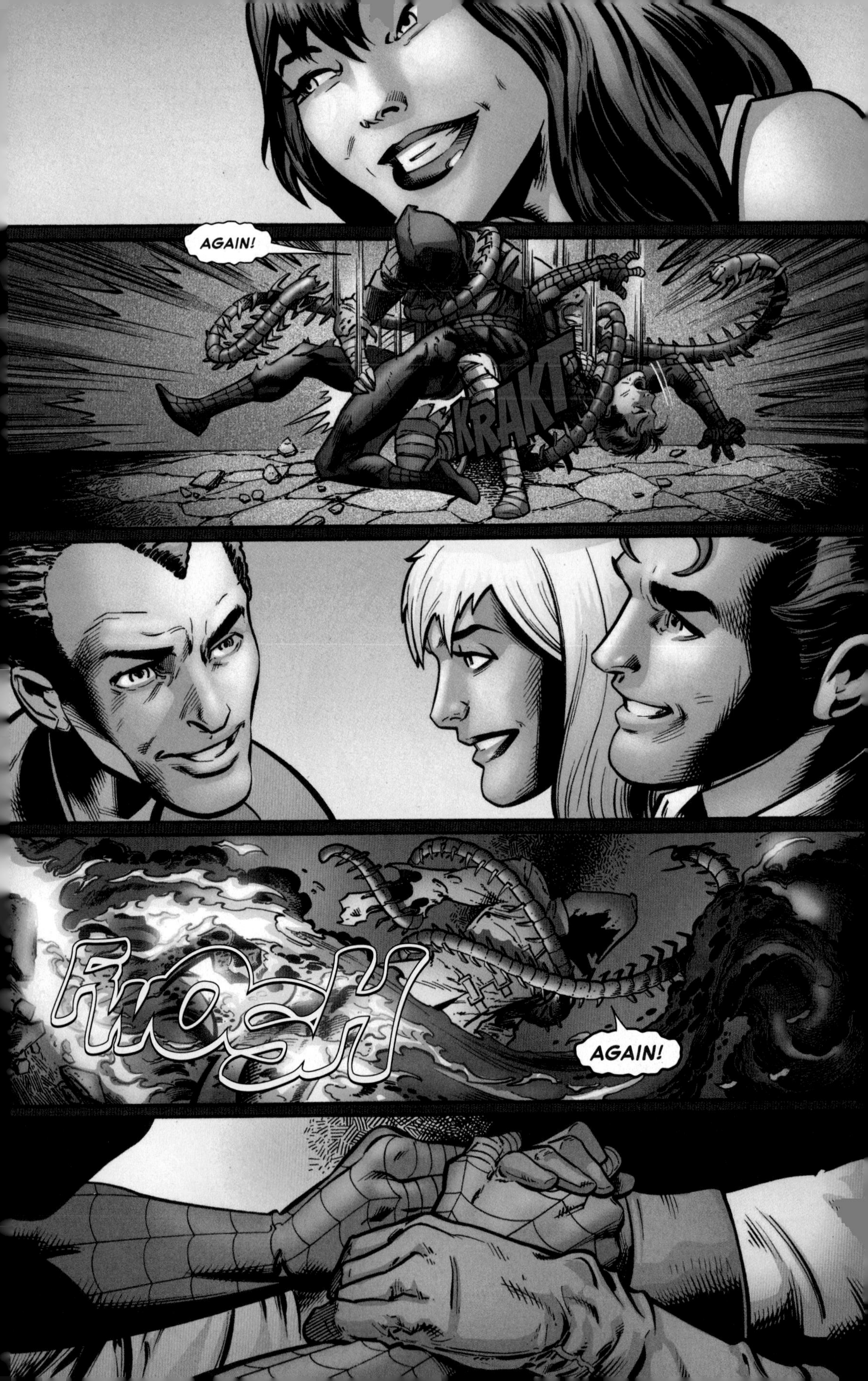
AGAIN!
KRAKT
FWOOSH
AGAIN!

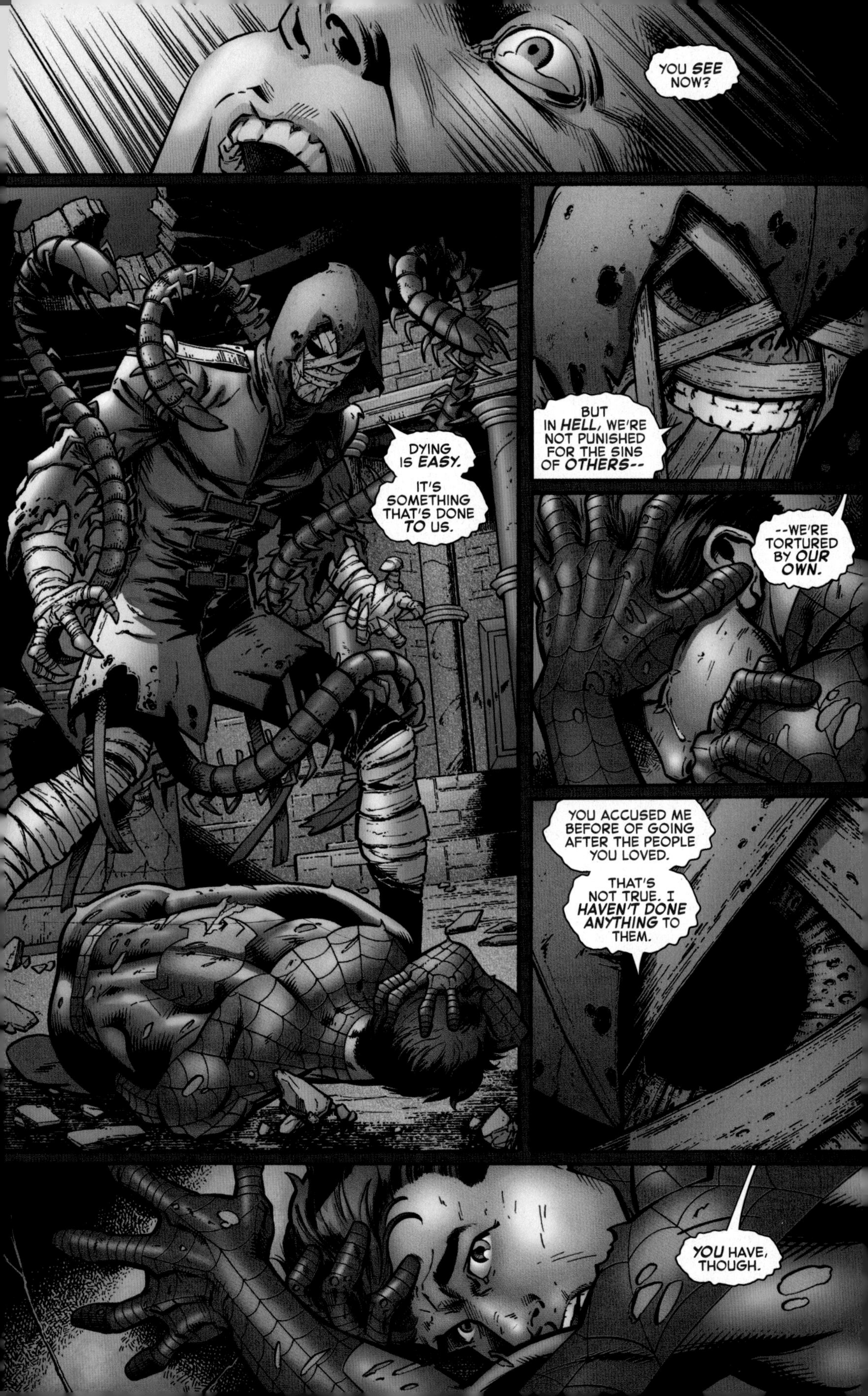
YOU SEE NOW?
DYING IS EASY.
IT'S SOMETHING THAT'S DONE TO US.
BUT IN HELL, WE'RE NOT PUNISHED FOR THE SINS OF OTHERS--
--WE'RE TORTURED BY OUR OWN.
YOU ACCUSED ME BEFORE OF GOING AFTER THE PEOPLE YOU LOVED.
THAT'S NOT TRUE. I HAVEN'T DONE ANYTHING TO THEM.
YOU HAVE, THOUGH.

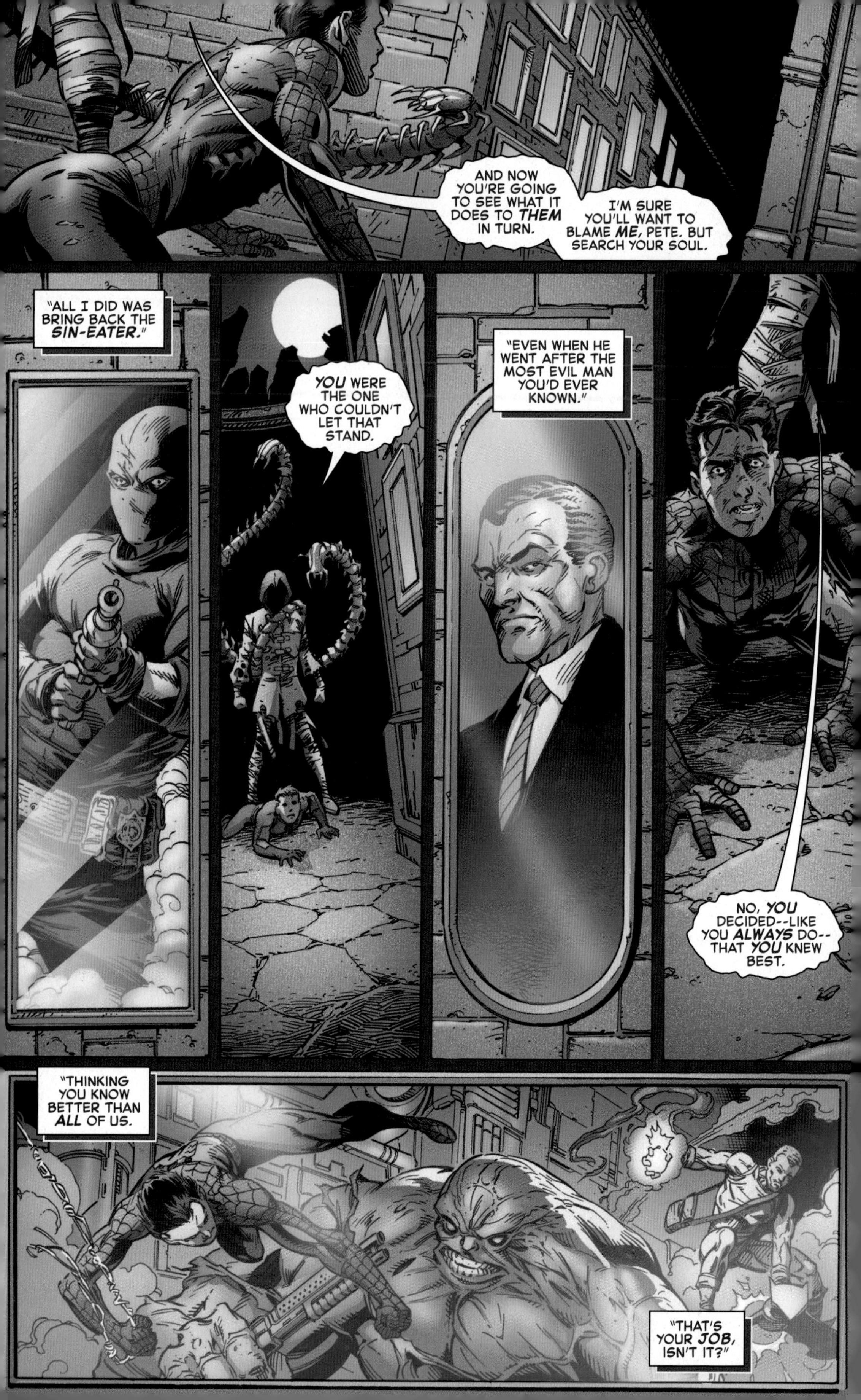
AND NOW YOU'RE GOING TO SEE WHAT IT DOES TO THEM IN TURN.
I'M SURE YOU'LL WANT TO BLAME ME, PETE. BUT SEARCH YOUR SOUL.
"ALL I DID WAS BRING BACK THE SIN-EATER."
YOU WERE THE ONE WHO COULDN'T LET THAT STAND.
"EVEN WHEN HE WENT AFTER THE MOST EVIL MAN YOU'D EVER KNOWN."
NO, YOU DECIDED--LIKE YOU ALWAYS DO--THAT YOU KNEW BEST.
"THINKING YOU KNOW BETTER THAN ALL OF US.
"THAT'S YOUR JOB, ISN'T IT?"

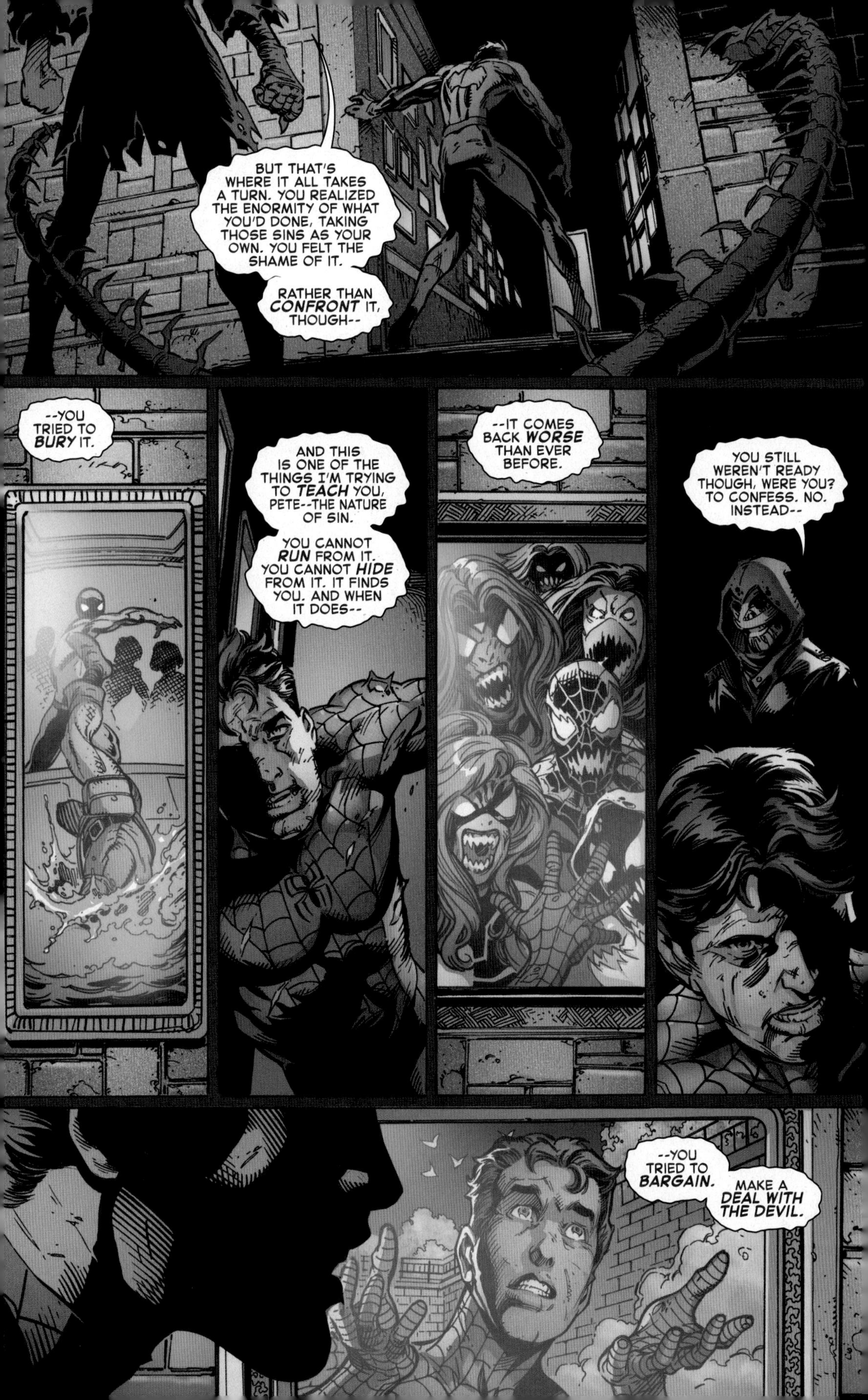
BUT THAT'S WHERE IT ALL TAKES A TURN. YOU REALIZED THE ENORMITY OF WHAT YOU'D DONE, TAKING THOSE SINS AS YOUR OWN. YOU FELT THE SHAME OF IT.
RATHER THAN CONFRONT IT, THOUGH--
--YOU TRIED TO BURY IT.
AND THIS IS ONE OF THE THINGS I'M TRYING TO TEACH YOU, PETE--THE NATURE OF SIN.
YOU CANNOT RUN FROM IT. YOU CANNOT HIDE FROM IT. IT FINDS YOU. AND WHEN IT DOES--
--IT COMES BACK WORSE THAN EVER BEFORE.
YOU STILL WEREN'T READY THOUGH, WERE YOU? TO CONFESS. NO. INSTEAD--
--YOU TRIED TO BARGAIN.
MAKE A DEAL WITH THE DEVIL.

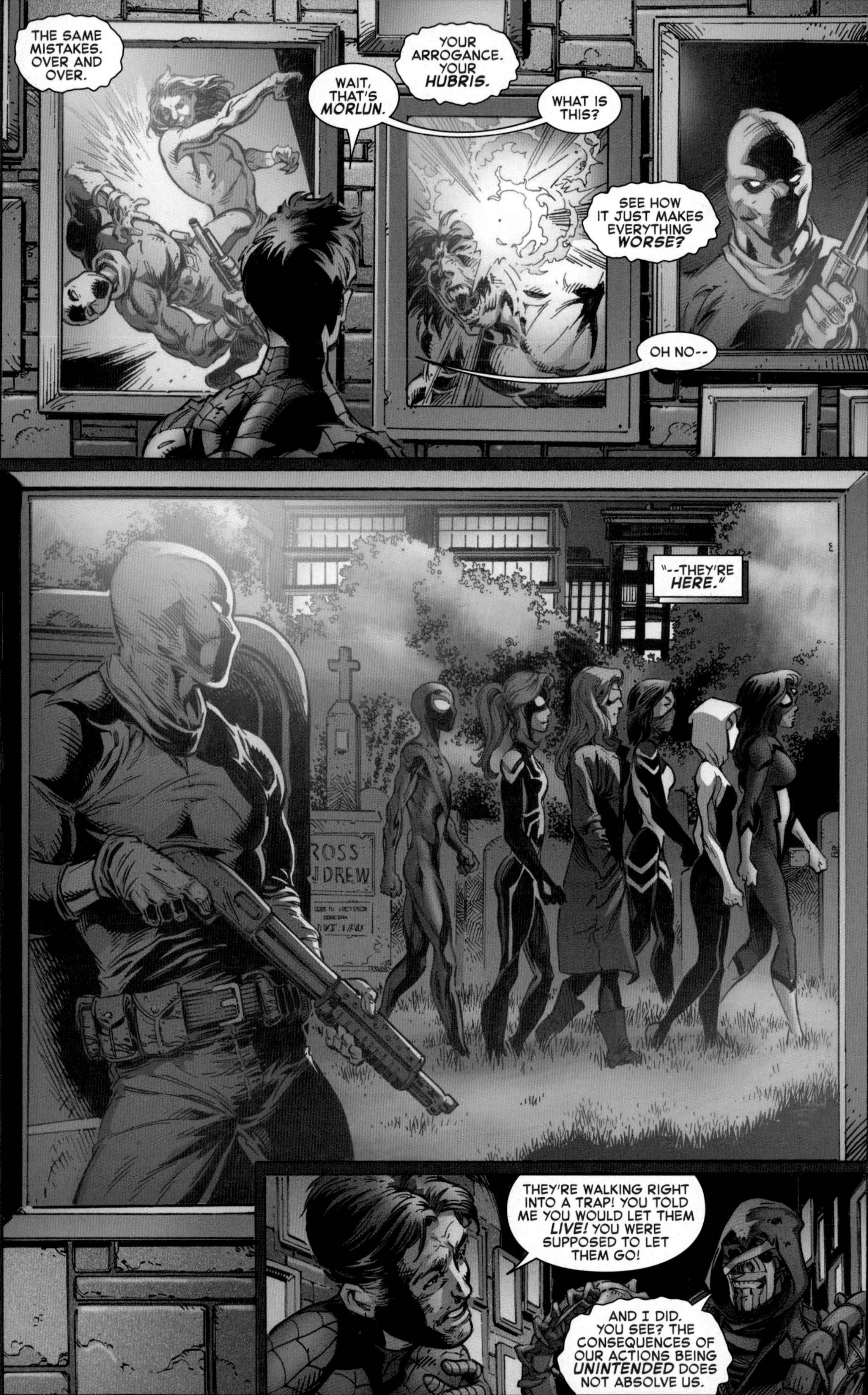
THE SAME MISTAKES. OVER AND OVER.
YOUR ARROGANCE. YOUR HUBRIS.
WAIT, THAT'S MORLUN.
WHAT IS THIS?
SEE HOW IT JUST MAKES EVERYTHING WORSE?
OH NO--
"--THEY'RE HERE."
ROSS
DREW
THEY'RE WALKING RIGHT INTO A TRAP! YOU TOLD ME YOU WOULD LET THEM LIVE! YOU WERE SUPPOSED TO LET THEM GO!
AND I DID. YOU SEE? THE CONSEQUENCES OF OUR ACTIONS BEING UNINTENDED DOES NOT ABSOLVE US.

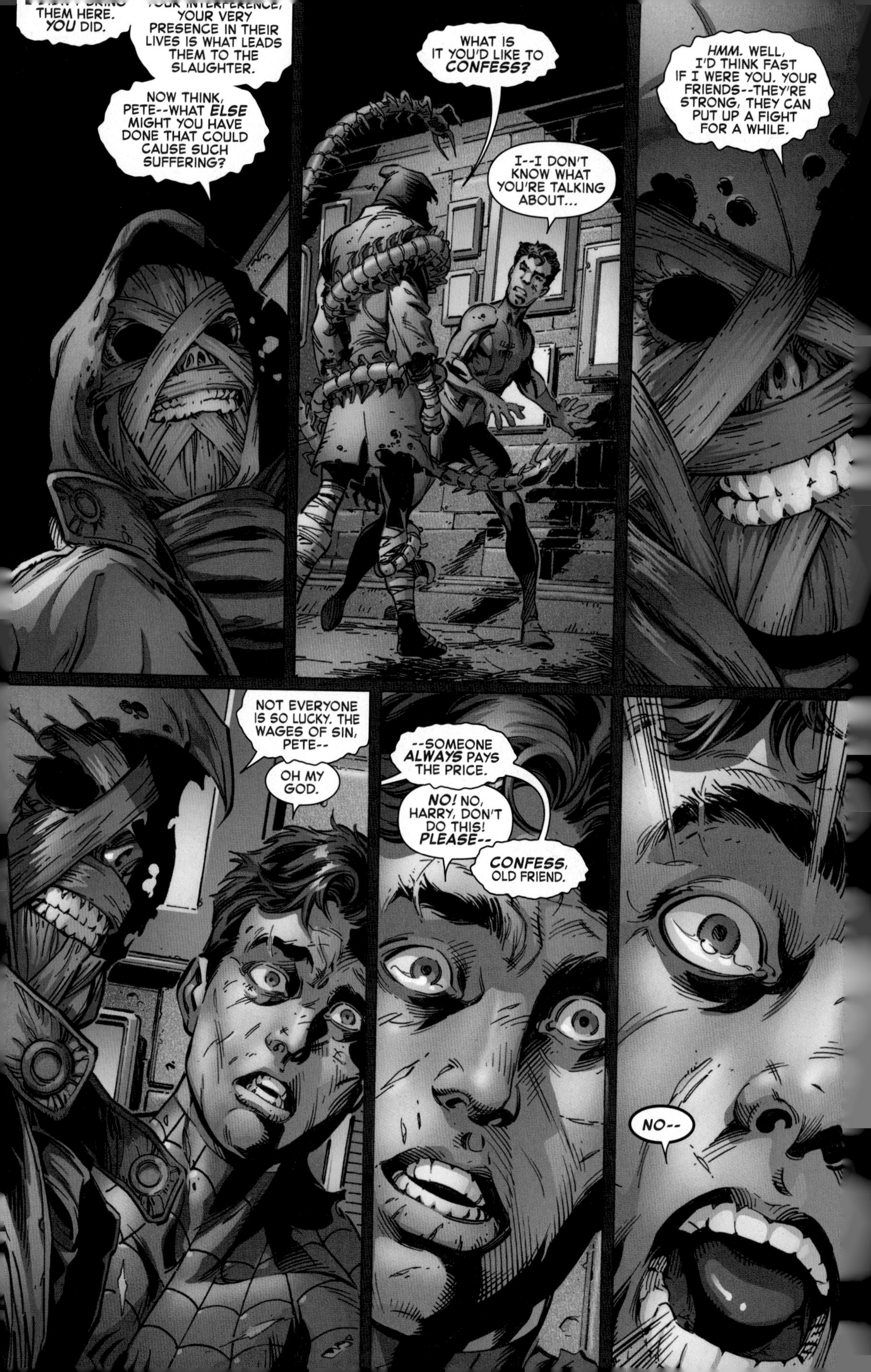
THEM HERE. YOU DID.
YOUR VERY PRESENCE IN THEIR LIVES IS WHAT LEADS THEM TO THE SLAUGHTER.
NOW THINK, PETE--WHAT ELSE MIGHT YOU HAVE DONE THAT COULD CAUSE SUCH SUFFERING?
WHAT IS IT YOU'D LIKE TO CONFESS?
I--I DON'T KNOW WHAT YOU'RE TALKING ABOUT...
HMM. WELL, I'D THINK FAST IF I WERE YOU. YOUR FRIENDS--THEY'RE STRONG, THEY CAN PUT UP A FIGHT FOR A WHILE.
NOT EVERYONE IS SO LUCKY. THE WAGES OF SIN, PETE--
OH MY GOD.
--SOMEONE ALWAYS PAYS THE PRICE.
NO! NO, HARRY, DON'T DO THIS! PLEASE--
CONFESS, OLD FRIEND.
NO--

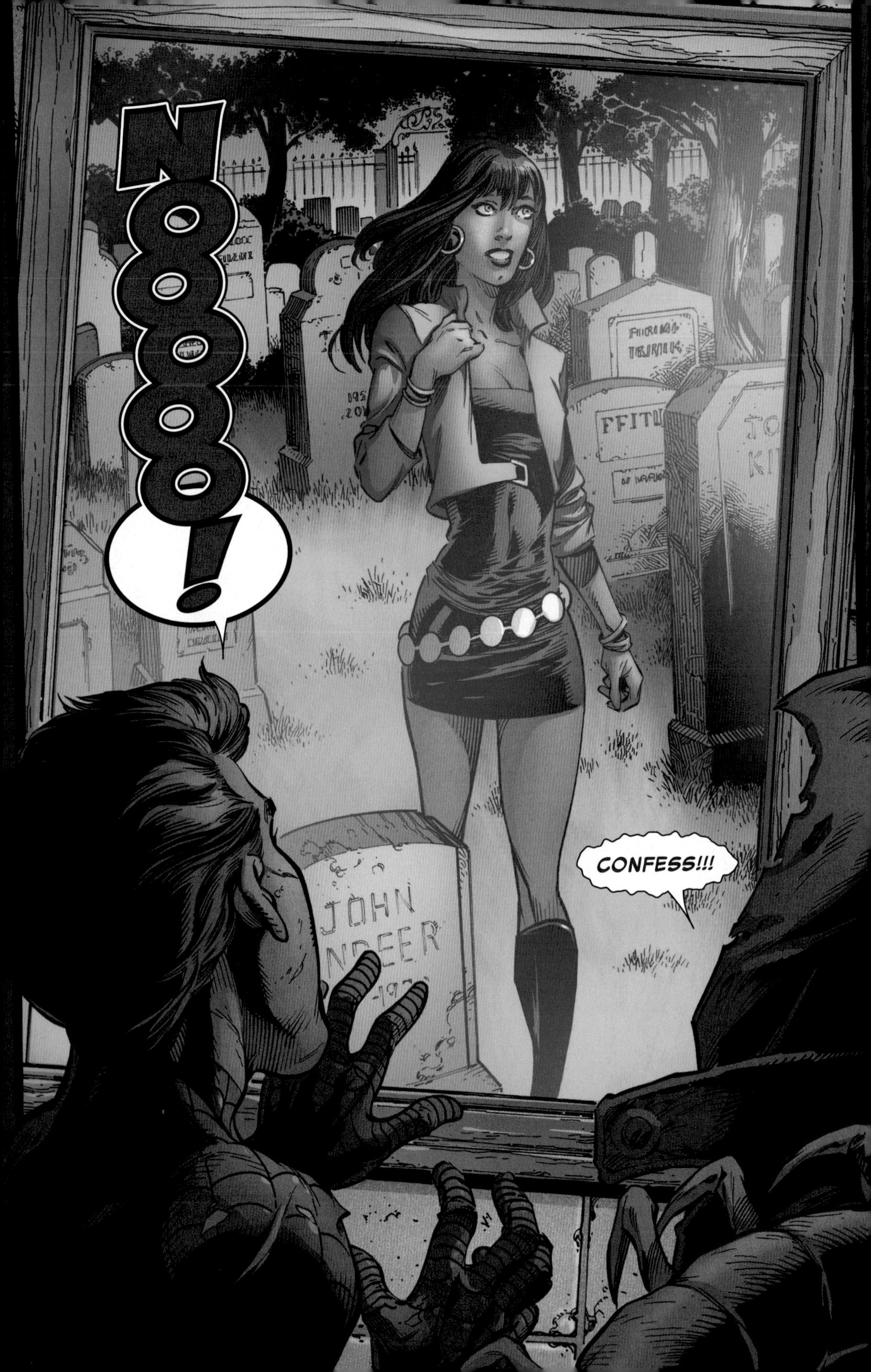
NOOOOO!
CONFESS!!!

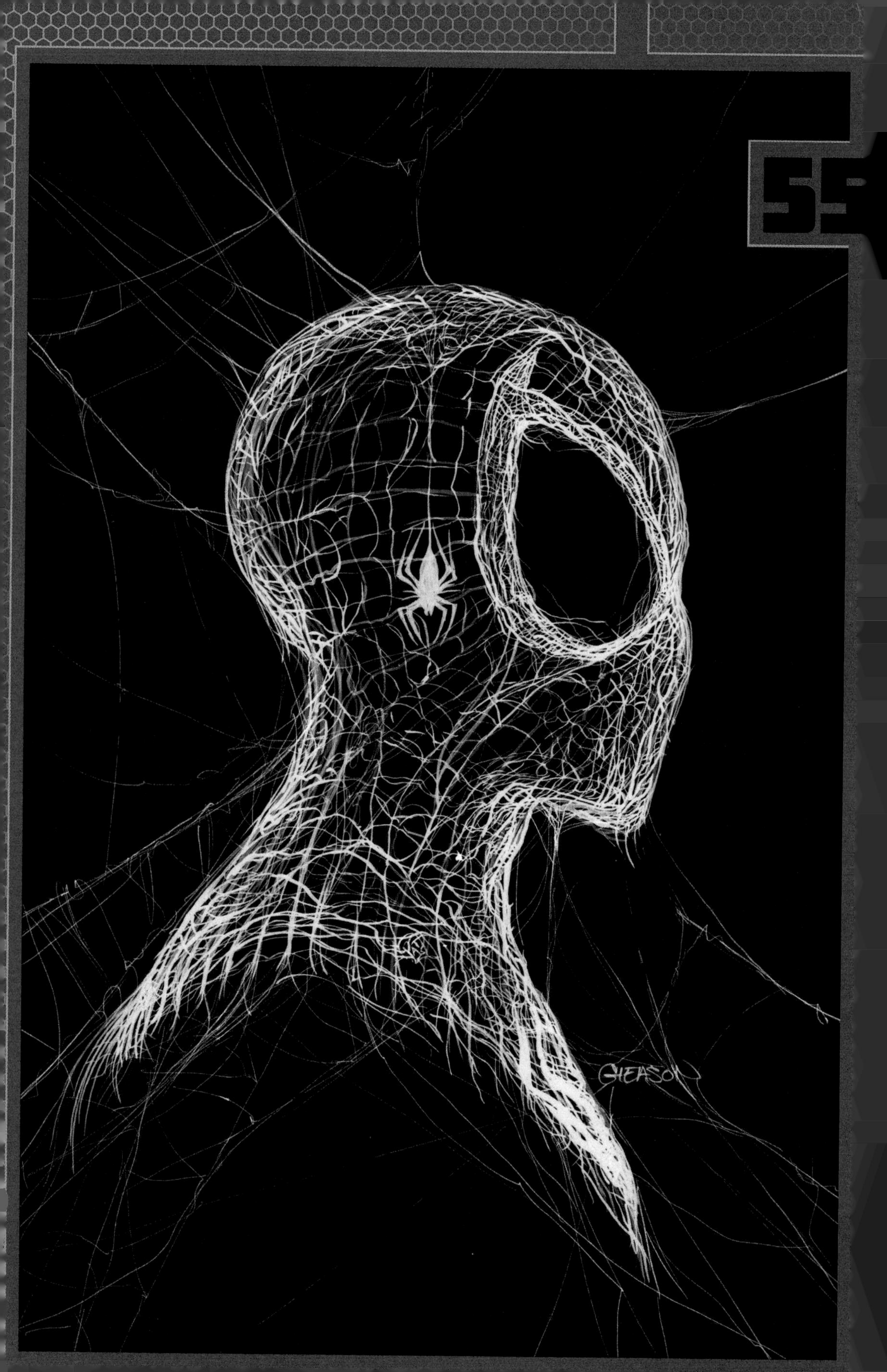
GLEASON

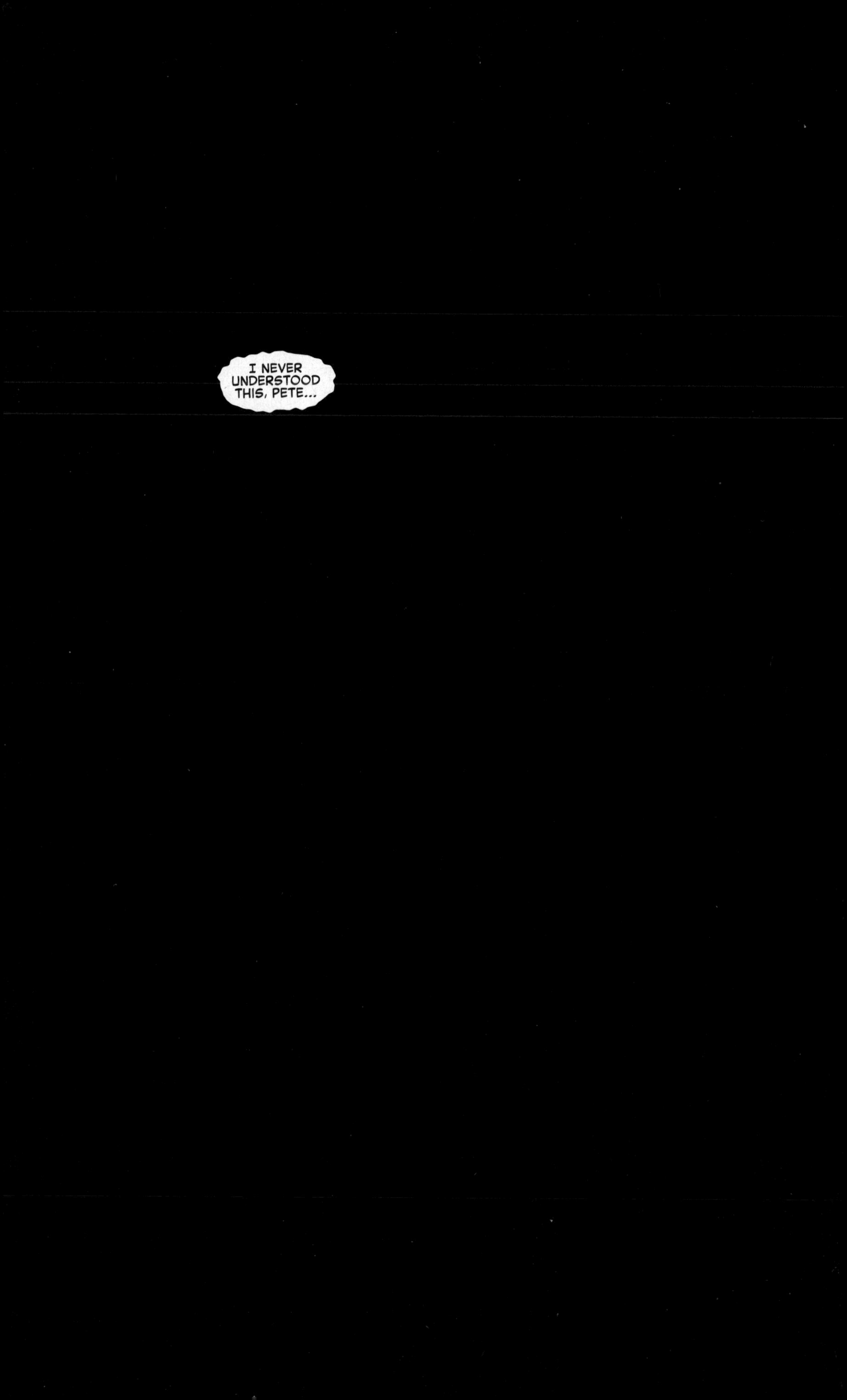
I NEVER UNDERSTOOD THIS, PETE...

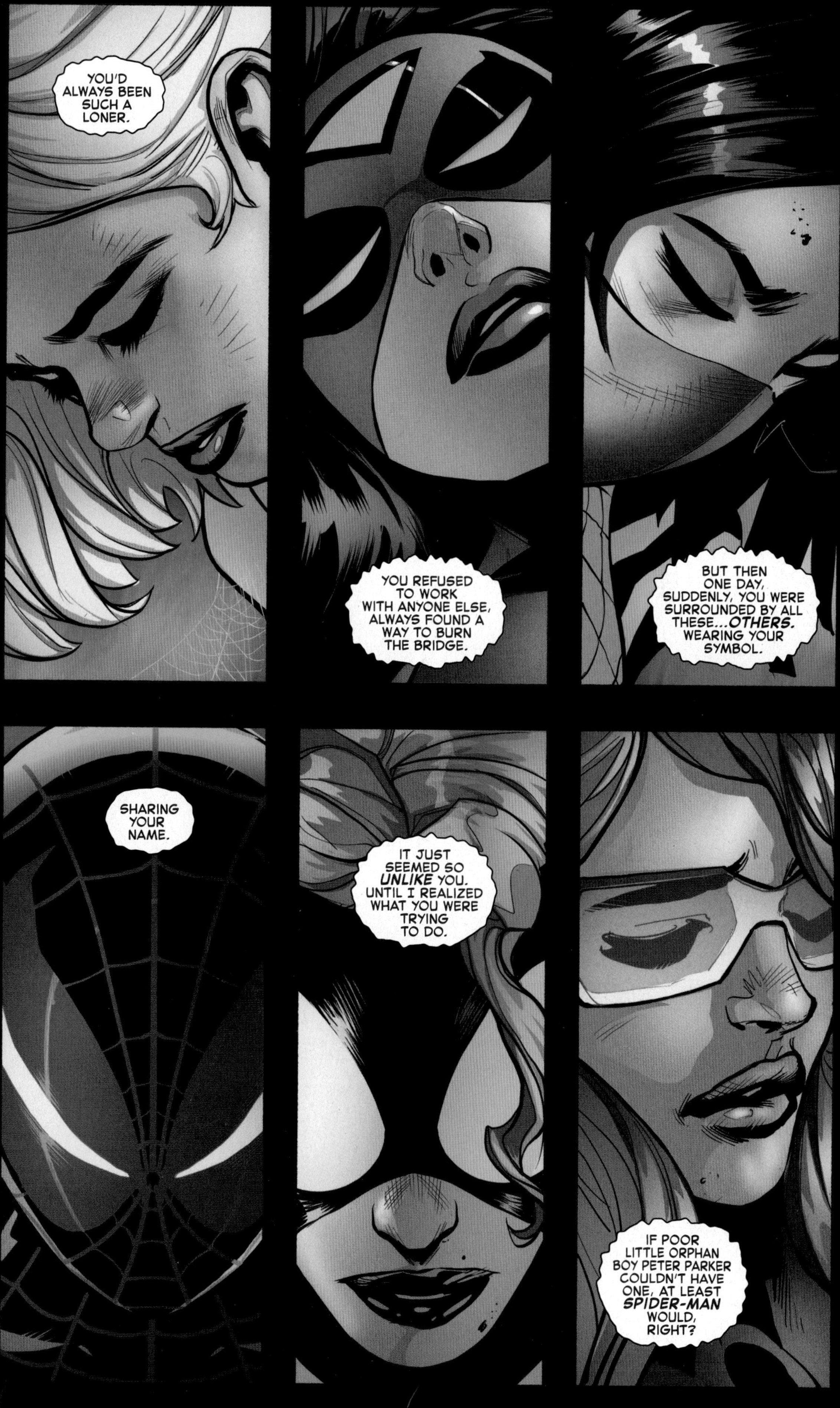
YOU'D ALWAYS BEEN SUCH A LONER.
YOU REFUSED TO WORK WITH ANYONE ELSE, ALWAYS FOUND A WAY TO BURN THE BRIDGE.
BUT THEN ONE DAY, SUDDENLY, YOU WERE SURROUNDED BY ALL THESE...OTHERS. WEARING YOUR SYMBOL.
SHARING YOUR NAME.
IT JUST SEEMED SO UNLIKE YOU. UNTIL I REALIZED WHAT YOU WERE TRYING TO DO.
IF POOR LITTLE ORPHAN BOY PETER PARKER COULDN'T HAVE ONE, AT LEAST SPIDER-MAN WOULD, RIGHT?

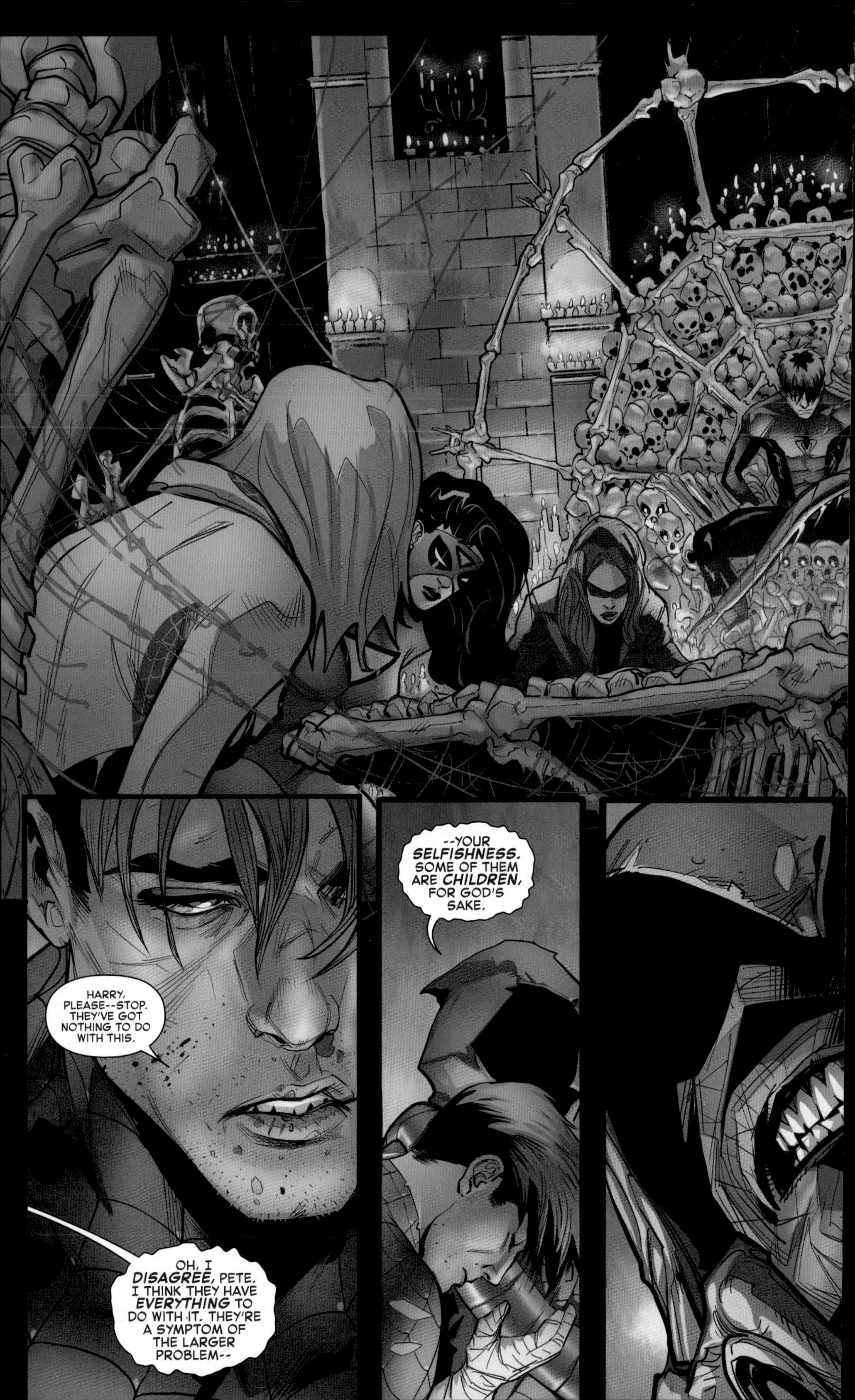
HARRY, PLEASE--STOP. THEY'VE GOT NOTHING TO DO WITH THIS.
OH, I DISAGREE, PETE. I THINK THEY HAVE EVERYTHING TO DO WITH IT. THEY'RE A SYMPTOM OF THE LARGER PROBLEM--
--YOUR SELFISHNESS. SOME OF THEM ARE CHILDREN, FOR GOD'S SAKE.

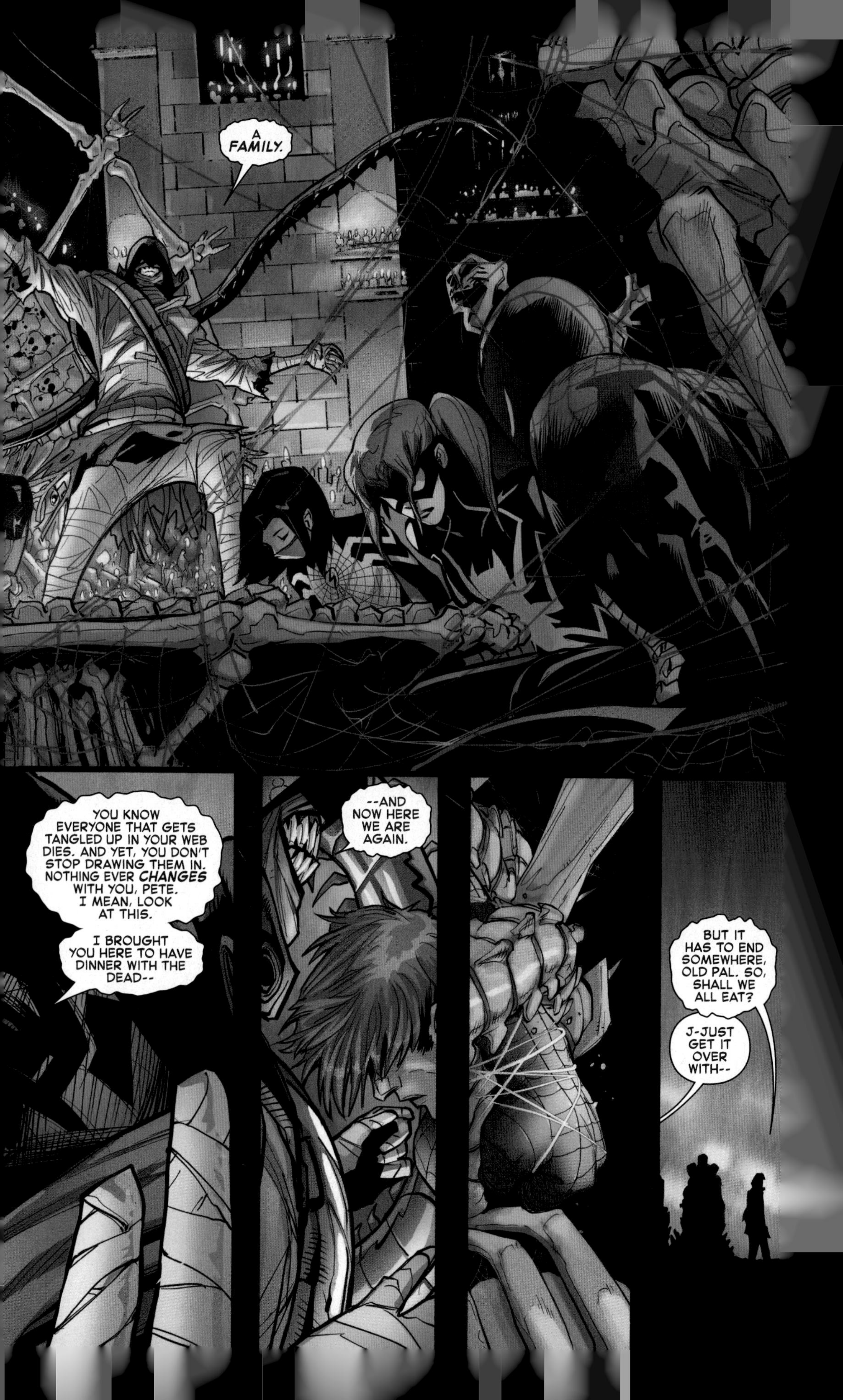
A FAMILY.
YOU KNOW EVERYONE THAT GETS TANGLED UP IN YOUR WEB DIES. AND YET, YOU DON'T STOP DRAWING THEM IN. NOTHING EVER CHANGES WITH YOU, PETE. I MEAN, LOOK AT THIS.
I BROUGHT YOU HERE TO HAVE DINNER WITH THE DEAD--
--AND NOW HERE WE ARE AGAIN.
BUT IT HAS TO END SOMEWHERE, OLD PAL. SO, SHALL WE ALL EAT?
J-JUST GET IT OVER WITH--

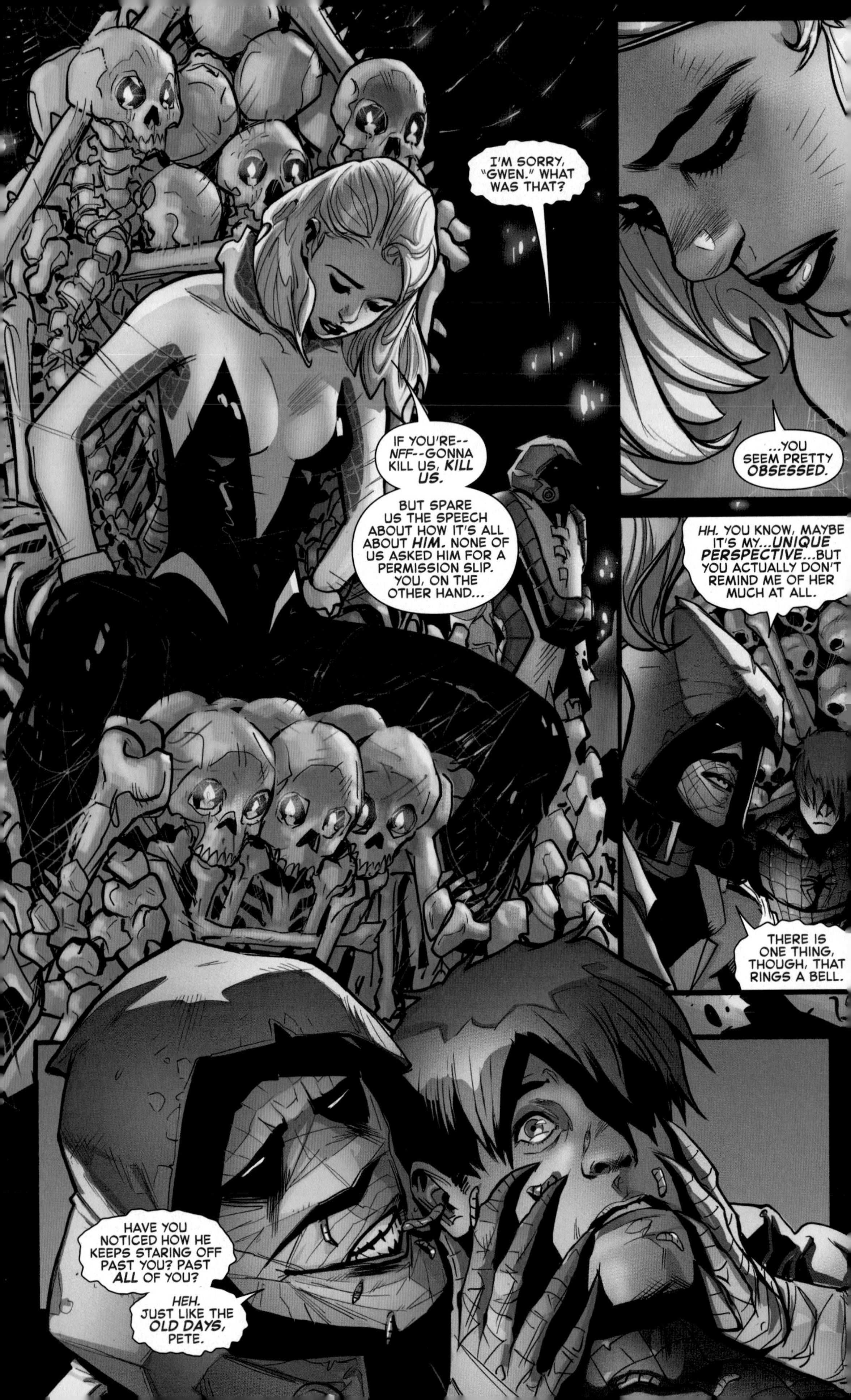
I'M SORRY, "GWEN." WHAT WAS THAT?
IF YOU'RE-- NFF--GONNA KILL US, KILL US.
BUT SPARE US THE SPEECH ABOUT HOW IT'S ALL ABOUT HIM. NONE OF US ASKED HIM FOR A PERMISSION SLIP. YOU, ON THE OTHER HAND...
...YOU SEEM PRETTY OBSESSED.
HH. YOU KNOW, MAYBE IT'S MY...UNIQUE PERSPECTIVE...BUT YOU ACTUALLY DON'T REMIND ME OF HER MUCH AT ALL.
THERE IS ONE THING, THOUGH, THAT RINGS A BELL.
HAVE YOU NOTICED HOW HE KEEPS STARING OFF PAST YOU? PAST ALL OF YOU?
HEH. JUST LIKE THE OLD DAYS, PETE.

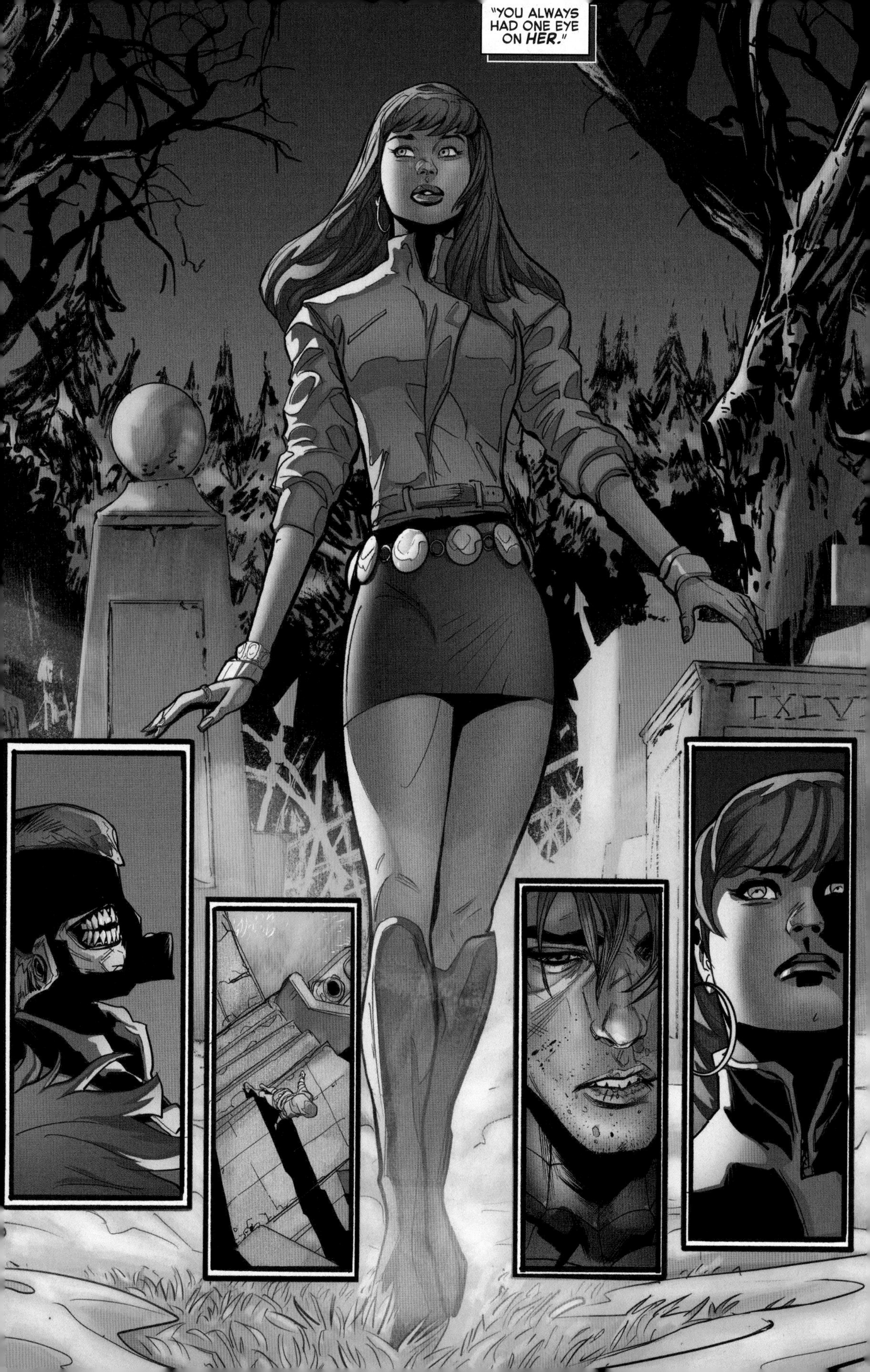
"YOU ALWAYS HAD ONE EYE ON HER."
IXIV

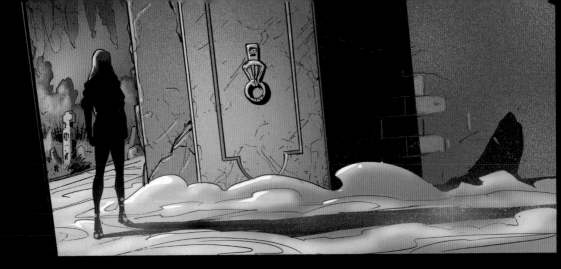

MJ!
NO--GET
OUT OF
HERE!

NONSENSE, PETE.
MJ, DON'T LISTEN
TO HIM.
PLEASE--

--DO
COME
IN.

YOU DON'T
KNOW HOW
MUCH IT WARMS
MY COLD, DEAD
HEART--

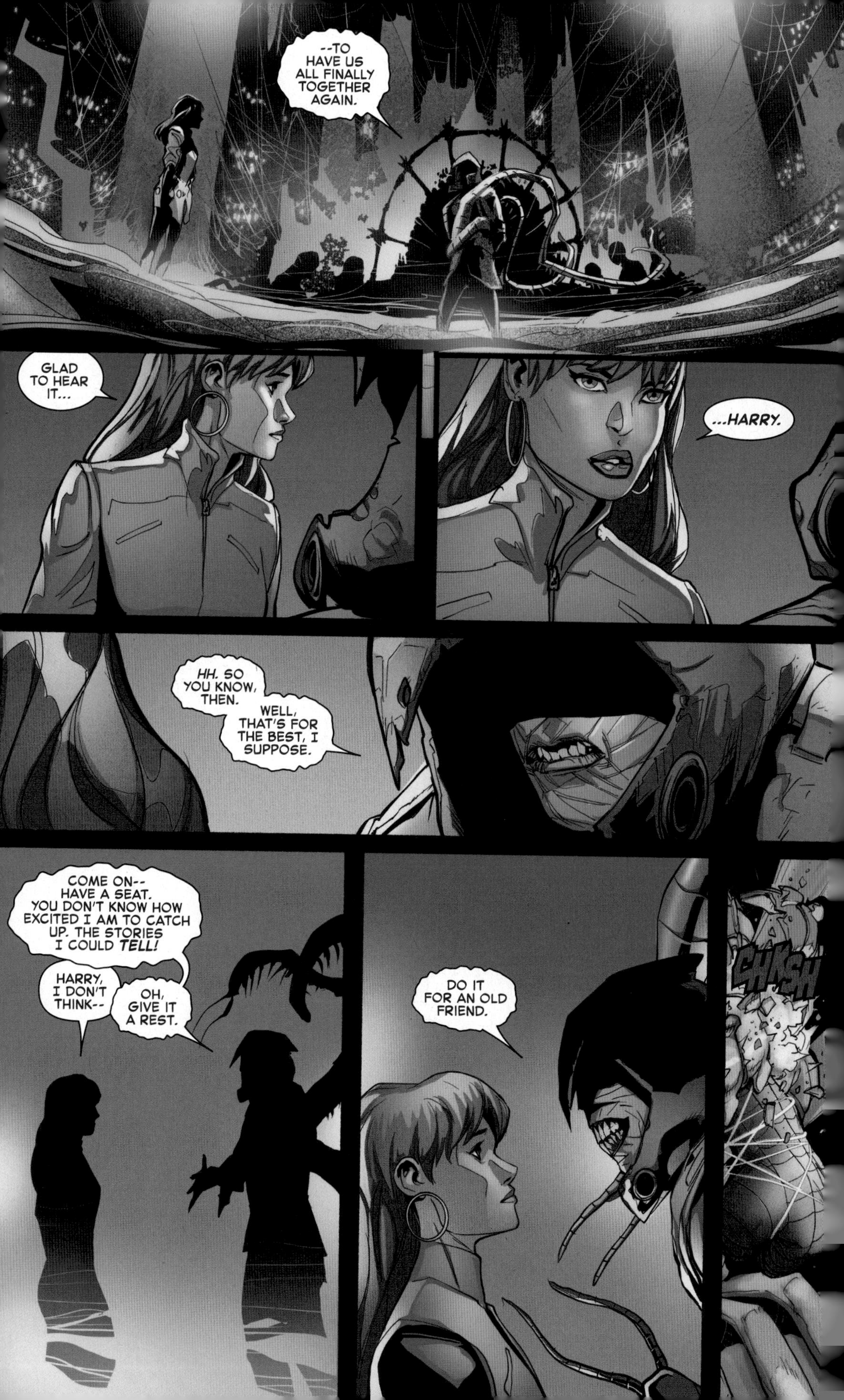
--TO HAVE US ALL FINALLY TOGETHER AGAIN.
GLAD TO HEAR IT...
...HARRY.
HH. SO YOU KNOW, THEN.
WELL, THAT'S FOR THE BEST, I SUPPOSE.
COME ON-- HAVE A SEAT. YOU DON'T KNOW HOW EXCITED I AM TO CATCH UP. THE STORIES I COULD TELL!
HARRY, I DON'T THINK--
OH, GIVE IT A REST.
DO IT FOR AN OLD FRIEND.
CHKSH

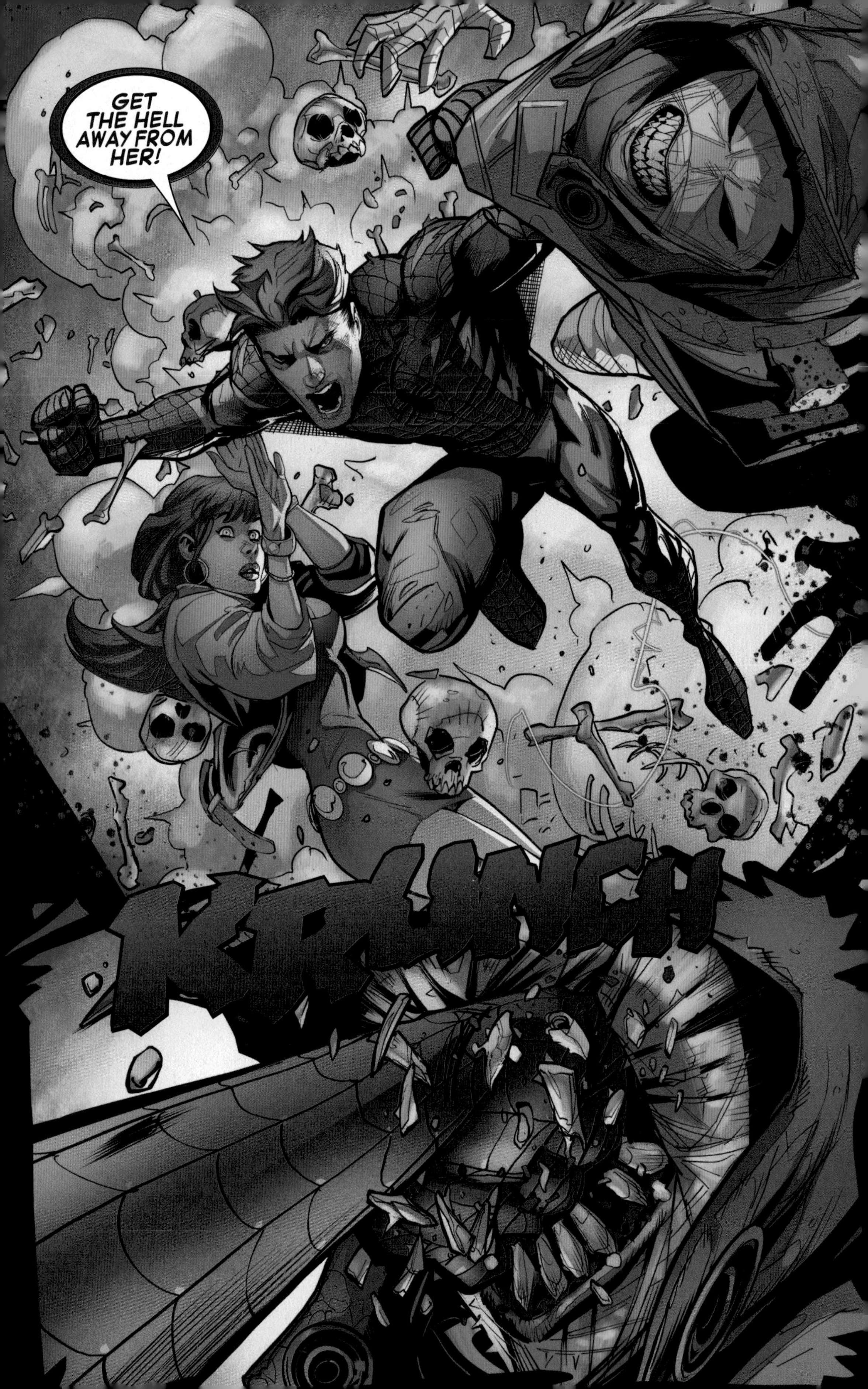
GET THE HELL AWAY FROM HER!
KRUNCH

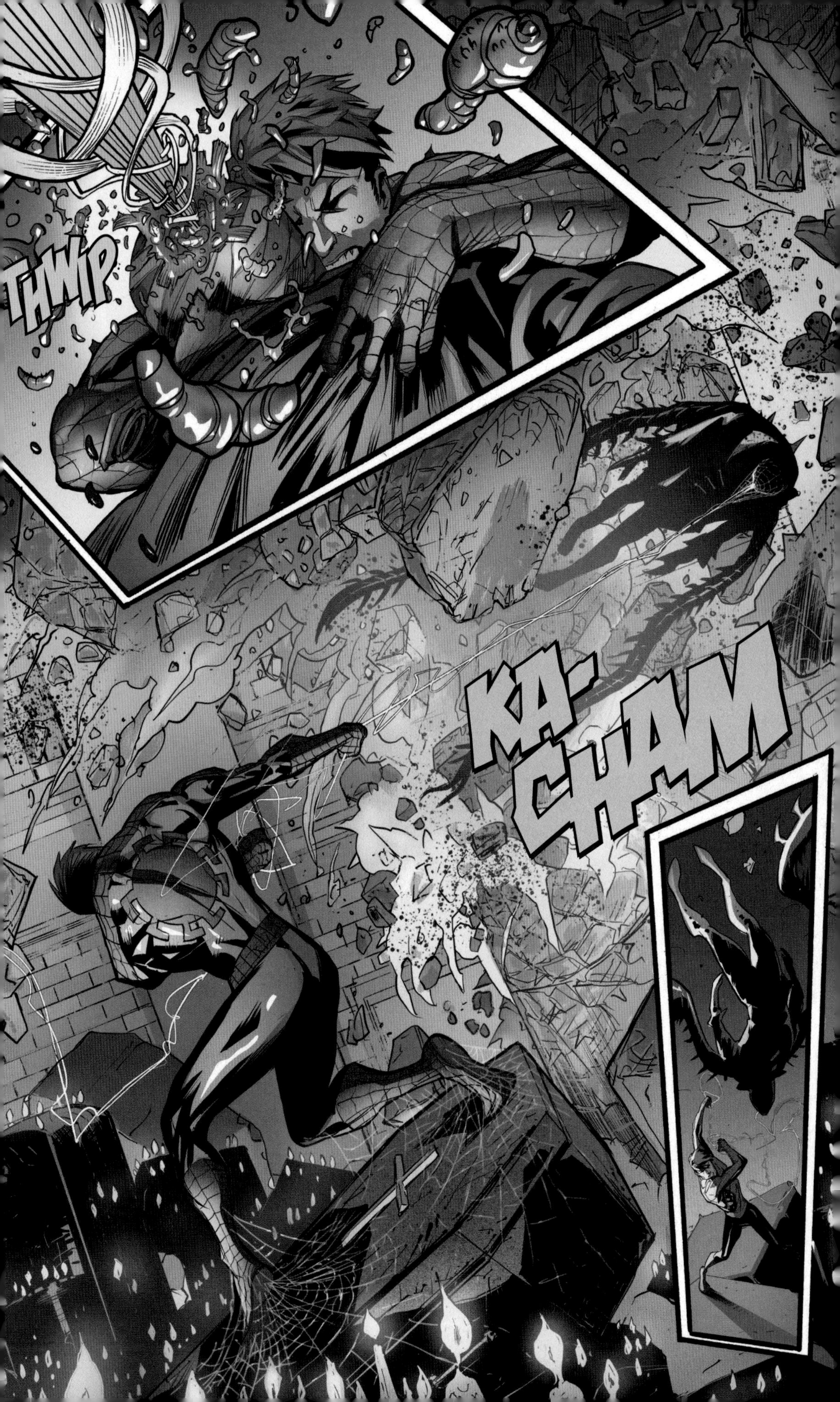
THWIP
KA-CHAM

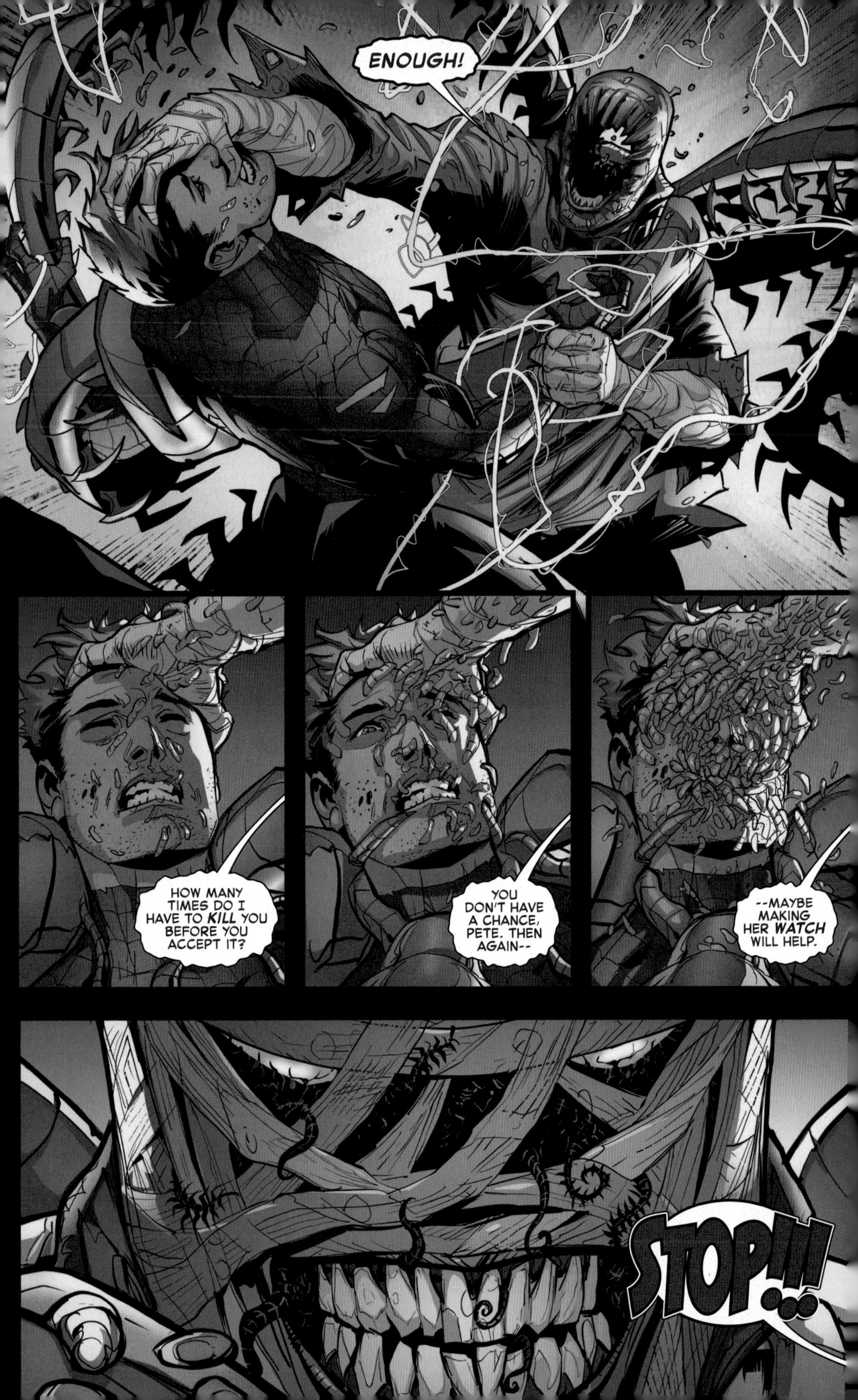
ENOUGH!
HOW MANY TIMES DO I HAVE TO KILL YOU BEFORE YOU ACCEPT IT?
YOU DON'T HAVE A CHANCE, PETE. THEN AGAIN--
--MAYBE MAKING HER WATCH WILL HELP.
STOP!!!

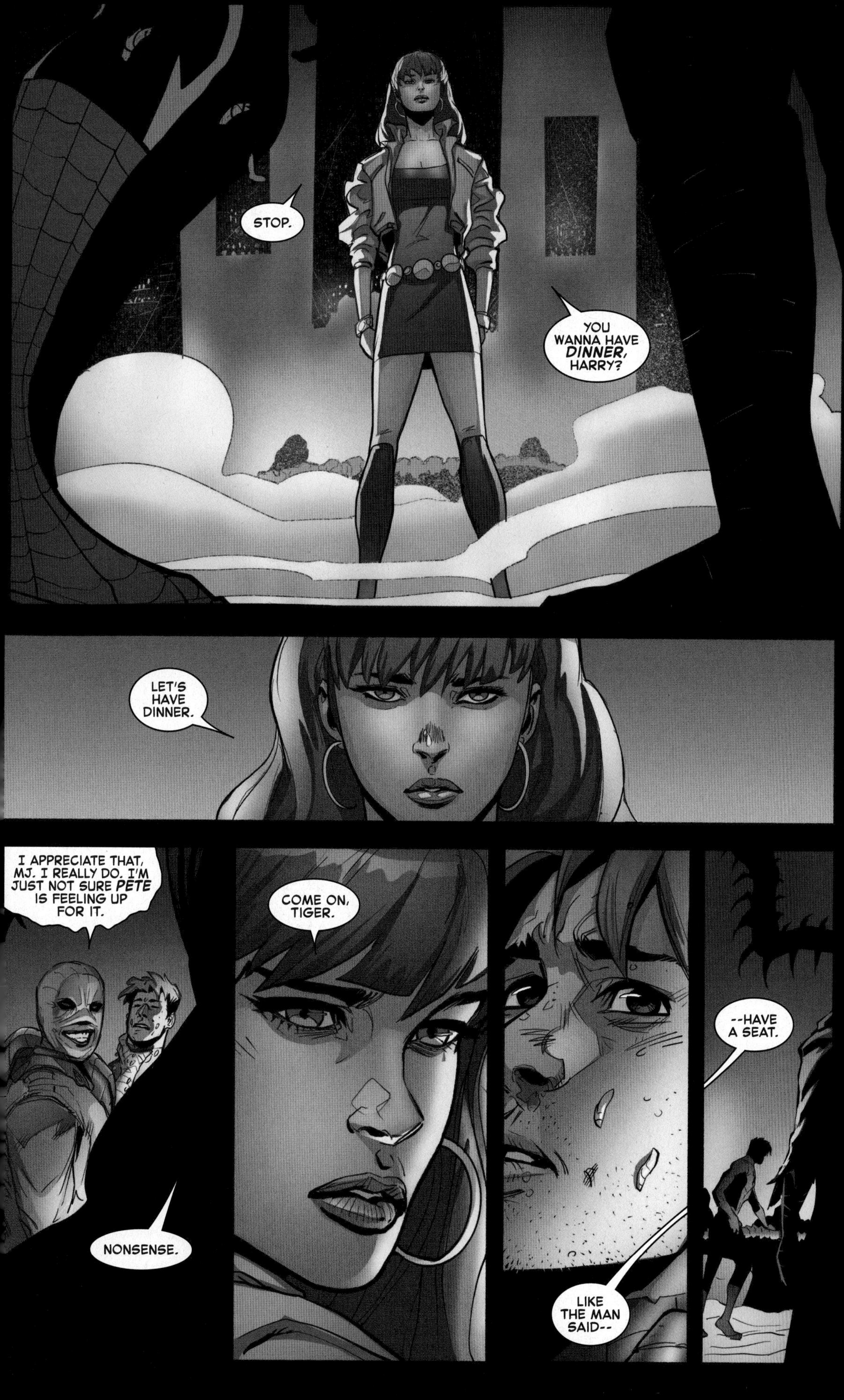
STOP.
YOU WANNA HAVE DINNER, HARRY?
LET'S HAVE DINNER.
I APPRECIATE THAT, MJ. I REALLY DO. I'M JUST NOT SURE PETE IS FEELING UP FOR IT.
NONSENSE.
COME ON, TIGER.
LIKE THE MAN SAID--
--HAVE A SEAT.

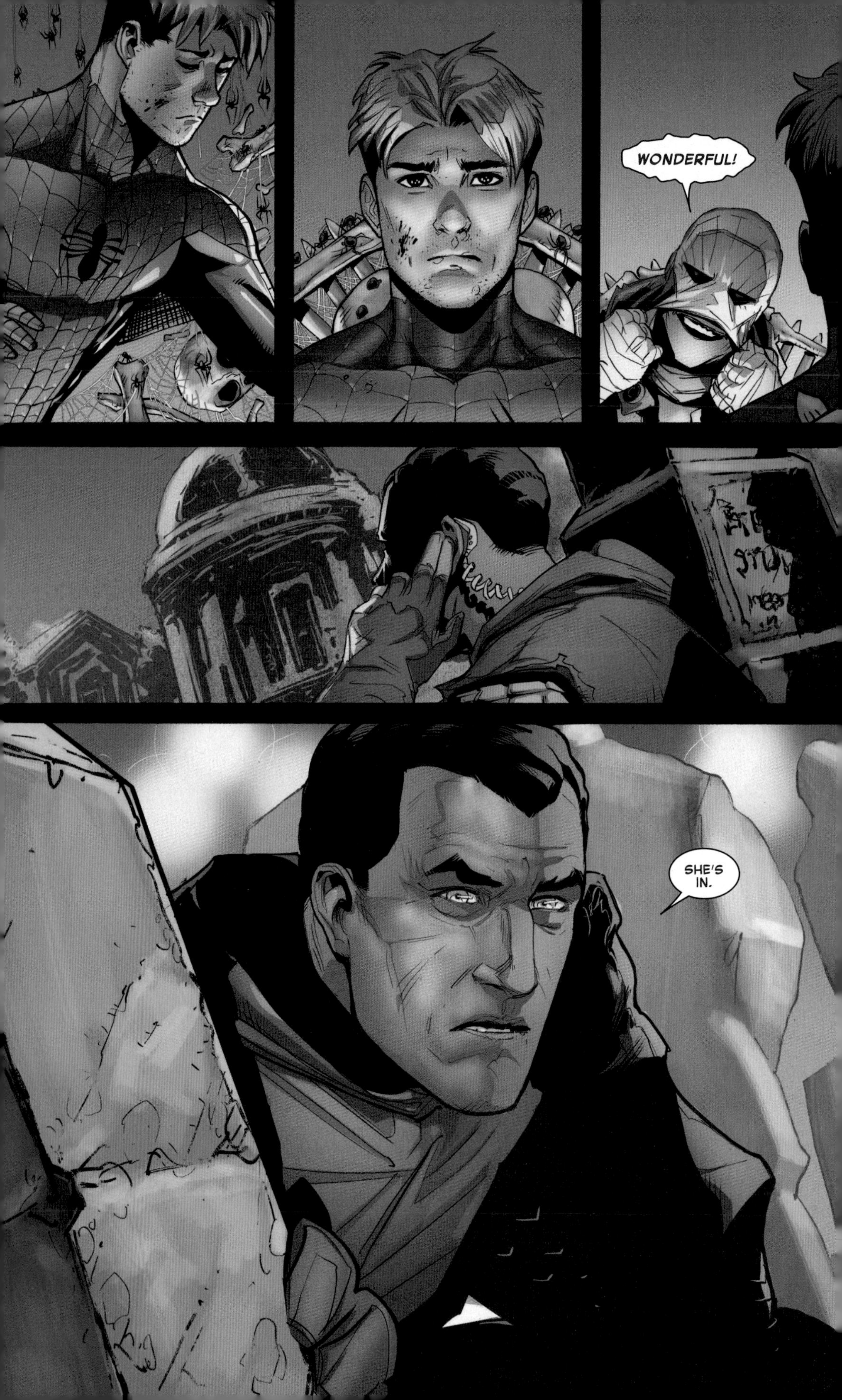
WONDERFUL!
SHE'S IN.

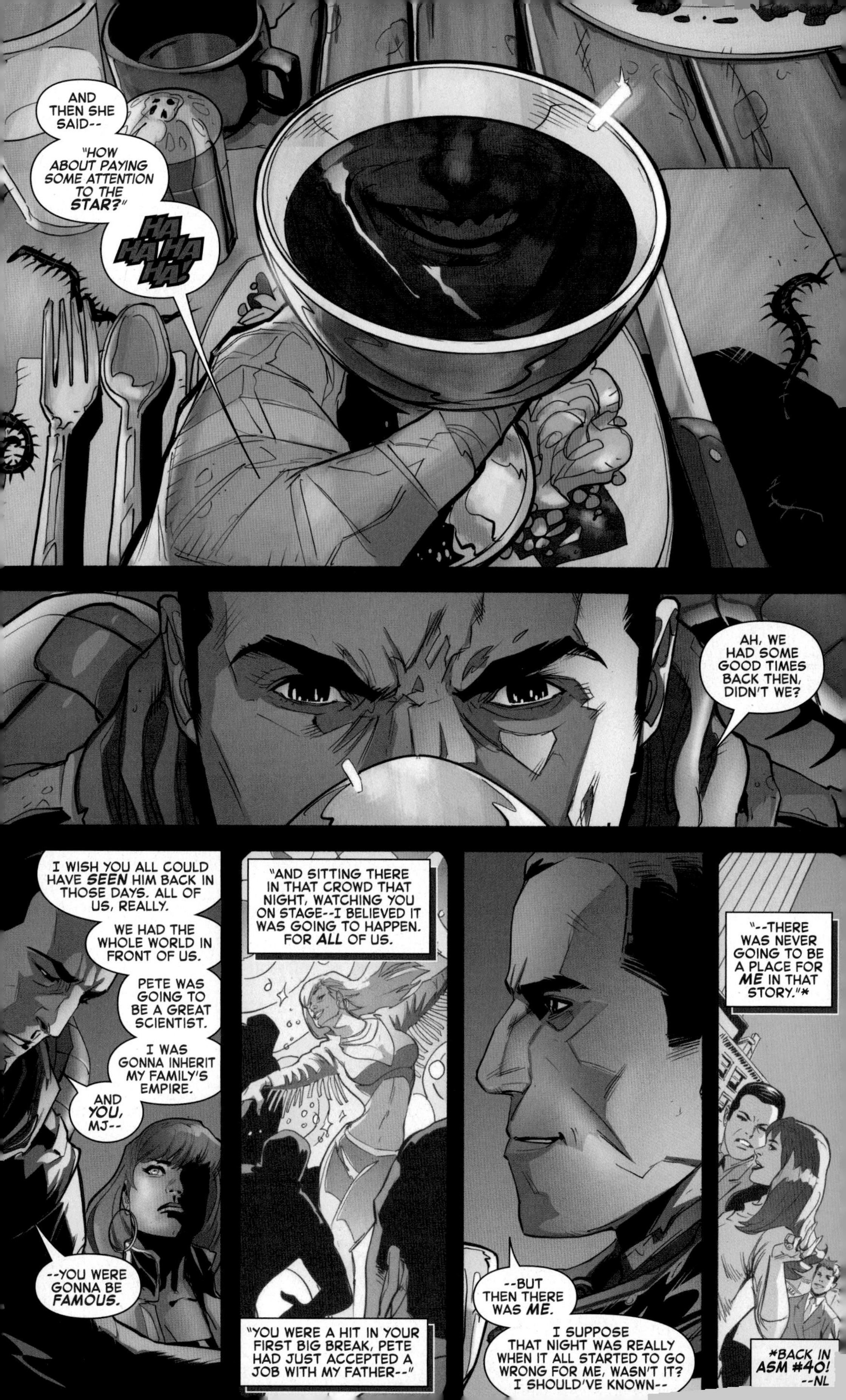
AND THEN SHE SAID--
"HOW ABOUT PAYING SOME ATTENTION TO THE STAR?"
HA HA HA HA HA!
AH, WE HAD SOME GOOD TIMES BACK THEN, DIDN'T WE?
I WISH YOU ALL COULD HAVE SEEN HIM BACK IN THOSE DAYS. ALL OF US, REALLY.
WE HAD THE WHOLE WORLD IN FRONT OF US.
PETE WAS GOING TO BE A GREAT SCIENTIST.
I WAS GONNA INHERIT MY FAMILY'S EMPIRE.
AND YOU, MJ--
--YOU WERE GONNA BE FAMOUS.
"AND SITTING THERE IN THAT CROWD THAT NIGHT, WATCHING YOU ON STAGE--I BELIEVED IT WAS GOING TO HAPPEN. FOR ALL OF US.
"YOU WERE A HIT IN YOUR FIRST BIG BREAK, PETE HAD JUST ACCEPTED A JOB WITH MY FATHER--"
--BUT THEN THERE WAS ME.
I SUPPOSE THAT NIGHT WAS REALLY WHEN IT ALL STARTED TO GO WRONG FOR ME, WASN'T IT? I SHOULD'VE KNOWN--
"--THERE WAS NEVER GOING TO BE A PLACE FOR ME IN THAT STORY."*
*BACK IN ASM #40! --NL

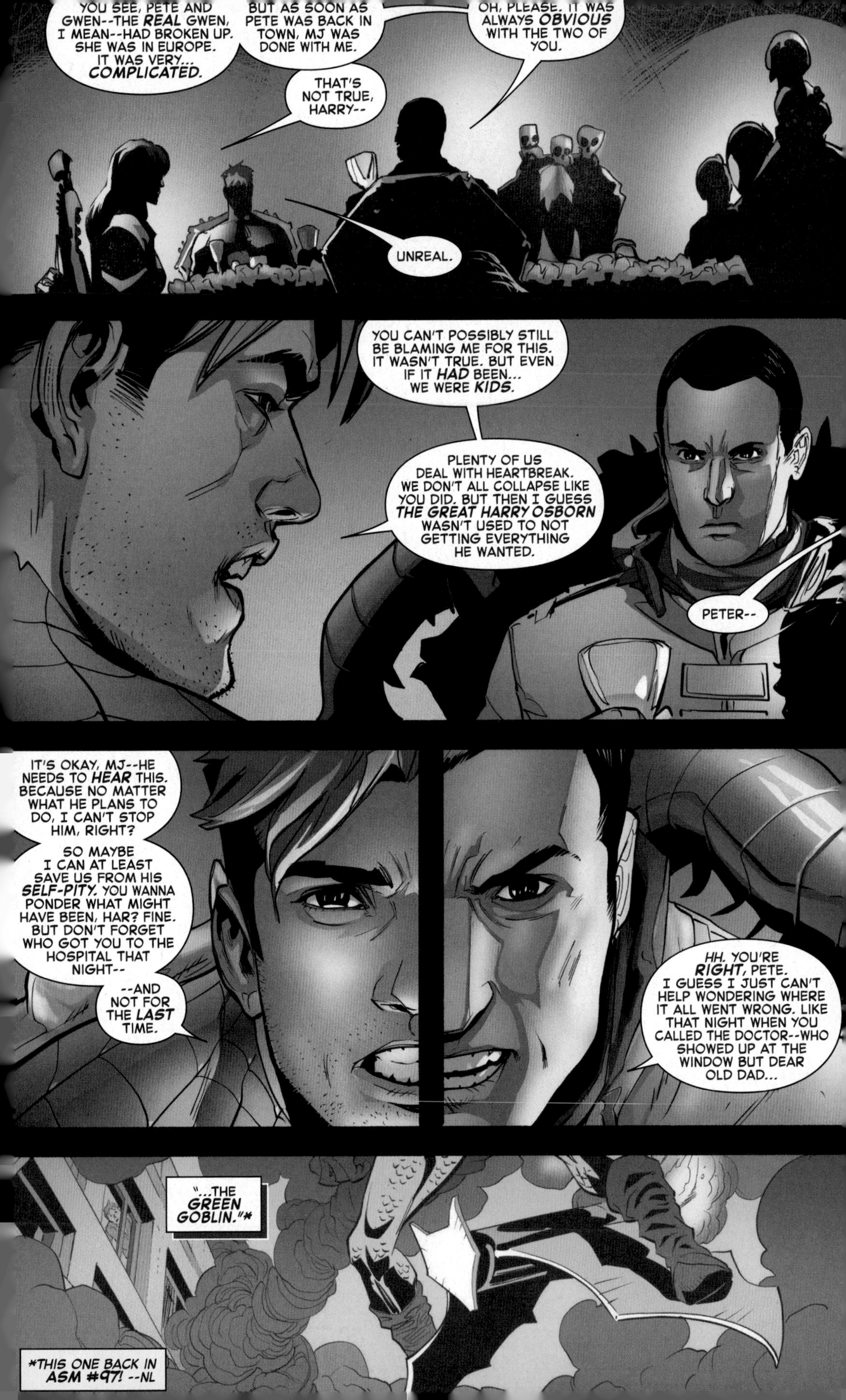

YOU SEE, PETE AND GWEN--THE REAL GWEN, I MEAN--HAD BROKEN UP. SHE WAS IN EUROPE. IT WAS VERY... COMPLICATED.
BUT AS SOON AS PETE WAS BACK IN TOWN, MJ WAS DONE WITH ME.
THAT'S NOT TRUE, HARRY--
OH, PLEASE. IT WAS ALWAYS OBVIOUS WITH THE TWO OF YOU.
UNREAL.
YOU CAN'T POSSIBLY STILL BE BLAMING ME FOR THIS. IT WASN'T TRUE. BUT EVEN IF IT HAD BEEN... WE WERE KIDS.
PLENTY OF US DEAL WITH HEARTBREAK. WE DON'T ALL COLLAPSE LIKE YOU DID. BUT THEN I GUESS THE GREAT HARRY OSBORN WASN'T USED TO NOT GETTING EVERYTHING HE WANTED.
PETER--
IT'S OKAY, MJ--HE NEEDS TO HEAR THIS. BECAUSE NO MATTER WHAT HE PLANS TO DO, I CAN'T STOP HIM, RIGHT?
SO MAYBE I CAN AT LEAST SAVE US FROM HIS SELF-PITY. YOU WANNA PONDER WHAT MIGHT HAVE BEEN, HAR? FINE. BUT DON'T FORGET WHO GOT YOU TO THE HOSPITAL THAT NIGHT--
--AND NOT FOR THE LAST TIME.
HH. YOU'RE RIGHT, PETE. I GUESS I JUST CAN'T HELP WONDERING WHERE IT ALL WENT WRONG. LIKE THAT NIGHT WHEN YOU CALLED THE DOCTOR--WHO SHOWED UP AT THE WINDOW BUT DEAR OLD DAD...
"...THE GREEN GOBLIN."*
*THIS ONE BACK IN ASM #97! --NL

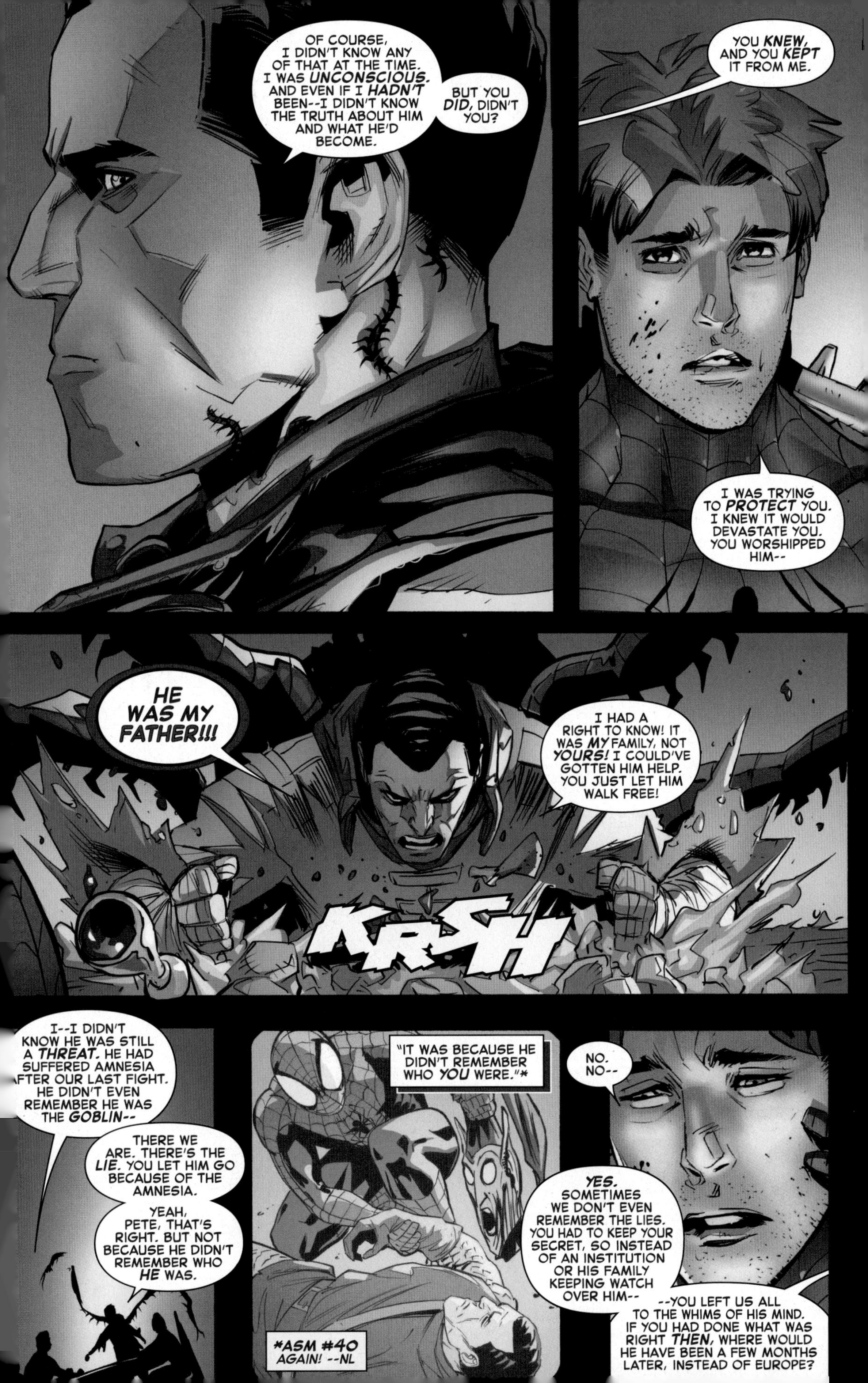

OF COURSE, I DIDN'T KNOW ANY OF THAT AT THE TIME. I WAS UNCONSCIOUS. AND EVEN IF I HADN'T BEEN--I DIDN'T KNOW THE TRUTH ABOUT HIM AND WHAT HE'D BECOME.
BUT YOU DID, DIDN'T YOU?
YOU KNEW, AND YOU KEPT IT FROM ME.
I WAS TRYING TO PROTECT YOU. I KNEW IT WOULD DEVASTATE YOU. YOU WORSHIPPED HIM--
HE WAS MY FATHER!!!
I HAD A RIGHT TO KNOW! IT WAS MY FAMILY, NOT YOURS! I COULD'VE GOTTEN HIM HELP. YOU JUST LET HIM WALK FREE!
KRSH
I--I DIDN'T KNOW HE WAS STILL A THREAT. HE HAD SUFFERED AMNESIA AFTER OUR LAST FIGHT. HE DIDN'T EVEN REMEMBER HE WAS THE GOBLIN--
THERE WE ARE. THERE'S THE LIE. YOU LET HIM GO BECAUSE OF THE AMNESIA.
YEAH, PETE, THAT'S RIGHT. BUT NOT BECAUSE HE DIDN'T REMEMBER WHO HE WAS.
"IT WAS BECAUSE HE DIDN'T REMEMBER WHO YOU WERE."*
*ASM #40 AGAIN! --NL
NO. NO--
YES. SOMETIMES WE DON'T EVEN REMEMBER THE LIES. YOU HAD TO KEEP YOUR SECRET, SO INSTEAD OF AN INSTITUTION OR HIS FAMILY KEEPING WATCH OVER HIM--
--YOU LEFT US ALL TO THE WHIMS OF HIS MIND. IF YOU HAD DONE WHAT WAS RIGHT THEN, WHERE WOULD HE HAVE BEEN A FEW MONTHS LATER, INSTEAD OF EUROPE?

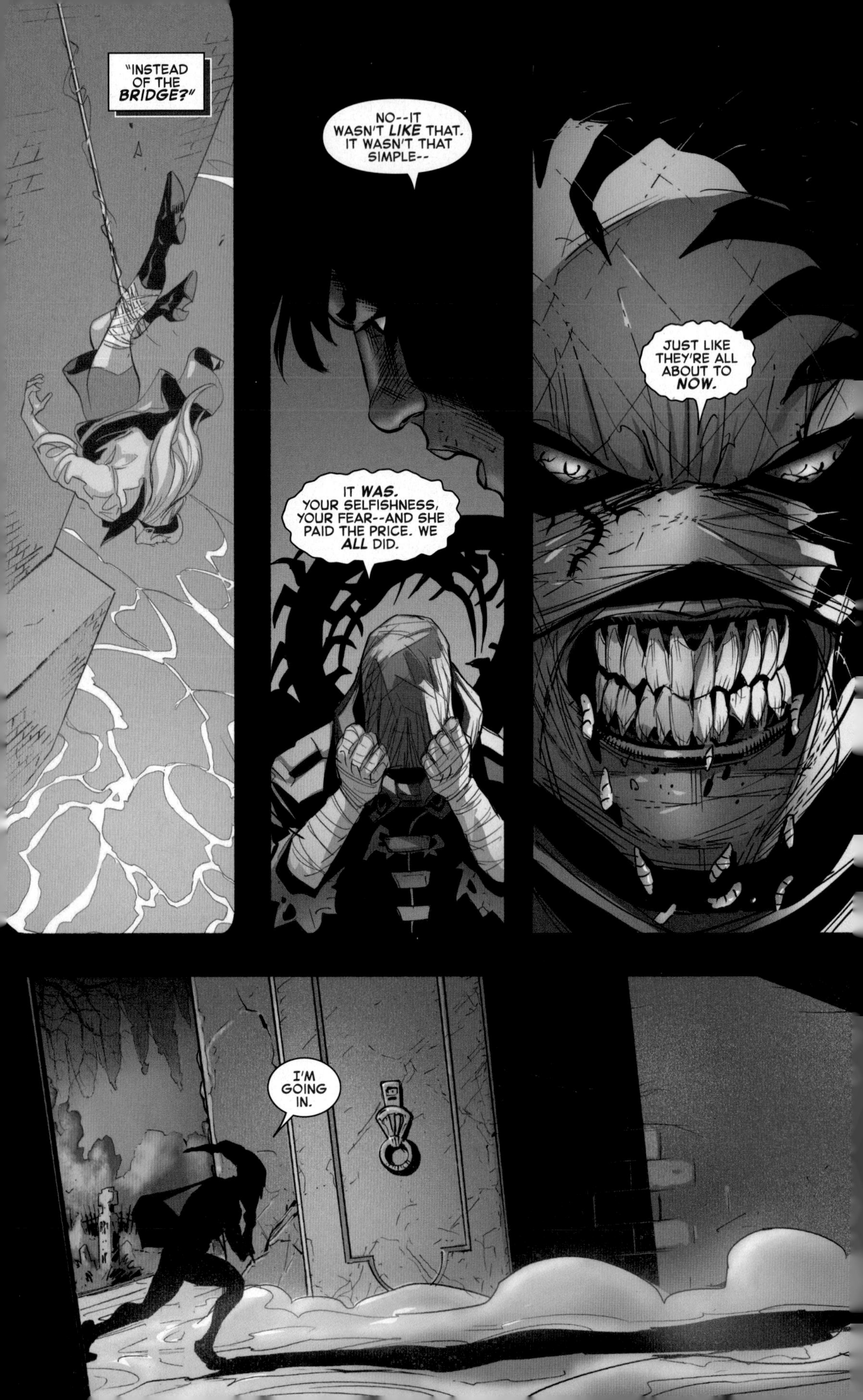
"INSTEAD OF THE BRIDGE?"
NO--IT WASN'T LIKE THAT. IT WASN'T THAT SIMPLE--
IT WAS. YOUR SELFISHNESS, YOUR FEAR--AND SHE PAID THE PRICE. WE ALL DID.
JUST LIKE THEY'RE ALL ABOUT TO NOW.
I'M GOING IN.

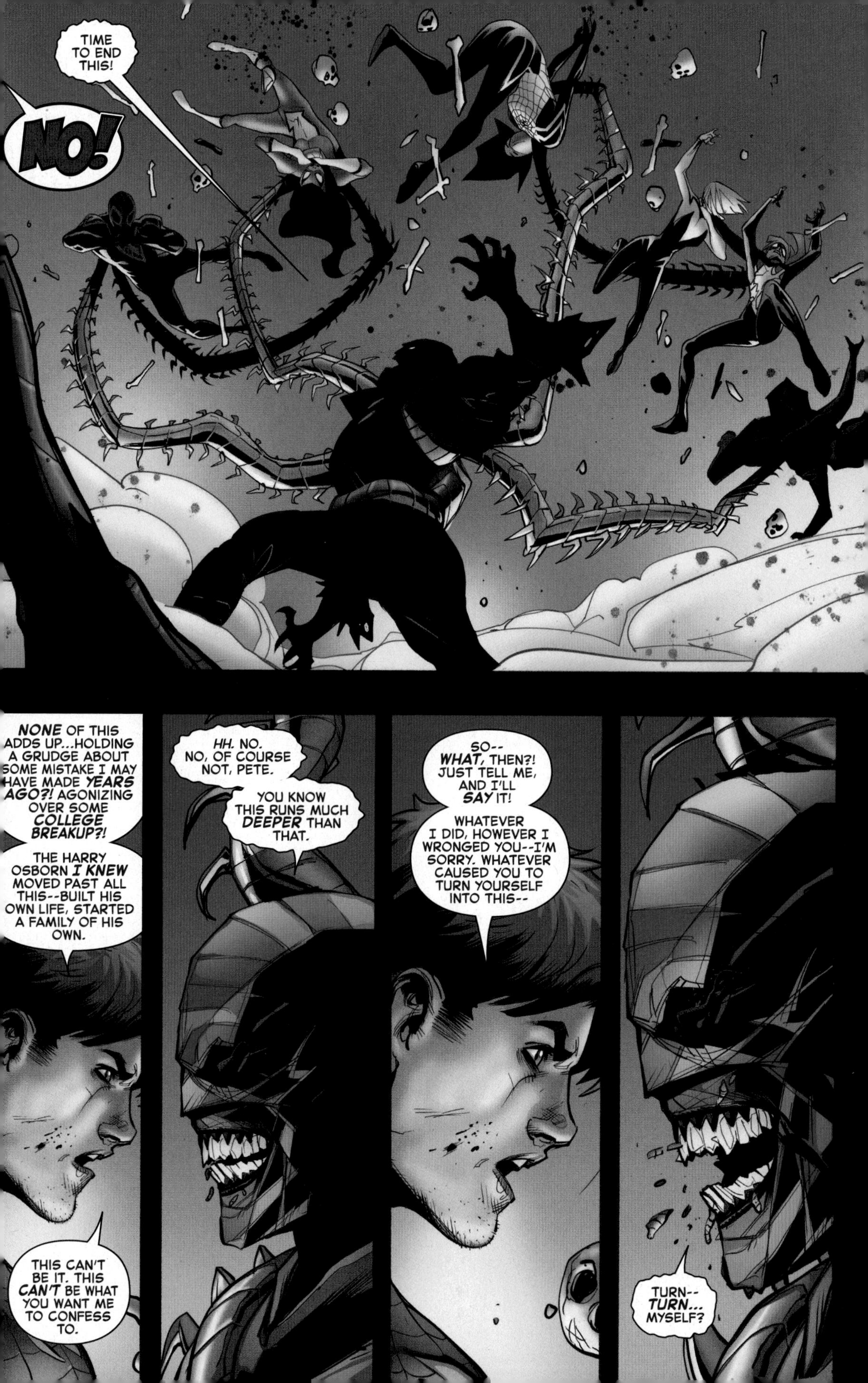
TIME TO END THIS!
NO!
NONE OF THIS ADDS UP...HOLDING A GRUDGE ABOUT SOME MISTAKE I MAY HAVE MADE YEARS AGO?! AGONIZING OVER SOME COLLEGE BREAKUP?!
THE HARRY OSBORN I KNEW MOVED PAST ALL THIS--BUILT HIS OWN LIFE, STARTED A FAMILY OF HIS OWN.
THIS CAN'T BE IT. THIS CAN'T BE WHAT YOU WANT ME TO CONFESS TO.
HH. NO. NO, OF COURSE NOT, PETE.
YOU KNOW THIS RUNS MUCH DEEPER THAN THAT.
SO-- WHAT, THEN?! JUST TELL ME, AND I'LL SAY IT!
WHATEVER I DID, HOWEVER I WRONGED YOU--I'M SORRY. WHATEVER CAUSED YOU TO TURN YOURSELF INTO THIS--
TURN-- TURN... MYSELF?

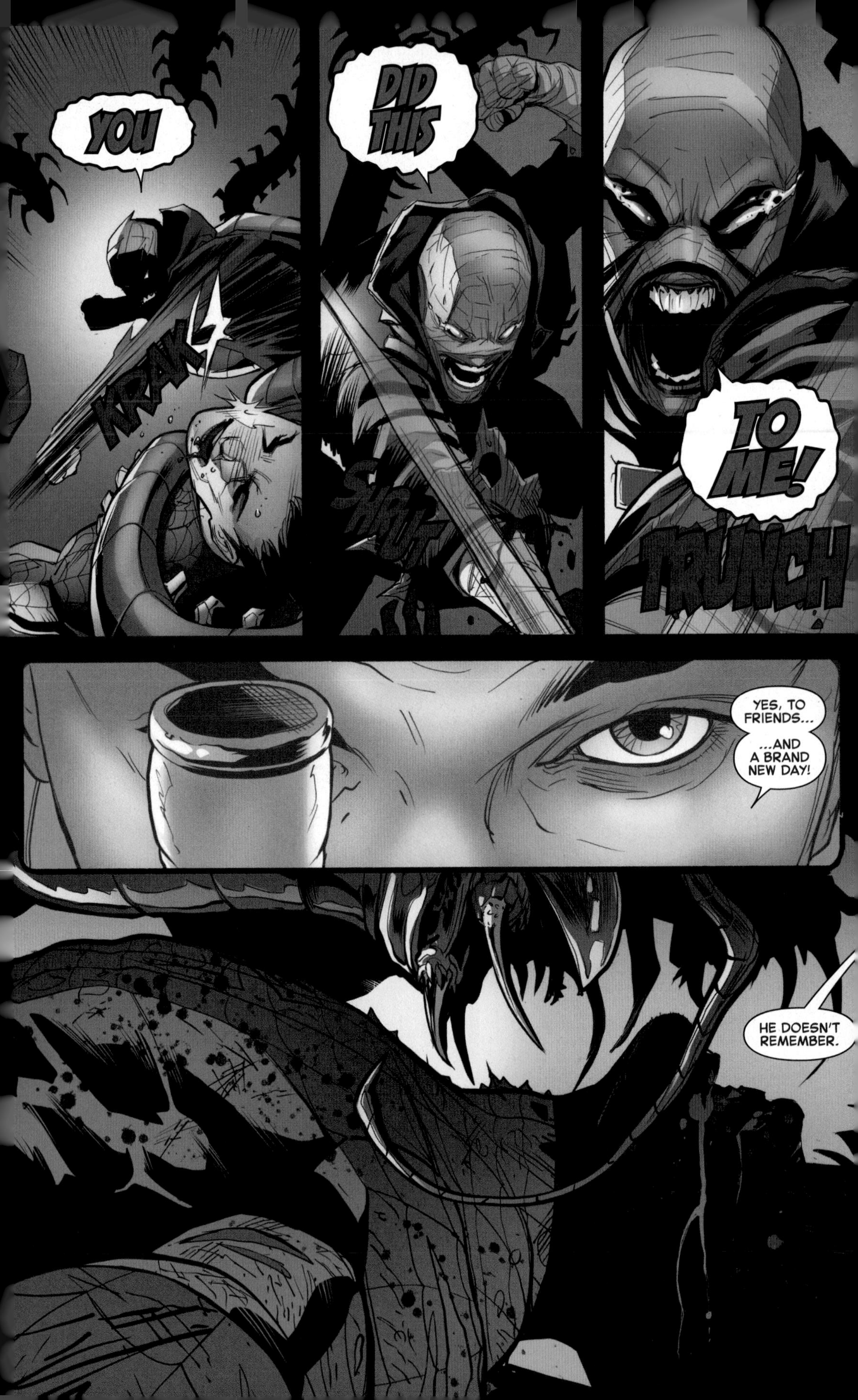
YOU
KRAK
DID THIS
SHLUT
TO ME!
TRUNCH
YES, TO FRIENDS...
...AND A BRAND NEW DAY!
HE DOESN'T REMEMBER.

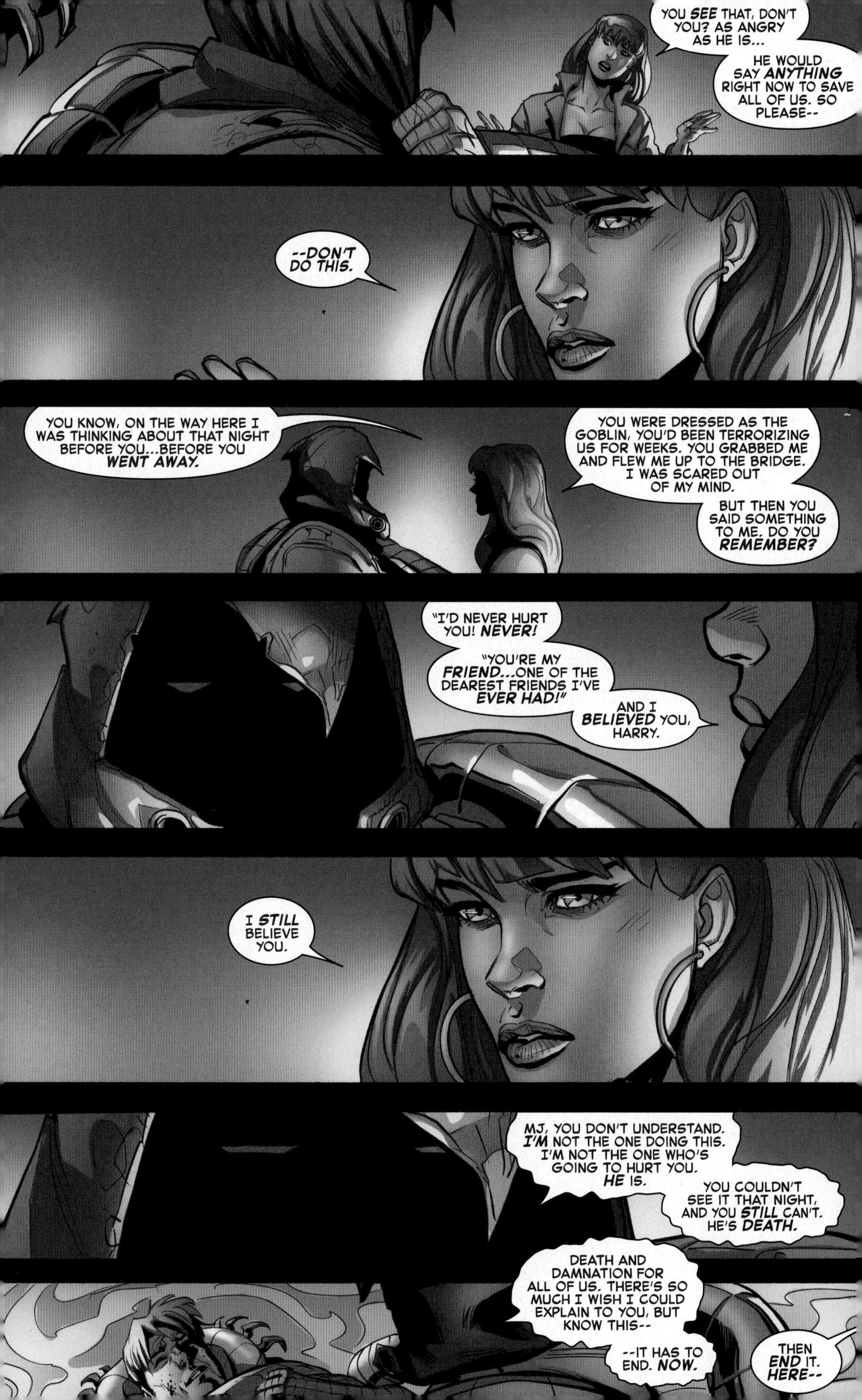
YOU SEE THAT, DON'T YOU? AS ANGRY AS HE IS...
HE WOULD SAY ANYTHING RIGHT NOW TO SAVE ALL OF US. SO PLEASE--
--DON'T DO THIS.
YOU KNOW, ON THE WAY HERE I WAS THINKING ABOUT THAT NIGHT BEFORE YOU...BEFORE YOU WENT AWAY.
YOU WERE DRESSED AS THE GOBLIN, YOU'D BEEN TERRORIZING US FOR WEEKS. YOU GRABBED ME AND FLEW ME UP TO THE BRIDGE. I WAS SCARED OUT OF MY MIND.
BUT THEN YOU SAID SOMETHING TO ME. DO YOU REMEMBER?
"I'D NEVER HURT YOU! NEVER!
"YOU'RE MY FRIEND...ONE OF THE DEAREST FRIENDS I'VE EVER HAD!"
AND I BELIEVED YOU, HARRY.
I STILL BELIEVE YOU.
MJ, YOU DON'T UNDERSTAND. I'M NOT THE ONE DOING THIS. I'M NOT THE ONE WHO'S GOING TO HURT YOU. HE IS.
YOU COULDN'T SEE IT THAT NIGHT, AND YOU STILL CAN'T. HE'S DEATH.
DEATH AND DAMNATION FOR ALL OF US. THERE'S SO MUCH I WISH I COULD EXPLAIN TO YOU, BUT KNOW THIS--
--IT HAS TO END. NOW.
THEN END IT. HERE--

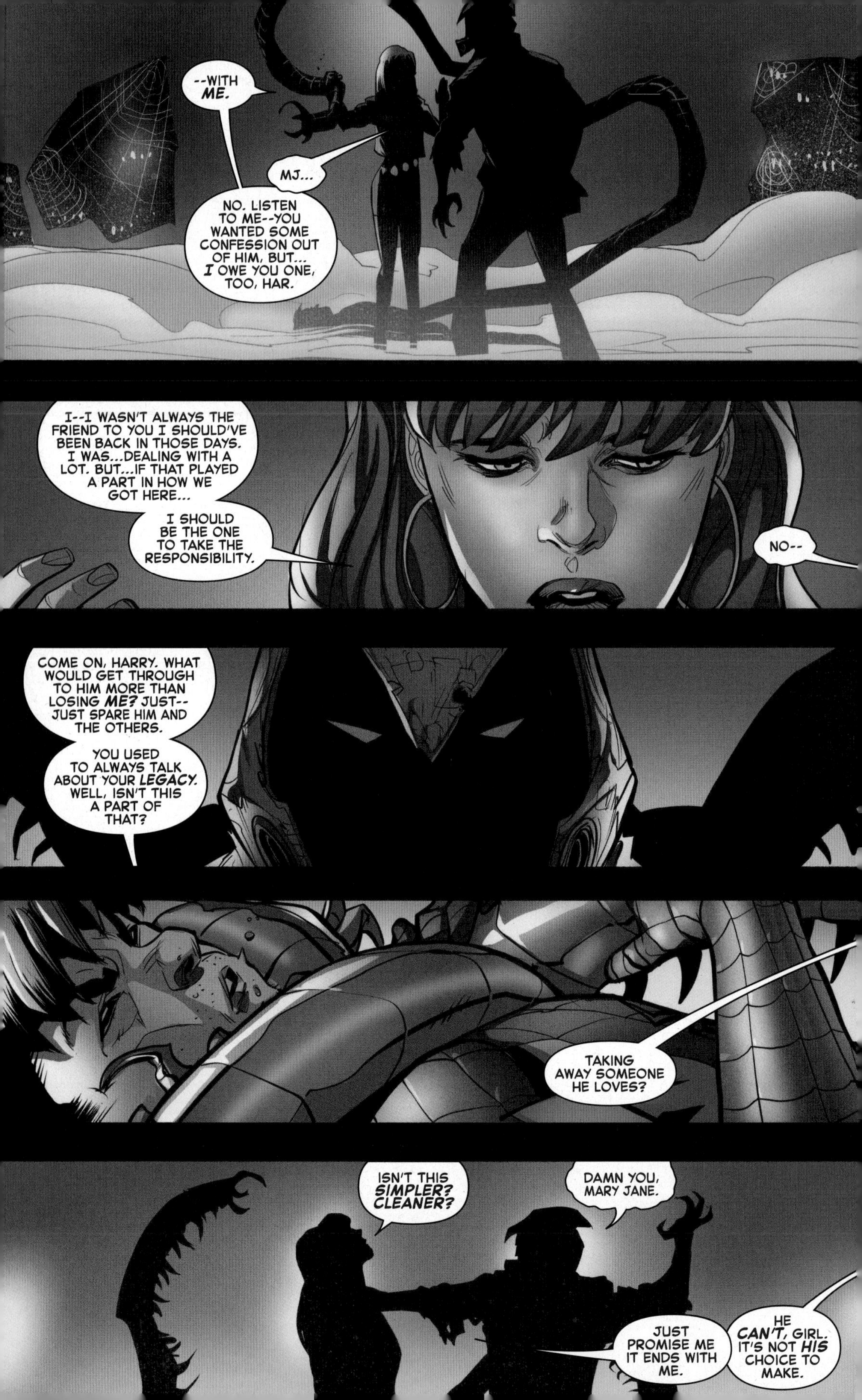
--WITH *ME.*
MJ...
NO. LISTEN TO ME--YOU WANTED SOME CONFESSION OUT OF HIM, BUT... *I* OWE YOU ONE, TOO, HAR.
I--I WASN'T ALWAYS THE FRIEND TO YOU I SHOULD'VE BEEN BACK IN THOSE DAYS. I WAS...DEALING WITH A LOT. BUT...IF THAT PLAYED A PART IN HOW WE GOT HERE...
I SHOULD BE THE ONE TO TAKE THE RESPONSIBILITY.
NO--
COME ON, HARRY. WHAT WOULD GET THROUGH TO HIM MORE THAN LOSING *ME?* JUST--JUST SPARE HIM AND THE OTHERS.
YOU USED TO ALWAYS TALK ABOUT YOUR *LEGACY.* WELL, ISN'T THIS A PART OF THAT?
TAKING AWAY SOMEONE HE LOVES?
ISN'T THIS *SIMPLER? CLEANER?*
DAMN YOU, MARY JANE.
JUST PROMISE ME IT ENDS WITH ME.
HE *CAN'T,* GIRL. IT'S NOT *HIS* CHOICE TO MAKE.

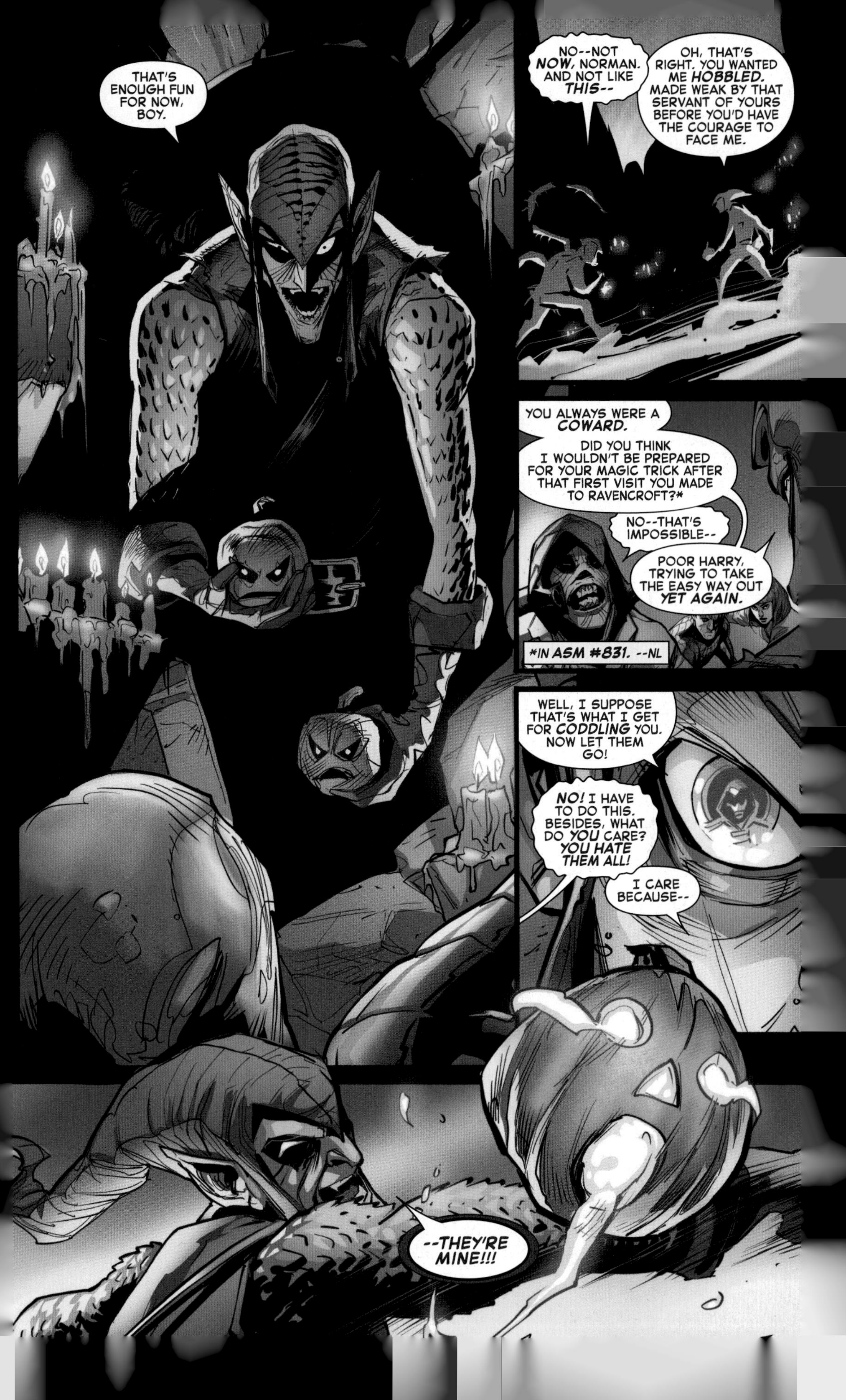
THAT'S ENOUGH FUN FOR NOW, BOY.
NO--NOT NOW, NORMAN. AND NOT LIKE THIS--
OH, THAT'S RIGHT. YOU WANTED ME HOBBLED. MADE WEAK BY THAT SERVANT OF YOURS BEFORE YOU'D HAVE THE COURAGE TO FACE ME.
YOU ALWAYS WERE A COWARD.
DID YOU THINK I WOULDN'T BE PREPARED FOR YOUR MAGIC TRICK AFTER THAT FIRST VISIT YOU MADE TO RAVENCROFT?*
NO--THAT'S IMPOSSIBLE--
POOR HARRY, TRYING TO TAKE THE EASY WAY OUT YET AGAIN.
*IN ASM #831. --NL
WELL, I SUPPOSE THAT'S WHAT I GET FOR CODDLING YOU. NOW LET THEM GO!
NO! I HAVE TO DO THIS. BESIDES, WHAT DO YOU CARE? YOU HATE THEM ALL!
I CARE BECAUSE--
--THEY'RE MINE!!!

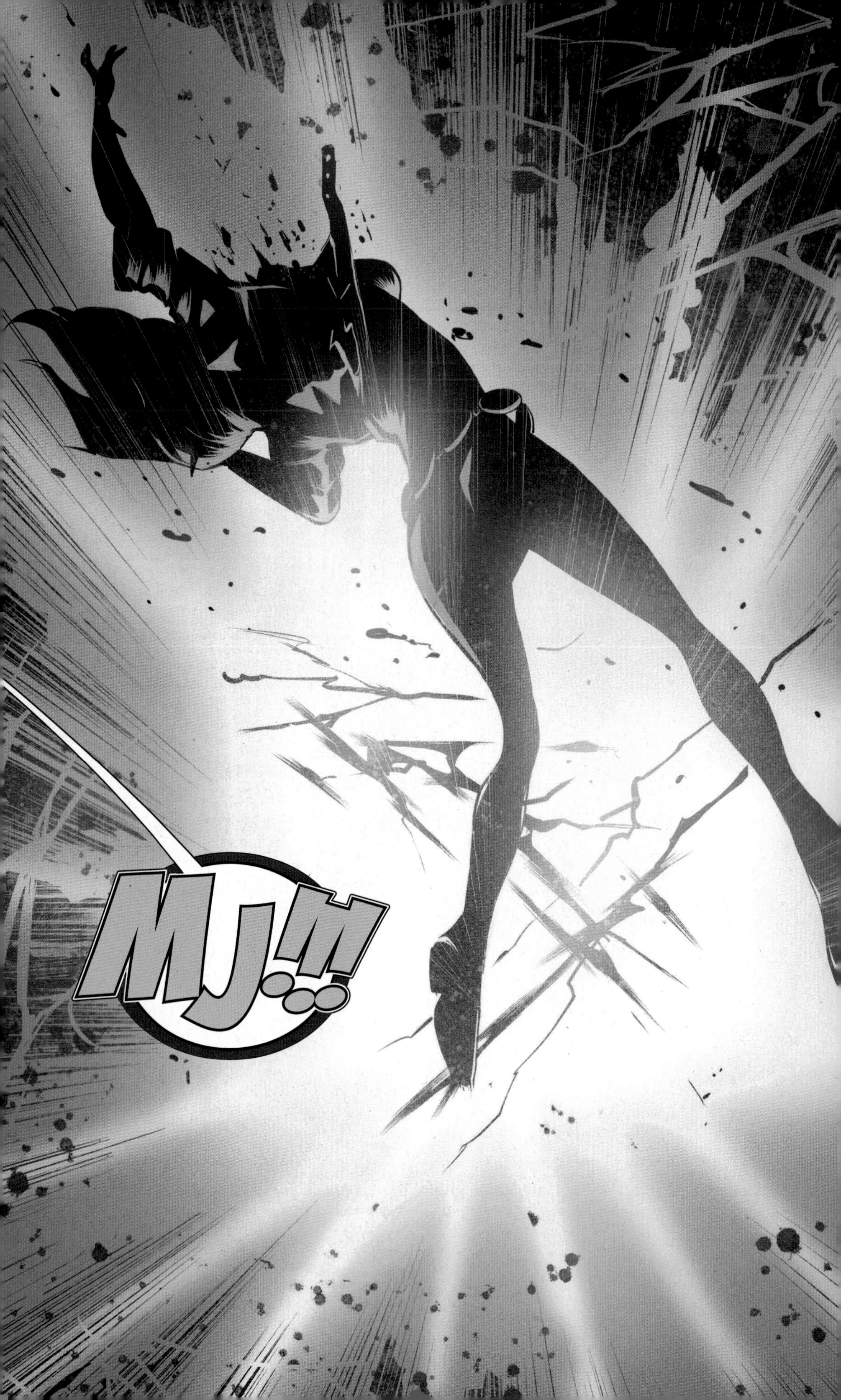
MJ...!!

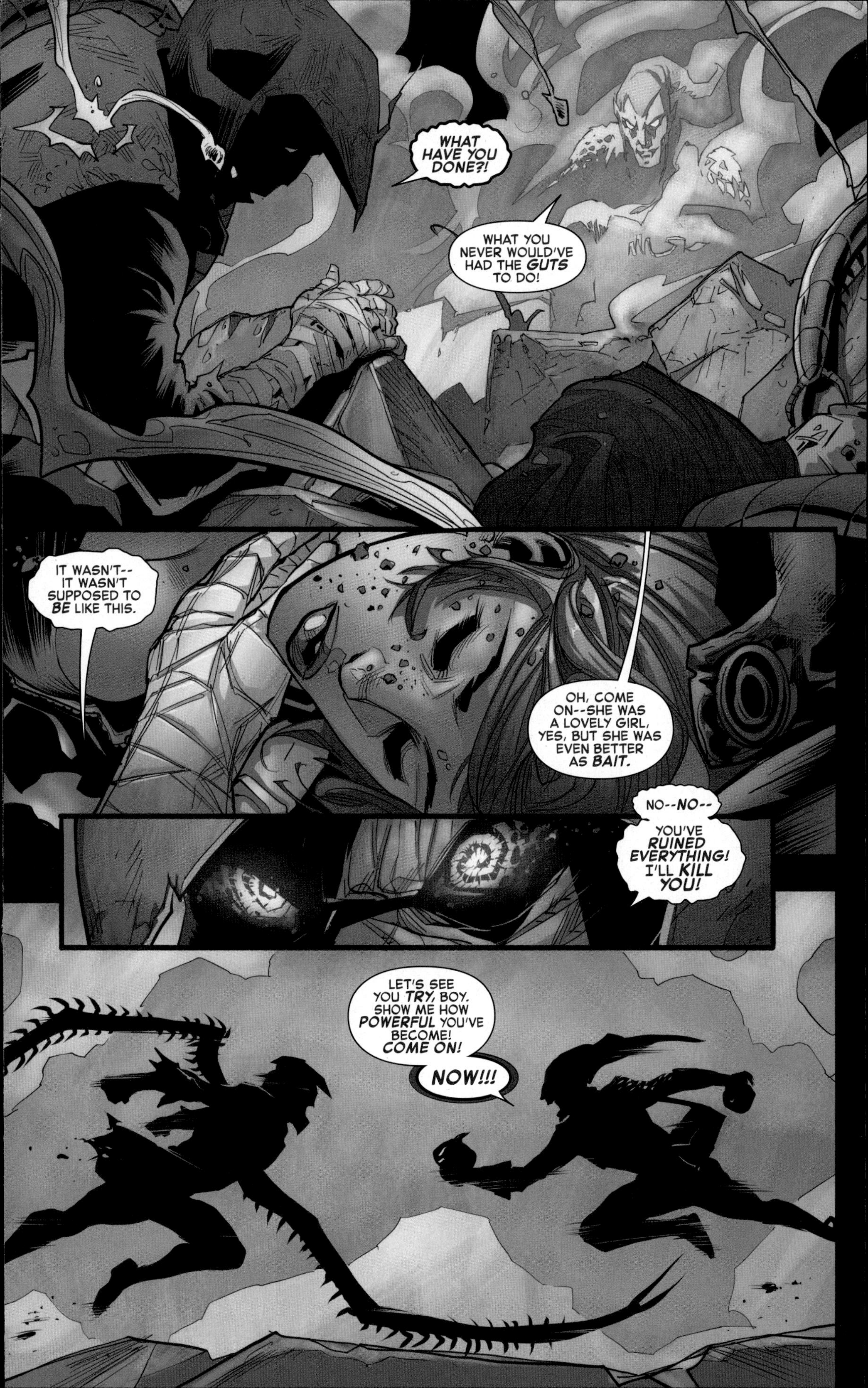
WHAT HAVE YOU DONE?!
WHAT YOU NEVER WOULD'VE HAD THE GUTS TO DO!
IT WASN'T-- IT WASN'T SUPPOSED TO BE LIKE THIS.
OH, COME ON--SHE WAS A LOVELY GIRL, YES, BUT SHE WAS EVEN BETTER AS BAIT.
NO--NO--
YOU'VE RUINED EVERYTHING! I'LL KILL YOU!
LET'S SEE YOU TRY, BOY. SHOW ME HOW POWERFUL YOU'VE BECOME! COME ON!
NOW!!!

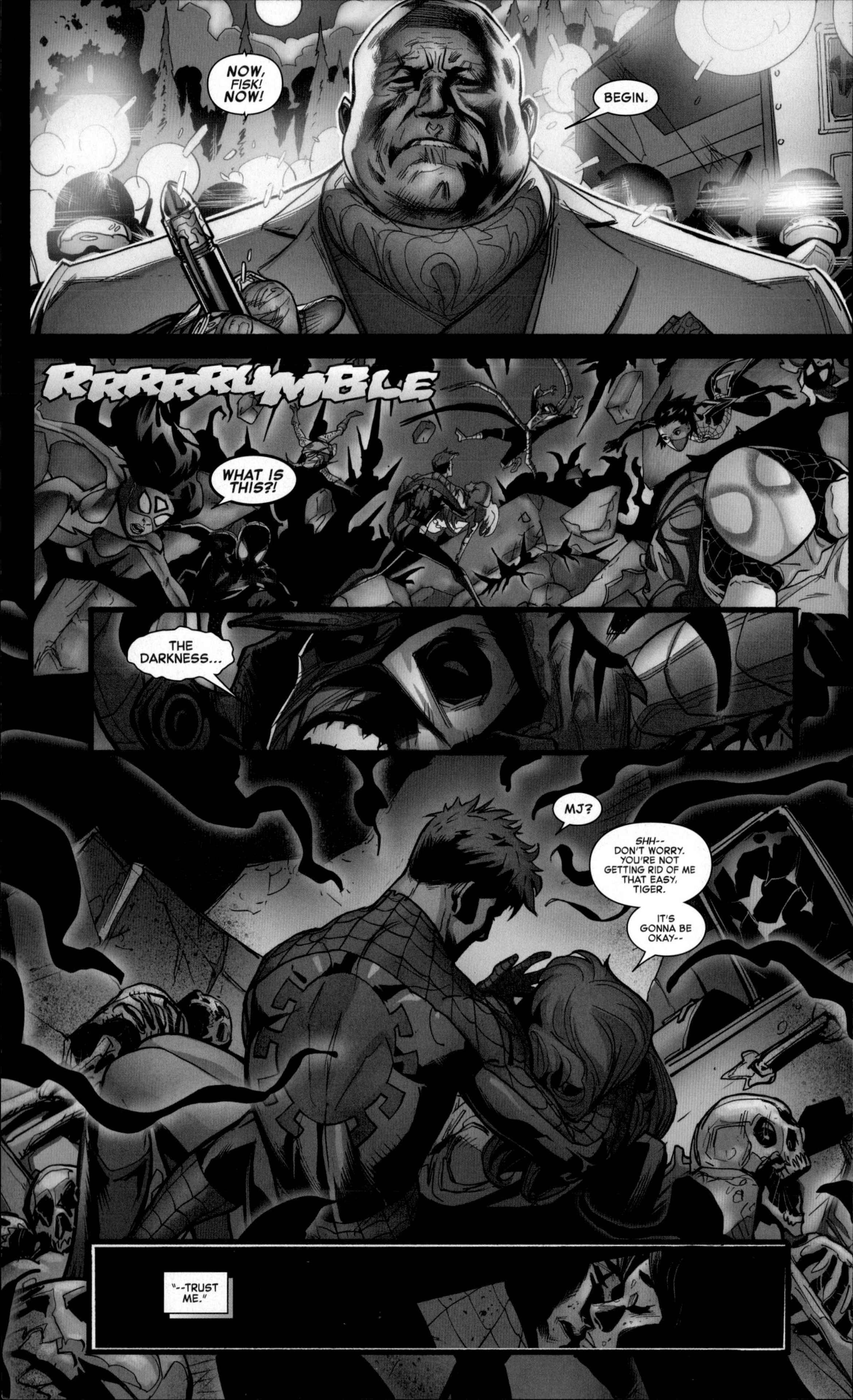
NOW, FISK! NOW!
BEGIN.
RRRRRUMBLE
WHAT IS THIS?!
THE DARKNESS...
MJ?
SHH-- DON'T WORRY. YOU'RE NOT GETTING RID OF ME THAT EASY, TIGER.
IT'S GONNA BE OKAY--
"--TRUST ME."

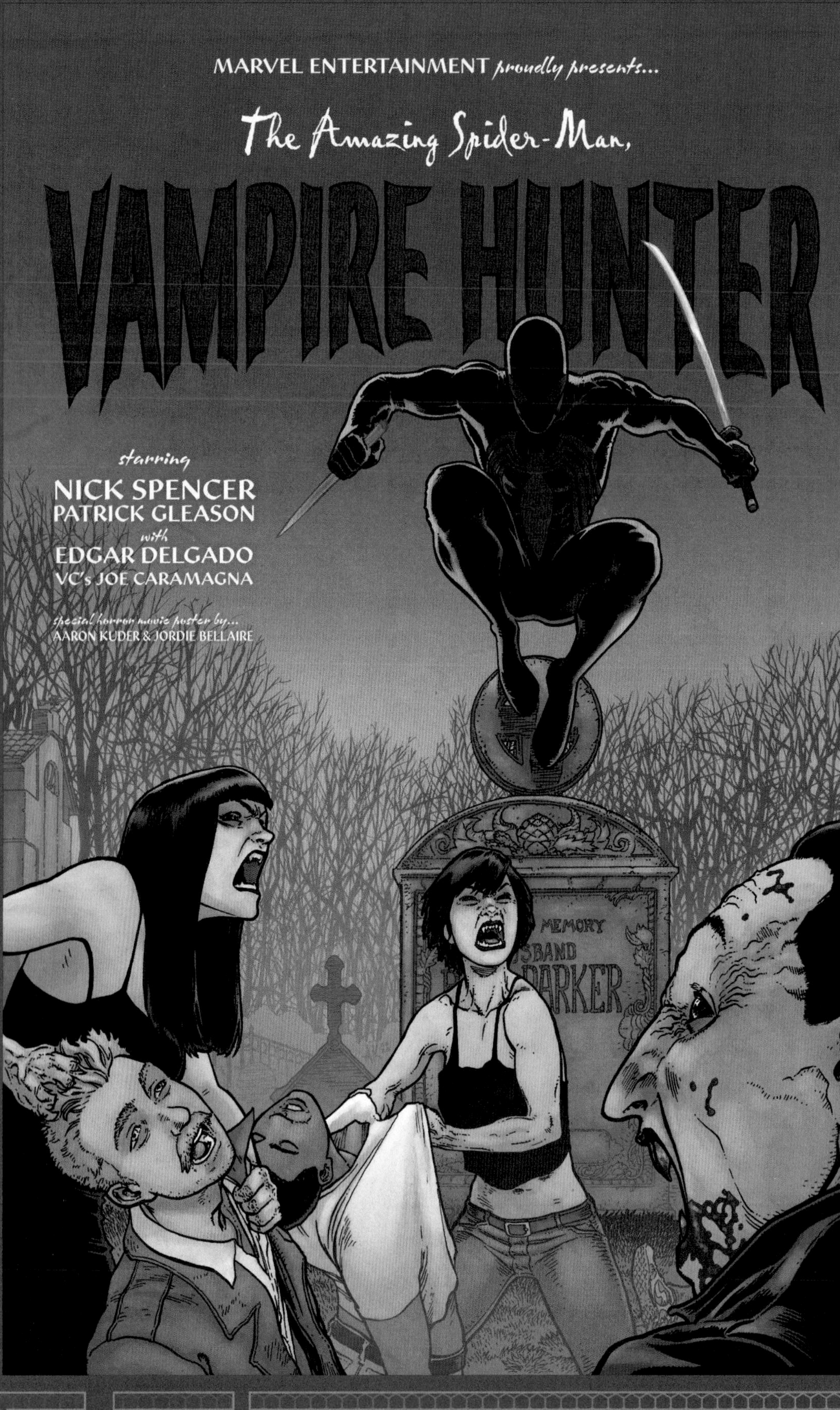

MARVEL ENTERTAINMENT proudly presents...
The Amazing Spider-Man,
VAMPIRE HUNTER
starring
NICK SPENCER
PATRICK GLEASON
with
EDGAR DELGADO
VC's JOE CARAMAGNA
special horror movie poster by...
AARON KUDER & JORDIE BELLAIRE
MEMORY
SBAND
PARKER

#50 HORROR VARIANT BY AARON KUDER & JORDIE BELLAIRE WITH ANTHONY GAMBINO

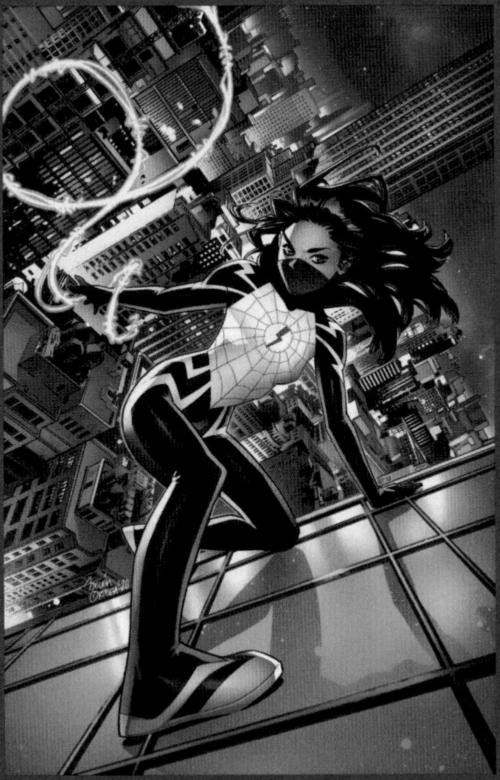

#50 VARIANT BY
BELÉN ORTEGA & DAVID CURIEL

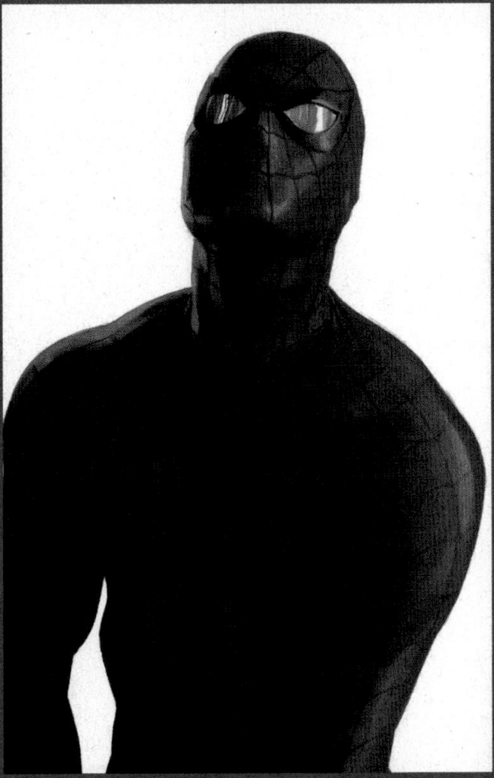

#50 TIMELESS VARIANT BY
ALEX ROSS

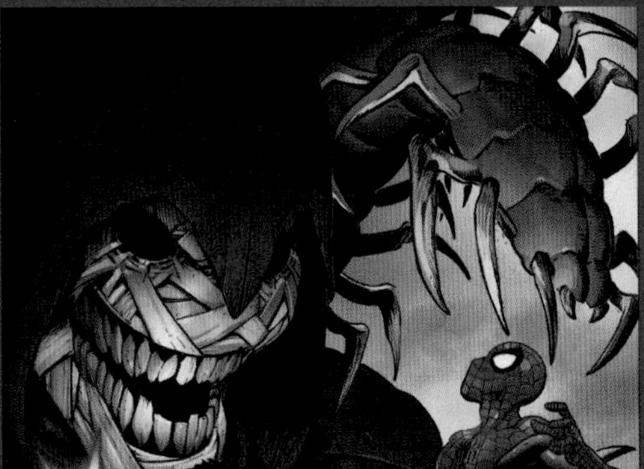

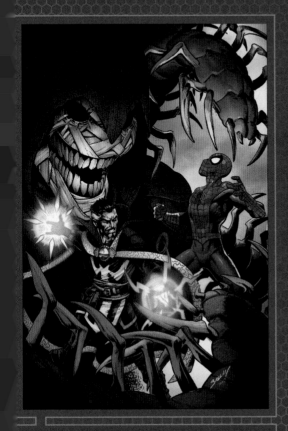

#50 VARIANT BY
MARK BAGLEY & DAVID CURIEL

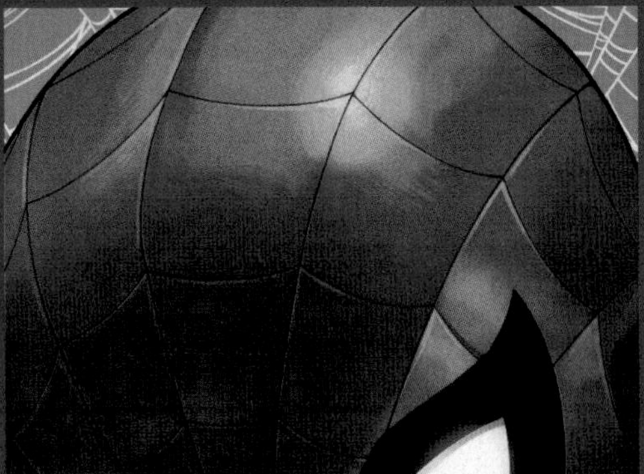
NAUCK

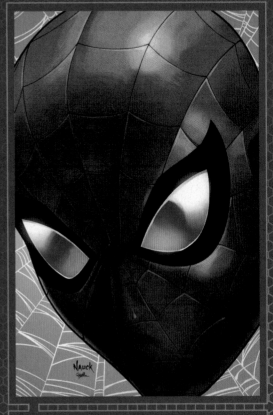

#52 HEADSHOT VARIANT BY
TODD NAUCK & RACHELLE ROSENBERG

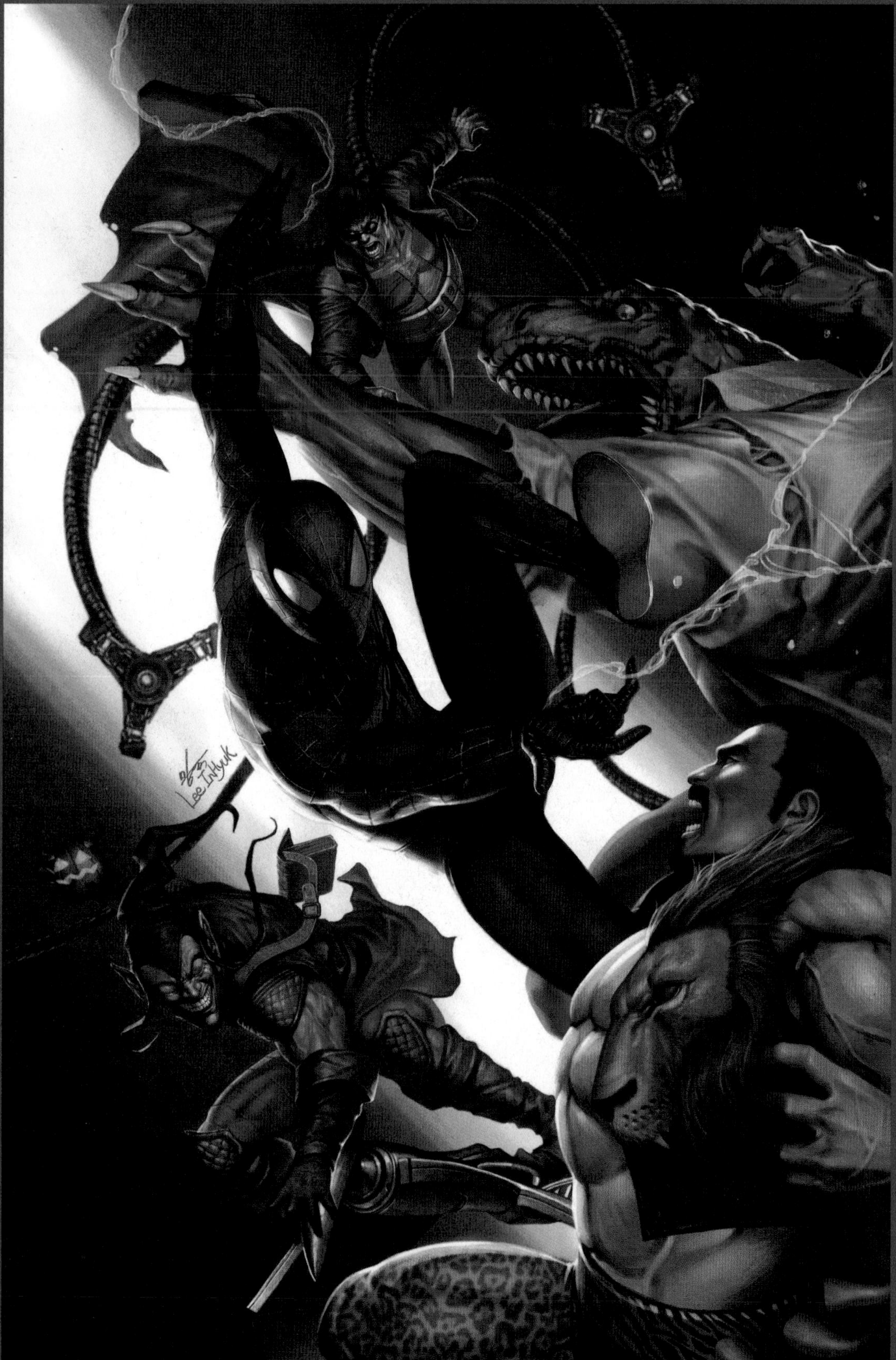
Lee InHyuk

#51 VARIANT BY INHYUK LEE

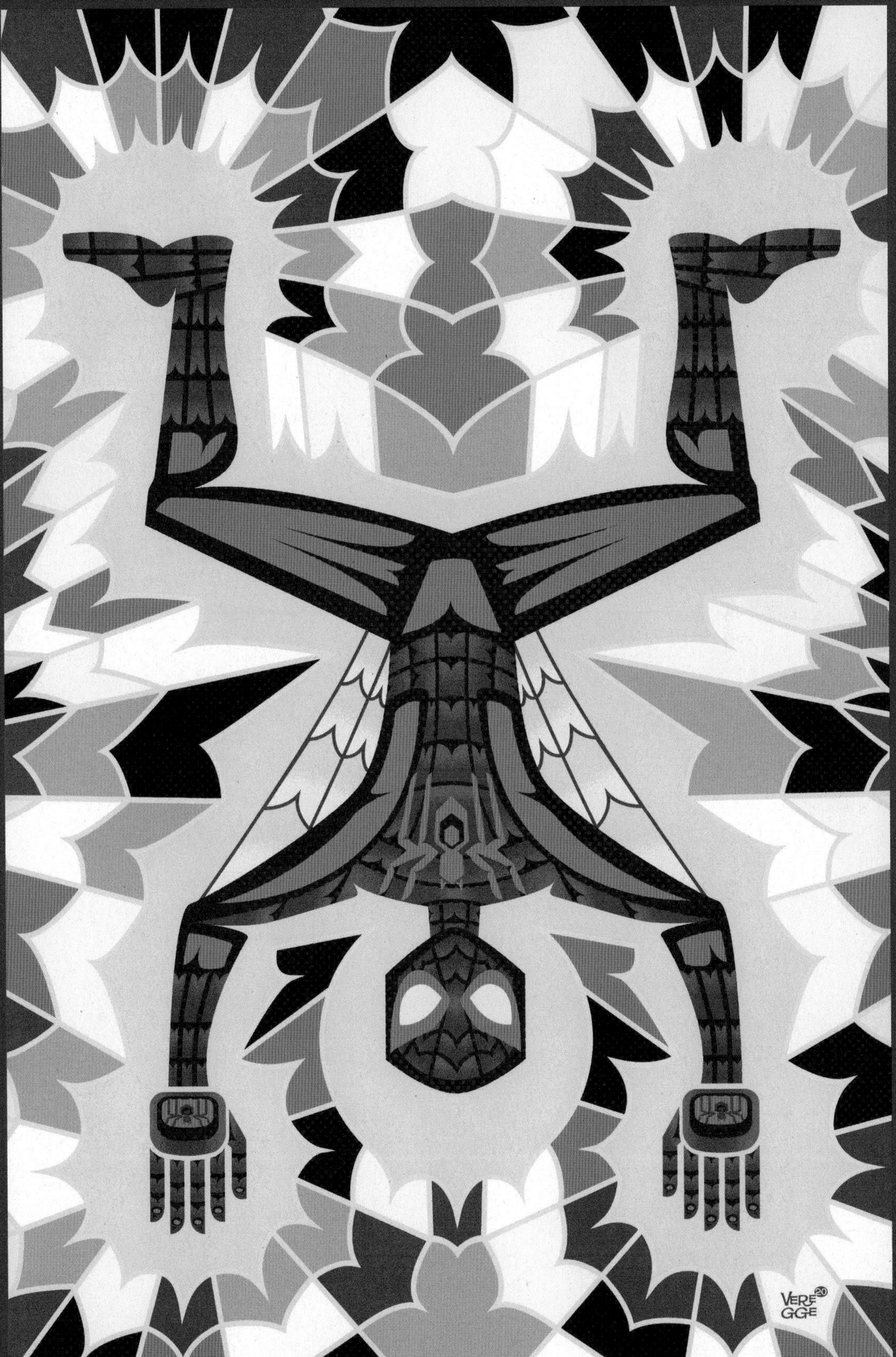
VEREGGE 20

#52 VARIANT BY JEFFREY VEREGGE

#53 VARIANT BY
HUMBERTO RAMOS & EDGAR DELGADO

#54 VARIANT BY
MARK BAGLEY, JOHN DELL & DAVID CURIEL

#54 KNULLIFIED VARIANT BY
PAULO SIQUEIRA & RACHELLE ROSENBERG

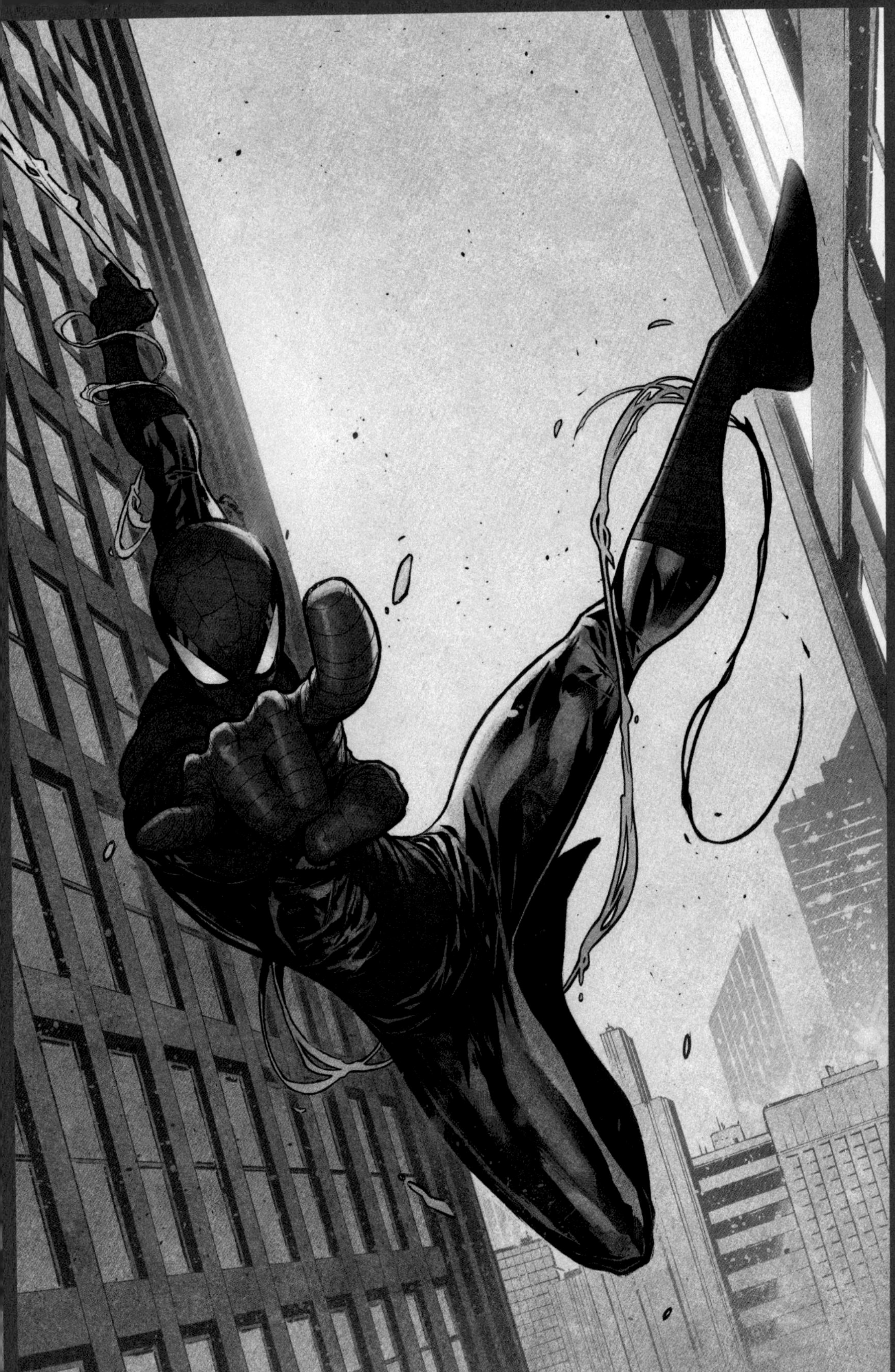

#54 STORMBREAKERS VARIANT BY IBAN COELLO

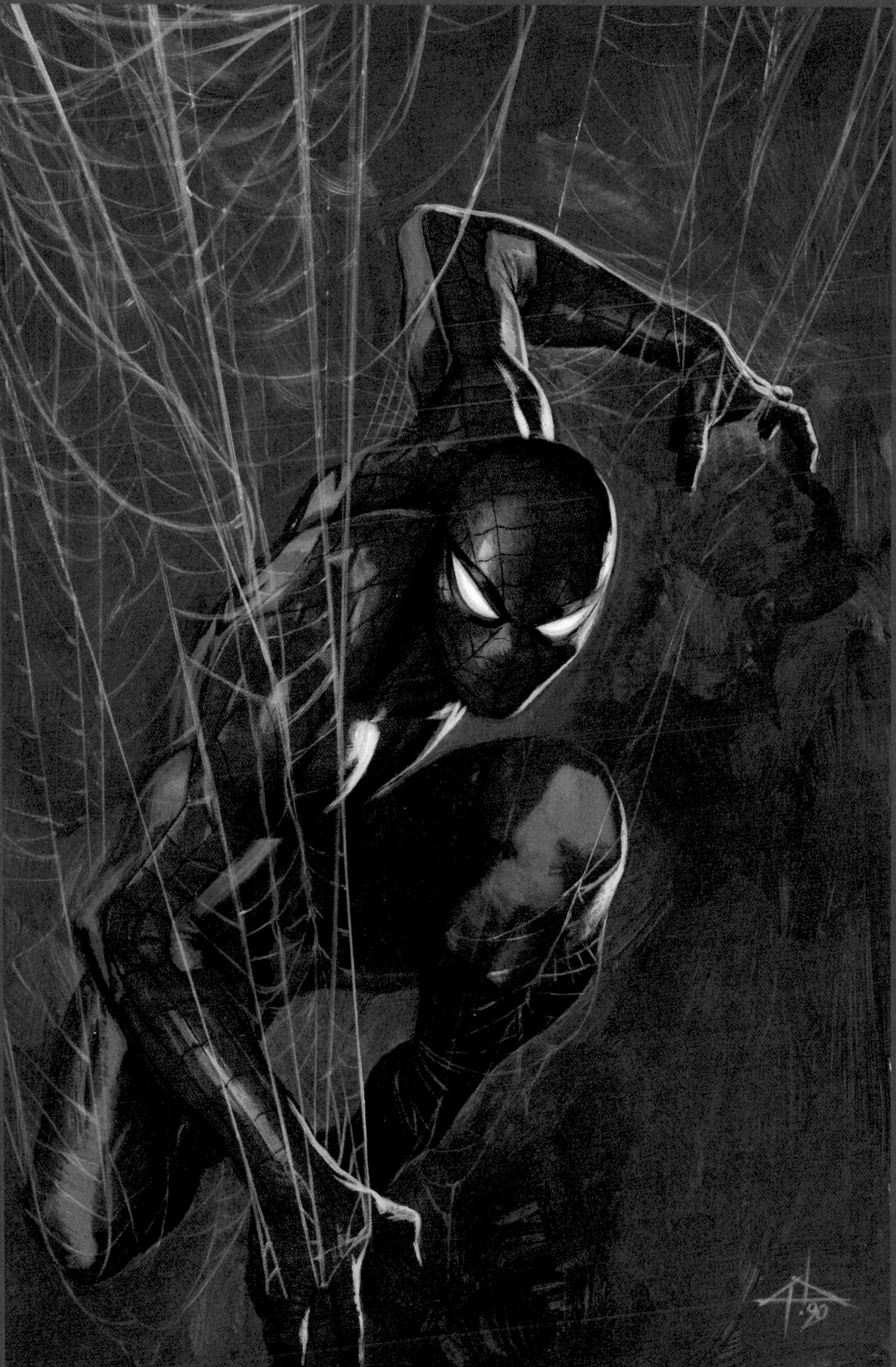

#55 VARIANT BY GABRIELE DELL'OTTO